I Sh●t
My Bridge Partner!

by **Matthew Granovetter**

FOREWORD BY ALFRED SHEINWOLD

Cover & Illustrations
by Nels Anderson

Granovetter Books
18 Village View Bluff
Ballston Lake, NY 12019
(518) 899-6670

With the exception of Roth and Kaplan,
the people in this story are the author's
creation and any resemblance to real-life
persons is completely coincidental. The
events in this book are also fictional.

Printed in the United States of America
ISBN 0-940257-05-X

I Shot My Bridge Table

TABLE OF CONTENTS

ILLUSTRATIONS *by Nels Anderson*

FOREWORD
BY ALFRED SHEINWOLD

T HIS IS a classic murder mystery.
The victim is shot at the bridge table just as he begins to play
a fascinating hand. (Perhaps most declarers should be shot, but
surely it's polite to wait until they've misplayed the hand.)

Three other players and an assortment of kibitzers are unable
to see who fired the shot because the lights are out. Why would
four sane people be playing bridge in the dark? Moreover, maybe
the problem isn't who fired the shot but how he should play the
hand.

Before you get an answer to these questions you meet the
author, Matthew Granovetter, a college freshman 20 years ago.
You also meet such fictional bridge players as the beautiful Chops,
Frankenstein, "Pizza" McCarver, together with such real-life per-
sonages as the great Al Roth, as he presided over the famous
Mayfair Bridge Club on West 57th Street in the New York of the
60's and 70's.

You won't understand and enjoy these daft denizens of the
bridge domain unless you're a bridge player yourself. But if you're
a player, you'll learn a lot, as the youthful Matthew did, about
getting the most out of a partner, bidding to the best contract,
when to stay out of the bidding, how to defend, how to play the
dummy, how to pay your bridge debts with counterfeit money.

And while you're turning these ideas over in your mind you'll
also be absorbed in the plot, the interplay of character, the question of who committed the murder. And just when you think
you've solved *that* problem, you find out you're wrong, smack in
the middle of another bridge hand.

It's crazy, it's logical, it's instructive—but most of all it's screamingly drop-dead funny.

In case you don't know the present-day Matthew Granovetter, he's one of the world's best bridge players, owner-publisher of *Bridge Today*, author also of *Murder at the Bridge Table*.

You can trust anything he says about bridge. But maybe he'll confuse the daylights out of you when you're trying to solve the murder.

A final word of advice: save this book. A hundred years from now, Granovetter first editions will be worth much more than you paid for this copy. If our present-day Matthew Granovetter isn't shot by an envious bridge partner, he should be good for several more hilarious histories of the bridge scene; and the wise collector will have first-edition copies of each of them.

—*Alfred Sheinwold*

INTRODUCTION

M Y DAD had a favorite Fort-Dix story he used to tell. It went something like this:

He was sent to Fort Dix as a private during World War II for basic training. One night at the barracks, the sergeant called out his name and ordered him to report to a lieutenant for special duty. The lieutenant accompanied him to a house. When they arrived, a colonel opened the door and asked him what he would like to drink. Then he was ushered to the table—the card table. His "special duty" was filling out the foursome in the colonel's bridge game.

I asked my dad how they knew that he played bridge. He told me they found him through the records. When he enlisted, he had no job except rubber bridge. On the line that asked for his profession, he wrote "bridge teacher." From 1943 to 1945 he played rubber bridge at Fort Dix. That's right—he never was sent overseas. No fool colonel would send the fourth overseas.

Who knows what would have happened if he had gone to war? I was born five years after the war, and grew up with the crazy notion that I owed my life to the game.

This book is a fictionalized version of my first rubber-bridge experience and other firsts as well. Two real-life characters from this book are Edgar Kaplan and Alvin Roth. They are not only great bridge players but great sports for allowing me to fictionalize them. The bridge hands and bridge concepts within these pages are real and, I hope, educational to any reader who wishes to learn something about the peculiarities of rubber bridge or the game of bridge in general.

I'd like to thank a few people for their advice and help in producing this book. My wife, Pamela, whose rubber bridge days are more recent than mine, offered many tips and scenarios that I incorporated. Some fascinating deals and concepts were furnished by Sandy and Paul Trent, Zia, Victor Mitchell, Ira Rubin, Jack Dreyfus and Jimmy Cayne.

Alfred Sheinwold was a great source of moral support, but more important, worked very long hours in editing much of my poor grammar in the early stages of this book.

Also, thanks go to Bob Nichols for his editing and Phil de Bourbon for his counseling.

Matthew Granovetter — October, 1989

I Shot
My Bridge Partner!

This book is dedicated to the memory of my dad, who warned me of the dangers of rubber bridge and also taught me never to tell a lie. Sometimes you listen to your father and sometimes you learn your lessons the hard way. This book is about the hard way.

CHARACTERS

At home:
YOUNG MATTHEW (the author, at 17 & 18)
MY DAD
STANLEY KESSELMAN (my friend)

At the Quad:
BIG AL
SHORT LARRY
LES THE MESS
PETE THE POET
J. B.
RAMONA (Quad book-keeper)

At the Mayfair:
ALVIN ROTH
MICHAEL (PIZZA) MCCARVER, JR.
CHOPS
BOBBY (Chops' baby boy)
FRANK STEIN (FRANKENSTEIN)
CATHY (Frankenstein's 7-year-old daughter)
BORIS (DOCTOR B.) BELLYARD
GUSSIE ADDLES
OTTO (ROCKEFELLER) MARX
MAGGIE JOHNSON (Mayfair cook)
POLICE SERGEANT O'ROURKE
CAPTAIN MCHALE

Other Characters:
DETECTIVE KENNEDY
ESTHER
MR. KEEWOOD (English professor)
MISS TILDEN (a student)
THE FAT LADY (on train)
OLD LEROY
STELLA and the rest of Leroy's gang
FORTUNATO
EDGAR KAPLAN

PROLOGUE

*COLD STEEL—A SHOT—ONE BRIDGE PLAYER
LESS—NIGHTMARES—THINKING BACK.*

T HE MAYFAIR Bridge Club, 119 West 57th Street, New York
City. Friday, December 12th, 1969. 9:18 p.m.

—I was the dummy. The contract was seven hearts—doubled.
The lead was the ace of spades. The declarer, Pizza McCarver,
was still studying his hand when the lights went out.

"I thought they called it off," somebody said to my left.

"It's a clazy theeng. I'll get my flashlight," said Otto, his accent
unmistakable.

We waited in the dark for 30 seconds, maybe 35. I could
barely see the outlines of the cards, and Pizza's head bent over in
thought. I heard Otto at Roth's desk. It sounded like he opened
up a drawer or a toolbox. A few more seconds passed in silence.

"Where's the dummy?" someone asked in a whispery voice, a
voice I couldn't quite place.

"Here I am," I said.

Suddenly I felt the cold steel across my cheek. I stiffened.
The arm across the left side of my neck rested firmly on my
shoulder. I started to resist. There was a shot. A match was lit and
I felt hot and faint. I was sure I had been shot. I was sure it was
Stanley taking revenge for my having ratted on him earlier in the
evening. Another match was lit. A red liquid was spreading over
declarer's cards, which were lying face down on the table. That is
except for one card, the queen of clubs, which was face up, a
piece of the upper right corner blown to bits. I hadn't given my
partner the chance to evaluate that card in the bidding. Now I

3

was glad to see it was there. Then there *he* was, facing me, head downcast, with a red hole through his shirt pocket. Was that the tomato stain I had seen earlier that day on his T-shirt?

"He's still thinking," said Gussie.

"It's a played card," insisted Chops.

Feeling very dizzy now, I grabbed the closest thing to me—something, anything to hold onto. It turned out to be the gun. That's when the lights came back on.

I woke up to that scene last night—it wasn't the first time. Nightmares are usually dark and gloomy affairs, and this was no exception. Yet we all know that dreams can shed light on our innermost desires. What is this light emanating from darkness? If it comes from a dream of the future, it may be something we wish for or hope to accomplish. But, as in the case of this particular nightmare, if it comes from a dream of the past, it is a burning sensation that ruins our cool sleep—it is a punishment for the dastardly deeds we once committed.

I dream about bridge matches that were lost on the last deal. I dream about contracts I could have made and bids I shouldn't have. I dream that I'm back in my seat again, given a second chance to stop my partner from going wrong on defense. But most of all I dream about the night I shot my bridge partner.

It's been nearly 20 years since I was accused of the crime. It seems to me that's long enough to risk opening old wounds. Besides, most of the members of the Mayfair Club who were there that night have either passed away or slipped into obscurity with no forwarding address. Yes, a few, like Roth himself, still remember the night. But only I can tell all the facts, because I knew things that weren't written in the newspapers—sparse accounts that didn't even mention the crucial deal.

Today, I no longer stalk the jungles of New York City. Today, I've retreated to the country life, hiding behind trees and telling secrets to the wind. I even play home bridge games with neighborhood farmers, who point out troubled patches in the garden and occasional failures to break up a double squeeze. What can I say? I'm happy to be alive. I have a beautiful wife and two wonderful sons (ages two and four, who sometimes throw the 52 cards into the air—where perhaps they belong). I should have thrown *my* cards into the air that night, but I didn't. I was so very innocent then. At 18, we are puppies, even more so than at the age of four. At four, we are veteran roots; at 18, we are only the buds of manhood. I was less than that. I was a seed on a rocky knoll, and weeds were growing all around me.

Thinking back to those days, I can now see things in my mind that I never saw in real life. Isn't it strange how time will sharpen rather than dull the edge of perspective? The seemingly innocent incidents of the months preceding the shooting became the clues to motives that no one saw until the shooting occurred. So often, the smallest facts are not noticed until they are later analyzed—like the postmortem of a bridge deal, when only at the conclusion does declarer realize how that innocent card played at trick three was the clue to the opponents' distribution—like the postmortem of a murder . . . and the events leading up to it . . . .

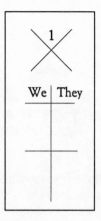

Through a Window

1

CARDS AND ACNE—STANLEY SHOWS ME UP—
ENVIOUS THOUGHTS.

M<small>Y GROWTH</small> to adulthood was severely restricted by an early career in duplicate bridge. There's no doubt trumps are in my genes. When I was six, my Grandpa Max played two-handed pinochle with me. When I was 10, I kibitzed weekly bridge games at my other grandparents' home. Come to think of it, I don't remember learning to play the game at all. Like speaking or walking or turning on an electric switch, I learned bridge by being there. When I was 12, I read the Ruth Cohen 1-2-3-4 book on point-count bidding, then broke a handball date for a session of local duplicate. I was soon hooked. At my second duplicate, an older man who was to be my partner stood me up. I insisted we call his mom to make sure he was punished. On another occasion, a very pretty woman (an old woman in her 20s) passed my jump-shift rebid. I insisted we tell her mom also.

Two years later, I organized the first bridge club of Lincoln High. At the second meeting I dared to introduce the idea of the Goren point-count. "We're not ready for bidding systems, yet," said Miss Roark, the teacher in charge. "Let's just keep it to bridge for now."

Most of my good partners came from outside the school world. They were my dad's cronies, who liked to have another Grano-vetter to play with when my dad was tired out from working all day or was partnering someone else. My dad, Mannie Grano-vetter, who was the first Life Master of Jersey City, occasionally played with my mom. He would shake his head in dismay all night

8

as my mom held back tears. Those were the nights they won.

My older brother also played bridge. He was a scholar and bought all the latest books. In 1964 we played the Kaplan-Sheinwold system. In 1965 we played Schenken. In 1966 we played the Roman Club, the Big Diamond, the Marmic Forcing Pass and the Little Major. In 1967, the whole family had settled down to a modified Roth-Stone, and my mom breathed a sigh of relief. No more fights over the dinner table on whether to bid again with a minimum 5-2-2-4 shape after a one-notrump response. "One notrump is forcing! Finish your soup."

The one schoolmate I did play bridge with was Stanley Kesselman—though I didn't actually play bridge with him until we were in college. He was a skinny, brainy type of boy, and we grew up on the same block. We played tennis together and went to the movies a lot. We even went out with girls a few times, but I had acne and was very nervous about my looks. If I could hold 13 cards in front of my nose, I could relax a lot more. So instead of dancing or rollerskating—something I had no idea how to do—I would suggest card games.

On one such occasion, the girls condescended to play hearts. I explained the rules. "Deal out the whole deck. The idea is to not take any tricks with hearts; they're worth a point each; oh, and the queen of spades—don't get stuck with that one either—that's worth 13 points."

"What's a deck?" asked Mary.

Eventually we did play a game. The other girl, Eileen Schwartzberger, (the one Stanley was interested in) was very impressed with my ability to shuffle without touching the table. Later we all got pizza on the cards and moved into the basement for a quick game of spin-the-bottle. By then, both girls had made quite a fuss over my card tricks and Stanley was pouting. He never agreed to go out with me and the girls again.

It was in our senior year that Stanley started to disappear. Mostly it was on weekends, although strange things were occurring in the middle of the week as well. I remember once in physics class, Stanley arrived after the bell in wrinkled trousers, a pizza-stained shirt, and smelling like tobacco and stale sweat. (I don't think he had gone to bed the night before.) The teacher, Mr. Dove, asked whether he was demonstrating the vaporization of odor. The class

9

laughed while Stanley just shook his head and said, "Children, you're all children."

Despite a growing distance, Stanley and I were both planning to attend Rutgers in the Fall of '69 and signed up as roommates. Near the end of our senior year, we were in my kitchen about to have some chocolate chips and milk when he told me he was ready to learn bridge. "Just tell me how to play in 25 words or less. Don't drag it out, kid." (He was lately in the habit of calling me *kid*.)

Stanley had a very high I.Q. and had actually scored a perfect 800 on his math SATs, but grasping the game of bridge in 25 words or less was not possible.

"It's impossible to teach you in one sitting, Stanley. I've got a family tree of knowledge up my sleeve."

I took out a new deck and threw out the jokers. There were four suits stacked up in order. I spread them across the table face up. "Memorize those cards, Stanley. 52 pieces. Four suits of 13—ace is high, deuce is low."

"Got it." Stanley smiled and poured himself some milk. "Don't worry, I'm listening."

"Now shuffle them up and deal four bridge hands around the table. Then sort your suits. Spades are the highest ranked, then hearts, then diamonds, then clubs."

"Okay, okay, let's get to the mechanics, and make it quick."

The mechanics, I thought. And he wants me to make it quick. Well, it took 2500 words, not 25, and by the time I was through, he had eaten all the cookies. Then he suggested we try a deal on for size. So I cleared the kitchen table, and Stanley dealt out four hands. In bridge-column notation they looked like this:

North
♠ A J 7 4 3
♡ K 4 3 2
◇ J
♣ 4 3 2

West
♠ 9 8
♡ J 10 8 6
◇ 10 9 3
♣ 10 7 6 5

East
♠ Q 5 2
♡ A 7 5
◇ K Q 8 7 4
♣ J 9

South
♠ K 10 6
♡ Q 9
◇ A 6 5 2
♣ A K Q 8

"All right, wise guy," I said. "Suppose South is the dealer. What do you think he would bid?"

"One club," said Stanley.

"Well, that was easy. The ace-king-queen made it obvious. West bids next. What do you think he would bid?"

"Pass the bid."

"Why?"

"Only one picture card. Are you blind?"

"Shut up. All right, now North responds to the one-club opening bid. If you're so smart, Stanley, what does North say?"

"One spade."

"Again an obvious call. You dealt a hand that was too easy. Now what about East?"

Stanley took off his glasses and peered closely at the East hand. "Pass."

"There," I said, triumphantly! "You missed a chance. East can bid two diamonds with 12 points in picture cards and a good diamond suit. You have to learn how to code the hand. You have to read books about this. Bridge is not calculus, Stanley. You can't expect to conquer it in one afternoon!"

"You're right, kid. However, personally, I would not overcall two diamonds—not for money at least."

"Money?"

"Yeah, man. At the Mayfair you'd get bloodied up pretty bad. I mean, geeziz, you're bidding between two bidders with a passed partner. Now you wouldn't walk into the road with two cars coming from both directions, would you?"

"No, but—"

"Yeah, well, two diamonds gets doubled by South, and after an easy trump switch, East-West are lucky to take five tricks. Still that's not as bad as what might have happened if North-South reached a slam in spades."

"What slam in Spades?" I asked. "Are you crazy? South has 18 points and North has nine. Twenty-seven points makes game, Stanley—you'll have to learn that." I looked at the hands again. Yes, you could make a contract of four spades. Ten tricks were there for sure, but 12 tricks . . . .

"Do I have to bid it and play it for you? Look, I admit you wouldn't get to slam playing with a good player like Frankenstein."

"Who?" I asked.

"Frank Stein—don't tell me you never heard of him. He's the best. But say you were playing with Doctor B. or Otto or Pizza McCarver—"

"Pizza McCarver?"

"Any one of those clowns might have you up at the six level if you didn't watch your step. After a one-club opening and a one-spade response, they might jump to three or four spades with the South hand. Then if you didn't stop and check out who your partner was, you might Blackwood yourself into six.

"Well, six spades is a piece of pie. Here, I'll make it easy for you by moving the hand around so the long suit is the declarer:

North
♠ K 10 6
♡ Q 9
◇ A 6 5 2
♣ A K Q 8

West
♠ Q 5 2
♡ A 7 5
◇ K Q 8 7 4
♣ J 9

East
♠ 9 8
♡ J 10 8 6
◇ 10 9 3
♣ 10 7 6 5

South
♠ A J 7 4 3
♡ K 4 3 2
◇ J
♣ 4 3 2

"There are at least three or four ways to make six spades. The simplest after a diamond lead is to win the ace in dummy and lead the queen of hearts. West wins the ace and tries another diamond. Big deal. You ruff it in the South hand and finesse the spades by leading low toward the king-ten and stick in the ten. Kapeesh?"

"I know what a finesse is."

"Good. Next lead to the king of hearts and ruff a heart in dummy. Cash the king of spades and ruff a diamond in the South hand. Pull the last trump with your ace and claim. With four cards left, the position is a simple squeeze. Dummy has the A-K-Q-8 of clubs and you have a heart and three little clubs. East can't keep all four clubs without giving up the last high heart. Whatever he discards at trick nine, you claim the rest."

To tell the truth, I couldn't follow Stanley that well. I'd made one or two squeezes at the table, but I had to turn the cards over to see the position because I still hadn't had enough experience to picture the ending in my mind:

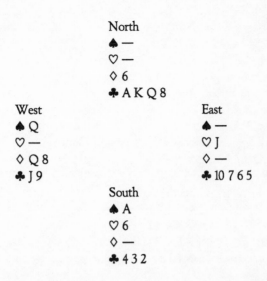

North
- ♠ —
- ♡ —
- ◇ 6
- ♣ A K Q 8

West
- ♠ Q
- ♡ —
- ◇ Q 8
- ♣ J 9

East
- ♠ —
- ♡ J
- ◇ —
- ♣ 10 7 6 5

South
- ♠ A
- ♡ 6
- ◇ —
- ♣ 4 3 2

On the lead of the ace of spades, dummy discards the six of diamonds and East can't let go of the heart jack without making South's six high. The discard of a club, however, permits dummy to take the last four tricks.

"Vienna coup variation or simple squeeze played like a double," said Stanley. "Call it what you like; *You're* the book worm."

(This hand stuck with me subconsciously for a very long time. It was seven months later when I realized how West could defeat the contract.)

Stanley had a good laugh that afternoon. Who would have thought that an innocent game of hearts among teenagers could provoke such a change in a person's life? But Stanley had been so furious about losing the adoration of Eileen two years earlier that he made up his mind to master the game of bridge to the point where he could show me up. And he did it in a way I was unfamiliar with: by playing at the rubber bridge club.

The only thing I knew about rubber bridge was that my dad played the game in the 1930s. One summer when I was 15, we were on the beach (playing with magnetic cards), and I asked him where he played rubber as a kid. He mumbled something about New York, the Mayfair and how I should forget rubber bridge and stick to good games like duplicate. It wasn't that he felt the gambling aspect was detrimental to my moral education. No, he was against the way rubber bridge players bid. "You wouldn't understand their ways. They don't believe in helping partner. When they have three trumps, they don't raise partner's one-spade opening to two. They first start with one notrump."

"But that's just Roth-Stone, dad," I said, believing I was the knowledgable one.

"Well then, maybe that's where Roth and Stone got it from. The problem with rubber is that everyone is different. There used to be a guy in my army game who liked to jump raise with only three-card support."

Somewhere along the line, I got the idea that there were evil elements in New York rubber bridge clubs. During the summer of '69, the thoughts of gangsters, card sharks, worldly women and high stakes began to swirl in my mind like an ocean's wave. I was flooded with the envious notions that others, like my dad (and Stanley, damn him!) had experienced these terrible, wonderful things, and I would never get to live the same experiences.

I must have been a demented 17-year-old. What can I say? Other young men are warned off smoking, drugs, burning the flag or houses of prostitution. I was told to avoid rubber bridge clubs. Meanwhile, Stanley had been actively taking part for nearly two years! And when I heard him mention the name of the club my father had misspent his youth in—and warned me against—it was only natural that my desire to see that hellish place grew and grew like a burning passion.

My summer job of 1969 was on the tennis courts. Day after day, taking quarters down at the city park in the bright, hot sunshine, I longed for the dark—the secret, cool blackness of a place called the Mayfair. Stanley was there, I thought with envy. Stanley was playing rubber bridge. Stanley was gambling, shuffling, making simple squeezes, and cavorting with people who were called Frankenstein and Pizza McCarver. I wanted to see that club like a normal 17-year-old wants to see a naked woman. (I wanted to see a naked woman too, but, hey, first things first.)

2

M Y OCCASIONAL evening sessions at the local duplicate did not come close to quenching my thirst for what was imbedded in my consciousness as the real thing. However, at the end of August, it was time to go to New Brunswick for two weeks of Freshman orientation, and this endeavor watered my hot desires for a brief spell.

I had not seen Stanley on the tennis courts for an entire month, but because we were to share a room, my dad offered to drive both of us to the campus. On Sunday, when we went to pick him up, however, his mother told us he had left on Friday. I did not tell her that no student activities were scheduled until Sunday night and that Stanley had probably headed East, not South. My dad and I took the 30-mile trip down the New Jersey Turnpike and when we got to the dormitory there was no sign of my friend.

Rutgers is a green, lush, 200-year-old school spread out along the banks of the Raritan River, which George Washington and the troops crossed on their southbound flight to Philadelphia in the first year of the Revolutionary War. A little known fact about the father of our country is that George played a lot of whist in those days—and for lots of money to boot.

My dormitory was known as the Quad. Located a block from the river, it was nothing more than a group of quaint three-story brick buildings encircling a vast courtyard. There were four bedrooms on each floor of each building, and at the top of the stairs on the first landing lived the preceptor—a senior whose job it was to maintain discipline and offer Freshmen the helpful advice they were used to receiving from their parents back home—which meant, of course, that all the boys were happiest when the preceptor was not around.

All the rooms were similar—two single beds, two small dressers, and one desk. There was one oblong window in the rear, but my particular room had an airy feel because of the high ceiling.

That Sunday afternoon, I said my goodbyes to my dad (promising to study hard), unpacked and went for a walk. The Quad was mostly concrete and brick, but outside on the streets were large numbers of trees and grassy knolls where students already were lying, reading, talking and generally partaking with joy in a new-found freedom.

That night was a combined welcoming dance of freshmen from Rutgers and first-year female students from Douglass College, the sister school across town. I went to the dance and met two girls. One was a fat girl with bee-hive hair, who I was sure kept examining my acne in curiosity. If she said one word about it, I was going to poke her jowls. The other was a very pleasant-looking blonde named Esther. I invited her on to the dance floor during a fast number, which was a mistake. After I had stepped on her toes and bruised her ankle about five times, she gave me the brush off. I couldn't blame her. There was no doubt in my mind, however, that if I'd had access to a deck of cards and could have revealed my debonair side, I'd have made her mine.

Oh well, I was a failure at the freshman ball and, to tell the truth, bored out of my mind. When I got back to my room, I took out my required reading list, checked off one or two books I had actually perused, then tossed it aside and got my August *Bridge World* magazine out of the back of my suitcase. Perhaps I had skipped one of the articles on my first two readings, and the night wouldn't be a complete waste. No, I had read every page, even the bidding challenge. So I settled on rereading an article called "Mayhem at the Mayfair," about a cut-around rubber-bridge game held recently at Al Roth's Mayfair Club.

English Comp. 1 (req.)
Calculus 1
Latin 3
Political Science 1
World History 1 (req.)

These were my courses, and by the second week of classes, I felt more like a student than a card player gone good. Little did I realize that this course schedule would change soon. Before the semester was over it would look like:

The guys in the dorm, seemingly immature at first compared to the sophisticated crowd I was used to at the local Temple duplicate, turned out to be just as nervous about who was going to be living with them for two semesters as I was. In fact, a few fellows actually dabbled in pinochle, and were easy converts to bridge. Once you know what a trump is, it's really pretty easy to make the switch.

It wasn't long before regular games were scheduled at 10 p.m. and ran until one or two in the morning. Pete the Poet, my first convert, was always on time and anxious to try new bidding systems—many of them homemade. My second convert was Les the Mess (from the second floor—unfortunately, a very serious student, thus quite unreliable). Then there was Big Al. Big Al loomed on the far side of the top floor with Short Larry. (That's right, loomed—he was 6 feet 6. Poor Short Larry was 5 feet 8, but had to live with that nickname because of his roommate.)

It fast became tradition in the game to accuse Big Al of peeking, but the truth is Big Al had no clue—as they say in the game world. If you showed Big Al a queen, he would still end up leading from the wrong hand. This was Big Al's idea of a back-ward finesse:

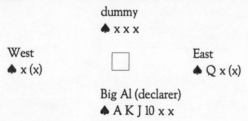

dummy
♠ x x x

West
♠ x (x)

East
♠ Q x (x)

Big Al (declarer)
♠ A K J 10 x x

Let's say you were playing this suit for no losers. Odds are you would cash the king of spades, and if everyone followed low, you would lay down the ace. Alternatively, and against the odds, you might go to dummy before leading the second round; then play low toward the ace-jack, finessing East for the queen.

Because we had no card table in the dorm, it became conven-

It wasn't long before regular games were scheduled at 10 p.m.
and ran until one or two in the morning.

ient to play in my room on the floor with two players situated on Stanley's empty bed. Thus, Big Al often did get a visual clue to the missing queens. Trouble was, even though he could see the queen, he couldn't picture the suit in his mind.

For example, on the previous layout, he would spot the key queen in the East hand. First he would go to dummy to play a spade to his king. (Big Al was a technician first and proud of it.) Then, knowing the queen was on his right, he would take a backward finesse, leading the jack out of his hand, which inevitably lost to the queen. Big Al would always look amazed that his play failed, and sometimes would curse at whoever was sitting East, "Yankee bastard." Big Al was from Boston and, though Bob Cousy, the basketball star, should have been his hero, he was a die-hard Red Sox fan.

Once, Pete the Poet and I cornered Big Al in the showers and explained to him what a real backward finesse was. I pointed to the current *Bridge World* issue (my dad forwarded his subscription to me) that described the following suit combination:

Dummy
♡ A 7 6

West   East
♡ Q 8 4   10 5 2

Declarer
♡ K J 9 3

The declarer made four heart tricks by taking a backward finesse. He led the jack of hearts from his hand, and West covered with the queen; then, after winning the ace in dummy, declarer led a heart back to his nine, finessing against East's ten. The reason it's called a backward finesse is that the normal 50% play is to cash the ace and lead low to the jack. The bidding on the hand, however, had indicated that West was very likely to hold the queen. Even Pete the Poet, who was not particularly strong in math, explained that the backward finesse had a 25% chance of success because declarer needed *two* cards placed correctly, not just one.

Big Al (who *was* a math major) was impressed and studied the hand all through his shower, completely ruining my September issue. Later that evening, playing as my partner, Big Al was declarer in a diamond slam with this trump layout:

Dummy (me)
◊ K 9 7 6 4

West (Pete the Poet)   East (Les the Mess)
◊ Q 10   ◊ 2

Declarer (Big Al)
◊ A J 8 5 3

Big Al led the jack of diamonds from his hand. West, Pete the Poet, covered with the queen, captured by dummy's king. The light bulb lit in Big Al's head. He led a low diamond back, and when Les the Mess, who was simultaneously reading a Roman History book and eating a double-tunafish sub, and was therefore prone to revoke—and indeed did revoke on the average of four times per session—showed out, Big Al stuck to his guns and stuck in the eight.

It might be advisable to explain at this time the form of scoring used in the Quad. We played traditional rubber straight out of the *According to Hoyle* rule book that Les the Mess bought for us on one of his frequent visits to the New Brunswick Bookstore. Traditional rubber is still played in some parts of the world today and in most home bridge, but rarely in American money bridge clubs. In fact, when we speak of rubber bridge today, we usually mean Chicago, which is the predominant form—more on Chicago scoring later.

The term "rubber bridge" not only implied a form of scoring, but had a connotation that money was involved. My dad's early warnings against rubber bridge were against "money" bridge and how that "ruined" the reliable-partnership concept I had learned from duplicate; the warnings were not against the form of scoring.

In the Quad, we played for a very small stake: a twentieth of a cent. That meant every point was worth 1/20 of a penny. To win a dollar you had to be up 2,000 points at the end of the night. (At the other end of the spectrum, in today's high-stake games, the stakes have been known to go as high as two dollars a point (making 2,000 points worth $4,000!)

Here is a sample score pad from our Quad game that shows a complete traditional rubber with a total difference of 2,000 points, an enormous amount:

We	They
	1400
100	500
500	700
120	60
	180
90	
30	
840	2840

Trick scores are written below the horizontal line, bonus scores for games, slams, honors and all penalties are written above. You have to bid and make a game or slam to get vulnerable, and you can receive a game bonus upon completion of the rubber only. Once you make a game, you wipe out the partscore of your opponents and a new horizontal line is drawn.

Penalties for doubled contracts are the same as in duplicate, and in those days were 100, 300, 500, 700 and so on for non-vulnerable doubled undertricks. (Today, a recent rule change makes the fourth undertrick worth 300 points and so on; e.g. down four doubled non-vulnerable is minus 800, down five 1100.) Vulnerable doubled sets were and still remain 200, 500, 800, 1100 per trick, and so on.

As you can see from the sample scorepad, you do not have to complete the rubber to win the rubber. In this case "We" *completed* the rubber with two games, but "They" *won* the rubber with numerous penalties. The bottom line in all forms of rubber is the total difference in points, which at the end is rounded to the nearest hundred.

After a couple of weeks at the Quad, I had to admit I was enjoying myself. The bridge games weren't what you would call high level, but they did have an element that was missing from my former duplicate adventures—they were rough-and-tumble.

I actually took to a couple of my academic courses as well, particularly English Comp. 1. Besides being lucky enough to be in one of the few experimental coed sections held across town at Douglass, I had a weird and wonderful professor, Mr. Keewood.

Strange as it may seem, Mr. Keewood resembled the professional wrestler, Johnny Valentine. He was in his mid-thirties, had long blonde hair that went down to his shoulders, and sported a flower in his lapel on occasion. He was a rebel, no doubt, and had failed to earn tenure in three other colleges prior to Rutgers. The first thing he told us was that he didn't believe in grades. We weren't sure how this belief would affect us at the end of the term, but for the most part, we were happy with the concept. He was a contrary fellow, and enjoyed pointing out the opposite of any more-or-less accepted literary criticism. I'm not sure whether he did this just to get his students to think or because he really believed in his upside-down ideas. Certainly, his favorite trick-of-the-trade was to begin each class with some outrageous remark or question, which invariably caught everyone's attention and interest. Some examples:

"The only true game is Russian Roulette. Everything else is just passing time."

"Do the Ku Klux Klan wear white because they think of themselves as the good guys or because the color white represents fear?"

"Alcohol is not much better for you than pot."

This one he wrote on the blackboard: "Is it possible to make love while people are being killed in Vietnam?"

As you can see, Mr. Keewood did not have his head buried in books. However, he was knowledgeable in his field, and he planned for us to read, discuss, and write about the following four books: *The Autobiography of Malcolm X, The Autobiography of Ben Franklin, Heart of Darkness* by Joseph Conrad, and *The Collected Short Stories of Edgar Allan Poe.* What these four books had in common I didn't know, but certainly the first was a study in contrast. The name, Malcolm X, was forbidding. I knew little of the man except that he was a black leader who had been shot to death. Until I read his autobiography, I thought he was a violent man; and a feeling of fear was branded on my brain, perhaps from distorted media coverage. The truth is he was a non-violent man who rose from an early street life of drugs, pimps, and corruption to become a minister in the clean, intelligent and proud Moslem community. The colorful writing of his early life, however, made an impression on me. It was a bad but exciting life, and I secretly wished I could experience just a little of that badness, so long as later, of course, things would all come out okay.

Near the end of September, there began to be some scuttlebutt about the whereabouts of my roommate. One night, the preceptor, John Bartholemew III (J.B. for short), while eating the second half of Les the Mess's tuna sub deluxe, was declaring a three-notrump-redoubled contract. J.B. was filling in because Les the Mess had quit early to study for an Astro Physics quiz.

J.B., who was an honor student majoring in Classics, was not a great declarer, and in fact, made Big Al look like the next Tobias Stone. J.B., unable to grasp the concept of what a trump was, always converted suit contracts to notrump, always got doubled on general principle and always redoubled to show who was boss in the dormitory. In this particular hand J.B. had about 11 or 12 tricks on top and was therefore an even-money shot to make his nine.

While he was examining the dummy, some tomato fell out of his sub onto the bed, and it suddenly occurred to the preceptor, as he looked down to see numerous other tomato-stained marks (that Les the Mess had made), that the bed had been unoccupied since the beginning of the semester. "Hey guy," said J.B., "did I miss something or is this room a single?"

I told him that my life-long friend, Stanley, had been missing since the day my dad drove me to school, but that he was a pretty brilliant kid and would probably have no problem catching up on his work when he did show up. This caused considerable laughter, a month being a long time to catch up on.

J.B., who incidentally made his three notrump redoubled by accident after Big Al shifted into dummy's tuna-fish-covered club suit that was more solid than originally appeared, called me into his room the next morning for more information on Stanley. "Listen guy, I have to report directly to the dean of student services. Are you trying to tell me your roommate never showed up at all. I mean, he never even registered for classes?"

"I don't know, I only know I haven't see—"

"Well, I do know, guy! Here's his record. He pre-registered for five courses in July. Look:"

```
Stanley Kesselman - Freshman
Student I.D. 154-4329

English Comp. 1 (req.)
Calculus 2
Physics 1
German 3
World History 1 (req.)
```

"Are you telling me you haven't seen him since the semester began? Because if he doesn't show by next Monday, I'm duty bound to report him." Wham! He slammed the palm of his hand into his forehead—a habit that would make him a Tylenol addict later in life. "Look here, guy. I don't like to fill out a report. It makes me look like I forgot to check him out in the first place. Makes me look like I forgot to do my job. But honesty is the best policy, so there's going to be no cover-up."

"I'm sorry," I said, having no idea what to say.

"Don't be sorry; just find him for me, okay? Do you have any notion where this Stanley guy is?

"Perhaps."

"I hate to come down hard on you, guy, 'cause it's not your fault; but, I'm setting a 1 a.m. curfew on all bridge games until you bring him in." Suddenly he put both arms on my shoulders and said, "Be off with you, guy, and heed this advice: 'Neither a borrower nor lender be.'"

I wanted to take the moment to ask him about his own debt (give or take $17, which is a lot of loot to be owing at a twentieth), but I didn't have the nerve. Besides, a sudden rush of excitement had returned to my blood—that old urge to venture into the dark arena of my dad's past. Yes, I had a very good notion where Stanley was.

3

O CT. 3, 1969. It wasn't a long ride on the Friday afternoon Raritan Express from New Brunswick to Pennsylvania Station. I had my "Autobiography of Ben Franklin" with me and I planned to do some work on a paper that was due Monday morning—contrasting this with Malcolm X's Autobiography. My placemark was a fresh copy of *Bridge World* magazine, which I had purchased through the mail directly from New York after my last issue was ruined in Big Al's shower.

I had a seat by the window with an empty seat on my left. When we boarded, a very fat lady almost sat next to me, but luckily for me she spotted a seat by herself in the front of the car. I now had room to pull up my knees and get into a comfortable reading position. Then I considered what travel must have been like in Franklin's day. Out across the Raritan River banks, through to the Elizabeth seaport, and then out to the Atlantic Ocean, was the same route taken by Ben Franklin when *he* traveled between Philadelphia and Boston. Only he did it by boat, not train.

I opened to the part where Ben lists 13 virtues, which he is determined to acquire, one week at a time:

1. Temperance.
Eat not to Dulness
Drink not to Elevation.

2. Silence.
Speak not but what may benefit others or yourself.
Avoid trifling Conversation.

3. Order.
Let all your Things have their Places.
Let each Part of your Business have its Time.

4. Resolution.
Resolve to perform what you ought.
Perform without fail what you resolve.

5. Frugality.
Make no Expence but to do good to others or yourself: i.e. Waste nothing.

6. Industry.
Lose no Time. Be always employ'd in something useful. Cut off all unnecessary Actions.

7. Sincerity.
Use no hurtful Deceit. Think innocently and justly; and, if you speak, speak accordingly.

8. Justice.
Wrong none, by doing Injuries or omitting the Benefits that are your Duty.

9. Moderation.
Avoid Extreams. Forbear resenting Injuries so much as you think they deserve.

10. Cleanliness.
Tolerate no Uncleanness in Body, Cloaths or Habitation.

11. Tranquillity.
Be not disturbed at Trifles, or at Accidents common or unavoidable.

12. Chastity.
Rarely use Venery but for Health or Offspring; Never to Dulness, Weakness, or the Injury of your own or another's Peace or Reputation.

13. Humility.
Imitate Jesus and Socrates.

I looked outside the window and saw the train speeding through the Jersey oil refineries. I had thought Ben Franklin was a fun-loving experimenter who liked to play with lightning. How could anybody follow these precepts in today's society?

Still, Malcolm X had done something similar. But then that

was after his wilder, misspent youth.

In the distance I could see the light from a slowly setting sun shining across a factory of steel. White static swept past my eyes, and I lowered the window shade half-way. Then I bent the page for my placemark and took out the *Bridge World.* Everything was cooler now as I spotted an interesting article by a man called McCarver:

The Theory of Exhaustion
by Michael P. McCarver Jr., *NYC*

Recently in my rubber game at the Mayfair Club in New York, I picked up the following hand:

♠ A J 9 5 4 2 ♡ — ◊ K Q 10 3 ♣ 6 4 2

First deal, the player on my right opened one heart and I overcalled one spade.

At this point everybody squawked. Apparently I had misheard the opening bid. It had been *three* hearts. I thought they said *two* hearts, so I overcalled *two* spades. When it was made clear to me that the opening bid had been *three* hearts, I had no difficulty; I overcalled *three* spades.

Later in the evening, it occurred to me that had the opening bid been *four* hearts, I would have risked a *four*-spade overcall as well. Had the opening bid been *five* hearts, I might even have risked *five* spades. What would I have done over a *six*-heart opening? I wasn't sure at first, but surely six spades is not out of the question at favorable vulnerability if I trust the opening bidder. In fact, over a six-bid, the overcall seems to have even more to gain, preventing the bonus for a slam. Of course, over a *seven*-heart opening, *seven* spades becomes a clear bid, almost as clear as that one-spade overcall back at the one-level! Quite amazing, isn't it?

As the overcaller, there doesn't seem to be anything one can do about it. You are at the mercy of the opening bidder. However, as the opening bidder, the power to destroy is yours—if you know what the next hand is holding.

Unless you peek, you never do know, so that power

to force your opponent into a sacrifice position is not applicable. However, the reverse is often applicable: When you have a very long suit and wish to buy the contract, you will want to bid in such a way as to *prevent* the sacrifice. This is the reverse of a poker, or bluff, tactic; it risks missing the game you could have opened with in the first place. However, in most cases when you hold wild distribution, others also hold wild distribution.

This "McCarver Theory of Exhaustion" is applicable no matter what bidding system you play. It is the anti-preempt concept. Time your calls in such a way as to allow your opponents to bid all their suits and make all their raises, thus exhausting their bids so that they will have no more bids left by the time you reach the level you were aiming for. This is also known as "walking the dog," though in the McCarver version you may apply it to coping with your dog of a partner as well.

My reading was interrupted by a screech. We were making a stop in Newark. I looked up and saw a group of nice-looking coeds climb aboard, then returned to the safer world of my magazine.

A prime example:

♠ — ♡ A K Q J x x x x ◇ Q J x x ♣ x

You are dealer, first hand of the rubber. What is your opening bid? If you open four hearts, you will invariably find yourself under the gun at the five-level or six-level. The object is to buy this hand at four or five hearts, if possible. Of course six or seven might be cold, but then what good is it if the opponents bid six or seven spades?

Applying the McCarver Theory, you open the bidding one heart. As the bidding develops you bid hearts at the lowest level on each succeeding round. At some point your exhausted opponents will let you buy the hand, you hope at game, sometimes doubled! Here is an example from a recent rubber bridge game.

Fourth Deal:

29

NORTH
- ♠ —
- ♡ A 8 7 3 2
- ◊ K 8 6 2
- ♣ Q 6 5 3

WEST
- ♠ 2
- ♡ K 5 4
- ◊ A Q J 9 7 5
- ♣ A J 9

EAST
- ♠ K J 5 4
- ♡ 6
- ◊ 10 4 3
- ♣ K 10 8 7 2

SOUTH (McCarver)
- ♠ A Q 10 9 8 7 6 3
- ♡ Q J 10 9
- ◊ —
- ♣ 4

SOUTH	WEST	NORTH	EAST
Pass	1 ◊	1 ♡	Double
1 ♠	2 ◊	Pass	Pass
2 ♠	3 ◊	Pass	Pass
3 ♠	Pass	Pass	4 ◊
4 ♠	Pass	Pass	Double
(All Pass)			

Well, that was pretty good, I thought, as I gazed at the bidding. Then I turned my head for a brief moment toward the window. We were roaring across the New Jersey marshlands. Not much time was left, and I wanted to read the analysis.

My opening pass was taking the theory to the limit. It takes a lot of guts to do this, so those chicken-hearted players out there should skip to Kantar's article on partscore play. The rest of you, stick with me.

You will note after the one-diamond opening bid, and one-heart overcall, I was now in position to bid to at least the five level. Sticking to my guns, however, I bid only one spade after East's Sputnik double. This gave West the chance to rebid his diamonds at a safe level (safe for me) and, following the theory, I returned to the auction with two spades. This allowed West to exhaust himself with a third bid of three diamonds. I advanced with three spades.

30

East now "put it to me" with four diamonds and, with the opponents totally exhausted by now, I bid four spades. East's double was a little extra kicker for my side.

Had I opened the bidding four spades, or jumped later to four spades, there's no doubt West would have bid five diamonds. My partner would double and I would be left with the unhappy guess—leave it in and go minus 750 or pull it to five spades and go minus 200.

Skeptics: Note that had I been passed out in three spades, I still would have done at least 400 points better than had I opened with four spades!

As for applying the McCarver Theory against partner, this will usually occur when you hold hearts and she holds spades. For example . . .

A jolting plunge into the Lincoln Tunnel flipped the page. We were going across the Hudson River. The lights went on and off and I replaced the magazine into my Ben Franklin. I tried to review the 23-bid auction mentally. The darkness of the tunnel did not stop my study of the deal. I could picture the cards and the details of the bidding in my head. Whether this was because the concentration of a bridge player does not get easily disturbed by blinking lights, train-wheel screeching, or conductor catcalling—"Last stop, Pennsylvania Station, New York. . . Check your seats for your belongings. . . Last stop. . . Peeeeeeennsylvania Station, Thirty-third street, New York City"—or because I had the young and fertile (empty) mind of a 17-year-old college freshman, I had no idea.

All I knew was that I had arrived in New York on my mission to retrieve Stanley. No problem. I'd go collect him at the bridge club. No problem. The fact that New York is a city of four million people, the fact that I was only guessing that Stanley would be at the club, the fact that even if he were there was no reason he should want to come back with me never crossed my naive mind. No problem—not at the age of 17, anyway.

Suddenly I had a strange sensation, a tingling in my brain of doing wrong. Was it one of Franklin's virtues grasping at my conscience? My mom probably thought I was back in the Quad studying the decline and fall of Roman civilization; my dad would be wondering if I had made a date with some well-developed coed for the weekend dance. Oh well, I figured they would have the sense not to phone me on a Friday night. Meanwhile, in my shirt pocket, I checked again to make sure I still had the address of the Mayfair written on my train schedule.

People were everywhere, walking, talking, folding newspapers, speeding past me, left, right, bump. I felt like I was the deuce of clubs being shuffled in a pack of human playing cards. I looked up. The clock in the station read 5:30. If I could get to the Mayfair by six and quickly convince Stanley that he should come back with me, we could still make the 8:00 train back to New Brunswick.

Which way was out? There were the telephones, the men's room, shoe shine, Orange Julius. The phones! Why hadn't I called first?! Suppose Stanley wasn't there. I couldn't worry about that now. Did I really care if he was there? Was it really to retrieve my friend from the dark abyss of the gambling world that I had made this pilgrimage? Or was it because I finally had a good excuse to see that abyss, to enter within, to bite the apple myself?!

Bump. Ouch! Sorry. Shouldn't philosophize in the middle of rush hour at Pennsylvania Station. Wait. Was my wallet still there? Check it. Okay. The men's room again. Pit stop, just for a sec.

I go to the urinal. Franklin under my arm. The magazine falls out. Set it up, there, on the urinal. Hmm. Where was I? . . .

> As for applying the McCarver Theory against part-
> ner, this will usually occur when you hold hearts and she
> holds spades. For example . . .

Zip . . . shadow to my left . . . shadow to my right. Ohhhh . . . back pain. "Not a word, boy." Hand in my pocket . . . pushed forward . . . ouch. Suddenly people again. Where were they a second ago? Was my wallet still there? Check it. No more wallet. My Ben Franklin. Still under my arm! Sweat pouring down my forehead. Must sit down. Right away . . . right away. Outside, wait, the *Bridge World*, okay . . . .

Orange Julius stand. "May I have some wa-water, please. S-some-body just took my wallet."

"Get lost."

Back into the crowds. Against the wind I steer forward until I can see through the cataclysm the silver escalators of people mov-

ing down to me. Must get out. Where's the up? No up. I climb
the stairs, higher, higher, and finally, triumphantly reach the top.

"Excuse me, son, you got some change to spare for a cup of soup?"
Thirty-third Street and Eighth Avenue. Taxi stand. I don't have
any change to spare. I reach into my shirt pocket. The address of
the Mayfair on my train schedule: 119 West 57th Street. Twenty-
four blocks north. I start walking. "Which way is uptown?"
    "Get out of my way, you idiot."
    Thirty-second street. Wrong way. Turn around. A group of
men and one woman fly by me. "I had the ninth race, I'm tellin'
ya." "Don't kid me man." "Hold it baby, I think Stella's got the
ticket." They enter an old white car parked at the corner, and it
takes off with a screech. I move forward, uptown, clutching my
Ben Franklin under my arm.

After seven blocks it begins to drizzle. I hold the book over my
head. Thunder. Great. I duck into a coffee shop on 41st and
Broadway. "Coke, man?"
    I want a coke, but don't have any money. I shake my head no.
"Okay, dude, how 'bout some good grass, then?"
    I run out of the coffee shop into the rain. In a few seconds
I'm drenched. Ben Franklin is drenched. The September *Bridge
World* is drenched.
    At 47th Street I pass the Roseland dancehall. This was where
Malcolm X did the boogie-woogie in his earlier days. I'm impressed. At 51st Street I start to get the shivers. There's an old
newspaper in the garbage can. I look around to make sure nobody's looking, then take it out and put it around my neck and
over my head. Ben returns to my arm. At 53rd Street the rain
subsides a bit. Crossing the street, I stick out my hand to see how
bad it really is. Someone puts a quarter in it. "Get a job."

What can I buy in New York on a quarter? My breath must be
bad, I think. Better get some mints before I get to the club. The
rain has stopped. I throw the newspaper into the gutter and find a
newspaper stand at the corner of 57th and Seventh. "Any gum for
a quarter?" A one-armed man tosses me a pack of bubble gum
from inside the booth. "Gimme the quarter."

Carnegie Hall. I can't believe it. Tonight, George Gershwin's

Rhapsody in Blue. Restaurant. The Russian Tea Room. I peer in the window. Black ties. Red and Green glitters. The numbers are getting smaller, even on the right side of the street, odd on the left. I cross over. Screech. A taxi stops short. "Watch where you're going, jackass!"

Sixth Avenue. One-forty-five, 143, 141, 139, . . . New York City Opera, . . . Gucci Shoes, . . . Greek Food . . . 121, 119. Mayfair Club, third floor.

I walk into the lobby and find the elevator. "See you later, Meester James," says a man in grey overalls. "Goodnight, Rockefeller." Where was Rockefeller? The man in the overalls? The doors open at the third floor. I move down a corridor. The Mayfair Club. I start to ring a bell. The door opens and a man in a grey flannel suit rushes past me. It is a big room, smoke, food cooking, buzzing, four hearts, pass, no bid, shuffling . . . I take a deep breath.

I have arrived.

———————

At the desk in the corner was the famous Alvin Roth. I recognized him instantly. I had played against him once with my dad in an open pair tournament. He was partnered by a beautiful woman named Barbara. She must have been younger than I thought at the time, because in the postmortem he called her "a child." I don't think she was his daughter, however.

Mr. Roth looked up from his desk and spoke to me. My heart was pounding.

"Can I help you?"

I stared. It was a simple question, but I was tongue-tied.

"Do you play bridge?"

"I-I once played against you."

"You played against me? It must have been quite an experience. What happened? Did you get overboard?"

"Overboard?"

"Bid too much. Most of my opponents bid too much, especially the young ones."

I was suddenly feeling very tired. I looked around the room for a chair. There were plenty of them.

"May I sit down?"

"You want to kibitz the great players here? See how they overbid?"

What was he talking about? Couldn't he see I was about to collapse?

"I'm looking for a friend of mine. His name is Stanley Kesselman."

"Not *the* Stanley Kesselman! Oh, he's one the great players of our club. So you're a friend of Stanley Kesselman. We've been looking for a friend of the great Mr. Kesselman."

A woman, an older woman, maybe 25, 26 years old, brushed my shoulder. She smelled wonderful. Her hair was dark black in bushels flowing down her back. "Can you change five for me, Al?"

"Change five? What do you need, sweetheart? Singles, change?"

"I have to make a call."

"The phone's out of order. Here, use this."

He handed her the desk phone. She dialed a number.

"Ex-excuse, me, " I said. "Mr. Roth, is Stanley here?"

She turned around. Her eyes met mine. She was not just beautiful. She was startling. Her eyes were wide, sad and slightly slanted. She smiled at me with wide lush lips.

"Stanley's in the back room," said Roth. "If you want to kibitz, sit down and keep quiet."

"Hello," she said.

I said hello back. I was a nitwit. She was talking to the receiver.

"Serena?"

I averted my eyes. She didn't even know I existed. Then I noticed her see-through blouse and, that being the year bras were out of fashion, what I did see was something I had never seen before.

"Everything all right? . . . Just give him the bottle anyway. . . No, just tap water, how many times do I have to tell you? . . . Okay, okay. I'll call you later."

Bang went the receiver. I quickly moved away from her toward the windows.

There were four tables in play, and I edged my way around. I didn't see Stanley anywhere. Roth had said the back room. I must have been dizzy. Around the corridor I saw a kitchen and a small lounge. A cook was busy over the stove. It smelled pretty good. She turned her head to me, then shook it, muttering under her breath. It was something like, "Lord have mercy, look what the cats dragged in."

35

I looked into the lounge again, spotted a coat rack and parked my Franklin. Then farther down the hall I saw the entrance to the "back room." The door was open, and cigar smoke permeated the air. It was warm in there, only one window slightly open. Near that window a little girl sat reading a book by the light of the setting sun. She couldn't have been more than seven. There were a couple of backgammon boards on the tables, and around another table were five people, four playing and one kibitzing—she was the woman who had just been talking on the phone. I barely recognized the declarer, who was studying a four-card end position. Stanley had a thin mustache, and his hair hadn't been cut for a long time. The woman put her hand to Stanley's neck and rubbed it. He brushed it off, something I never would have done.

Stanley was wearing some nice clothes, including a silk shirt. His partner, the dummy, was even better dressed. He was middle-aged and sported a dark blue suit with a wide Italian tie. He was drumming his fingers on the table, very anxiously. "Play a card, c'mon already," he said. I leaned over to see Stanley's hand:

> dummy
> ♠ —
> ♡ 9 8
> ◇ —
> ♣ A 4
>
>
> Stanley (declarer)
> ♠ —
> ♡ —
> ◇ —
> ♣ K Q 10 3

It was obvious that Stanley had three top club tricks. What was he thinking about? Playing the ace and finessing on the next round, leading low to the ten?

Finally Stanley did cash the ace and did lead low to the ten. The man on his left, a ghoulish-looking man with very thick glasses, thumbed the jack on the trick and tabled the queen-jack of hearts. "Ooooh, he's counting again," the ghoulish man said. His partner, a pock-marked chubby fellow wearing a poker shade

Near that window a little girl sat reading a book
by the light of the setting sun.

around his forehead, reached for the cigar in the corner ashtray and started chuckling. "What are you chuckling at?" said the ghoulish man. "You don't even know what happened." Stanley turned the chuckler's cards over. They were all small clubs.

"Don't tell me I don't know what happened; if they were playing the Theory they'd stop in *one* notrump."

"Shut up, Big Baboon."

"You shut up or I'll make you shut up."

"Come on, don't you know by now when Frankenstein is joking?" said the ghoulish man with thick glasses, leaning across the table and tapping his partner on the wrist. "Let's go to work."

His partner subsided and wrote "100" in the top left box of the scorepad, then pushed a deck of cards toward the man who had just been dummy. Instead of cutting, he knocked the deck twice. The pock-marked man started to deal very methodically. Then, as his partner, Frankenstein, swept the cards in for the shuffle, Stanley's partner looked at the scorepad in surprise.

"Down one?" he asked.

"I'm sorry," said Stanley.

"You're sorry. I'm sorry. The whole world is sorry. But you had two more tricks in your hand." He rubbed his hands on his temples. "You're giving me a headache with your expert plays."

"It was five-to-two odds, Doc," said Stanley. "In the long run, I'm right. If I go down twice in seven times I lose twice my 70 partscore, 140 points. But if I make an overtrick five times out of seven, I score five times 30 for 150 points."

Doc just shook his head. Frankenstein, on Stanley's left, finished shuffling. His partner, on Stanley's right, finished dealing and wrote a "4" on top of a huge X on his scorepad. Suddenly a rapid-fire argument took place while everyone sorted his cards. It was so fast, I could hardly follow it:

"Partscores are worth more than 70 points."

"One hundred bonus on the last hand for incompletion."

"And what about if we complete it?"

"He forgot to calculate the overtrick he already had."

"How did he even know the distribution? How is he so smart? Did the clubs have to break five-two, eh?"

"Frankenstein showed me his distribution."

"Frankenstein is suddenly on your side when he plays against you? C'mon, deal already, I'm late."

"Five to two, those were the odds. The trouble with you is

you don't understand odds."

"Who is that gaping clown? The guy looks like he just came out of a well."

"Sit down if you want to kibitz!" screamed Stanley from the side of his mouth. If he saw me, he certainly didn't recognize me.

I pulled up a chair from one of the backgammon tables. Stanley picked up:

♠ 10 9 7 6 ♡ 6 5 ♢ J 10 4 2 ♣ A K Q

He passed and his left-hand opponent opened one notrump. Doc, Stanley's partner, passed, his hands shaking now, and the dealer responded two clubs, which I recognized as the Stayman convention. Stanley doubled with his A-K-Q of clubs. This was lead-directing, of course, but when the notrump opener bid two hearts, Doc came in with a bid of three clubs. This got doubled, everyone passed, and Stanley jumped out of his seat banging my knee while running to the other side of the table to see his partner's hand..

Then he rushed out of the room and I heard a door slam. I stayed and watched. Doc wasn't a great declarer from what I could tell, plus he was missing a lot of trumps. At the end of the hand, the defense had eight tricks, which meant 1400 points.

The beautiful dark-haired woman without the bra, whom I had completely forgotten about, got up and leaned across the table. She was trying to reach a folded paper on the other side. Doc, the declarer, said, "What do you want from *me*? Who doubles on a three-card suit, eh?"

"I'm not discussing bidding theory with you!" she cried. "I just want to see the score." Slap! The pock-marked man slapped her wrist. Her face got all red. I wanted to stand up in protest, but I just sat there in fear and awe. He put his plump hand into his inside jacket pocket and pulled out a pencil filled with lead. With that, she stormed off, and I soon heard another door slam.

Doc looked at me. "So he wanted the lead? I need his help for the lead? Wouldn't you bid three clubs on my hand? Anybody have the time? My watch has stopped."

I stared at him. I think I was mesmerized by the whole proceedings. Doc did have four clubs, plus an ace and a singleton. But on the other hand, he was vulnerable, and he had probably missed the fact that Stanley was a passed hand. On a high level, the double was clearly for the lead, not for competing.

However, *high level* doesn't always work at the table. I remember the time, many years later, I made a similar vulnerable double of a cue bid. I held the A-K-Q of spades. The opponents bid to slam in diamonds, but my partner, who had never made a bid (and had had an opportunity to do so at the one level) suddenly jumped in with six spades (he held seven little spades and out)! This vulnerable sacrifice went down 1400 points also. My partner was an expert player of national ranking. If he misinterpreted my lead-director as inviting a bid, then anybody could. But on that earlier occasion, at the Mayfair Club when I was only innocent kid, I thought Stanley's partner had been pretty stupid.

I kept quiet, however—which was just as well, since before I could say a word, the guy with thick glasses, known as Frankenstein, pointed at me and told me to shut up. In the meantime, Doc had looked at Frankenstein's watch, muttered something about a hospital and rushed out of the room. I later learned that he was a surgeon at NYU Medical Center, and a very respected one at that. With luck, none of his patients had ever played bridge with him, or they would have seen his hands shake.

The pock-marked man who had slapped the woman was studying a long rectangular pad that opened up in the middle and spread across the table. "Stake $5" was written in the top left-hand box. The names of the players were in the left-hand vertical column, and boxes in horizontal rows had numbers in them. Apparently, these were the scores. This is what it looked like:

Stake $5	④	⑦	⑮		
PLAYERS	7	8	9	10	11
Gussie ($2)	-3	-3	-3		
Pizza	-8	-15	0		
Doctor B.	-15	-8	-23		
Frankenstein	+19	+26	+41		
Stanley K.	+7	0	-15		

In the column across, marked "9," he wrote the number "-3" in the horizontal row that had a woman's name at the far left. I believe it was "Gussie." Then, in the next row, he wrote "0" and shook his head. "All that work, for nothing." The name in that row was "Pizza." Next came Doctor B's row. He got a minus sign and "23." Frankenstein's row followed, with a plus sign and "41." Last was Stanley's row. His final figure was "-15."

A boy walked in with a box of pizza and placed it on a nearby table. "Not on the notebook!!" screamed the pudgy, pock-marked man. He ran to the table and took a huge black notebook from under the pizza, cradling it as if it were a baby. At the same moment the woman from the kitchen rushed in with a tablecloth.

"I'm late. . . ." She looked over at the man. "Lord have mercy, that's two in one day." She quickly placed the backgammon board on the floor, spread the cloth over the other table and took the pizza from the boy. The man clutched his notebook and placed it carefully on a chair, then sat down to his pie.

"I'm hungry," came a high voice from the window. The little girl was looking up from her book, and put it on the window sill. "I'm hungry, daddy" she said again.

Frankenstein got up from the card table and took her by the hand. "C'mon, Beauty, we'll go out for Chinese."

"I want pizza, daddy."

"That girl needs herself a good home-cooked meal," said the woman with the apron.

"Only big baboons eat pizza. Beauties eat Chinese."

"Look what I drew, daddy." She handed him a piece of colored paper with a sketch on it. I leaned over and saw a sketch of the pock-marked man. It was quite good.

"Very nice, Beauty; we'll call it 'Big Baboon in Action.' Now put it away and let's go; the smoke from that cigar is ruining my appetite."

"Did you win, daddy?"

"Frankenstein always wins."

"You better, or I'll tell mommy."

"C'mon, let's go get some won-ton soup. I'll dish it out."

"No, I'll dish it out. Oh please, daddy, let me this time, just once."

After they left, the woman from the kitchen shook her head back and forth, and shook her apron. "Lordy, lordy. That poor girl lost her mama nearly two years 'go. Must be talkin' to a ghost."

In a few moments the room was empty except for me and the pock-marked man. He was hunched over the backgammon table chomping away at his pizza. He took a moment to swallow and said, "You look hungry, kid. You want me to order you a pie?"

"No thanks, I've got to find my friend."

"Come here, kid." He waved his chubby middle finger. "Come here. What's your name?"

I walked over to the table and looked down at him. "Matthew Granovetter."

He stuck out his thick paw. "Michael P. McCarver." I shook his hand and came up with oil and cheese. "My friends call me *Pizza.*"

4

THE BONUS SYSTEM—A CLAZY THEENG— SPOT OF BLOOD.

As I passed the lounge, I could hear the argument.
"You can't keep taking money out of an account that's minus," Stanley insisted.

"If you wouldn't go for 1400, there wouldn't *be* a minus account," she returned.

"Look, you teach me gin; I'll teach you bridge."

"I have to teach you a lot more than gin."

"Stop that!"

I looked down. She had her left hand inside the back pocket of his trousers, her right hand on the crotch area.

"Okay, okay, okaaaay, here's your money. Don't let Roth see it, that's all."

"I've already got it," she said, holding up a wad. She put the bills in her purse.

"Give me one," he said.

"Just a second."

She handed him a white pill and he swallowed it whole. I

spotted my Ben Franklin on top of the coat rack, so I stepped into the room to retrieve it. I certainly didn't want to leave it here. My damp *Bridge World* was still inside. Moving past them again, I cleared my throat.

"Err, excuse me, but Stanley, don't you remember me?" (I left out, "You remember. We went to high school together—just last year.")

"What the hell? Matt, what are *you* doing here?!" He grabbed me around the shoulders and gave me a hug.

It suddenly dawned on me why I *was* there. And it sure seemed ridiculous now. Could I really say: *Stanley, I'm here to take you back to school?* The Mayfair Club was on a totally different planet from the Quad.

His friend started to walk out of the room.

"Hey, Chops, this is the kid I was telling you about, the one I went to high school with."

"M-Matthew," I said. "I'm visiting from Rutgers. That's where we . . . uh . . . I, go to school."

"Gimme a break," she said, brushing past my outstretched hand.

"She's a little high strung," said Stanley.

"Wait a second, Chops. This is the kid who taught me what a deck of cards was."

She turned back from the doorway. "You play bridge?" she asked—a small turnaround in her interest.

"He plays duplicate," interrupted my friend. "Doesn't know a thing about money bridge, but he's a great duplicate player, wins a lot of tournaments."

"SUPPER!" came a cry from the kitchen.

"C'mon, let's eat," said Stanley, and he dashed out of the room into the back. Chops looked me over from head to toe like I was a piece of kielbasa hanging from the butcher's rope.

"I judge a man by his ability to make the right bid at the right time," she said with a smile. "Do you think that's evil of me?"

I shook my head no, and wished to heaven I could improve my competitive judgment. Then I erred. I said, "Personally, I think declarer play is the most interesting part of the game."

"Gimme a break, anyone can play a hand. Your partner's out of your way and it's you against the world. Any moron can follow a defensive signal, too. But when you and your partner bid a hand together, and are on the same wavelength—" Her eyes began to film up. "Well, that really is the limit."

Swallowing hard, I got my courage up and said, "You know, I once bid a slam with my dad on only 25 high-card points."

"That's what they all say." She turned around and headed out again. I followed her, running to catch up, then bumped her elbow by accident. "Oh, you," she said. "So you're a great duplicate player, huh?"

I nodded my head, yes, yes, yes.

"I went to a duplicate club once. It was very boring. There were no stakes, nothing. And all that fuss over extra tricks. I couldn't really get into it. But Al says it's an interesting game."

"Al?"

"Al Roth. He said I could learn a lot by just playing rubber for a few years, sort of make it my training ground. But I don't know if I could ever get worked up over an overtrick. Do you?"

I shook my head, no, no, never.

We entered the back room, which had been changed into a dining area. About eight or nine people already were seated around the tables, eating, drinking and theorizing over the late-afternoon rubbers. She looked around the room, then looked back at me. "You don't look like a great duplicate player. You look awfully young."

Oh god, she was looking at my acne. I pretended to sneeze, covering my nose. "I am. I mean I am young but, well, I'm not any younger than Stanley."

"Stanley is real good. But he loses too many points trusting the other players. That's what Frankenstein says. Anyway, you must be good, if Stanley says so. But I like to judge things for myself. Personally, I go strictly by the bonus system."

"The bonus system?"

"That's right. A partscore nets you nothing. Bid and make a game, that's worth a kiss. A slam, that's worth—well, you know."

I didn't know. "What about a grand slam?" I asked.

She smiled. "A grand slam?" She whispered in my ear what that was worth.

The advantages of the bonus system at rubber bridge were growing in importance to me as I sat down to supper. All the tables were covered with cloths, silverware, napkins and glasses. I saw that Stanley was sitting at Pizza's table. Pizza had just finished his last slice, which appeared to be only his appetizer—for now a plateful of lamb chops and mashed potatoes was heading in his direction—and he was licking his fingers. I gazed around the room. There was his precious notebook on the empty chair by the window.

Chops got Stanley's attention and crossed her eyes, pointing to a different table. But Pizza already was standing up, napkin in shirt, moving the adjacent table next to his. "C'mon kids, sit with me. We'll make a party of it. C'mon, no hard feelings." Chops, a bit annoyed, sat on Stanley's right (the other side of Pizza) and I sat across from her for a good view. On my right, between Pizza and me, sat an elderly woman (elderly to a boy of 17—I doubt she was over 60) who later was introduced as Gussie. I was hoping Mr. Roth would join us on my left, but he took one glance in my direction and went to the far corner. Suddenly, the man with the janitor's uniform, whom I had seen earlier in the building's foyer, approached the table with a bow and asked if the seat was occupied. "Whad'ya want, an engraved invitation?" squealed Gussie.

The thin man sat down and thanked everybody. Then he turned to me and held out his left hand. "Ahh, a new face. Let me intloduce myself. Otto."

"Matthew," I said, eyeing the mashed potatoes that were just put before me.

"All right, Rockefeller," said Pizza. "What did Polaroid do today?"

"It's a clazy theeng, that Polaroid," answered Otto, "Up thlee points at the opening, then never moving all day. I theenk my elevator had more ups and downs than Polaroid"

"Just as long as it was up." said Pizza.

"I theenk one day a camela is invented that takes the *inside* of what someone is. That would be sometheeng, heh?"

"Just keep it out of *here*," squealed Gussie.

Otto turned to me. "So what you say your name is, heh? It's a clazy theeng, the number of new people you meet here."

What's so crazy?" squealed Gussie again. "It's the only place in town you can eat on credit."

"Tlue, tlue," said Otto. "Everytheeng is credit, these days. In the old countly . . . ."

The woman from the kitchen looked down at me and asked if I was having salad with my meal. I said yes, please, and she gave me a bowl next to my lamb chops and potatoes. I didn't even check

45

to see if the ladies at the table were served. I dug right in. After my fourth bite, my attention turned to the argument at the far end of the table.

"This is why I say you must play a structured system," Pizza was explaining.

"What's it got to do with system?" Stanley whined. "If a double is lead-directing, it's lead-directing, and that's all there is to it."

Pizza took a glass of ice water and emptied the whole thing in one gulp. "In my system, when you double Stayman, you must have at least five clubs to two of the top three honors. If you and Doc played my system, you couldn't go wrong."

"C'mon, man. Are you trying to tell me it's my fault? With ace-king-queen of a suit?"

"I don't know anytheeng about the hand," said Otto, waving his arm "but maybe the boy's got a point."

"If you don't know anything about the hand," squealed Gussie, "keep your trap shut. That's what *I* always say."

"No system is gonna help playing with Doc," insisted Stanley.

"Well then, if you know that," said Chops, "why did'ya double?"

Stanley did not respond. Then Pizza shook his head, a few crumbs falling to his left and right. "First rule of rubber bridge, kid, don't invite an overbidder to the party. Pass the ketchup. Maggie! Where's the ketchup?!"

The woman from the kitchen, Maggie, charged over to the table with a plate of ketchup, spilling some of it on Pizza's napkin. "Thanks, kid."

"Don't call me kid, Mr. McCarver. I'm old enough to be your mother. And my lamb chops do not need ketchup."

"Women!" said Pizza. "You're all alike; you all gotta make a fuss over me."

Gussie dropped her fork. Then she picked up her plate and moved to another table. "I'm trying to digest my food."

This was the first time I had ever heard the concept of bidding out of fear of your partner. In fact, this was the first time I'd ever heard *any* discussion of bridge strategy. Most of the discussions after duplicate sessions are about which systemic bids worked and which didn't. Sure, system was mentioned here at the Mayfair, but the crux of the table-talk was psychological. I was brought up on duplicate and tournament bridge—which, in the foremost sense, is based on partnership trust and system. After a duplicate session, conversation tended to be biased. "That bid didn't work because our system is wrong. Let's change the meaning of the bid." Here, the remark, "don't invite an overbidder to the party," was far more general, yet far more applicable in any partnership, playing any system.

Before that night, I'd have judged Stanley's double on the basis of whether he used the bid in the proper context. Suddenly a new element was foremost—who is your partner? Doc was a weak player, an overbidder, somebody Stanley should never have risked bidding with regardless of what the bid meant!

This lesson could easily be applied to duplicate or partnership bridge as well. To put it simply: If your bid might confuse partner, don't make it. Partnerships of long standing often get into ambiguous sequences. The simple solution is to avoid the questionable bid and discuss the situation afterward.

"I never have this kind of problem with Doc," bragged Pizza. "I pass throughout with him. Next time we play together, you'll see. Doesn't matter what my hand is, Nooooo bid. Roth taught me that."

"Did I hear my name in vain—for the two thousandth time?"

Al Roth sat down on my right. "All right, what's the problem?"

Stanley told Al the auction and the 1400 result. Al looked at me and told me to be careful what kind of people I hang out with.

"First of all," he continued, pointing at Stanley, "you don't belong in the game." Stanley started to object. "Don't get so insulted. *None* of you belongs in the game." That seemed to make Stanley feel better.

"You're all children. And the reason is you don't know the value of money." Maggie came by with some chocolate layer cake.

"Who's having dessert? Mr. Pizza, I made your favorite tonight."

"No sweets for me," said Pizza, who cut himself a slice, anyway.

"But Al," Chops asked in a high-strung voice, "was Stanley's double lead-directing or inviting a bid?"

"Hold on, little girl," said Al. "In all my years, I never heard of

47

a lead-director on a three-card suit." Chops gave Stanley an evil stare. "Don't get me wrong, now," Roth continued, "it was lead-directing. And it might have worked. But he was playing with the wrong partner. Doc's an excitable guy. He doesn't appreciate that his partner is simply trying to help him out with a lead. He's like most bridge players, always wanting to get into the act. When you play with people like that you're better off passing, losing a point here or there rather than creating a catastrophe by bidding." He turned to me, now. "You like your cake? You ate it awfully fast. My final words to you and all you children are: Learn the value of the word *pass*."

With that, he rose and went into the kitchen. Otto nodded. "It's a claaazy theeng, but he's right again, dammit."

"Of course he's right," said Pizza. "The first rule of rubber bridge is: Learn to say pass. That's what *I* say."

With that, Pizza rose, burped a big one, and went over to the window where his notebook lay. Taking a pencil from his jacket pocket, he sat down and began to write.

"What is that?" inquired Otto. He was looking at my book.

"Just a school book," I said. "Actually it's an unfinished autobiography—"

"No, that," he interrupted pointing to my *Bridge World.*

"Oh, this is the latest issue—"

"No, that!" he demanded, his finger on the heading of one of the articles listed on the front cover: "The McCarver Theory of Exhaustion."

He grabbed the magazine from me and found the article. "Dammit," he said. "First he steals my ideas, then he publishes them under his own name! I'm going to keell him one day." Otto looked up suddenly and pointed his chin to Pizza, who was still busy writing in his book in the corner. "See, now he steals Roth's system. Oh, if only the boys back in Boodapest could see how he's distorted every single one of the bids."

"You mean the theory written up in this month's Bridge World magazine?" I asked, trying to remove it from his grip.

"Ahh, don't give me that. Is only the Boodapest system in disguise. You ever play this system?"

When I next looked up, Chops and Stanley had left the table, and I was stuck there alone with the building's janitor telling me about his bidding system from the old country. I suddenly noticed Otto's watch. It was seven forty-five. I had no chance to catch the eight o'clock train. I felt my shirt pocket. The schedule was still there, albeit wrinkled and damp. The next train to New Brunswick on Friday nights was the 10:55. A little late, but what could I do?

"Are you going to pay cash or do you have an account, young man?" asked Maggie, who was clearing the tables.

I felt into my pants and came up with nothing. I had forgotten about my stolen wallet. Not only did I not have money to pay for dinner, I didn't have a return train ticket.

"Put it on Stanley's account," I said.

"That's between you and Mr. Roth."

BANG! Otto had smashed my magazine on the table. "Sonofabitch Pizza thief! It's a clazy *theeng*, but both systems appear to be the same. Yet history proves the Boodapest System, which I intloduce to this country, has come first. You tell me now, what do you theenk?"

"I theenk, I mean I think . . . I mean I don't think it's a system really, just a theory or so. . . ."

"I theenk I have another cup of tea, Maggie. Is good for the nerves."

"Yes, sir, Mr. Rockefeller. Say, did you see that new stock listing, IBM?"

"Maggie, is no good. Tlust me. Computers are kaput."

"But Miss Gussie says you advised her to buy computer stocks only last week."

"Did I?" said Otto. "I don't remember—wait—yes, yes, I did. But I don't theenk they did very well."

I ran into Chops on the phone at the desk where Roth was writing on some 3-by-5-inch index cards. "Don't give me that," she said into the receiver. "You were supposed to stay till twelve tonight. All right, all right, give him another bottle. I'll wait."

A couple of tables were already in play for the evening session. Frankenstein was back, his arms waving in protest. I could see him across the room yelling at Otto, who had just sat down with his tea to kibitz. Frankenstein had forced him to change seats and kibitz on the other side of the table. The sounds of shuffling and table talk grew louder, like the rising sounds of a symphony in the final movement. There was almost no breeze coming from the windows; it had gotten dark outside and was going to be a warm, humid night.

"She's over your head, kid." Pizza gave me a wink as he walked by the desk, then asked Roth to get Gussie's account. I couldn't help seeing the white index card with various numbers, fees, dates, written with black and red ink.

"The usual transfer?" asked Roth.

Pizza nodded. "Don't worry, Al; the lawyers settled this afternoon."

He turned and gave Chops a squeeze on her rear with his enormous, plump hand. She turned around, phone in hand, and smashed the back of his ear with the receiver. I thought his skull had cracked, but it was thick, very thick. Pizza stumbled back, then felt the back of his neck. He reached quickly into his inside jacket and pulled out a handkerchief. Wiping a spot of blood, he exhibited a lecherous smile, then walked over to the corner, rapping his knuckles on the table where Stanley and three other players were already bidding a hand.

"I'm gonna kill that jerk, someday," said Chops between her teeth. In the meantime, she had lost her connection and hung up. "I have to go home, darnit."

She looked around the room, spotted Stanley and rushed over. Then she stopped suddenly—I think because she saw Pizza kibitzing—and turned back toward the exit.

"Excuse me, Mr. Roth," I said. "I have a problem concerning the cost of the dinner."

She grabbed my arm, and before I could say anything else, she had moved me down the hallway past the backroom. The last thing I saw was the shadow of Frankenstein's little girl, sitting in her chair by the window in the back room, writing something in a book, a tall lamp behind her providing the light.

5

IT WAS a short cab ride across town and I had to lie, saying I had no small bills, when it came time to pay the fare.

Her apartment was on the top floor of an old five-story brownstone. It was a walk-up, and it reminded me of an old movie I had seen with my dad on television, called "Room at the Top." Chops wasn't exactly Simone Signoret, nor was I Lawrence Harvey. But the room was at the top.

Chops unlocked the door, but it was chained from within. I heard a radio, then heard it go off. The babysitter opened the door. She looked very young (she was my age) and got her purse as soon as we came in. Chops paid her, and there we were in the living room, a high-ceilinged, musty smelling room with a couch, chair, card table, and an old RCA record player with the Beatles' "Sergeant Pepper's Lonely Hearts Club Band" lying next to it. There were two bed pillows on the couch and a sheet sticking out of the cushion.. Some books were set up on a shelf built into the far wall next to a solitary window.

Chops went into a back room and I followed. It was hardly a room, more like a big closet. A baby lay in a crib. He was sucking on a bottle, but seemed to be sleeping at the same time. Chops touched his forehead—he stirred—and she quickly lifted her hand and pushed me back into the living room.

"Would you like a joint?"

"Yes, this is a nice joint," I said.

She looked at me like I was nuts. Then she opened a closet, reached up and pulled down a cardboard box. Inside were some small one-inch-square papers and what looked to me like dirt.

"Do you roll?" she asked.

"Dice?" I said.

"Oh, c'mon now, gimme a break." She rolled a cigarette out of the paper and dirt, then lit a match. After inhaling deep into her throat, she held the smoke for a while before letting it out.

"That's better," she said, then handed me the cigarette.

"Where's the ashtray," I asked.

"Ashtray? Don't waste any of it. It's Peruvian."

"Oh."

I handed it back to her.

"Well, how about wine?"

"Sure," I said, though I didn't drink wine either—but was afraid to admit it.

She went to the kitchenette, a small enclosed area that sported a sink, old stove and half-sized refrigerator. Above was a cabinet, from which she took two glasses and a bottle. I saw something move in the closet. It was some kind of bug. Chops scooped it up and tossed it down the drain. I wondered if I could let the hand that touched that bug ever touch me.

"Where should I sit?" I asked.

"I don't know; I'm not your keeper."

Unable to make up my mind between the couch and the card table, I wandered over to the the the bookshelf and read the titles. "According to Hoyle." "Bridge is a Partnership Game" by Roth and Stone. "Five Weeks to Winning Bridge" by Alfred Sheinwold. "Watson's Play of the Hand." "Websters Scrabble Dictionary." "The Backgammon Book" by Jacoby and Crawford. Bridge World Magazines 1967-1968.

I suddenly realized I'd left my Ben Franklin at the club, and my September *Bridge World.* She handed me a glass of wine and clinked my glass. "Here's to Stanley holding cards tonight."

"How late does Stanley usually play?"

"He won't be back till dawn, unless he's really hot."

I took that to mean he would quit early if he won some money, but had understood it wrong. The professional gambler continues when he's hot, when he's doing well, and quits when he's cold. It's another one of those psychological strategies. The theory is that you play better when you're optimistic, but you start pressing and making poor decisions during a losing streak.

She moved over to the couch. I followed suit. Suddenly I saw tears on her face. I didn't know what to do. I took out my train schedule and tried to wipe one away.

"What's that thing?" she said, pushing the paper aside. "I'm so embarrassed. Look at this place. It's the pits, right?" She sniffed a few times and took another puff. Then she relaxed again. "Can I ask you something, seriously? I need some advice on life."

I nodded, although I was probably one of the last people on Earth to seek advice from.

"Say you . . . well, say for example you had a chance to move from a place like this to the East Side. You know, one of those nice apartment buildings with a doorman, a real kitchen, air conditioning."

I nodded again.

"Would you think it so bad to . . . say, well you know, for example, suppose there were this older woman who you found slightly repulsive, but could afford to get you this nice place. Would you . . . turn a few tricks just to get it?"

I thought about it. I had played with some pretty awful women on occasion when I went to the duplicate without a partner. But what the heck.

"That's not bad if it means getting a new apartment," I said.

She smiled now, and put her hand on my leg. "C'mon," she said, "let's bid some hands."

We moved to the card table. She made herself another joint and poured me more wine. Then she put some cards from a deck on the side of the table and dealt us each 13 of the remaining. I sorted my hand.

♠ K Q 6 5 ♡ A 7 ◊ K 10 8 7 6 ♣ Q 4

Chops opened one heart. I responded two diamonds. Chops rebid two hearts. Now I had a difficult decision. She didn't promise six cards in hearts with her rebid because on many hands she might not be able to bid anything else. For example, with:

♠ x x x ♡ K Q x x x ◊ A x ♣ K J x, two notrump could easily place the contract from the wrong side of the table, the spade lead coming through partner's tenace. If she had three little clubs opposite my queen doubleton, a notrump contract from either side would be wrong.

For now, I bid two spades. She rebid two notrump. So I bid three notrump. She held:

♠ A 9 ♡ Q J 10 9 5 4 ◊ A 5 ♣ K 6 5

"Not so hot," she said. If they lead a club from a five-card suit and the heart king is offside, I go down."

She was a fast analyzer, but I had to agree. The best contract was four hearts, which was practically laydown for five. Maybe I should have hedged over two notrump with three hearts, but, having bid diamonds followed by spades, a three-heart bid would have implied a singleton club.

"Why not make a convenient response, one spade?" asked Chops. "Look how easy the auction would have gone:"

Chops	Me
♠ A 9	♠ K Q 6 5
♡ Q J 10 9 5 4	♡ A 7
♢ A 5	♢ K 10 8 7 6
♣ K 6 5	♣ Q 4
1 ♡	1 ♠
2 ♡	4 ♡
pass	

"My two-heart rebid after a one-level response guarentees a six-card suit. You don't have to look further after knowing the eight-card fit is there."

This was true, but I always thought you responded in your longest suit first. The argument against responding in spades is that you can miss a diamond slam when partner holds ace-third of diamonds and a huge hand. But then again, how likely is that? I made it a point to remember this "convenient-response" concept.

"C'mon, deal the next hand," she said. The night was young. "No, not with those." She grabbed the cards I had picked up from the side of the table and threw them on the floor. "No two's or three's. The idea of a practice session is to deal out some game and slam hands. Games and slams get bonuses. Or have you forgotten already?"

How could I forget?! I dealt myself:

♠ A 10 6 5 ♡ K 10 8 7 5 ♢ 4 ♣ A Q 6

"What system are we playing?" I asked. It was a perfect hand for Flannery (an opening bid of two diamonds to show a minimum hand with four spades and five hearts).

"Stick to *Mayfair Standard.* That's what we play at the club. Five-card majors, forcing notrump, weak jump responses, weak two-bids—two notrump the only force, forcing Stayman, Jacoby

Transfers, negative doubles . . . that's about it."

"What about Pizza's theory? The one he stole from Budapest?"

"Gimme a break."

"Flannery?"

"No Flannery. Al hates Flannery."

I opened one heart. She responded one notrump, forcing. I rebid two clubs. She bid three clubs. I didn't like it, but there was nowhere to go on my minimum, so I passed. "Nothing to that hand," she said.

"Wait a second," I said, turning her cards over. "I want to see what would have happened playing Flannery."

Me	Chops
♠ A 10 6 5	♠ Q 7
♡ K 10 8 7 5	♡ 4
◇ 4	◇ A 9 8 7 5
♣ A Q 6	♣ J 10 9 7 4

Our auction:

1 ♡	1 NT
2 ♣	3 ♣
pass	

Playing Flannery:

2 ◇	?

"You're wasting time," she said, shuffling the cards. "It must be your duplicate training. Too much concentration on conventions and partscores. The idea is to think and communicate and always keep in mind a possible game."

I couldn't help but notice Chops had raised me with only seven high-card points. With all that distribution, however, three clubs looked iron-clad; I'd probably make an overtrick without a trump lead.

"Wait a second," I said. "What would you have bid with 10 points and the same hand?"

"Two spades."

"On queen doubleton?"

"I didn't respond a spade. That makes spades an impossible suit, so if I bid it later on, it means that I fell in love with your last suit."

She dealt a new hand, but her answer was sensational. She had bypassed spades the first round; thus two spades had become a totally impossible call. "I fell in love with your last suit!" I was starting to love this conceptual way of bidding. Had she gotten all these ideas from the Mayfair Club?

Chops handed me the joint and I took a puff without thinking. I started to cough. "Here," she said, "drink your wine." I did, and then picked up my new cards:

♠ A 10 9 7 5 ♡ A K Q 6 ◇ 5 ♣ A 8 5

Chops opened one diamond. I responded one spade. She jump-raised me to three spades.

Thinking a small or grand slam, I decided not to leap, but instead investigate with a cue bid of four clubs. Whether this was the wine, joint, or my own brain slowing me down, I don't know; but surely no one would criticize if I had gone straight to Blackwood or the grand slam force. My four-club call had a good effect, I think, because Chops sat up in her seat visibly excited. Six clubs, she bid.

I stayed calm. What was this jump to slam all about? Probably some other bidding technique from rubber bridge that I knew nothing about. Was she void in clubs? At duplicate we play unusual jumps to show singletons and voids. I tried six hearts. What could I lose by cue-bidding my ace-king-queen? She went back to six spades.

I was wasting time again. What could she have? If she were indeed splintering in clubs, she would have to hold at least one ace and the trump king-queen for her bold leap. In fact, she *must* be void in clubs! After all, with only one ace, how could she be sure we weren't off two of them? Even with one ace and a void, she was taking a chance. The hell with it. I looked up from my cards and proudly bid seven spades.

Here were the two hands:

Chops	Me
♠ J 8 6 4	♠ A 10 9 7 5
♡ —	♡ A K Q 6
◊ A K Q 8 4	◊ 5
♣ K Q J 9	♣ A 8 5

1 ◊	1 ♠
3 ♠	4 ♣
6 ♣	6 ♡
6 ♠	7 ♠
pass	

"How was I supposed to know your trumps were so bad when you leaped to slam?" I said, defending my seven-spade bid.

"What suit did I leap to," she asked in return, "spades or clubs?"

"Can I have another puff of that stuff?"

She had leapt to clubs—*clubs*.

"You need more than a drag. I thought you said bidding was your forte."

"But I held 17 of the finest points!" I protested. "Why, I could almost bid seven spades over three spades and not feel guilty."

"What are these feelings you're talking about? Guilt? Why don't you just bid your cards like a man? You're supposed to be investigating a slam; you're supposed to be bidding where your values are, not counting your points. Why did you bid your ace-third before your ace-king-queen-fourth? Bid your suits first; otherwise how can partner know how to evaluate his hand?"

I sat back and took the blows.

"Okay, I'll give you this much," she continued. "Your exploratory call of four clubs turned out lucky. But now, when I bid six clubs, you had to understand the basic meaning of jumps. Roth says whenever a lower bid in a suit is forcing, a jump in that suit shows good trumps. Okay, you didn't know clubs were trump yet. But only a . . . a . . . a millionaire would leap to slam in a second suit without absolute solidity."

"A millionaire?"

"Yeah, somebody who doesn't care about money, somebody who wouldn't mind if partner passed the bid and he lost a hundred dollars."

I nodded. I wasn't so sure, but I nodded. The hands said we

could make seven clubs, but it looked like a dream. Dare I mention out loud that I played her for a club void? How could I have been so wrong? Let's try again, I thought.

$$\spadesuit \text{A K 8 6 5} \quad \heartsuit 5 \quad \diamondsuit \text{K J 8} \quad \clubsuit \text{A Q 10 6}$$

I opened one spade. She bid one notrump. I rebid two clubs. She rebid two spades. What now? She could have as little as six points and a doubleton spade. I had 17 highs. I had to make another move. Wait. Gotta stop counting points all the time. What do I need for a game? That's the question I should ask myself. Well, how about the jack of clubs, queen of diamonds, queen of spades? That's five points. Five crummy points! If I raise to three spades, how will she know to bid four with that hand? Suddenly I felt a chilly breeze. There was a thunder clap! Then a baby cried from the distance. Chops rushed to the bedroom.

What about that impossible bid thing? Suppose I bid a red suit now at the three level. What would it say? I fell in love with your last bid? Okay. But, there's two red suits. Probably I should bid the one where I have length. Then she can evaluate her high cards, perhaps discredit points in the heart suit, knowing I have a singleton there.

Chops came back. "It wasn't Bobby," she said.

"I bid three diamonds."

She looked at her cards and bid four spades. I put my hand on the table.

Me	Chops
♠ A K 8 6 5	♠ 7 4
♡ 5	♡ 10 8 7 6 4
◇ K J 8	◇ A Q 10
♣ A Q 10 6	♣ J 9 8
1 ♠	1 NT
2 ♣	2 ♠
3 ◇	4 ♠
pass	

What a bid! What a contract! Assuming a heart lead, I ruff the second heart, cash the ace-king of trumps, go to dummy and finesse in clubs. If the spades are at worst 4-2 and the club finesse works, I make the game, losing only two trumps and a heart. If the club finesse loses, there is still a chance of a 3-3 trump split with one opponent running out of hearts.

"You're finally learning to bid out your shape," she said with a smile. It was good to see that smile. I hadn't bid a hand smartly until now. As she dealt the next hand, it started to rain. The combination of rain on the window and shuffling is a pleasing one—a sound that soothes the nerves. One more sip of wine. She leaned over and clinked my glass. Suddenly her face was closer to my face than the wine glass. Her lips were heading to my lips. What do I do with the joint in my hand? My neck was stiff. My face felt hot. C'mon, now, relax. Here it comes. . .

SLAM!

The door banged open against the wall. "What the hell's going on here?" asked Stanley.

I dropped my joint in the wine.

6

CUE BID AT THE SIX-LEVEL—BABYSITTING—
I AM THE WHEEL

THE BABY was awake and crying. Chops retrieved him from the crib.

"We've been minding the baby," I said. "Here, have a drink." I handed him my wine glass, and we both stared down at the joint.

"You were bidding hands," he said to her. "You were giving away all my secrets."

"*Your* secrets," said Chops. "They belong to the club. And what about him? He's supposed to be your friend."

"Someday *he'll* be playing in that game, and you know as well as I do that nobody there is anybody's friend." Stanley was furious. It was hard to believe he was so wrapped up in the rubber-bridge game.

"Here, take the baby, and tell me what happened," said Chops.

Stanley waved his arms in the air. "I'm not taking the baby; don't give me the baby. Give *him* the baby."

She did. And there I was holding the baby. I tried to burp him, but burped myself instead.

"It's that idiot, Pizza. I'm gonna kill him someday, I swear it," said Stanley. "First he goes down in a laydown game, which I don't mind, okay, 'cause what can I do about his declarer play? But then, on the third deal, with us vulnerable, he passes me in a cue bid at the six level."

I had to laugh.

"What are you laughing about? You think it's funny to lose two thousand points in one hand?"

"No, I . . . er . . . we, Chops and me, that is, had just had a similar misunderstanding and got to seven spades off the king-queen of trumps."

Stanley looked at me like I was mad.

"What's wrong with you, man? This was for money, this was business!"

Chops moved close to Stanley and put her hand on his neck. He brushed it away. "Now, c'mon, tell us what happened and we'll make it better," she said.

Stanley snapped his fingers. She went to her purse and gave him a white pill. He swallowed it whole. "Here, I'll lay out the cards."

The baby threw up on my shirt. "He did something on me," I said.

Chops shook her head. "You should have put him down before he did that."

"Put him down? Where do I put him?"

"I don't know. Am I your keeper?!"

"There," said Stanley. "Tell me this isn't cause for homicide."

I put the baby on the couch and went over to the table to see the hand. The cards were laid out:

```
♠ —                    ♠ A K x x
♡ x x x x x            ♡ A K x x
◇ x x                  ◇ A K x
♣ A x x x x x          ♣ K x
```

"I held the big hand," said Stanley, "the best hand I've held in a week. So after a pass on my right, I start with two clubs. No

60

interference. Pizza bids two diamonds, waiting, and I rebid two notrump. Now Pizza bids three diamonds, transfer to hearts, and I have this moose. Okay, so I jump to four hearts."

"You might have cue-bid, darling," said Chops.

"I might have cue bid, but which suit? Spades or diamonds? I bid spades, he'll think maybe I got a long suit, I bid diamonds, he'll think I don't have the ace of spades. Besides, why confuse matters? My hand screams for a slam in hearts, so I bid what I have, four hearts, great hand, great hearts."

"Too bad," I said. "If you had bid three spades, you could hear four clubs, then bid a slam."

"You don't know what you're talking about, kid. Go play a few rubbers before you talk. You think I'm playing with duplicate partners? Pizza's got a one-track mind. If I bid three spades, next thing I hear will be four spades."

"Then you bid five hearts," I said.

"Then he'll bid six spades, idiot!"

Then you bid seven hearts, I said to myself.

"All right, already, I know what happened," said Chops.

"You know what happened?" said Stanley. "How is it you're so smart all of a sudden? I'll lay you two-to-one you can't call his next bid."

"At least he bid again," I said.

"I'll take the bet, five dollars. He bid five clubs," said Chops.

"Very bright," said Stanley, nodding his head. "Yes, he bid five clubs."

"Give me my fiver."

"I don't have it. You'll get it tomorrow."

"How much did you lose tonight?"

"Nothing. I just can't take money out every single second."

"All right, already, what happened now, Stanley?"

"I cue-bid six clubs."

"Oh brother, gimme a break," she whined. "What are you, the bank of England? You think you can go ahead and make any bid you damn please. Do you think money flows out of the faucet?! When are you gonna grow up?!!!"

"That's why the two of you will never understand the game," Stanley said.

"I didn't say anything," I objected.

"Stop it!" she screamed, looking up at the ceiling. "Now you're listening to Pizza. I know, I know it all. You and him talking bridge again. I remember the whole discussion. Bypass two suits and the trump suit to cue-bid the fourth suit means a key card there, plus first-round control of the other suits."

"And that's exactly what I had."

"So," she said, "what went wrong, Mr. Brilliant?"

"He passed me, and the clubs were four-one. We would have made six or seven hearts."

"That's seems unlucky," I said, trying to calm things down.

"You know as well as I," she said, "he can't remember his own inventions. You know that's why he writes them down in his book. You know he's all theory and no practice."

"All right, all right, all right. I'm sorry. Here I make the perfect bid, I lose a fortune at the club, I come home and get no sympathy. . . ."

"It really wasn't so bad," I said again. He turned around and stared at me as if for the first time.

"What the hell are *you* doing here?" he said.

"Uh. . . minding the baby."

"THE BABY! Where's Bobby?!" screamed Chops.

"I left him on the couch."

All eyes went to the couch. No baby.

"Bobby, Bobby. . . ."

Stanley went to the table and finished the last of the wine. I looked around the room—nothing. Under the couch—nothing. Through the window—nothing. Oh my god! Who opened the window?! I heard a cry. Chops came out of the bedroom with the baby.

"Look, he wanted back in his crib. Isn't he a sweet thing, my Bobby?"

As babies go, he *was* a sweet thing that night.

There were no more trains back to New Brunswick until the next morning, so I figured I might as well see a few sights the next day before returning to the Quad. Chops was all excited over the idea of showing me around. Even Stanley thought it would help my education. That's when I finally got around to telling Stanley what I *was* doing there—bringing him back to college. He went into an uncontrollable laughing fit and told me I had a better chance of winning the fifth race double at tomorrow's Belmont card than him chucking the high life of New York to become a student again. I took a good survey of the apartment and agreed with him:

it would be difficult to leave all this.

"Besides," he told me in confidence, "Roth is planning to make me a partner."

"A bridge partner?"

"No, a partner in the club. You know, run the late-night action and things."

Chops made a list of activities for us. We'd start at the Statue of Liberty, take a ferry there and back, then work our way up-town. Through Wall Street and Chinatown (Chops said she knew a great restaurant there), then over to Little Italy for expresso. It sounded charming. After that we'd head to Greenwich Village and visit some art galleries, go to an exotic shop she knew of, but hadn't had time to visit yet, then have tea at Washington Square. It sounded romantic. Then we'd go to Macy's, buy me a clean shirt, and finally wind up the tour at the Empire State Building for an overall view. It sounded thrilling.

"All of us can go, me, you, Bobby and Stanley," she said. With that, Stanley yawned and agreed it sounded like a nice change of pace, but he was going to bed.

The sleeping arrangements were a problem. There was only the pull-out sofa and Stanley absolutely refused to sleep next to me. "But we used to as kids," I said, thinking it was only a few years since we bunked together on holidays and summer camp. "No dice, Romeo," he said. "I'm older now and it makes me itchy to sleep next to another body of similar sex."

That left only one option: Chops in the middle. This was not a good thing for my getting a decent night's sleep; so I spread a few cushions on the floor next to the sofabed, laid my head down and went straight off to dreamland.

Sometime shortly after dawn, I heard a gurgling sound. It was coming from the bedroom. Chops, leaning over the bed, reached down and touched my cheek with the tips of her fingers. "Be a good guy and give him his milk, 69 degrees, use tap to mix."

"Sure," I said.

"Oh, and change his diaper while you're up; they're in the third drawer down, pins in the second."

About two hours later, all was in hand. The secret to my success was to make three bottles at a time. That way I could keep feeding him while I worked on the safety pins.

It was now around 8:00, a good time, I thought, to get started on our day's activities. However, Stanley and Chops were still sleeping so I let them be and went to the bookshelf. There I selected Roth-Stone's "Bridge is a Partnership Game."

I had never read the book until now, though for the five years I played bridge I had played most of Roth's methods. Five-card majors, the forcing notrump, negative doubles all seem to have become standard, and nobody thinks of them any more as conventions. I read with interest the chapter called "Isms." Here was a list of rules to follow for practical success, rather than just bidding theory. One of these was about my own bad habit of counting points and not evaluating those points. It was number 13:

Pay No Attention to Point Count on Some Hands
(The Roth-Stone Theory of Distribution).

Throughout the history of bridge, it has been customary to describe many bids by the so-called expert as the expert's prerogative because "he has card sense." Point count and card sense have no relationship.

(This was underlined in red pen, apparently by Chops.)

This card sense is nothing more than a knack of evaluating your hand based upon the bidding and determining the number of possible winners or losers. That knack (or card sense) may be translated into the following rules:

1. When a trump fit has been established, the laws of probability are affected as follows:

a. If you have a side suit of five cards or longer, your partner is likely to have no more than two of that suit.

b. If you have a singleton or doubleton, your partner is likely to have three or more cards in that suit.

2. If you have three or more cards in a suit bid and raised by the opponents, your partner will probably have no more than two.

Thus you can vuisualize your partner's probable distribution and act accordingly.

One of the illustrations given was:

♠ A Q x ♡ x ◇ A K J x x x ♣ A x x

Partner opens three spades and you must decide whether to bid slam. A table is given:

Partner's probable distribution	Possible losers
♠ 7 (possibly 6)	None
♡ 3 or more	One
◇ 1 (or 2)	None
♣ 2 (or 1)	None

The book goes on to say:

> Thus, bid 6 ♠. Point count is unimportant. Partner should have a reasonably long and good spade suit. Partner's hand was:
>
> ♠ K J 10 9 x x x   ♡ x x x   ◇ x   ♣ x x
>
> Slam was laydown.

I continued reading another page. However, the baby was up again. I didn't know what to do and I didn't want to wake up my hosts, so I dressed the kid, found the stroller, and decided to take him outside for a walk. Before I left, though, I figured I would need some money for a little breakfast, so I went through Stanley's trousers. There I found about ninety bucks and I took a ten-spot, promising myself to return it later.

Five stories later I was out on the town with Bobby. We circled the neighborhood until we found a coffee shop. I had two eggs over easy, the kid had a donut and apple juice. I bought a newspaper. Thunderstorms expected to continue in the city tonight. I turned to the bridge column. It concerned a battle for an overtrick in a board-a-match team championship. The contract was one club at both tables and one side scored two for plus 90 while the other side made only one for plus 70. Chops was right; it was pretty boring. I suppose it was one of those deals where you had to be there for it to be exciting. When we got home it was 11:30 and they were still asleep.

I put the baby in his crib for a nap and went back onto the floor for one myself. In about an hour, I heard Stanley mumbling something about being late for the races. He got out of bed, dressed and ran out the door. Chops seemed dead to the world, so I stayed there thinking sexy thoughts. Maybe she would wake up to a sudden urge of passion, though I wasn't sure how that passion might manifest itself, being a little behind in the educa-tion-of-passion department. Of course, you can't score a slam un-less you're in it, and I wondered if I should slip up next to her in the bed.

After a while, however, I fell asleep again, and somewhere around three o'clock I woke up to the shuffling of cards. I looked up from the floor. Chops was dressed and at the table ready for action again.

"You gonna sleep all day?" she asked.

I rose, and she gave me some toothpaste, soap, and a towel. Then she made me put on one of Stanley's shirts before announc-ing the news that we had blown the sightseeing. I suggested we at least have lunch before I go back to New Brunswick, and she said that we could eat at the Mayfair. With that, we (me, Chops and Bobby) left the apartment without making the bed and hailed a cab to 57th and Sixth.

At the club, Roth greeted us and suggested we make up a two-cent game. I wondered who was going to hold the baby, the dummy? Then, as luck would have it, Frankenstein arrived with his daughter. "Just doing a little sightseeing with my beauty here," he said.

"We went to Chinatown for dim sum," said the little girl, very proudly. She was overjoyed to see somebody closer to her age, even if he was only a one-year-old, and she took Bobby into the back room to play among the chess clocks and backgammon boards.

The two-cent game was pretty awful, though not nearly as bad a game as the one at the Quad. Still, it was a good place for me to start, since I learned some new rules and got some early lessons on how to handle weak, and dangerous players. Surprisingly, even though I was far and away the best player in the game after Chops, I had a very difficult time winning—and I wasn't holding bad cards either! Part of my problem was the money angle. With about six dollars left over from breakfast in my pocket, I could not afford to lose more than three points. Two-cents-a-point meant that a vulnerable three notrump, for example, was worth twelve dollars. Thinking about the money made me tight, and as I picked up the cards to each deal I kept looking for the aces, a bad habit to get into. Another problem I had was my slowness to adjust to my partners. It was not until the fourth wheel that it came to me I was playing against three people, not two. And the most dangerous of the three was the person opposite!

The other two players in the game were Gussie, the elderly woman who had sat at the supper table with us the night before, and the Hungarian janitor, Otto, the fellow sometimes referred to as "Rockefeller." Otto was basically a pinochle player who found rubber bridge a fascinating diversion. "It's a clazy theeng, having a partner over there to contend with." Gussie was, on the other hand, a veteran bridge player who occasionally ventured out to the tournament world. She had even won a few Women's Pairs. She was quite a timid player, rarely bid, and even less rarely doubled a final contract. On the plus side, when she was your partner, you knew that she always had her bid, so she was far less prone to disaster than Otto.

Chops was in a different catagory. She was a student of the game, always learning, always applying what she learned. She had that rare ability to listen to what others were saying and, still rarer, to distinguish good advice from bad. If there was one player to emulate at the Mayfair, it was Chops. I was sure she was destined to become one of the world's best players. At that time, however, she stuck to the two-cent game rather than a higher stake. This was purely a financial choice, I assumed.

We played Chicago scoring at the Mayfair. Four deals constituted a "rubber." The deal passed clockwise around the table. The first deal, nobody was vulnerable, the second and third deals, the dealer's side was vulnerable, and the last deal, everyone vulnerable. Bonuses for games and slams were the same as in duplicate; for example, 300 for a nonvulnerable game and 500 for a vulnerable one. Doubled contract penalties were the same also. The only differences from duplicate or team scoring were partscores and honors. The partscore counted below the line toward the next deals, so long as the opponents did not wipe it out with a game or slam. Honors were traditional, 100 for four of five top honors in the trump suit, 150 for all five or all four aces in notrump.

The wheel was a club policy. At the beginning of the game, the cards were spread out face down on the table. Everyone picked a card. The two highest and two lowest were partners. Also, the highest card was the wheel. That person would start the deal rotation on each of the next three rubbers. After each rubber, the wheel remained seated as the other three players moved around the table—first two to the wheel's right switched, then two to the left.

This was a fair way to play because you had to partner everyone in the game an equal amount of time. When a fifth came into the game, it became more complicated, but still worked. A cut of cards produced an order of sit-outs which was listed on the scorepad, one person coming in and one going out after each rubber.

I was the wheel on my first experience at the Mayfair. My partner was Gussie, who was kind to me. "I hear you play duplicate. Just don't try anything too fancy, and we'll get along," she said in her high screechy voice. I was given the choice of red or blue deck. I chose the blue. Gussie shuffled and gave the deck to Otto for a cut. I dealt the cards. My first hand was:

♠ — ♡ A Q J 9 2 ◇ K Q J 10 7 ♣ A 7 4

I opened one heart. Otto, on my left, bid two clubs. Gussie passed. Chops, on my right, bid two spades. I was about to jump to four diamonds when I realized the McCarver Theory of Exhaustion might apply. If I took it slowly maybe I'd have a better chance of buying the contract. So I only bid three diamonds. Now Otto jumped to four spades. I thought he knew the theory from Budapest. Then why was he blasting to game?

Gussie passed. And when Chops passed, I considered bidding five diamonds. Was this one of those hands not to count points, but imagine the final contract instead? I had only four losers in the hand at the most. If Gussie had a little for me over there, I might even make five of a red suit. So I bid five diamonds. No bid, by Otto. Pass, by Gussie. Double, by Chops. This came around to Gussie, who hemmed and hawed and finally made a call of five hearts. Chops doubled this too and everyone passed. The ace of diamonds was led. How bad could *that* be?

My dummy was:

♠ Q 10 9 8 5 ♡ 4 3 ◇ 3 2 ♣ Q 10 8 3

On the ace of diamonds, Chops played the four. Otto switched to a low spade. I ruffed Chop's ace and quickly led out the ace and queen of trump. Chops won the king and played a diamond. Otto ruffed it and led a club. Chops ruffed it and I still had to lose a club trick for down three. That wasn't too bad considering that I would have been down five if Otto had respected Chop's suit-preference signal at trick one and switched to a club.

"They could have beaten me five," I said.

"I think that's what we beat four spades," she answered.

"Sorry, I thought at worst it would be a good sacrifice."

"You shouldn't keep bidding when you hear me passing," said Gussie.

"Maybe you could have doubled four spades," I suggested.

"Under the spade bidder?" cried Gussie.

Meanwhile I realized that Otto had a ridiculous hand for his jump to four spades. He had completely fooled me by blasting into a game he had no intention of scoring. The mad Hungarian tapped the deck to get Gussie's attention. She cut and he dealt the second deal while Chops shuffled. This was an etiquette I had to learn. The partner of the dealer shuffled and placed the cards on the right side of the table, ready to cut for the next dealer on the right.

On the second deal I held:

♠ K J 4 3 ♡ 9 8 7 ◇ 2 ♣ A J 9 8 3

Otto, on my left, started with one heart. Gussie passed. Chops responded one notrump. We had favorable vulnerability, and I wanted to slip in a two-club bid, but all I could think about was that I was minus ten dollars and hadn't even had lunch. So I passed, in fear, and Otto rebid two diamonds. Gussie passed (Gussie almost always passed) and Chops bid two hearts.

Now I knew I should double, both black suits were staring me in the face. But I analyzed their bidding instead of bidding my cards. Otto had five hearts and probably four diamonds. Chops, who bid one notrump and merely preferenced, had a doubleton heart and at most three diamonds. That gave my partner three hearts and at least five diamonds, thus very few black cards. Surely this was a misfit hand all around. I passed, and so did Otto and Gussie.

The first thing that hit dummy was three-card heart support to the king. The next was four diamonds to the jack. There were two more queens there, and when the hand was over, and Otto had made his two hearts, I realized Gussie's hand had been:

♠ A 10 7 6 ♡ J 2 ◇ Q 9 8 6 ♣ K 10 2

We were cold for two spades, and two finesses away from four spades! "That was better," said Gussie to me. "I didn't have a thing, so you did well by passing."

Now they had a partscore, and that made matters worse. They only needed 40 points to complete the game.

Gussie dealt and I shuffled. I put the cards down on my left and was corrected by Chops. I noticed she was very quiet, and deadly serious. One would hardly have guessed that she had just spent the night in the same room with me. Perhaps she was demonstrating to me the virtue of silence at the table. She hadn't even said a word to Otto when he misdefended earlier.

My new hand was:

♠ A 4 3 2 ♡ A Q 7 5 ◇ 7 6 5 2 ♣ 3

Gussie passed. Chops opened one notrump. "Weak or strong?" I asked Otto.

"When we have a partscore, we don't like to say."

Hmm. Did we play Landy? I couldn't remember if two clubs showed the majors or not under the house conventions. Anyway, we were vulnerable, so I passed.

Otto bid two hearts and Gussie passed. Chops bid two spades. I passed and Otto passed. Apparently two hearts was a transfer bid. Gussie now sprang to life with three clubs! I tried to remain calm waiting for the double. But Chops passed. I passed and Otto now bid three hearts. Gussie passed and Chops bid a quick three spades.

What was going on here? Had Otto forgotten the transfer? There was definitely confusion. But I was happy to be out of three clubs. I passed, Otto passed and Gussie passed.

I led my singleton club. This was the dummy:

♠ Q 5 ♡ J 10 9 8 6 4 ◇ J 8 ♣ J 6 5

Chops played it well for down five. I felt like an idiot for not doubling. Not only that, but we were cold for four clubs, partner holding six of them to the king-queen-ten.

"You never raised me with ace-queen-ace?" asked Gussie.

"But I only had a singleton club."

"I was vulnerable!"

"I should have doubled," I said. "But there was so much confusion, and also it was a partscore."

"They already had a partscore," squealed Gussie. She was right! How could I have forgotten? It was absolutely free to double. If they made it, it was game anyway.

"This hand demonstlates why pinochle is a better game," said Otto.

"No more transfers over notrump," said Chops rather curtly.

"No more tlansfers? Who tlansferred?"

I picked up my cards to the fourth deal, cursing my lost opportunity.

♠ 9 ♡ A Q 6 5 ◇ Q 10 8 6 ♣ J 9 7 4

Chops opened one notrump again. This time everyone passed, but I had to remember we were defending a game, not a partscore. With 60 on below the line, 40 points would mean 540 points. I had no clue what to lead, so I stuck to a traditional fourth-best heart lead. Dummy held:

♠ A 5 4 2 ♡ 9 8 7 ◇ 4 3 2 ♣ A 10 2

With two aces in dummy, it certainly appeared hopeless for us. I had nine points and dummy had eight. Even if Chops had only 15, Gussie would hold only eight.

Chops won Gussie's jack with her king and led a club to the ten. Gussie won the queen and returned a heart. I cashed both honors, everyone following. Then I played the 13th heart. Dummy threw a spade, Gussie threw the jack of spades, Chops threw a spade.

We had four tricks in. Now what? It looked like Gussie held the king-jack-ten of spades, so I shifted to my spade. Chops played low and Gussie won the king. Then Chops tabled her cards: ♠ Q ♡ — ◇ A K J ♣ K 8 6.

"I win any return in my hand," she said, "then cash the queen of spades before going to dummy with the club ace. I have two spades, one heart, two diamonds and two clubs—seven tricks."

"Too bad," said Gussie. "If only you could have found that

71

lead at the beginning of the hand."

Whatever Gussie had said so far that afternoon was wrong, and this was no exception. I should not have led a spade, not at the beginning of the hand, and certainly not later on! My spade shift at trick six gave Chops the contract on a silver platter. Look at the whole diagram:

Dummy
♠ A 5 4 2
♡ 9 8 7
◊ 4 3 2
♣ A 10 2

Me
♠ 9
♡ A Q 6 5
◊ Q 10 8 6
♣ J 9 7 4

Gussie
♠ K J 10 8 3
♡ J 4 2
◊ 9 7 5
♣ Q 5

Chops
♠ Q 7 6
♡ K 10 3
◊ A K J
♣ K 8 6 3

After Chops won the heart lead, she attacked clubs. Gussie won, and led back my suit. I cashed hearts and on the last heart, dummy threw a spade and Gussie signaled high in spades. Chops had to make a choice of discards. She didn't want to give up the diamond jack or one of her clubs, which could be the 13th if the suit divided 3-3. So she threw a spade. This was a mistake. Assuming Gussie's signal was honest, by keeping three spades, Chops could always lead one to her queen for two tricks. However, I did her work for her. My spade shift established the seventh trick.

Instead of thinking for myself, I had woodenly followed my partner's signal. Since the club ten was gone, I had a very safe club shift. I could play the jack or the nine; they were equals. Chops probably would have tested clubs before falling back on the diamond finesse for down one.

This was a bitter lesson. First, never give up. Second, don't just look at partner's signal; apply it to the hand. In this case, that meant counting declarer's tricks. That's all I had to do to realize the spade shift would give her the seventh.

Here's what the scorepad looked like:

We	They
	500
250	500
	60
	40

⑨

Minus 850 points. A "9" was circled on the pad now. (All fifty-point-or-greater scores were rounded off to the next hundred.)

"We lost the pip," squealed Gussie as she opened up the long white sheet. I looked around for it on the floor, but saw nothing. Then it was explained to me that the pip was the extra 50. If we had been minus only 840 points we would have "pipped" them and been minus only *eight* points.

She wrote "-9" in the column next to my name. This meant minus nine points. At two-cents-a-point, it translated to 18 dollars in the hole . . . plus the card fee.

Chops and Gussie rose from their chairs and exchanged places. However, just as I was about to deal the first hand of the new rubber, an ugly fat fist pounded the table. It belonged to Pizza McCarver, who was "knocking" into the game. "This is a two-cent game," said Chops.

"I know that, darling, but that's all there is right now. I'm sure I can sink to your level." With that, he took the other deck and spread the cards out. Gussie picked the three of spades, Otto picked the nine of hearts and Chops picked the three of clubs. That meant Chops was low and out first. There went my chance to recoup my losses. Chops left the table with daggers in her eyes. Pizza sat down in her place. I noticed the bandage across the ear that she had smashed the night before.

"All right, kid, now that the women are out of the game, we can play rough."

"Thanks," said Gussie.

"Are you familiar with my latest theory of bidding slowly and buying the contract?" Pizza asked.

"A little," I said, dealing the cards. "Let's just stick to Mayfair Standard."

"Kid thinks he knows a lot," said Pizza.

"He's not so bad as he looks," said Otto, coming to my rescue.

Pizza gave me a wink as I picked up my cards. I tried to take after Chops, keeping my mind in my own little bubble, not allowing these characters to affect my concentration.

$$\spadesuit J 6 \ \heartsuit Q 3 2 \ \diamondsuit 10 9 8 7 \ \clubsuit 7 5 4 2$$

I passed. The Theory of Exhaustion was quickly bypassed by the mad Hungarian. Otto opened three hearts. Pizza overcalled three notrump. Gussie doubled. That ended the auction. Gussie led out her ace of spades. "You can't win with dummies like that," said Pizza. Gussie continue the king-queen of spades and four more, followed by the ace and king of diamonds. Pizza took the rest. Down five. Minus nine hundred. Minus another 18 dollars.

Otto dealt. Pizza said, "I had *my* bid." And I suppose he did. His hand was:

$$\spadesuit 9 8 7 \ \heartsuit A K \ \diamondsuit Q J \ \clubsuit A K Q J 10 3$$

However, when Gussie, who never doubles without a sure thing, doubled, it would have been prudent for Pizza to run to safety. Even if four clubs were doubled—which it couldn't be, Pizza holding such good trumps—we would still be plus 50 after honors were added. I mentioned this to Pizza, in as nice a way as I could. He shook his head.

"You don't run from a double, kid, or they'll be doubling you out of cold contracts from here to Canarsie. That's game theory."

"We can make four spades," said Gussie.

"Then why don't you bid it?" complained Otto.

$$\spadesuit A K J 10 4 \ \heartsuit A 8 7 \ \diamondsuit J 2 \ \clubsuit 6 5 3$$

Otto opened one vulnerable spade. I was thankful. It was the first time he had started at the one-level. My partner passed. Gussie raised to two spades. I passed. If this were Christmas, I thought, Otto would jump to four spades. Otto did jump to four spades! Pass. Pass. I couldn't believe it, I savored the moment, four spades, vulnerable—I paused, then doubled.

Otto: "I wouldn't redouble." Taps the table.

Pizza: "Me neither, ha ha." Lights up a big fat Havana and bids four notrump.

Gussie: "Pass."

When the smoke from that Havana cleared, I was down only three in five clubs doubled. Pizza's hand:

$$\spadesuit - \heartsuit 4\,3\,2 \ \diamondsuit Q\,10\,7\,5\,4 \ \clubsuit Q\,9\,8\,7\,2$$

My hands began to shake. I reached for the table to keep steady. Pizza winked at me. "Good sacrifice, kid."

"I make four spades, dammit" said Otto, tossing in his cards with anger.

"Wh-what are you talking about?" I said. "I've got f-four top tricks."

Pizza pushed the 52 cards over to me as Gussie cut the red deck.

"Don't try to analyze every deal," instructed Pizza. "It'll ruin you for the next hand."

$$\spadesuit - \heartsuit A\,5\,4\,2 \ \diamondsuit A\,9\,8\,7 \ \clubsuit A\,8\,5\,3\,2$$

Pizza opened three spades, vulnerable. I was closing in on a state of shock. Gussie passed. I passed, praying for no reopening double. Otto hemmed and hawed. Finally he tapped the table. "You win," he said.

Gussie led a club. Pizza announced, "Honors," then spread seven solid spades face up on the table as proof. Otto cursed. Gussie wrote it in on the scorepad. Then Pizza played out the hand methodically for an overtrick when nobody revoked.

"Rule of one-two-three and four," said Pizza. "We should have been playing my preempt system It's the corollary to—."

Otto looked at him, red in the face. "Don't say *your* system. You know I intloduce this system from Boodapest."

Pizza chuckled. "You *are* a pest."

Otto slammed the table with his fist. "I cannot play at the

table with this thief! He provokes me, I—I—I. . . someday, I tell you!"

"Calm down," said Gussie, who had finished dealing the new hand and was already counting up her points. There was no doubt about it, she finally had a good enough hand to bid with. When she stopped counting, she lifted up her head and said two clubs. I passed with:

$$\spadesuit J 5 4 3 \quad \heartsuit 10 9 8 \quad \diamondsuit 2 \quad \clubsuit 7 5 4 3 2$$

Otto bid two hearts. Pizza thought for a few seconds, checked the scorepad, then considered. Finally he stepped in with three diamonds. Gussie never hesitated. Three hearts, she said. I passed and Otto bid four diamonds, a cue bid. Pizza sang out a double and Gussie sang out louder with a redouble. Finally, Otto leaped to six hearts, ending the excruciating auction. This was the whole deal:

Gussie (Dummy)
♠ A K Q 2
♡ Q J
◇ A 6
♣ K Q J 10 8

Pizza
♠ 8 7 6
♡ 6 5 2
◇ K J 10 9 8 3
♣ A

Me
♠ J 5 4 3
♡ 10 9 8
◇ 2
♣ 7 5 4 3 2

Otto
♠ 10 9
♡ A K 7 4 3
◇ Q 7 5 4
♣ 9 6

Gussie	Me	Otto	Pizza
2 ♣	pass	2 ♡	3 ◇
3 ♡	pass	4 ◇	double
redouble	pass	6 ♡	(all pass)

Pizza led the ace of clubs. Then he paused for quite a spell. From my point of view, it was hopeless unless Otto was missing one of the trump honors. Finally, Pizza shifted to the king of diamonds. This annoyed me, because I thought he held the queen, and was upset that he hadn't led the diamond king to begin with. Otto won the ace in dummy and played the queen of hearts. We all followed and Otto next played the jack of hearts, on which I falsecarded with the ten. Otto started counting to himself in Hungarian, and finally played low, protecting against a four-two split. However, now he had to get back to his hand to draw the last trumps. And suddenly it occurred to me I could get him to play a club if he thought I held a singleton spade. So when he played dummy's ace of spades, I dropped the jack.

Otto turned the trick over two or three times asking whose jack it was. Then he led the two of spades to his ten and drew the last trumps.

"It's a clazy theeng," said Otto. "If the jack of spades does not dlop, I come back in clubs and make the slam that way."

What was this mad Hungarian talking about?! Why would he try to return to his hand in *clubs* after the ace-of-clubs opening lead? Why wouldn't he ruff a third round of spades?

"Hey kid," said Pizza, "you better straighten yourself out. You only had one picture card, you should have held onto it."

I was speechless. I was afraid to look at the scorepad, but I did. This is what I saw:

We	They
150x	900
30	500
90	1430
270	2830

(26)

Minus 2,560 points. When I held good cards I did badly. When I held bad cards, I got murdered. In my anxiety, I failed to see three important points. First, if Pizza had kept his mouth shut and not bid over two hearts, there was a good chance Gussie would rebid notrump and the seven-card heart slam would never be found. Second, Gussie, who was a terrible player in most respects, revealed her one strength: She was a good partner. She raised Otto's suit with only two trumps, something many players—

especially egotistical ones—would never think of doing. Third, when that lunatic, Otto, had cue-bid four diamonds on four to the queen, Pizza had compounded his first error (overcalling three diamonds) by doubling the cue bid, allowing Gussie to show her diamond control with a redouble. I hated Pizza and I wanted him out of my sight.

Unfortunately, all he did was move to my left. Otto took a seat opposite me and Chops moved in on my right. "Cut me out," said Gussie. "It's time for dinner."

I could smell the food cooking now. It smelled great, but even if it hadn't, I would have wanted to go to dinner too. I wanted to go anywhere. But I had to think of etiquette and how it would look if I quit just as the mad Hungarian sat down opposite me. Then again, Chops and Pizza were my opponents. A partnership made up of two people who hated each other would surely dump some points my way. Chops had brought two cups of coffee with her and pushed one in my direction. That was very sweet of her, I thought. She must have seen the score, and felt sorry for me. But as I reached for the cup, she pushed it past my outstretched hand to Pizza! "Two sweet-and-lows?" asked Pizza.

"Two sweet-and-lows," said Chops. "Let's play cards."

I wondered if she was just putting him on, if that white powder floating on top was really cyanide. Or was it possible she could be so cool that when she sat down at the bridge table, all personal feelings, good or bad, would vanish from her soul? That she could turn on the charm for a man she hated just to get four good bridge hands out of him was more than I could stand. Cyanide, please let it be cyanide, I thought.

♠ Q J 7 6 ♡ Q J 9 8 ◇ 7 6 5 4 ♣ J

No aces, no kings. Life was becoming difficult. I passed and Pizza bid one notrump. Otto overcalled two clubs. Chops bid three notrump. What was Otto's two clubs? I was an idiot for not having straightened it out before when I thought about it. If it was clubs, my hand was good for defense only. If it was Landy for the majors, my hand was good for offense only. What to do, what to do? After a minute, I looked up at Chops. "Would anyone mind if I asked the meaning of my partner's two-club bid?"

"I don't mind," said Pizza, "the kid is new on the block, ha, ha."

"You can't ask," said Chops. "You'll have to learn the hard way."

Very nice, I thought. It's the last time I spend the night at *your* place. Clubs or the majors, I thought, clubs or the majors. Finally I decided to go with the odds. I had a singleton club and two four-card majors. The odds must be he's got clubs. So I passed. Otto's hand:

♠ K 10 8 5 4 ♡ A 10 7 6 4 ◇ 2 ♣ Q 3

Spades were 2-2 and the heart king was with the notrump bidder. We were cold for four hearts, but they made the first thirteen tricks in three notrump after a heart lead. Actually, this was an easy problem to solve if I had paid full attention to the clues in the bidding. The jump to three notrump by Chops was probably based on a long minor. Thus, my partner had the majors. Also, if partner's two clubs was natural, Chops probably would have doubled rather than bid three notrump.

"Nice bid," said Pizza.

"Gimme a break," said Chops.

"Maybe if I do not bid," said Otto, "you stop in only two notlumps."

Nobody addressed me. I didn't blame them. I picked up the cards to the next deal.

♠ — ♡ A K Q J 7 6 5 ◇ 4 2 ♣ A K Q J

Finally, something to work with. It had been a dry spell for a while. Pizza started with pass. Otto opened one spade. Wow. Chops passed. I decided to keep things simple. I would jump to four notrump. Then bid six or seve—

"What's that card on the floor?" said Pizza.

"What card?" asked Chops.

"I see it," said Otto. It was a red card face down. The three of them checked the backs of their cards, all red. "It's a clazy theeng," Otto said, "Look, I only have twelve cards. It must be mine."

He picked up the card and turned it over. The two of spades. "I theenk we just reshuffle." I started to object as cards were flung into the center. "Don't worry," Otto said to me. "I had a piece of clap for my opening."

Otto dealt me the following replacement:

♠ 4 3 2 ♡ 9 8 6 5 ♢ 6 5 4 ♣ 10 6 5

I was ready to cry, but I refused to in front of Chops. Pizza opened two notrump. Otto passed. Chops bid six notrump. My ten of clubs scored a trick when Otto held queen-jack doubleton; however, that was the only trick for the defense—making six, minus 1440.

"First time luck," said Otto with a big smile. "You don't have that ten of clubs, they make seven."

He dealt the cards. I shuffled the other deck, my fingers numb. I think I was getting a fever.

♠ K Q J 9 8 7 4 ♡ A 3 ♢ — ♣ Q J 10 3

Otto passed apologetically. "Sorry, partner, maybe I do better with you tomorrow." Chops also passed. I was about to open one spade when I realized it was third deal, we were vulnerable and they weren't. Perhaps a preempt was called for to keep them out of the auction. It would put Pizza in the hot seat if he had a close call. So I tried it. Four spades, I said. Five diamonds on my left. Otto passed and Chops passed. Now *I* was in the hot seat. Oh no. This was the hand I was supposed to "walk the dog." Why didn't I think of it before?

Now what? Could I really give up? If Otto held one or two cards for me, I might make five spades. But it wasn't correct in any book I ever read to preempt and then bid again without hearing from partner. Still, I couldn't bear to give up. Five spades, I said. Pass by Pizza. Pass by Otto. Six diamonds by Chops. I had already bid four and five, I couldn't bid six. So that ended the auction. Partner led the ten of spades. Pizza discarded a losing heart on dummy's ace:

Chops (dummy)
♠ A 6 5 3
♡ 10 8 7 6 4 2
♢ A 10 7
♣ —

Otto
♠ 10 2
♡ K 9 5
♢ 6 3 2
♣ K 9 8 7 5

Me
♠ K Q J 9 8 7 4
♡ A 3
♢ —
♣ Q J 10 3

Pizza (declarer)
♠ —
♡ Q J
♢ K Q J 9 8 5 4
♣ A 6 4 2

Then he led a heart off dummy at trick two. I couldn't duck without allowing four heart tricks to become established with a ruff on the next round. So I went up with the ace of hearts. However, declarer could still trump three clubs in dummy and made his slam. Not only that, but we were practically cold for five spades—only a far-fetched club lead defeats it. Chops had timed the bidding perfectly with her pass of five diamonds and then her slam bid over my reopening five spades. I, however, could not have timed the auction worse, leaping to game on the first round and guessing on the next round, when my whole purpose should have been to buy the contract—at any level.

On the last deal, I picked up:

♠ A 8 7 ♡ A 10 9 7 ♢ A 4 ♣ A J 3 2

Before Chops could bid, I heard my name called. It was Al Roth, looking down at me. "Are you Matthew Grano. . . somethingorother?" I was. I remembered that vaguely. "Well, there's a call for you on the phone." I rose, not without great effort. "Here," said Mr. Roth, "if nobody minds, I'll take the last hand for him."

As I headed to the desk, I heard Roth open one notrump, followed by three passes. It was just as well. I doubted I had enough sense to declare a hand at this point anyway. I picked up the phone. "Hello?"

"Hey, guy. Where are you?"

I looked around the room, then back at the receiver. "I'm in New York," I admitted.

"Well, this is J.B. at the Quad. You should have reported in 10 hours ago."

J.B., J.B. "Oh yes, J.B., it's you! Sorry. I've been . . . well, here."

"I know, I know," said J.B., "but you realize you're under my supervision. You were not in your room all last night. The guys and I waited till after 3:00 for you. I lost nearly two dollars!"

"Two dollars," I repeated.

"Now listen to me, guy. Have you located that roommate of yours, Stanley Kesselman?"

My head started to clear. "Yes, he's here, I'm working on him."

"Well, let's see that you bring him back tonight, guy."

"Yes, I'll do my best."

"Good. One more thing, if you have a moment. Do you have time for a hand?"

"A hand?"

"Yes, one of those Stayman sequences you were telling me about. I was partnering Big Al, and we started with notrump. He asked me for a major and I had both of them! Amazing, isn't it? I had to make a choice."

I could see my game breaking up in the corner. Did Roth make one notrump for me?

"Well, I thought about it for quite a while and decided to show him neither. After all, it seemed awfully crude to choose between two perfectly good suits. So I rebid two notrump."

I had to get off the phone. I was dying to see how much I was down on the score.

"I think you should have bid two diamonds if you wanted to deny a major," I said.

"Two diamonds is awfully risky, guy. Suppose he passed? Now over two notrump, Big Al says three clubs. So I now reveal my hand with three hearts which leaves him the option of bidding three spades. Instead he bids three notrump, which I am happy to pass. Have you ever heard such an auction?"

I told J.B., that I hadn't, and this seemed to please him. Then he gave me a further warning to be back at the Quad by midnight. Mr. Roth was back at the desk with the afternoon scores.

"Did you make one notrump?" I asked.

"What's the difference?" he returned. "I made one notrump,

you got your honors and you're still minus 50 points for the day."

What he meant was: I was minus 50 points times 100—at two cents a point, it translated to a hundred dollars. I reached into my pocket and pulled out six dollars and 75 cents. Roth did not look up. He was busy writing in the scores. I took advantage of the moment and slipped the money back into my pocket, then stole as quietly as I could into the hallway and the back room where supper was being served.

"AIIIII!!" It was a deathly scream; a chill ran through me as my soup spoon dropped to the floor.

7

T HE SCREAM had come from Frankenstein, who was sitting across from me at a table for four. He jumped from his chair and ran to the kitchen. "What happened?" I asked.

"The matzo balls," said Gussie, "they're not portioned."

"What? They're not the right size?"

"No, they're not portioned out equally."

I looked down at my plate. I had three matzo balls. I surveyed the other bowls. Gussie had two, the little girl had two and a half, Frankenstein had only one.

Suddenly Frankenstein was back with a huge heavy serving pot. "NOBODY TOUCH THE SOUP!" He added one and a half matzo balls to his soup, broke half off of one of mine and gave it to Gussie. Then he started in on the carrots. His daughter tried to take a mouthful. "Put that down! Nobody eats till Frankenstein divvies up."

Maggie came over to the table, her hands wringing her apron. "That man is crazy. Here, give me that ladle." There was a brief struggle, during which we all hid behind our napkins, but Frankenstein won in the end. "Lordy, lordy," said Maggie, "there's plenty of vegetables to go around."

"And what about the noodles?" asked Frankenstein with blood in his eyes.

I glanced down again. It was true, the soup was sparse on noodles. Suddenly a loud slurping noise came from the adjacent table. We all turned around. Pizza had a two huge bowls of noodles next to his soup. Assorted condiments like ketchup, mustard and grated cheese surrounded his plates.

"There's the culprit," said Frankenstein, pointing an accusing finger, "the Big Baboon."

"Mr. Pizza," cried Maggie, "how could you?!"

"You want some more noodles?" said Pizza. "Here, I'll give you noodles." With that he put on a big smile, took a plate of noodles, and flung them at Frankenstein. They were wet and sticky, however, landing for the most part across Maggie's face.

"Lord have mercy," she cried, "I'm going to kill that man." She wiped the noodles off, grabbed the soup ladle from Frankenstein and started toward Pizza. Gussie and Roth rushed over to stop her. Roth told everyone to get back to their seats or pay their accounts, and this seemed to control the situation. Pizza got up from his chair and offered to wipe Maggie's face with his napkin.

"Sorry, Maggie. Here, here, take this," said Pizza, handing her a ten-dollar bill.

"Don't put that dirty thing on me," she said, pushing aside his napkin. "Lordy, I'll be here all night cleaning this carpet."

She did take the ten-spot, however, and Pizza returned to his table, where Stanley and Chops also were seated, little Bobby on her lap.

Frankenstein retrieved the ladle and portioned the rest of the carrots, restoring order to the soup as well. Soon the conversation turned to bridge, and when I mentioned I was a duplicate enthusiast, Frankenstein looked down at me through his thick lenses and gave me a monstrous smile. "I heard about your hundred honors in spades."

"Which hand?" I asked.

"The one where you doubled four spades and your baboon removed."

"Well, what was I supposed to do, pass four spades?"

"Don't ask me," said Frankenstein. "If you can't figure it out, you should take up Parcheesi."

True, I thought. I had let Pizza back into the game when I doubled. Sure, the meaning of my double was clearly penalty, but then there was partner to contend with, we were favorable, and he was known to be holding a trump void. "I guess that's the main difference between duplicate and rubber, huh? In duplicate, you trust your partner, in rubber you don't."

"That depends on which baboon is sitting opposite you," corrected Frankenstein. "Take Gussie, she'd always pass your double."

"I trust my partners," said Gussie.

Sure, I thought, I have to pay more attention to my partner's idiosyncrasies. But that's difficult until you know the players better.

"I trust nobody," bragged Frankenstein. "That's the difference between rubber and duplicate. Duplicate players rely too much on partner, they make too many forcing passes and optional doubles. On defense, they're always signaling this and that instead of working out the hand for themselves."

Like the hand I had with Gussie, where I shifted to a spade after Gussie's high-spade signal. Instead, I should have been working out the hand.

"It's very easy to lose sight of the forest by concentrating on the tree," continued Frankenstein, his eyes staring into space, rather than addressing any particular individual. "You've got to picture the hand not only from your cards, but from your opponents'. That's the crux of the game; if you can learn to do that at rubber bridge, you can carry it over to tournament bridge as well."

"But what's the difference?" I asked. "Why not do that at duplicate, too?"

"Aaaawr," he barked, "you're too busy at duplicate worrying about what the rest of the idiot field is up to. What's the difference if they make a game or a slam? What's the difference if you don't outbid them for the partscore? All you care about in duplicate is duplicating or surpassing the rest of the field's terrible results."

"You can be mediocre and win at duplicate," squealed Gussie.

True, I thought. She'd won a good deal herself. And what about me? Still, you couldn't deny there were certain difficult skills applicable to duplicate alone, like sacrificing, doubling for a one-trick set, making the maximum number of tricks rather than claiming an easy contract. I proposed this argument to Frankenstein as Maggie came and cleared our soup bowls. "You can learn all those things in half the time playing rubber. Then when you're through, you can go play duplicate and feel like you've gone from fighting Mohammed Ali to spanking your seven-year-old." Frankenstein paused, then said, "Any experienced rubber player is a winner at duplicate. But you take a star tournament player and sit him down for a nickel-a-point for the first time, and he'll get crushed."

Maggie came back with roast chicken, stuffing, whole potatoes and corn. Frankenstein's little girl clapped her hands in joy. I'd forgotten she was there. The food smelled wonderful and I wondered how most of the Mayfair members remained skinny. Probably nervous tension, I thought. Frankenstein dug in but continued to pontificate between mouthfuls.

"Now you take those three little items you listed before. Sacrificing, doubling for a one-trick set and. . ."

"Overtricks," I said.

"Aaaaawr, overtricks. What are you, a lunatic? I make a hundred overtricks a day at rubber. They feed Frankenstein with overtricks. Everyone's so busy trying to defeat undefeatable contracts, overtricks are easy. Difference between rubber and duplicate is you're declarer, on average, six hands in three hours at duplicate. At rubber, you're declarer on six hands every hour."

Six hands per hour. Wait a second. That would mean about 24 hands played per hour if each player was declarer on an equal number. I objected.

"Objection denied," said Frankenstein. "If you know what you're doing, I mean. At duplicate you have to let the opponents play their share of contracts. At rubber, you steal hands left and right. If you're good, you even steal them from your partner. You don't want his mitts on the dummy and you certainly don't want to defend with some baboon when you can take full control by declaring against two baboons."

True, I thought, that's a three-baboon differential.

"Remember this: It's better to go down a couple hundred points then let them have the partscore. The value of a partscore is very underrated. Baboons have little notion how to bid with a partscore, but they have less idea how to compete against one."

"Partscores are very important at rubber," added Gussie. "I love to make a partscore."

"There," said Frankenstein. "Listen to her and you'll be busted in no time." He leaned over and whispered to me, "Get rid of all partscores as fast as you can. Games, bonus scores, that's where the money is."

"All right," I said, "so the idea is you're declarer a lot more often at rubber, which makes it a better practice field than duplicate."

"You don't sit around all day waiting for the rounds to be called," he added.

"Okay, and what about sacrificing and doubling for a one-trick set. How would playing rubber bridge help you improve in those areas?"

"It's hard to discuss bridge with a baboon. You *never* sacrifice at duplicate! That's the greatest fallacy in the history of fallacies!"

"Really?" I asked, surprised.

"It's simple mathematics," said Frankenstein, cleaning off his gravy with his third roll. "Say you sacrifice six times in one session. Once you go for too much and get a zero. Another time you'd have beaten their game, another bottom score for you. The other four times you're right. Their game is cold, but on most of those hands only a majority of the field has bid it, not everyone. Therefore, all you can score is average-plus. Maybe once you get a top. Even then, you've barely earned half of the matchpoints on the six deals. What good is it?

"If you want to sacrifice, do it at rubber, but only for a one-trick set. Sacrifice against partscores all the time, you almost never get doubled."

"What about against slams?" I asked.

"*Slams?!* Never at matchpoints—is that clear?! But at rubber, you could occasionally sacrifice against a slam if you figure on losing only a few tricks, but only if you're going to play the hand, not baboon over there."

This was all news to me, especially the duplicate strategy. Our main course was over, and the little girl asked, "What's for dessert?" She wasn't a bad little girl as little girls go, and kept her mouth closed while her father lectured. Anyway, we all had coffee and cheesecake that Maggie had picked up from Lindy's. After a few bites, Frankenstein finished his sermon.

"Now for your stupidicus one-trick doubling concept. You double a partscore at matchpoints for an extra one-hundred points, but I double a game at rubber for an extra *eight*-hundred points."

"Why can't I double the same game at matchpoints?" I asked.

"Don't be a baboon. At matchpoints, you can't double a game unless you're sure it's going down. At rubber, the double costs you very little if they make it, and when they go down *because* of the double, your reward is eight times your silly matchpoint doubles."

After dessert, when Pizza left the room, I switched tables and asked Stanley how he did at the track. "He lost every race," said Chops.

"Shut up," said Stanley, "it wasn't that bad. I practically broke even. If it hadn't been for the photo-finish in the fifth—"

Chops sprang up from her seat. "It's always some lame excuse or other. I'm getting sick of it." Then she stormed off, baby in arms.

I took the moment alone with Stanley to tell him about the ten dollars I had borrowed, and that our preceptor had phoned and requested our return to campus.

"Campus? Matthew, you're not seeing straight. Look around you. *This* is my campus. This is my learning ground. What more could any student of life ask for?"

It was true. There was Professor Frankenstein, from whom I had just received a short discourse on the comparative study of rubber and duplicate. Then there was Otto Rockefeller, the Hungarian scientist who introduced the Budapest system to America. He had moved over next to Frankenstein's little girl, patting her on the head and admiring her latest drawings. Then there was the Mayfair preceptor, Al Roth, educator and inventor. Ahh, mustn't forget Professor Pizza, bridge author and culinary expert. Suddenly I spotted Doctor B., honest-to-goodness special surgeon at NYU medical center, and my hallucinatory fictionalizations suddenly turned to reality.

"C'mon, c'mon, I've got two hours off," said Doc, looking at his watch. "What's the matter with you people, you all want to die of clogged arteries? Let's play cards."

"I hear the clinking of silver coins," said Frankenstein, rising from his table.

"I'm clearing as fast as I can," cried Maggie, who was hustling every which way.

Frankenstein bent down and gave his daughter a kiss on the nose, then took a book from a paper bag and gave it to her. She seemed pleased, rose from her chair and pushed it near the lamp by the window. Meanwhile, Mr. Roth was up and about, helping Maggie. Then he got a set-up of cards, scorepads and pencils.

"You playing?" Doc asked Gussie, who was finishing her coffee.

"Don't rush me. I'm digesting," she squealed.

"Where's Pizza?" asked Doc.

"He's writing in his book," said Frankenstein.

Doc went to the bathroom and opened the door. "Pizza! I got two hours; let's go!"

"You're still on night call?" asked Gussie, from behind her newspaper.

"This is absolutely the last time," said Doc. "Let the younger guys do it." He turned around and spotted Stanley and me. "What about you kids, you in?"

"I'm in," said Stanley, who hustled over to the table and started to sort through a deck.

I kept my mouth shut. I was already in a hundred-dollar hole and besides, this game was for a nickel, more than twice the afternoon stake.

"I'm gonna be another ten minutes," Pizza called.

"Are you crapping or writing?" Doc asked.

"Both," said Frankenstein.

Stanley spread the shuffled deck face down across the dark green velvet carpet of the table. Frankenstein picked the queen of hearts, Doc turned over the nine of clubs. "Pick," he ordered to Stanley.

"Youngest goes last," said Stanley.

"I'm picking for you!!!" yelled Doc.

"O-kaaaaaay!" cried Pizza from the bathroom.

Doc turned over a diamond, the two. Stanley quickly pulled an ace from the deck and sat across from Frankenstein. I pulled up a chair and saw Chops return to the room. She was burping Bobby and took a seat behind Stanley. Doc sat on Stanley's right and motioned to me.

"What?" I asked.

"Don't what, just take a seat. Until Pizza gets out."

So I moved into the designated spot between Stanley and Frankenstein. "Don't be shy, cut the deck," said Doc. I did and Stanley dealt. "I play no conventions," Doc told me, "just Stayman and Blackwood."

♠ A J 10 9 3 2 ♡ 7 ◊ A J 9 3 ♣ K 2

Stanley passed. I opened one spade. Frankenstein passed. Doc bid one notrump. Stanley doubled. I was about to make a two-spade rebid when I paused for a moment. Thirteen points, but . . . what if I pictured my partner's hand? Couple kings in the right places and I might make game, especially with Stanley holding a few key minor-suit cards on my right. I rebid two diamonds, to give Doc the chance to evaluate his cards. Frankenstein passed. Doc bid two spades. Stanley passed. Well, not much from Doc, but he still could have the right stuff. Three spades, inviting four, seemed right. "C'mon, c'mon," said Doc. "This is rubber bridge; we can't bid every hand like world champions." I bid four spades. He asked for it, he got it.

Frankenstein led a club. This was the whole deal:

Doc (dummy)
♠ K 4
♡ J 6 5 3
◊ K 5 4
♣ Q 7 6 5

Frankenstein
♠ Q 8 7 6
♡ Q 10 9 8
◊ Q 9 8
♣ J 10

Stanley
♠ 5
♡ A K 4 2
◊ 10 6 2
♣ A 9 8 4 3

Me (declarer)
♠ A J 10 9 3 2
♡ 7
◊ A J 7 3
♣ K 2

I caught a decent dummy, and there were hopes. I played low on the club lead and Stanley went up with his ace. He then cashed the king of hearts, and Frankenstein signaled with the ten, Next came the ace of hearts, which I ruffed. With ace-king-ace on my right, an original passed hand, there was little room for any other high cards, so I led the jack of spades and let it ride. It won the trick, and I played a second trump to the king. When Stanley showed out, I knew I was doomed to lose a trump trick despite my successful finesse. I had already lost a club and a heart, and there seemed to be no way to avoid a diamond loser, the diamond queen being a sure thing to be with Frankenstein. There was, of course, the chance it was doubleton. Anyway, I led a club back to my king and played the ace of trumps. Then it occurred to me, I might as well give up the trump. With three tricks in for the defense, Frankenstein was on play:

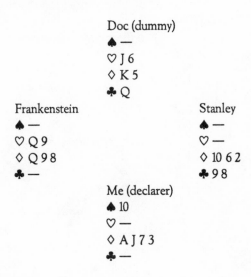

Doc (dummy)
♠ —
♡ J 6
◇ K 5
♣ Q

Frankenstein
♠ —
♡ Q 9
◇ Q 9 8
♣ —

Stanley
♠ —
♡ —
◇ 10 6 2
♣ 9 8

Me (declarer)
♠ 10
♡ —
◇ A J 7 3
♣ —

He could not lead either red suit without giving me my contract.

"Aiiii," screamed Frankenstein. "What are you doing?!"

Stanley sputtered something about the heart-ten signal.

"Heart ten? I'm just telling you what I have, you little baboon! Underlead the ace to my queen like a normal human being; don't cash all your high-cards endplaying Frankenstein."

In the meantime I looked up at Doc, proud as could be. "What took so long?" he scolded.

"I'll be right out!" yelled Pizza from the bathroom.

"Stay there all night, see if I care!" yelled Doc.

I already had the cards dealt to the second deal.

♠ A K Q J 2 ♡ A 6 5 4 2 ◇ — ♣ A 4 2

I opened one spade. Frankenstein passed. Doc bid two diamonds. Stanley passed. I bid two hearts; maybe I should have

He could not lead either red suit
without giving me my contract.

jumped. Frankenstein passed. Doc bid three clubs. Stanley passed. I was about to rebid my hearts when I realized that Doc might pass me. I was sure three hearts was forcing but playing the rule, "don't trust your partner," I took no chances. I bid six notrump. Doc nodded in approval of my bold leap and everyone passed. Frankenstein led the ten of spades.

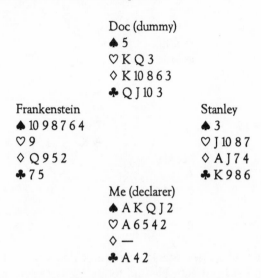

Doc (dummy)
♠ 5
♡ K Q 3
♦ K 10 8 6 3
♣ Q J 10 3

Frankenstein
♠ 10 9 8 7 6 4
♡ 9
♦ Q 9 5 2
♣ 7 5

Stanley
♠ 3
♡ J 10 8 7
♦ A J 7 4
♣ K 9 8 6

Me (declarer)
♠ A K Q J 2
♡ A 6 5 4 2
♦ —
♣ A 4 2

Not much in dummy this time, I thought. Still, I had avoided the diamond lead, and if the club finesse were onside, I would come to twelve tricks provided the hearts were three-two or both black suits divided evenly. Suddenly I heard a cry. I turned to my right. It was Chop's baby. Chops had moved the chair between Stanley and me in order to see my hand, and the baby had bumped his head. "He's okay," she said. I nodded, but when I returned my attention to the bridge hand, I suddenly realized I had pulled the deuce of spades from my hand. Thus Frankenstein won the first trick and I wanted to murder that baby.

In the meantime Frankenstein was looking around in amazement, while Stanley was sitting up in his seat. Obviously, he held the ace of diamonds and was hoping for a diamond shift. Frankenstein thought about it for a few seconds and finally played the nine of hearts. It was very difficult for him to find that diamond shift from his queen, of course.

I won the heart shift in dummy and took a couple of club finesses, followed by a club to the ace. Then I ran my spade honors, discarding diamonds from dummy. On the last spade, Stanley threw the king of clubs with the speed of lightning! I did not fail to notice it, however. Here was the ending that forced that incredible discard:

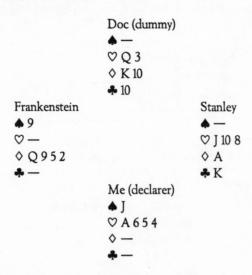

Doc (dummy)
♠ —
♡ Q 3
♢ K 10
♣ 10

Frankenstein
♠ 9
♡ —
♢ Q 9 5 2
♣ —

Stanley
♠ —
♡ J 10 8
♢ A
♣ K

Me (declarer)
♠ J
♡ A 6 5 4
♢ —
♣ —

On my jack of spades, Stanley could not throw a heart without setting up my heart suit. He had to choose between discarding the king of clubs and the ace of diamonds. It didn't matter. It was slow death. I led a heart to dummy and repeated the squeeze by cashing my ten of clubs.

"Aaawr," cried Frankenstein in agony.

"All you had to do was switch to diamonds," yelled Stanley.

"How am I to know I'm playing against someone from outer space?"

Doc wrote the score down and warned me not to duck any more tricks. But when I heard Bobby cry again, I saw a quizzical expression on Chops face. Yes, she had worked it out. The duck at trick one was the only way to rectify the count—before Stanley could signal Frankenstein that he held the diamond ace.

I patted little Bobby on the head and that seemed to calm him down. Of course, six hearts was cold. Even seven hearts would have been a decent contract. But six notrump making six was a success, and that was what counted at rubber—the bottom line.

Pizza made his appearance. He fingered the score with his

chubby paws, gave a little whistle and suggested I finish out the rubber. Stanley objected, but Frankenstein told him to shut up, it was only beginner's luck. Pizza sat down between Frankenstein and me, lighting up one of his humongous Havanas. Frankenstein started waving his arms in the air at the smoke as I picked up my new cards.

$$\spadesuit 43 \heartsuit KQ2 \diamondsuit 763 \clubsuit KJ962$$

Frankenstein opened one diamond on my left. Doc passed. Stanley bid one notrump. Feeling rather loose now, I slipped in a two-club overcall. This was really a terrible bid, but when you're on a roll as I was, you get a feeling of invincibility, and bids pop into your head (and out of your mouth) that you never would dream of under ordinary conditions. In fact, I could feel Chops's eyes bearing down on my cards in disapproval.

Suddenly the auction stopped. Frankenstein had rebid two diamonds over my two clubs and that was all I remembered. No one ever recalled Doc taking so long to make a call, but sure enough, it was Doc who was thinking. His hands were shaking, and it was all he could do to keep from spilling a few cards onto the table. Finally, he blurted out "six clubs." Everybody passed, and Frankenstein led the king of diamonds.

Doc (dummy)
♠ A 9 8 6
♡ J 10 5 4
♢ —
♣ A 7 5 4 3

Me (declarer)
♠ 4 3
♡ K Q 2
♢ 7 6 3
♣ K J 9 6 2

I give you this hand from my point of view because it was one of the few occasions in my life that my mind was more picturesque than the physical reality. In fact, the Mayfair had very poor lighting in the back room on this particular evening (mainly because the ceiling light was flickering on and off from some electrical problem), and the only good lamp was in the corner by the window, where Frankenstein's little girl was reading. My mind, as I said before, was clear and lucid, so much so that, before I made even the obvious ruff in dummy at trick one, I made the fastest and most memorable deduction of my bridge career: the clubs were three-zero! Stanley's one-notrump response denied a four-card major; thus, Frankenstein had to hold four spades and at least three hearts. Add that to his rebiddable six-card diamond suit and it left with 4-3-6-0 shape.

Therefore it cost me nothing to ruff the opening lead with dummy's ace of clubs—it might even help me. At trick two, I led a club to the nine and Frankenstein discarded. I could feel hot breath on my neck, now, the sweet combination of perfume and milk. I ruffed a second diamond and played a club to my jack. I ruffed my last diamond. Finally, I led a heart to my queen. Frankenstein ducked, so I drew the last trump and played hearts, claiming my slam. (Upon subsequent analysis, I saw that ruffing a diamond with the ace of clubs and double-hooking was absolutely necessary.) Suddenly a human hand was on my neck, a soft wonderful hand massaging me. I made no move to brush it aside. This was the full deal:

Doc (dummy)
♠ A 9 8 6
♡ J 10 5 4
♢ —
♣ A 7 5 4 3

Frankenstein
♠ K 10 7 2
♡ A 8 7
♢ K Q J 9 5 2
♣ —

Stanley
♠ Q J 5
♡ 9 6 3
♢ A 10 8 4
♣ Q 10 8

Me (declarer)
♠ 4 3
♡ K Q 2
♢ 7 6 3
♣ K J 9 6 2

Doc looked up. "Nice bid I made, hmm?" Frankenstein was shaking his head in dismay. Stanley had already left the table, but I didn't hear the bathroom door slam. Instead, I was paged.

"Excuse me," I said, getting up from the table. There was a phone call for me at Mr. Roth's desk.

"Hello?" I said into the receiver.

"This is Stanley, don't look surprised."

"What? Where are you?"

"I'm at the pay phone in the hall, you idiot."

"But we still have another deal to complete the rubber," I complained.

"Listen to me, jerk. You're playing for Pizza's account, not mine. All you're doing is costing me a fortune. Don't you realize I have extras with Pizza and Doc?!!"

"You mean all these good results are for nought."

"Worse than nought, you moron. You're killing me. You've got to give something back on the last deal."

"What?" I said, then hung up the phone.

"Everything all right at home?" asked Mr. Roth.

"Huh?. . .Yeah." I walked to the back room slowly. Dump? He wants me to dump him some points? But everyone will see me do it. Not only everyone. . . but Chops. I can't dump, I won't dump, it's just too bad.

Stanley was already seated at the table, and Doc was finishing the deal. I picked up my cards, secretly hoping for a bad hand. Unfortunately, all I saw were aces and kings:

♠ A K 6 4 ♡ 10 9 3 2 ◇ A 2 ♣ A K 7

Doc opened one club. Stanley jump overcalled two diamonds and stared at me. I looked down at my hand. How could I dump? It was impossible. Okay, I thought, I'll bid two spades, two hearts would be too obvious a dump. Frankenstein passed and Doc jumped to four spades. Rather unlucky of me to hit him with a fit like that. Stanley passed with vengeance in his eyes. What now? Chops was watching. The baby had started to cry again and I could feel her rocking him in tempo behind me. There was no way I could bid less than slam. In fact, if I passed I would only cost Stanley a sure six or seven hundred points. But if I bid a slam, at least I could go down. And with his preemptive two diamonds, Stanley might have some wild distribution that would mean bad breaks for me in slam. So I bid six spades and hoped for the worst.

Frankenstein led a diamond. This was the full deal:

Doc (dummy)
♠ Q 7 5 3
♡ A K 4
◇ K 3
♣ 10 5 4 2

Frankenstein
♠ J 10
♡ Q 8 7 5
◇ 7 6 4
♣ Q J 8 3

Stanley
♠ 9 8 2
♡ J 6
◇ Q J 10 9 8 5
♣ 9 6

Me (declarer)
♠ A K 6 4
♡ 10 9 3 2
◇ A 2
♣ A K 7

The baby was crying louder now, and I could hardly concentrate. All the better, I supposed. Maybe I could go wrong naturally. I won the diamond lead in dummy without stopping to analyze. Then I drew trump in three rounds and saw Doc's approving smile as I played on without thinking.

"We'll need a lot of luck for this one," I commented, trying to soothe Stanley. I next cashed the ace of hearts and, making a show of exasperation when no honor fell, did the most novice thing I could think of by switching suits in mid-stream. I played to my ace of diamonds, a silly and useless play. Then I cashed the two top club honors, closed my eyes and prayed for the queen-jack not to drop doubleton. They didn't, nor were they likely to, but something in the air was eerie, and I felt a miracle coming—a miracle that I never wished for in the dark.

This was now the position, with five cards remaining in each hand:

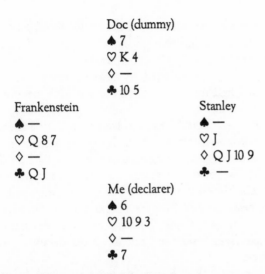

Doc (dummy)
♠ 7
♡ K 4
◊ —
♣ 10 5

Frankenstein
♠ —
♡ Q 8 7
◊ —
♣ Q J

Stanley
♠ —
♡ J
◊ Q J 10 9
♣ —

Me (declarer)
♠ 6
♡ 10 9 3
◊ —
♣ 7

I was about to lead my seven of clubs when a bolt of lightning flashed at the window. We all looked up. The little girl didn't stir. I think she had fallen asleep in her chair. A second flash of lightning lit up the entire sky. It was a horrific scene, the little girl suddenly turning white from the light, then black shadow again across the wall. I shall never forget that picture of her, never. (I dream of it even to this day.)

A loud thunderclap followed. The baby was crying uncontrollably, but somehow my concentration was fighting back against the storm. It's strange how a diversion can suddenly clear the bridge player's mind, allowing him to find the correct path of play he had been looking for in vain a moment before. And so it happened now, only this time it was not a path but a warning away from a path. This thought struck me: If Stanley wins the third club with the queen, he'll have nothing but diamonds left and be forced to give me a ruff and a sluff. Mustn't play a club, might make the slam by accident. Of course, Stanley should have dumped his club queen under my ace-king if he held it, but then, he may not have seen the endplay coming.

A trump was a hopeless play, and everyone would know I was throwing the hand if I did that. What about hearts? I realized I was thinking too long now. I couldn't make a really stupid play without getting caught. I needed to make a *subtle* error. I was sure that Stanley had no more hearts. He wouldn't have made a vulnerable weak-jump overcall between two bidders on a balanced hand. Yet how could I explain leading a heart instead of a club. Hmm. If Frankenstein still had the queen-jack of hearts, I could make believe I was trying to slip the nine by him. Not a great excuse, but better than nothing. So I led the nine of hearts.

Frankenstein played low. I started to sweat. Don't tell me he ducked with both honors! No, he couldn't have. Stanley must have the jack or queen. Good, I'll let it run, lose the trick, then lose a club trick. Even a sluff and ruff won't do me any good with two more losers.

Stanley won the jack of hearts and led a diamond. I threw my seven of clubs. Frankenstein hesitated:

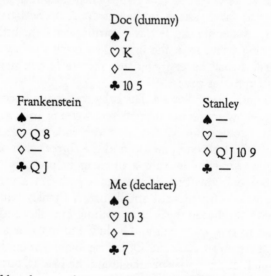

Doc (dummy)
♠ 7
♡ K
◇ —
♣ 10 5

Frankenstein
♠ —
♡ Q 8
◇ —
♣ Q J

Stanley
♠ —
♡ —
◇ Q J 10 9
♣ —

Me (declarer)
♠ 6
♡ 10 3
◇ —
♣ 7

If he threw a heart, my hearts would be good. If he threw a club, I could ruff a club in my hand and dummy's club would be high. Before I could fall back on a revoke, he threw the cards in. "You tamed Frankenstein," he said, rather quietly for him. Then suddenly regaining his old self, he rose and said, "C'mon Big Baboon (referring to Pizza), join the party."

Stanley got up, and I could see murder in his eyes. Suddenly I found myself running into the hallway to the elevators. In the darkest corner of my heart, however, I was counting up the score, three slams, two vulnerable, one game . . . 4210 points. Even if it did all go on Pizza's account, I was still proud. Then I saw a shadow approaching me at a horrific pace. Damn, I had forgotten to push the elevator button. I crouched down to defend myself.

8

IT WAS Chops. I stood up from my crouch. The baby was still crying. The elevator came and we were soon out on the street hailing a cab.

I could feel shock-waves in the muggy night air, but not a drop of rain. It took us 20 minutes on a Saturday night to get across town. The fare was three fifty, and I gave him a 50-cent tip. That left me with two dollars and 75 cents, enough to get me to Pennsylvania Station, I hoped. Maybe I could stow away in the dining car's lavatory. The thought of my little room in the Quad never seemed so appealing. But before I knew it, I was not on my way downtown to the train station. No, I was five flights up in the seedy brownstone with my best friend's girl and her baby.

I wondered if she were going to kiss me. We were sitting on the bed smoking a joint. The baby finally was asleep in the crib. The rain had started slowly, splattering across the window, forming silvery liquid drops in the blackness. She leaned over and brushed back my hair, allowing me to peek down the back of her blouse. She had her bra on tonight, and it looked complicated. I hoped she would be the one to take it off. I had always been bad at mechanical devices, especially hooks and metal. Perhaps that's why I took up bridge rather than racing cars or building model airplanes.

Then I remembered. No, it was to hide my acne. Oh god, she's looking at my face now. My dermatologist had suggested this once. He told me that sex was the best way to get rid of pimples. Really? I had asked. No, he said, but you'll have a lot of fun disproving the theory.

Her hand moved down my cheek to my lips, over a rough spot. Perhaps I was too self-conscious. The lamp was on, but I didn't dare make a move to it without risking the mood. I had to reassure myself, however, so I whispered in her ear, "When you look at me, do you notice any .. er . . . you know. . . ?"

"When I look at you I see the suicide ruff-and-sluff criss-cross trump squeeze. That's all I'll see for days," she said.

That made me feel better. I could relax now. Her hands moved down to my neck and her body edged even closer. I suddenly had to go to the bathroom desperately. I think I had felt something like this once before while reading a James Bond novel. Her face leaned forward. Her nose was on top of me. I had to be careful not to collide noses. At the last moment she tilted her head and the noses missed. She was very experienced at these things, I was sure of it. Our lips touched. My hands were at my side. Where were they supposed to go? There was a whole body there, yet I felt there was no adequate place to rest them. I felt a tongue. Oh my god, what was a tongue doing in the middle of a kiss? Her hand was moving downward across my shirt. Hot, getting very hot. Must be that horrible humidity. What do I do? Concentrate. Her hand was below the belt now. Somewhere in the distance I could see the black sky turn white; I heard a crackling sound, a drum roll, a thunder bolt. Then blackness. Was I dreaming? Uh oh. Uh ohhh. This was no dream, this was one of those game bonuses, no, this was a slam . . . . a small slam.

I opened an eye and awoke to the soft shuffle of the cards in a dark room. Where was I? I jumped up in embarrassment off the bed. "What time is it?"

"Some time after eleven, I don't know; the clock stopped." She was sitting at the card table, drinking tea and reading by candlelight Watson's Play of the Hand. She looked at me sheepishly and bent her head at a slight angle. "You finally got me interested in card play." She closed the book. "But enough's enough." She took a deck of cards and started sorting through them. My head was hazy. I got up and clung to the wall until I found the bathroom. There was my shirt from yesterday with the train schedule sticking out of the pocket. So much for the 10:55. It was the midnight express or nothing. When I came out, the cards were dealt. She ordered me to sit down and I obeyed. Then, leaning toward the candle, I sorted my hand.

♠ Q ♡ J 9 8 5 4 ◊ 10 8 7 6 ♣ Q 6 5

She opened one spade. I was about to pass and pick up thirteen cards from the undealt pile, then thought better of it. What the heck, she *could* have a two-suiter with hearts; let's just see what happens if I respond—after all, it's only practice.

I bid one notrump. She thought for a couple of seconds (unusual for her to take so long), then rebid two clubs. I passed. "Sorry, I'm just wasting time again," I said. I'd never been so conscious of time since I started playing rubber bridge. "But, I might have improved the contract. I'll tell you the truth, there's no way I would have responded in real life."

Chops	Me
♠ A K J 8 7 5	♠ Q
♡ 7 6	♡ J 9 8 5 4
◊ 5	◊ 10 8 7 6
♣ A K J 8	♣ Q 6 5
1 ♠	1 NT
2 ♣	pass

Four spades was a perfect contract. Two clubs could actually go down if the clubs were not three-three. I knew I was better off passing her one-spade opening. Still, what about the game we missed?

"Couldn't you evaluate your two black queens?" she asked. "That's why I rebid clubs rather than jump to three spades."

I couldn't really believe I was supposed to bid again over two clubs. I didn't even want to respond in the first place.

"Honestly," she continued, her voice starting to shake, "Your play of the cards may be all right, but your bidding is still the pits. Here I am trying to describe my hand to you so you'll be able to evaluate your cards, and you're just sitting there counting your stupid points."

"I realize you put a high premium on games and slams," I objected, "but aren't we overdoing it here? I mean, is bridge a game of absolute perfection? If I wouldn't respond in the first place, how can I be expected to keep it going on the same five points?"

"STOP IT ALREADY WITH THE POINTS!"

The baby started to cry again. I felt my head. Suddenly it was pounding. My hand hit an old wine glass from the night before; it toppled to the floor. As she went to the bedroom, I looked down at the cards. She was going nuts here with this evaluation thing. Then I had an idea. "Maybe we should call the Mayfair and get a second opinion."

"Fine," she said, as she came out holding the baby in her arms. "But the phone is dead. Must have been the storm. Everything's out."

Suddenly I realized that there were no other lights coming from the window. No wonder we'd been bidding by candlelight. I had naively thought she was being romantic.

"Why not try the pay phone outside?" she suggested. "It might just be this building. I'll wait here with Bobby."

I got up. "Who do you think I should ask?"

"Roth first. If he left, try Frankenstein. He's the one who taught me to keep the bidding open."

"With less than six points?"

"Gimme a break."

I stared at her. Standing there in her long grey night shirt behind the candle, her baby cradled in her arms, she was mystery personified, her tall frame casting a three-dimensional shadow across the floor and up the back wall. Had I been ten years older, ten years wiser, known the number of nights I'd lie awake in my bed and dream of such an image within my grasp, I would have bolted the door, placed the child back into the crib and blown out the candle. But let's face it: I was nothing more than a 17-year-old bridge junkie. All I could think was: Who is this creature to give *me* bridge lessons? This was going too far.

Suddenly she got up and put her arms around my neck,

balancing the baby between us. "Now don't forget to come back to me?"

"I wouldn't dream of it," I said. For a brief moment, I looked into her dark wet eyes and almost aged those ten years. For you could not look into those eyes very long without melting into the very spot you stood. I glanced away for a second and broke the spell. When I reached the hallway, I could hear her humming to the baby.

I should have taken an umbrella. Five stories was too long a climb to go back, so I stepped off the porch into the cold rain. When I got to the corner there was no phone. If there was, I couldn't see it. People were out on the street everywhere. Some were carrying flashlights. Others were laughing and playing games in the night. I jogged back down in the other direction, using the headlights of passing automobiles to guide me. There, only a few feet from her brownstone, was a phone booth. Suddenly there was a soft roar from the people. The lights had come back on. I wasn't sure they were happy about it.

I lifted the receiver. There was a dial tone. What was the number? I tried information. They answered as if nothing were wrong, as if storms and lightning and blackouts were just a daily routine hazard of the mad metropolis.

"593-0830."

I dialed. It rang about five times before someone picked up. A cab stopped close to me, and someone rushed out. Was it Stanley? I couldn't tell in the rain. The cab waited while the passenger went into the brownstone. Finally someone answered.

"Detective Kennedy?" said a voice.

"Hello?" I said. "Is this the Mayfair Club?"

"Is this the Mayfair Club? . . . Yeah, who *is* this?"

Something made me frightened. So I didn't give my name. "I, uh, want to talk to the manager, Mr. Roth, please."

"He's not here yet. He's on his way. What's your name? This is police Sergeant O'Rourke. There's been an accident here, and we'd like the name of anyone who calls. Could you please stay on the li—"

I hung up. Oh god, I shouldn't have done that. Police could trace the calls, couldn't they? What accident? Why should I be scared? I hadn't done anything wrong.

I started to walk back to the brownstone. A crazy guy rushed past me with a suitcase. Then he stopped. Stanley!

"Get in the cab," he said.

"But, what about Chops? I—"

"Just get in and keep your mouth shut."

I did as he said.

"Where to?" asked the cab driver.

"Where do you get the train to New Brunswick? Grand Central or Penn?"

Nobody answered. Stanley looked at me. "Wake up and answer!"

I must have been mesmerized. "Sorry, Pennsylvania Station."

"Move it."

When we got to 33rd and Eighth, Stanley jumped out of the cab. I gave the driver all the cash I had left in my pocket and caught up with Stanley before he could vanish into the brightly lit interiors of the station.

9

THROUGH A WINDOW—TRAPPED BETWEEN
CAR DOORS—AN IMPORTANT PARTSCORE—
A WARNING.

"NOTHING HAPPENED," said Stanley as the train sped through the tunnel. "The little girl fell out a window."

The little girl fell out a window! "What are you talking about, 'nothing happened'? Are you crazy!? She fell out a window!?"

"What I mean is nothing happened that anybody could do anything about."

About five minutes went by in silence. I listened to the sounds of the train, the whistle, the rough metal on the tracks, the swish of the air as we came out of the white tunnel into the black night. I looked out of the window into the black marshlands, but saw only the girl's white face, that horrible, beautiful face whitened by the lightning flash. She had been sitting up against the window then, also. All the details came back to me. The sight of her had stopped me from leading the seven of clubs in my six-spade contract.

The conductor came by for tickets. Stanley took out a wad of what looked like hundred-dollar bills and paid for both of us. His hands were filthy; his fingernails were filled with mud.

"Don't get worked up, kid," he said. "I'm sure she's all right. It was only the third floor."

I got worked up. "Please don't call me kid! I'm only two weeks younger than you, you know."

"Okay, okay, take it easy." He handed me a bill with Ben Franklin's picture on it. "Here, keep a hundred on account."

I took it, looked out the window again and watched the downpour. How high up was the third floor of a New York office building? Could it be that the third floor was only two stories up, the first floor being the foyer? I mentioned this possibility to Stanley.

"Now you're thinking, kid. Come to think of it, it's quite possible. I'm trying to remember the buttons on the elevator. . . okay, okay, I'm not sure, but that would certainly make all the difference."

I looked down at the hundred-dollar bill. Suddenly I realized my Ben Franklin book was still at the Mayfair. And inside the book was my September issue of the *Bridge World*. And on the front of my *Bridge World* was my name and home address! Oh god, there's only one hope. Maybe the rain had washed out the ink on the label.

I was convinced the police would find it and put it under a microscope. It was an obvious lead. But wait. Even if worst came to worst, I could easily tell my parents how I had been sent to the Mayfair to find Stanley. Then I could explain to the police how I had left early with Chops. Chops was my alibi. Chops! Waiting for me still in her apartment, the baby in her arms. Waiting for the answer to a bridge problem! I promised to return. Would she be angry with me? Would she go so far as to not back up my whereabouts at the time of the . . . of the what? The accident? If it was an accident, what was there to worry about? Hadn't the policeman on the phone said there had been an accident? Then why did he want the name of anyone who telephoned? Stanley said it was an accident. Why is Stanley racing around town like a wild man to get his suitcase and escape on the midnight express?

"Do you mind telling me exactly what happened?"

Stanley shrugged his shoulders. "I'm not really sure," he said. "I think lightning hit the building and the shock sent her out the window. There was a blackout, you know."

"But the window was opened just a little when I left."

"Well, somebody opened it more. Whadaya want from me? It was a muggy night."

"Who opened it?"

"I didn't see. If you must know, I was concentrating on a partscore the whole time."

"A partscore? How important can a partscore be when a girl is falling out the window?!"

"Would it make you feel any better if it were a slam? Besides, you shouldn't knock partscores. Very few people understand the value of a partscore. You let them make one partscore, you've got a terrible handicap on the next hand. Not only do they need only one more partscore to complete the game, but there's your partner to watch out for. They all go crazy against partscores. They all keep bidding on nothing and the next thing you know you're going for a number just to stop the second partscore."

I was about to object, quoting Chops and her esteem for games and slams, but then I was reluctant to give Stanley any clue to what went on between Chops and me. Certainly, he was living with her. Then there was Frankenstein's sermon. He also feared the partscore and what it could do to his partner's judgment on the next deal. Then there was Frankenstein's little girl, sitting so politely with us at supper.

"Are you telling me you were in the back room at the time? Playing this partscore?"

"Not in the back room—the front room! You don't listen to anything I say. What's wrong with you? You look sick. C'mon, I'll give you the hand, take your mind off things."

"I'm too upset to concentrate. . . . Write it down."

Stanley pulled out a green pencil that had "Belmont Park" printed on it. I handed him the back of my train schedule and he wrote out a hand:

$$\spadesuit J x x x \quad \heartsuit A x x \quad \diamondsuit Q J \quad \clubsuit J x x x$$

"It was the third deal. We were vulnerable and they had 40

partscore from the previous hand. I passed and Gussie on my left opened one diamond. I was playing with Pizza. He passed and Frankenstein raised to two diamonds."

"I'm sorry," I said. "Who was the dealer?"

He grabbed the piece of paper away from me in anger. "Go get some black coffee; I'm not gonna waste my time teaching you the finer points if you're not gonna stay awake. And get me some while you're at it. Oh, and here, throw this out for me."

He handed me some crumpled damp paper. I got up and headed forward, then hesitated. "Which way is the concession stand?"

"That way," said Stanley, "or that way. You got a 50-percent shot."

Left-right, left-right, the constant rattling of the train in my ears, I started bumping into seats and disturbed some dozing passengers. I put the crumpled paper in my pocket and tried to hold on to the tops of the seats as I stumbled onward through the aisle. I really did need the coffee, I thought, feeling very woozy. I passed a group of coeds who were whispering and laughing. Should I ask them if I was heading the right way? I opened the heavy door and when I got outside, the door slid shut behind me. I moved quickly to the next car, opened the sliding door, and stepped in before the rain soaked me. Coffee, that would help. My dad didn't drink coffee, I thought. What would he say if he saw me here going for a cup of coffee?

Down at the far end I spotted a lit booth. The train was rattling left and right as I made my way through the aisle. It was the lavatory. I opened the sliding door and suddenly I was outside again. Steady now. The next door slid open, and I tumbled back in. This getting coffee business was not so easy. I passed an old man with a cup of tea in his hand. It was a good sign. So I pushed onward. At the end of the car was a porter, snoozing. Behind him was a small bar with a coffee pot.

I hummed a little, but it didn't do the trick. He opened one eye and must have thought I was an apparition. Back to sleep he went. I jostled him slightly. He finally woke and shook his head. I ordered two cups of coffee. He packed them in a tray with covers and put in sugar, cream, and stirrers. I handed him the hundred. He said he couldn't change it. I pleaded with him to trust me until next time. He let me have the coffee and went back to sleep. I opened the door with my elbow and held it with one foot.

Out in the rain again, I suddenly realized I was going the wrong way. I tried to open the door again but it was stuck. I kicked it, the porter woke again and opened it. He shook his head as I apologized. Then I started back toward Stanley, trying to hold the coffee upright. When I got through the next door, I noticed the coffee cups had a leak. Luckily for me someone else was heading the other way and let me back in out of the rain. Only one car to go, I thought.

The train took a sharp curve, but I stayed with the coffee. One container of cream went flying, however. Finally the sliding door again. Out into the night. Bang it shut behind me. There didn't seem to be a way to open the final door, though. One foot on one car, the other foot on the other car. The rattling of the train was very loud now. I looked around for something to hold onto. There was a red fire extinguisher and an ax behind some glass. Ah, there was an aluminum gripping on the side of the door marked, "Warning! Do not lean."

Suddenly another curve, my foot slipping, one of the coffees tipping over. Owwwww. Burning my arm. Caught the other coffee. Nice catch. Hold on. My right arm stretched out, caught around the handle—YIKES!—outside open door, rear of the axle near foot—rain on my face. Can't move my arms now without falling off the train. Track below my head. Kick the door. Kick it. Can't reach. Scream. Why not? Must try something. Scream. I can hardly hear it, myself. Sparks from wheels. The window, the window. There's one of the coeds sitting by the window. Edge over a little. She will see me. Lift my body, further, further. She looked! Thank god. I smile, so I won't scare her too much. She shuts the window shade! Oh no. Edge back to the axle. Bang! What was that? A door slamming? Not my imagination. Somebody coming back. I kick at the door. He turns and sees me. Long arm reaching down. Thanks, thanks a lot. No problem. You all right? Yes, had to get some fresh air. On my feet, back into the car. Past the coeds. Where's Stanley? There, there he is, eagerly awaiting his coffee, anxious to tell me about the all-important partscore deal. I sit down, completely drenched in rain and sweat.

"They were out of coffee," I lied. He shook his head and pointed to the hand again.

♠ J x x x ♡ A x x ◇ Q J ♣ J x x x

"Pass, one diamond, pass, two diamonds to you. What's your call?"

I looked at the hand. It felt good to be alive. Hmm. Was there something I was missing in this problem? I passed.

"Okay," he said, "Just testing to see if you're awake. I passed and Gussie passed. Now Pizza comes back with a double and Frankenstein passes on my right. Now what?"

I forced him to write the auction down:

Gussie	Pizza	Frankenstein	Stanley
—	—	—	pass
1 ◇	pass	2 ◇	pass
pass	double	pass	?

"What can I do?" I said. "My cheapest suit is spades, so I bid it."

"That's why you know nothing," said my lifelong friend. "First of all, the double was balancing. You didn't hear it go one diamond-double immediately, did you?"

I shook my head.

"Well, now what do you suppose partner has? A singleton diamond and support for the other three suits?"

I shook my head.

"Of course not. Do you have any clue what he has?"

I shook my head some more.

"Right on, man. You have no idea and neither did I. That's because he was *balancing*, just trying to push them up a level to where we might beat them a trick. Pizza might be a stickler for system and all, but when it comes to basic rubber bridge tactics, he's not so stupid."

"So what did you do?" I asked.

"I bid two hearts. Can't you see that? Two lessons here, kid. First, he may not have spades; he might even be 2-4-3-4 shape with a doubleton spade, no telling."

I had to protest. "True, but then he'll correct if you're doubled." I was pleased that my brief experience on the axle of a moving train hadn't dulled my thinking.

"Once the doubling starts they'll get into a rhythm and everything will be doubled!" he rebuffed.

"Anyway, that's not the main point. I want a heart lead against three diamonds, so I help Pizza out with a little lead-directing response. He's not too bright on opening lead to begin with; and whenever you play with a non-expert, you've got to watch out before bidding suits without an honor. Next thing you know, they're leading their king doubletons and blaming you for your bid."

All very interesting, I thought. Outside the window we were passing the port of Elizabeth. I could see the last refinery tank with the tail of the Esso Oil Tigers lit up across its side. The cartoon creature made me think of the little girl. "Was she still asleep by the window while this was going on?"

"What are you, a district attorney? I was playing bridge, I wasn't watching the kibitzers. Now pay attention. After my two-heart bid, it went around to Frankenstein, on my right, who bid *three* diamonds."

"And that became the final contract?"

"No, not exactly. I passed, Gussie passed and Pizza bid *three* hearts." Lovely, I thought.

"Now Frankenstein, who can't stand to let the opponents have a partscore, took the push to *four* diamonds. *That* became the final contract.

"Now aren't you glad you bid two hearts rather than two spades?" Delighted. "Opening lead, as directed, deuce of hearts."

Stanley wrote down the lead and the dummy. It looked like this:

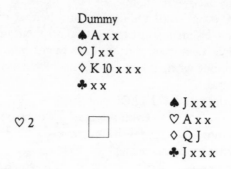

Dummy
♠ A x x
♡ J x x
◊ K 10 x x x
♣ x x

♡ 2

♠ J x x x
♡ A x x
◊ Q J
♣ J x x x

"On the heart lead, declarer plays low and you win the ace; what do you play back?" said Stanley.

"Fourth or third-and-fifth leads?" I asked.

"This is rubber bridge, man—fourth best."

I thought about it for a while. Declarer must have a heart honor; if it's the king, a heart return might be necessary. However, a club shift looks tempting. Partner might need a club return with the king behind the ace, or even the ace-queen behind the king. Hmm. What about spades? I sure don't want *partner* to lead a spade; the suit should be led from my hand first.

"This is impossible," I said. "My only entry was taken out at trick one, and now I have three important suits to lead from with only one opportunity."

"All right, I'll make it easier. What would you do at duplicate?"

Strangely enough, switching forms of scoring did make it easier. Right away I knew I would lead back a club, and I told him so. "That's dummy's weakness and looks like the most obvious play; if it's wrong at least others will be in the same boat."

"That's why duplicate is for babies. You can always fall back on, 'I'll make the same obvious play as everybody else.' At rubber, you gotta make the winning play or you lose. It doesn't do any good to theorize what others would do."

True, I thought. But let's have it already. "What did you do?"

"I didn't sit there and worry over every suit. I simply made some deductions and eliminated my horses."

He obviously picked up this type of thinking from the races. Years later I learned that handicappers eliminate first, then choose from what they have left.

"Partner might have the king or queen of hearts. If he has the king, a heart return can wait. If he has the queen, declarer can go up with the king and throw him in later, so what's the use of a heart return?"

I nodded. That seemed awfully easy.

"The spade picture was totally unclear. Maybe partner had a tenace, maybe not. I waited for a moment on that shift. Now, the club suit. How many clubs does declarer hold? If three or four, a club shift is going to set up pitches for him."

"Her, you mean," I interrupted.

"Him, her, what's the difference?"

"You said Gussie was declarer."

"Yeah, man. Good, you're paying attention. Now the point here was that only if she had a doubleton club—and specifically the ace-queen or king doubleton—would it be necessary to shift through her."

I nodded. A club shift was a bigger longshot than I thought, though I wasn't really convinced.

"Now back to spades. There were lots of tenace possibilities in that suit. Partner could have K-Q-9, K-10-9, Q-9-8, who knows? So I went with the odds and shifted to a spade."

"Nice play," I said. "I don't think many people would have found it."

"You're right. Here, don't you want to see the whole hand?" He wrote it on the inside of the schedule.

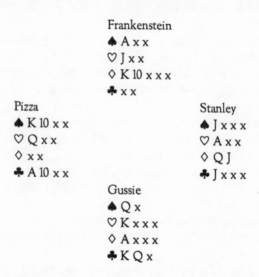

Frankenstein
♠ A x x
♡ J x x
◇ K 10 x x x
♣ x x

Pizza
♠ K 10 x x
♡ Q x x
◇ x x
♣ A 10 x x

Stanley
♠ J x x x
♡ A x x
◇ Q J
♣ J x x x

Gussie
♠ Q x
♡ K x x x
◇ A x x x
♣ K Q x

I looked at the diagram. Three hearts doubled would have been a nice spot.

Anyway, Stanley was right about my club return. Pizza would win the ace and exit a club, but Gussie could pick up trumps, ruff a club and lead king and a heart to endplay him.

What about a heart return at trick two? Gussie goes up king, draws trumps and throws him in. Likewise, he's endplayed—no, no he's not. He can get out with a low club. Wait a second. No, if he gets out a low club, dummy's second club can be thrown on Gussie's fourth heart. Hmm. A heart return doesn't work either.

Did that spade return at trick two really solve Pizza's problems?

"You figure it all out yet?" asked Stanley.

"Okay, you made the only shift, but it still seems a little lucky."

"Lucky? And what about my two-heart bid, I suppose that was

114

luck too? You would bid two spades and receive a spade lead, killing any chance for the defense."

Stanley remained silent and stared at the diagram. I suddenly realized he didn't give a damn about Frankenstein's little girl. All he cared about was his heart bid and spade shift.

The deal, the deal, the deal. There was something missing. Why should Stanley get away with a two-heart bid like that? Yes, Frankenstein was afraid of the partscore like everyone else, but would he really bid on to *four* diamonds?

I didn't like Stanley's defense, either. A club shift looks too good to be so wrong. Surely, there was a guess here. The sound of the tracks grew louder. We were going over the bridge across the Raritan River. Rutgers College was just over the embankment, the Quad was minutes away. I turned to him and asked him point blank, "Who the hell opened the window in the middle of a lightning storm?"

"I told you," he said, "I don't know. There was an explosion, a fight. It was . . .uh . . . Frankenstein. That's right, man. Earlier, when the smoke from Pizza's cigar was bothering him. He got all riled up; that's why we moved into the front."

Frankenstein! He opened the window that his daughter fell out of?!

A whistle blew in the distance. Suddenly the conductor's voice: "Nuuuuu Brunswick! Next stop Trenton, then Phiiiiiiladelphia."

"Okay," I said, "There was an argument. But there was also lightning, right? Somebody must have looked. Or did the lights go out before she fell?"

"That's it. The lights went out. How could anybody hear her with the lights out? The hand was over; there was a lot of screaming and yelling, there was the lightning, the lights went out and she must have fallen."

The train had slowed down and was coming to a halt in the station.

"There had to be more. Somebody must have seen her missing. Didn't anyone light a match? Was there a flashlight?"

We got up and moved to the door. There were the three coeds in front of us.

"I don't know, man, you're giving me a headache. She was there, then she was gone—poof. I don't think anyone noticed. We were all too involved."

The girls were talking about breaking curfew. There were lots of jokes and giggles.

"Hey, kid," whispered Stanley. "I didn't know we had girls here."

"They're from Douglass College," I explained.

"Maybe this won't be so bad after all."

We got off the train and I walked around to the front to find a cab. In the meantime, I could see that Stanley had struck up a conversation with the girls. There was one cab driver dozing over his wheel. I woke him up and went to tell Stanley. He insisted we all ride together even though the two colleges were in opposite directions. When we got to Douglass, the four of them got out. "What's the number of our room?" Stanley asked.

"It's on the far left, first floor, Quad number one."

"See you later," he said. "Take care of the baggage."

We drove back across town and the fare was 12 dollars. I had to give the driver my hundred. He said he had no change, so he'd come back on Monday night to collect the fare. I dragged Stanley's suitcase into the Quad, past the late-night sandwich truck, and into the building marked number one. The lights were all out, thank goodness, because I didn't feel like talking to anyone.

I dropped Stanley's suitcase on his bed and it popped open. There were some clothes, a bottle of white pills, and some shaving cream. I didn't want him unpacking in the middle of the morning while I was sleeping, so I put the stuff in his dresser. At the bottom of the suitcase was a black notebook. I opened it. At the top of the cover page in handwritten caps was:

PRIVATE PROPERTY—M. P. McCARVER

Underneath it said:

> *WARNING to anyone touching these notes: Unless you'd like to go for a midnight swim in the East River, get your hands off this.*

Underneath this was some kind of diary-like note:

> That idiot, Otto, tried to read my
> notes today while I went to the
> john. I caught him with it by the
> window. Next time I said, he goes
> out the window! From now on I
> take the book to the bathroom
> with me.

And underneath that was a red and white smear—it looked like a combination of tomato and mozzarella.

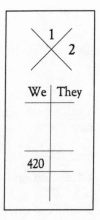

Hearts of Darkness

10

NEWSPAPER ACCOUNT—ANALYZING UNDER
A TREE—A NEW FRIEND—THE LOTTERY.

THE COMBINATION of exhaustion and fear inhibited me from reading Pizza's notebook. What was it doing in Stanley's suitcase? It was a question I didn't want to deal with. So I went straight to sleep and didn't even hear Stanley when he came in through the window at dawn. I slept so soundly that even my subconscious refused to disturb my rest. No dreams, thank god, no images of little girls sitting by windows lighting up in the dark—only the distant chirping of country birds outside the dormitory.

When I woke it was Sunday afternoon. Stanley was at his desk, going over his class schedule. He seemed like a different guy—like the old Stanley from early high school days. It made me feel good to watch him checking off items in his notepad.

Notepad! I remembered it now. I looked around the room. There up against the wall was his suitcase. Was Pizza's notebook still in there? And why did Stanley have possession of it? Had he stolen it? This was the book that Pizza never let out of his sight!

J.B. dropped by and had a chat with us. Stanley did most of the talking—not a word, of course, about a black notebook, nor about a little girl who had fallen from a window in the middle of a partscore.

Stanley made it sound authentic when he explained his tardy arrival to Rutgers as a debt he owed to a friend of his father's. He had worked all summer in New York as an accountant for a respectable club, and still had a month to go before the debt was repaid. Now all was fine and dandy, he was happy to be here and eager to get caught up in his studies. J.B. thought it remarkable that a modern young scholar should take so much responsibility for his family's honor and immediately nicknamed Stanley "Honest Abe." I didn't mention the fact that Stanley's dad had left home when he was two years old and has never been heard from since.

"I'd have been here even sooner," said Stanley, pointing to me, "if this kid hadn't got into trouble at the card table. I had to drag him away."

I started to object but thought better of it. What difference did it make anyway? Stanley was here, and J.B. was content; his duties as preceptor were back in order. That night, some of the guys returned from weekend visits. Some of them were curious to know where I was when the lights went out. When I explained I was with Stanley's girlfriend, minding the baby, they seemed disappointed.

Stanley hit it off quite well with the boys and there even was a bridge game that lasted till 1 a.m. Stanley explained the rules of Chicago scoring, and the boys took to it right away, especially Pete the Poet, who fancied the concepts of the wheel and precisely four deals per rubber at varying vulnerabilities. "Like a red and white wheel of fortune," he said, "that spins and slows down at four sequential quadrants—but never stops, no, never stops."

The Monday morning *Times* had no article about the accident. The New York *Post* had nothing either. I went back to the library rack, but couldn't find the *Daily News*. But why should the *News* have the story if no other paper did? There were plenty of stories in the Sunday papers the day before, all concerning the blackout, the lightning storm and Con Edison, which promised to conduct a test in the near future that would prove to the public the company's efficiency in times of crisis.

There were interviews, asking people where they were when the lights went out. There were articles about the theaters and the mass exits, the restaurants and the free champagne offered to customers. There were 17 separate columns about rapes. There were 23 articles dealing with theft. There was not a word of a little girl falling from a window.

It was almost 11:30 on Monday and I had an 11:45 English

class across town at Douglass. We were supposed to start our study of Conrad's *Heart of Darkness*. I had the book with me, but had yet to turn to page one. When I arrived, I also realized I had never written that paper on Ben Franklin and Malcolm X.

Mr. Keewood had left a note on the door: "Class cancelled today for preparation of rally." What rally that was, I didn't know. Anyway, it was lucky for me. My next class, a history lecture back at Rutgers, was not until 4:30. I decided to try the Douglass library to see if the *News* was there. It was a warm, bright day and I could have used sunglasses. When I reached the entrance of the building, I was happy to get in out of the sun. I spotted the *Daily News* on the rack immediately. The front page had one big headline and two smaller ones at the bottom:

Nixon OKs Cambodia Raids

'Mazing Mets Win Division (back cover)

Lightning Causes Girl's Fall (page 7)

I carried the paper over to the nearest table where a blonde girl was reading. I swear that newspaper weighed a hundred pounds.

Page seven. There was a photograph of the Frankenstein and the Beauty! She was sitting on his lap looking up at him with adoration. He looked "spacy" behind his thick glasses, as if he were calculating the odds of a redoubled slam. The caption read: "Frank Stein and victim-daughter, Cathy." I moved quickly to the article underneath. There it was in black and white. I clutched the table as I read:

LIGHTNING CAUSES FALL
FROM GAMBLING CLUB

MANHATTAN CLUB CLOSED AFTER FALL FROM WINDOW

Special Report—On Saturday night, Oct. 4, a 7-year-old Manhattan girl fell two stories to the wet bushes beneath the rear windows of 119 West 57th Street, located between Sixth and Seventh avenues. She was discovered in the courtyard at approximately 11:40 by a man carrying a flashlight, Mr. Otto Marx, a handyman employed by a group of 57th Street office buildings in the area. Mr. Marx identified the girl as Cathy Stein, the daughter of an associate, Frank Stein, a lifetime member of a bridge club called the Mayfair, which has its rooms on the third floor of 119 West 57th Street. The girl was taken to NYU Medical Center where she underwent surgery for head and neck wounds. She was last reported in critical condition by Doctor Boris Bellyard, special surgeon at the hospital.

Early investigation shows that the girl was leaning her head against a window at the time of the fall, after going to sleep in a chair. Lightning struck the area a number of times Saturday night, and at 11:15 P.M, a 20-minute blackout occurred. The lightning was presumed to be a catalyst in jarring the child off the chair, but the precise time of the accident was not confirmed by police because no one in the club at the time noticed her missing.

"It's the first case of its kind," said Captain McHale of the 17th Precinct. "These people were too busy playing cards or Parcheesi or something to notice the fall. Can you beat that?!"

Famous Proprietor

The Mayfair Club is owned and operated by Alvin Roth, one of the country's most famous bridge players and writers. His 1957 book, "Bridge is a Partnership Game," co-authored with Tobias Stone, was built upon the Goren point-count methods and has set the cornerstone for modern bidding systems. Mr. Roth, who was not in the club at the time, was called at his home at midnight. He told police that the game in the back room of the Mayfair was for a higher stake than most bridge games and very serious. "From time to time we get famous players like

Johnny Crawford, Ozzie Jacoby, Phil Feldesman. But last night only our regulars were there." When asked how it's possible for somebody to fall unnoticed from a window in the middle of a lightning storm, Mr. Roth responded, "Players get very wrapped up in bridge. Few people realize how fascinating the game is. Recently in London, a nude woman was brought in to kibitz a well-known player. It was a bet to see if he would notice her and lose concentration. But he never looked up from his cards."

On a more serious note, Mr. Roth was most grieved about the accident and promised to put in an air conditioning system with closed windows in the near future. "Unfortunately," he said, "I understand there was some kind of argument going on at the time, which is not abnormal. There was a doubled slam contract. I don't know all the details, but as usual I believe one pair was a couple tricks too high."

Club Shut Down

When police discovered the members' account cards, the club was closed until further notice. "Where there's dice and cards, there's gambling," said Sergeant O'Rourke, who first responded to the call. "It's up to me to close the joint down. Personally, I don't see anything wrong with it, but I've got to do my job."

The illegal gambling charges were denied by Mr. Roth. "It's ridiculous. Just plain ignorance. Bridge is a game of skill, and has been proven so. This happens every so often, here, so I don't worry about it. Besides, all our cash flow is on account, and the house takes no percentage of the winnings." However, police also reported backgammon and klaberjass games in progress when they walked in.

A statement this morning by Detective Kennedy of the 17th Precinct, who as of today was placed in charge of the case, revealed that Mr. Roth was correct. "Bridge is purely a game of skill," said Kennedy, a junior master with nine rating points earned at the bridge-tournament level. "The club will probably be reopened within a few days."

Asked why a special detective was appointed for an

124

accident of this kind, Kennedy would not comment, except to say that lightning storms are not generally the cause of window falling and therefore "must be investigated. The blackout may have been a factor, too, of course."

Missing Money

Police also reported an unloaded registered handgun found in Roth's desk drawer, next to a cash box containing $1,200. A reported $500 in hundred dollar bills was missing from the cash box, and police are also investigating that. "Although this may be totally unrelated to the accident," said Detective Kennedy, "it certainly seems a coincidence." Police Sergeant O'Rourke had his own opinion at the scene of the crime. He told reporters, "I suspect this was an inside job. No one saw anyone near the desk, except earlier in the evening when a suspicious character in wet, wrinkled clothes was spotted hanging around the vicinity."

Suspicious character in wet, wrinkled clothes!! I forced myself to read on, my eyes burning red with tear-stained grief.

The police said they had some leads and were investigating. (See p. 93 - GIRL'S FALL)

I turned to page 93, with—Shall I say it?—the speed of lightning.

GIRL'S FALL
The McCarver Foundation

A figure of some prominence, Michael McCarver Jr., son of the Nobel prize winner for bio-chemistry in 1935, was in the bridge game at the time of the girl's fall. Mr. McCarver, whose nickname at the club is "Pizza," is the controlling shareholder of the McCarver Foundation, which makes donations to hospital charities in New York and is sponsoring a new wing at the NYU Medical Center.

As a bridge player, Mr. McCarver is a notable theorist and author of a contract bridge system. He told police that two young boys were at the club that evening, one of them a regular member. "With young riffraff like that you never know what to expect," said McCarver. "Instead of joining the armed forces—like we did when we were their age—they hang out at bridge clubs, which, uh, I don't mean to say is necessarily a bad thing—bridge being a very intellectual pastime." During World War II, Mr. Mc-Carver was a training officer at Fort Dix, and served in Europe from 1945 to 1947.

Other Witnesses

Another witness, Miss Gussie Addles, of the Bronx, told reporters that there were many players that evening, and that so-called suspicious characters were an everyday occurrence at the club. "You can never tell a book by its cover. Even the nice, respectable people look suspicious. Look at me, for instance."

Maggie Johnson, chief cook at the Mayfair for more than 20 years, was interviewed by telephone at her apartment on West 128th Street. She testified that she had left the club early Saturday night after clearing the supper tables, but had seen the suspicious individual (in wet, wrinkled clothes) both on Friday evening and Saturday night around six o'clock. "Oh, he was nothing special," she claimed. "Just a poor boy—didn't have the money to pay for his supper." When asked about the little girl, and why she was there so late on a Saturday night, she responded, "Lord have mercy, I knew something was gonna happen if this kept up. I always said this is no place to bring a little girl. But that poor Mr. Frankenstein, widower and all, trying to save every dime he can for his child's education—I know from the tips I get—he's a little chintzy when it comes to Christmas bonuses. But Lordy, I do feel sorry for him now."

Frank Stein, the former mathematician and Rhodes scholar, employed for six years (1958-1964) at the Mc-Carver Foundation and now unemployed, was treated for shock before hospital officials released him to the police for questioning. Mr. Stein later returned to the bedside of his daughter and would not speak with reporters.

126

That was it. That was enough. That was *more* than enough! I removed my hands from the table. They were red and sore from gripping the edge. The blonde girl was staring at me.

"Are you all right?"

I didn't answer. I had seen her somewhere before. She went back to her book. I swallowed hard.

"Sorry," I said, "I didn't mean to snub you. Where's the water fountain?"

"Over there, near the entrance."

I rose with an effort. Then slowly, like a walking corpse, I stepped quietly toward the doors. I needed more than water.

When I got back to the table, the girl was getting ready to leave. Now I remembered. She was the girl whose feet I had stepped on during the Orientation dance, though it seemed many years had passed since that time—not just one month.

I don't know what made me do it. Perhaps it was the fear of carrying all this weight by myself, perhaps because she looked like a nice girl—the sort you played with in open fields, swam with in lakes, held hands with in the sunshine, but never went with in the dark. "Don't leave," I said. "I'm in terrible trouble."

"I'm on my way to psych. C'mon." I rose and stumbled briefly. "You walk like you dance," she said. I was overjoyed that she remembered.

We walked in silence to the exit and out to a small park-like enclosure at the rear of the library. There wasn't a single cloud in the sky and my eyes were hurting from the glare. Except for a few trees, the only shade was provided by a circular group of old ivy-covered buildings. She pointed to a huge oak tree on the lawn. "Wait there. It'll be about an hour."

I nodded, moved to the tree and watched her enter a building nearby. Then I sat down on the grass. Oh God, I was wearing the same wrinkled pants I had worn on the weekend. I should have burned them.

She was gone now. What was her name? I'd completely forgotten.

Something in my rear pocket was sticking into me. It was a crumpled piece of paper. There was no trash can around, so I folded the paper into my Conrad. Then I noticed another piece of paper had fallen from my pants. It was my train schedule with Stanley's partscore diagram. Hmm. The newspaper account said something about a slam hand, not a partscore. Did Stanley leave the Mayfair before the slam? No, he knew about the girl's fall. Yet no one saw the girl fall. She wasn't discovered until Otto passed her on the street. The partscore hand must have come first. Of course it did—Stanley had said that the fight for the partscore was important. It would affect the next deal. That next deal must have been the slam hand—the hand that caused the argument. But Stanley had said she fell during the heated discussion over the partscore hand. How could he know that unless he saw her fall? And if he saw her fall, how could he continue to play the next deal without saying something?! And how could that deal be played in the dark?!! And why was there no mention of Stanley in the newspaper—only me?!!!

Maybe Stanley left right after the partscore. So he never played the fourth deal—the slam. But still, he would have mentioned the girl's fall to someone. And someone would have taken his place in the game. But who? Was it Otto? He was the one with the flashlight. Maybe it was in reverse. Maybe Stanley *did* see the girl fall. The game had moved to the front room, Stanley told me. Well, maybe he left something in the back room and there saw her fall. Maybe he returned to the game, then left during the argument over the partscore while Otto filled in during the slam hand. Then after Stanley located the girl on the pavement, maybe he phoned the club and maybe Otto came down with his flashlight and reported the girl's fall while Stanley got into a taxi. Only one problem—that's a lot of maybe's.

I looked at the partscore again. Was this really a hand that could cause enough commotion to drown out the sound of a girl falling from a window? Under the diagram I jotted down the entire auction.

Frankenstein
♠ A x x
♡ J x x
♦ K 10 x x x
♣ x x

Pizza
♠ K 10 x x
♡ Q x x
♦ x x
♣ A 10 x x

Stanley
♠ J x x x
♡ A x x
♦ Q J
♣ J x x x

Gussie
♠ Q x
♡ K x x x
♦ A x x x
♣ K Q x

Gussie	Pizza	Frankenstein	Stanley (dealer)
—	—	—	pass
1 ♦	pass	2 ♦	pass
pass	double	pass	2 ♡
pass	pass	3 ♦	pass
pass	3 ♡	4 ♦	(all pass)

The auction seemed suspicious to me when Stanley reported it on the train. Hmm. Didn't Stanley say it was third deal and that his side was vulnerable? That would mean Frankenstein had allowed himself to be pushed to four diamonds by vulnerable opponents. This didn't seemed likely.

What about that 40 partscore from the previous deal? It's true, Frankenstein might stretch to four diamonds if he had a 40 partscore. But it would not explain Pizza's three-heart bid. A nonvulnerable sacrifice against three diamonds would be reasonable. But would Pizza risk a *vulnerable* sacrifice? I wasn't sure, but I was sure of one thing: This was no partscore deal—this just *resembled* a partscore deal.

How did the play go?. . . Pizza had led a heart to his partner's ace. Then Stanley found the brilliant spade shift, the only play to defeat the contract.

Assuming this scenario was true (there was no reason for Stanley to lie to me about a bridge deal), Gussie might have criticized Frankenstein for bidding four diamonds. Frankenstein might have criticized Pizza for bidding three hearts. Pizza might have criticized Stanley for bidding *two* hearts. But how much could you argue? Four diamonds, down one—so what?

I stared at the deal. It was like staring into a microscope. No, it was more like a telescope to another world. Not only did the hand contain bits and pieces of esthetic evidence born from a natural order of suits, it also contained people behind them, their thinking, their moves, their postmortem arguments. Beyond them was the back room where the cards were dealt, the little girl by the window, the lightning, the fall.

Still there was more to this. I forced myself to concentrate on the diagram. Were the exact spots on the cards important? It didn't appear so. Like most players when they write out a hand, Stanley had inscribed only the honor cards, ace down to ten. . . Hmm, he had forgotten the ten of hearts. But tens weren't so important, usually. . . .

The ten of clubs was important because if Gussie held it instead of Pizza, she could have set up a club pitch for dummy's third heart.

The ten of diamonds was important because it gave declarer an option of finessing on the second round of the suit. Gussie had refused the finesse, I suppose because she was the sort who always played for two-two splits.

The ten of spades was key to the defense on this deal. If Frankenstein or Gussie held it instead of Pizza, Gussie would only have to play low on the spade return to force out the king.

But the ten of hearts—it wasn't there. Hmm. Perhaps, Stanley wrote only the tens he thought important. Stanley was an expert analyzer and would have realized the card's irrelevance.

Then again, maybe he simply wrote in all the tens, regardless of relevance, but forgot about the ten of hearts. Why was that card bothering me anyway?

I stared further into the diagram. That spade return bothered me on the train and bothered me now. Why not a club shift? Hmm. Change the cards slightly and the deal could look like . . .

Frankenstein
♠ A x x
♡ J x x
◇ K 10 x x x
♣ x x

Pizza
♠ K 10 x x
♡ K x x
◇ x x
♣ K 10 x x

Stanley
♠ J x x x
♡ A x x
◇ Q J
♣ J x x x

Gussie
♠ Q x
♡ Q x x x
◇ A x x x
♣ A Q x

Now a club return is crucial before Gussie has the chance to set up her fourth heart for a club discard from dummy. I knew a club return was reasonable! The problem was that there didn't seem to be a way for Stanley to know which suit to shift to. His claim that a spade was more likely because there were more possible tenaces in spades was nonsense!

"Don't tell me you haven't moved from this spot for an entire hour."

I looked up at her. Not only had I not moved, I had completely forgotten where I was. At least a hundred students were swarming the area. A bandstand was being erected 20 feet from me. The hammering and drilling were suddenly loud and irritating.

"What's happening?" I asked.

"The Vietnam rally tonight. Are you that out of it?"

Her name was Esther. I remembered now from the dance. As we walked toward the commissary, she asked me what was bothering me so much.

During the hour of analysis under the oak tree, I had completely forgotten about my real-life troubles. Now I wasn't sure how much I wanted to tell this innocent-looking stranger. But I was hungry—bridge analysis always works up an appetite.

"Forget the commissary," I said. "I'll take you to lunch at a little Hungarian place I know."

The Red Tulip didn't open till four, but the cook was there early, so they let us order a late lunch.

She had chicken paprikash with noodles. I had goulash. She told me her hopes for the future. I told her my fears of the past. She held nothing back—her radical political feelings, her passion for classical music, her claustrophobia. I held a lot back—getting robbed in the Pennsylvania Station men's room, my seduction in a rundown Westside brownstone, my enchantment with the dark.

When the check came, I flashed Stanley's hundred-dollar bill, hoping it would impress her. She told me her mother wanted her to go to Radcliffe, but she had insisted on a State school because she couldn't stand spoiled rich boys. I told her the hundred was borrowed from a loan shark in New York, that I needed a scholarship just to pay for the 400-dollar tuition.

"You're really some kind of nut," she said affectionately. I was a nut (being pleased that she thought I was). "You spend hours playing a card game while the world's falling apart, and you get upset over a newspaper story when you know you weren't involved."

"True," I said, not having any clue that the world was in such trouble. The waitress brought back the Franklin-note and told me she couldn't change it now, she'd trust me for the check till tomorrow.

"And besides," Esther continued, "you said yourself you have a perfect—What do you call it?—"

"Alibi."

"Alibi. With that Chops fellow that you spent the night with." I nodded.

We each had one more class to attend, and made plans to meet afterward back under the oak tree for the six o'clock rally.

She was there, waiting for me when I arrived. They were protesting the Vietnam war, the draft and the lottery that went with it.

"Hey," I said, "that's my English prof."

Mr. Keewood was on the platform. He brushed his long blond hair from his eyes and addressed the assembly. "If scientists can put a man on the moon, we can end the war in Vietnam!" Cheers went up from the crowd. "If doctors can transplant a human heart, we can end the war in Vietnam." More cheers. "If the New York Mets can reach the World Series . . . WE CAN

END THE WAR IN VIETNAM!!"

There were other speakers, and the gist of the evening's protest was that at 7:30 that night, the United States government was going to conduct a lottery of birthdates to determine the order of conscription from the local draft boards around the country. Assuming you wanted to stay in school and not be drafted, the lottery worked in reverse—you *didn't* want to hear your birthdate called because, for example, if you were born on the date that was selected first, you would be the first one drafted. The second picked would be second and so forth.

"My birthday is December 12th," I told Esther.

Some of the students had radios to listen to the lottery. However, Esther suggested we go to her dorm so I could hear clearly.

Upon entering, she signed me in, and we went to a room on the second floor. We found the local station broadcasting the lottery, and she offered me a glass of coke. We sat next to each other on the bed with our backs to the wall as we listened to my fate. The coke was refreshing and it wasn't long before the pressures of the day began to subside. It was a short relief, however.

When the first birthdate was called off, I made a joke about moving to Canada. When the second date wasn't mine, I let out a yawn. When the third date was December 11th, I spilled my coke.

As the numbers were called off faster and faster, I grew more and more tense, whispering in the air, "not December 12th, not December 12th." When they had reached number 100, and I had not heard my birthdate, I started to relax again. It was around 150 that I resumed my worry. "Maybe," I said, turning to Esther, "we missed December 12th."

"Between the two of us we would have heard it," she reassured me.

Still, after 200, I began to root for December 12. I came from Jersey City, a large community. I didn't think the draft board would get past 200 in one year's time. At 250, I grabbed the closest thing to me for security, which was Esther's left hand. At 275, I began to panic. How many days were there in a year anyway?! At 300, I jumped up from the bed and began pacing. At 307 or 308, Esther's roommate came in and I thought I had missed the call. "It was November 12th," Esther insisted. The roommate grabbed some books and left. We were alone again for the final 50.

At 314, we heard December 12 clear as a bell, and embraced. Then we looked into each other's eyes. "I'm still a reactionary when it comes to kissing on the first date," she said. She took my hand and walked me out of the building. Then she gave in and I felt a quick peck on my cheek.

That peck meant a lot more to me than it should have—more than my brief affair the night before. It stayed with me all the way home. But the bubble soon burst. When I reached the gates of the Quad, the police were waiting.

11

NOVICE DETECTIVE—GRILLED—DEEP IN A
HOLE—THE TORN PIECE OF PAPER—
A TOMATO STAIN.

I HELD out my wrists and waited for the handcuffs. Instead, the cop handed over my Ben Franklin book. I thumbed through it. The *Bridge World* was missing. I wondered if they were keeping it as evidence.

J.B. looked downtrodden. I must have been a huge disappointment to him. "This is Detective Kennedy," he said, introducing the man standing next to the cop. He was a young oval-shaped man with horn-rimmed glasses. Carrying a small attache case, he resembled a Wall Street businessman rather than a city detective. "He's already talked to Stanley," continued J.B. Then in a concerned voice he said, "We've been waiting for over an hour for you. Where've you been, guy?"

I wasn't sure it was a good thing to tell the police I'd been to an anti-war rally. "I was with a girl." That seemed to make everyone a little looser. The cop put on a big grin and said he was going for a cup of coffee. Then Detective Kennedy suggested we go somewhere and "chat."

"We could go to my room," I suggested.

"No," said J.B., rather quickly with a funny grin of apology.

"My room would be best for this sort of thing."

Before we reached the entrance to Quad number one, J.B. turned to me and said, "By the way, guy, you owe me 12 dollars. A cab driver was here collecting from a ride you owed him for, and I took care of it."

I reached into my pocket and pulled out the Franklin-note. "That's all right, guy," said J.B., "I'll just have it transferred on the account card."

I didn't know what he meant by that, but when I slipped the hundred back in my jeans, I noticed the detective staring at my pocket.

J.B. said good-by to us in the hallway, and the detective and I entered J.B.'s room, turned on a dull overhead light and took seats by the desk. The detective opened his attache case and whipped out a notepad and pen. Then he began to grill me.

"Name?"

"Matthew Granovetter."

"Date of birth?"

"314."

"What?"

"I mean December 12, 1951."

"Occupation."

"Bridge, er, student."

"Present address."

"Rutgers University, the Quad, number one, New Brunswick, New Jersey."

"Telephone number?"

"Uh, there's a phone on the desk there."

"I see it."

He wrote down the number, then looked up at me.

"I suppose you know what this is all about."

"I think so."

"Well, don't be nervous. Is this the first time you've ever had to talk to a detective?" I nodded. "Well don't tell anyone, but this is only my third case. I just got my badge two weeks ago."

I relaxed a little. It made me feel better to know he wasn't *that* experienced.

"Now, just tell me what you know, tell the truth and everything will be fine." I nodded again. "Were you at the Mayfair Bridge Club in Manhattan Saturday night?"

"Yes."

"Did you play bridge in a game with Michael McCarver, Frank Stein and Gussie Addles?"

"Some of them, I think. But—"

"But what?"

"Well, I know them better by their nicknames."

"Let's see," he said, thumbing through his notes. "Pizza and Frankenstein. You know these people?"

I nodded.

"What about Stanley Kesselman? You know him of course."

"Y-yes, he's my roommate, and uh. . ." The detective waited. "He was my best friend for many years."

"Were you with him last night at the club?"

"Yes."

"And you're familiar with a girl friend of his, a young lady who goes by the name of Chops?"

"Yes." (How familiar did he mean?)

"By the way, did you know a foreign substance was found at her apartment?"

"A what?"

"Pot. Hash. Reefer. Marijuana. You do go to college, don't you?"

I shook my head, no, then quickly changed it to yes.

"Were you ever inside this woman's apartment?"

I shook my head, no, for sure this time. What made me do it? Was it the line of questioning? Was it self-preservation? "Was she arrested last night?" I asked, rather stupidly.

"No," he answered. "Why should she be arrested? Do you know something about her activities last night?"

"No, but. . ."

"But what? She says here, let's see. . . " He thumbed through some notes. "Said she was home last night with her kid, Bobby, and your school roommate, Stanley. Anything wrong with her statement?"

I shook my head, no, not knowing what I was saying anymore. Then I asked another dumb question. "Is Stanley involved with drugs?"

"Nobody's involved with drugs. This woman had a misdemeanor charge, when drugs were found in her apartment three months ago."

Three months ago!

136

"Pizza and Frankenstein. You know these people?"

"You don't look like a kid who takes uppers, but that's the first thing I like to check out when I interrogate suspects."

Suspects!

"Now, getting back to the Mayfair. You were seen there playing in a bridge game when lightning struck, the lights went out and this 7-year-old girl, Cathy, fell out a window. Tell me everything you remember about the incident."

"What?"

"Just take it slowly. Start with anything; it doesn't have to be in chronological order. Any details will do."

Good God, what had I gotten into? Could I now go back and say I was with Chops Saturday night? Then he would think I was a liar and never believe *anything* I said. Details. What did I know? Must think fast. "I was in a partscore."

"You were playing rubber bridge, right?"

"Yeah, it was a four-diamond contract."

"Hold on." He thumbed through his notes again. "Four diamonds, you say. Let's see here. You know I play duplicate bridge myself. My wife taught it to me after we got married last year. I have 7.4 masterpoints." He looked up at me proudly. "That's why they put me on the case—my knowledge of the game. I actually have another case I'm working on, but I when I heard my Captain mention the word 'bridge,' I volunteered for the assignment." He returned to the notes. They seemed to be disorganized.

Suddenly I remembered that this was the detective I read about in the newspaper account. Detective Kennedy—I had *heard* that name before, also. I remembered now. When I phoned the Mayfair from the street, the cop on the phone asked if I were Detective Kennedy.

"You play duplicate or just rubber bridge?"

"I, uh, I was raised on duplicate," I said.

"Okay, here it is. According to Mr. McCarver, the declarer of . . . no that was six spades, not four diamonds. Here, four diamonds was the deal before that. Mr. McCarver at first testified you were the declarer. This was refuted by Gussie Addles, who said the girl's father, Mr. Stein, was declarer, and that she was only a kibitzer. She claimed that when she's in the game, she's generally a defender and sometimes the dummy, but rarely the declarer—and that he—the girl's father that is—played it against someone by the name of Doctor B. and Stanley Kesselman; she said that Mr. McCarver was the dummy. Whereupon Mr. McCarver changed his testimony—said it was hard to remember who declared every hand, especially an insignificant hand as a partscore—but insisted it was you partnering Doctor B., not Stanley, because he remembers there was a commotion afterward about you misdefending at trick two, permitting, uh, Frankenstein, to find some kind of endplay position in which your partner had to give declarer . . . I can't read my own handwriting."

"A sluff and a ruff," I said.

"That's it, thank you. Sluff and a ruff. Nice ring to that. I recall one of my duplicate opponents last week mentioning the phrase in connection with *my* defense to a hand. Anyway, let's see now, we have corroboration from the Chops girl that Stanley was with her all evening. And of course Stanley's statement—he didn't recall any partscore deal. Claims to have played a few deals after supper at the club, won quite a big rubber I understand, and then left with Chops and her baby son.

"Well, you agree, you were defending at the time, not declaring. It's important, you see, because I want to know who was sitting in the seat with the direct view to the corner window. Anything you notice about the girl by the window? Do you remember seeing Cathy during that deal?"

Things were getting out of hand. How could I have the direct view when I wasn't even there? And why was everybody twisting the facts? Sure, Stanley didn't want to admit he was there, but he shouldn't be lying to the police. And maybe Chops was angry at me for never returning to her apartment, but why should Pizza McCarver claim *I* was his opponent during the partscore deal? Surely Gussie wouldn't lie; if she said she was kibitzing, I'm sure she was. Then why had Stanley said that she was declarer, and why had he given me the deal with Pizza as his partner?

Detective Kennedy was waiting. Then I remembered something important. "The girl fell out the window in the back room, but then the game moved into the front."

"Ah, good," said the detective, "you remember now." He started to scribble something in his notepad. "And when you saw the girl in the back room, where were you sitting?"

"Facing the window," I said.

"Good, good. Now, let's concentrate on the slam. Do you remember seeing the girl during the slam hand?"

"Yes, I saw her," I said, thinking of the slam hand that I had played earlier in the evening.

"Did you see lightning? Was there thunder?"

"Yes, both, we all looked up. She was sitting there when the lightning struck." But wait, I thought, you've got the wrong hand; that was another slam hand, the one that capped my 42-point rubber, the one that took place in the *back* room.

"Now we're getting somewhere." He looked at his notes. "And your partner was Doctor B., correct?"

Yes. My partner was Doctor B. Pizza was kibitzing, I was filling in the first rubber for him. "Yes," I said, "Doctor B. was my partner." Though that was much earlier—right after supper.

"Were you in a position to see the girl most of the night? Were you what they call. . . the wheel?"

"Part of the time," I said. "The only thing I remember clearly is the little girl sitting by the window when she was reading a book. But that was on Friday afternoon. On Saturday night I kind of remember seeing her asleep by the window and I think there was some lightning, or did I already say that?" I was getting myself deeper and deeper in a hole, telling bits of truth mixed with white lies. If only I could go back to the beginning of this testimony.

"Now, you mentioned a book. Was it a notebook per chance? A large, black notebook?"

"A black notebook?" *The black notebook at the bottom of Stanley's suitcase in my dormitory room.* I couldn't possibly tell the detective about the notebook, not without ending up with handcuffs and a ride to the station, not without a phone call to my dad to come bail me out of jail!

Snap! "Can you make anything of this?" asked Kennedy. He had taken what looked like a cigarette case out of his inside jacket pocket and snapped it open. With a tweezer he pulled out a torn piece of paper, somewhat wrinkled, and laid it out on the desk. Then he turned the lamp up on J.B.'s desk. The paper appeared to be the bottom right-hand corner of a page with the fragmented words "nerable," "erable," and "rable" in a column. Also, there was a noticeable red smear near the edge:

nerable
erable
rable

"What *is* this?" I asked.

"That's what I want to know," said Kennedy. "It was found in the bushes next to the girl's body. It could be nothing, but then it could have been within the girl's clenched fist when she fell. If you ever come across any manuscript or paper that's missing this corner, I want you to phone me immediately. Here, the lab made a copy."

I took the piece of paper he handed me and suddenly felt very sick. "You mean those are blood stains over there?" I asked, pointing to the red marks.

"No," said Kennedy. "The lab reported it as dried tomato. So you see, there's no direct connection to the case, and it might just be some innocent piece of garbage unconnected to the accident. Maggie, the cook, told us she served soup and chicken for supper that night, let's see . . ." He looked at his notes, "yes, with a brown gravy, no tomato sauce. Anyway, enough of this. I'd like to get back to the partscore deal for a second." He slipped the paper back in the case and shut it.

Tomato. Tomato. Of course, tomato. Pizza's tomato.

"When do you recall missing the girl? During or after the partscore deal? Or was it during the slam hand following? By the way, that was a nice lead you made."

What lead? He must mean Stanley. Stanley must have made a good lead—whatever it was. But Stanley said he left after the partscore. He wasn't involved with the slam hand. But neither was I, at least not with the slam hand he was talking about, the one that was played while little Cathy was lying in the bushes of 57th Street. This had gone too far. I had to come clean; I just had to.

Lowering my head shamefully, I said, "I . . . I have to tell you the truth; I . . . wasn't there."

"You mean you left the back room before her disappearance was noticed?"

"I, uh, yes. I had to catch the midnight train back to campus, you know."

"So that would mean you left the club between 11:20 and 11:30?" he asked, jotting down a new note, "before the lights came back on."

"I guess so. I don't wear a watch." It was true, at least, that I didn't wear a watch.

"One last question. Did you complete the last deal—the six-spade contract—before you left? I mean, surely you didn't let a kibitzer sit in for you."

I was in a quandary. How should I know if I completed the deal? I never even saw the deal! "Wait," he said, "maybe this will refresh your memory."

He showed me a page from his notebook and placed it directly beneath the lamp; perhaps it would be the six spades I had played earlier in the evening; then at least I could explain the play. However, this is what I saw:

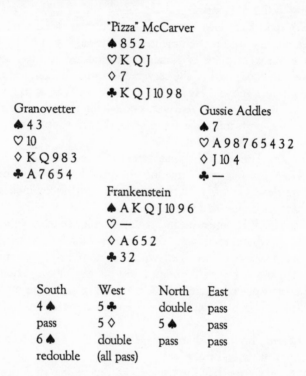

"Pizza" McCarver
♠ 8 5 2
♡ K Q J
♢ 7
♣ K Q J 10 9 8

Granovetter
♠ 4 3
♡ 10
♢ K Q 9 8 3
♣ A 7 6 5 4

Gussie Addles
♠ 7
♡ A 9 8 7 6 5 4 3 2
♢ J 10 4
♣ —

Frankenstein
♠ A K Q J 10 9 6
♡ —
♢ A 6 5 2
♣ 3 2

South	West	North	East
4 ♠	5 ♣	double	pass
pass	5 ♢	5 ♠	pass
6 ♠	double	pass	pass
redouble	(all pass)		

"Can you tell how you found the killing lead?" he asked.

I stared and stared and tried to analyze fast. Six spades looked cold? No, of course it wasn't. The lead of the ace of clubs followed by a club would beat it. But would someone lead an ace with a king-queen on the side? The diamond lead looked better before you saw all 52 cards. It was impossible to analyze so fast under pressure. My train of thought kept slipping to the lies and inconsistencies. Why was my name over the West hand?

"I have to confess," I said. "I never played this deal. I left the club right after the partscore."

Detective Kennedy smiled. "Right. That's what your friend Stanley said, too. Then you picked him up in a cab at Chop's apartment about 11:45 and drove to Pennsylvania Station. I apologize for my methods, but I had to be certain you were telling the truth. I put your name over the West hand to test you, to see if you'd lie to me and say you *had* played the hand. You seemed a bit nervous you know—only natural. But then, a good detective studies the manner of his suspects, not just the facts."

He smiled as he said this. Then he took out an eraser and cleaned my name off the slate, putting Otto Marx in its place. "The two kibitzers, Gussie Addles and Otto Marx, filled in for the fourth deal. Doctor B. was late for the hospital—you see, by coincidence he's the same Doctor Bellyard that operated on Cathy only a few minutes later. And you, of course, were late for your train. Then, after the slam, the girl was discovered missing, and it was Mr. Marx who located her in the courtyard below."

That wasn't true, I thought. Stanley had known the girl was gone *after the partscore deal*. But I was absolved, and I breathed better. When I brushed my hair back, I could feel the sweat dripping down my forehead. I looked down at the floor. The train schedule had fallen out of my pocket. The partscore hand was lying there exposed under the desk! I edged my foot over to cover it.

"That's it, for now," he said, standing up. "Oh, one more question. Do you remember precisely what you were doing when the lights went out?"

I paused. Yes I remembered. I was in Chops' apartment.

"Just tell me what card you were playing."

"The . . . uh . . . hand was over. Then the lights went out," I said, adding one more lie to the mess I had created.

"Thank you. If I have any other questions, I'll phone you."

I looked up at him, keeping my shoe over the schedule. "You're not going to report this to my parents, are you?"

He looked down at me and squinted his eyes. "To tell you the truth, I hadn't thought of it, but maybe it is a good idea—"

"Please don't," I pleaded. "I've only been to the Mayfair once, and may lightning strike me if I ever step in there again." We looked at each other. It was a stupid oath. The little girl by the window in all her eerie whiteness came back to me.

"Okay," he said. "But I will have to round up everyone again if the girl doesn't come out of her coma."

I let a minute pass after he left the room, then retrieved the train schedule. I had to copy that partscore to another piece of paper and burn the damn thing. I just sat there for a while at J. B.'s desk, feeling numb. There was the black and white photocopy of the torn paper. The grey smudge was tomato stains the lab had reported. Finally I rose and moved slowly out into the hall and toward my room. I was too tired to think any more—in the morning, in the morning. Right now, all I wanted to do was go to bed and forget. When I got to the door, it was locked. What was this now? Locked doors were forbidden in the Quad.

I knocked. Les the Mess opened up and peeked through. "Hi, it's you. C'mon in. Shh. J.B.'s in four notrump redoubled and he's playing for extras."

12

THE MINI-MAYFAIR—J.B. DECLARES— PLAYING YOUR OPPONENT.

I N LESS than 24 hours, Stanley had converted our room into a miniature Mayfair. There was a cashbox on his dresser, scorepads and pencils strewn across my bed, even a braless brunette leaning on Stanley's shoulder as he examined Big Al's dummy in four-notrump redoubled. I looked over our preceptor's shoulder and saw:

Big Al's Dummy
♠ A J 9 8
♡ A 8 4 3
◊ A Q
♣ A 5 4

◊ 10

J.B.
♠ K 10 5 4
♡ K J 10 9
◊ K J
♣ J 7 6

Four-four fits in both majors. What were they doing in four notrump? "How'd the auction go?" I whispered to Big Al. The brunette glanced at me and wrinkled her nose. "Not very well," she said, crossing her eyes.

Pete the Poet came over and told me Big Al had opened one club. "I opened *two* clubs," corrected Big Al.

"You wouldn't remember *what* you opened," insisted Pete the Poet. "He opened *one* club and J.B. responded one heart."

"That's right," said Big Al.

"Then Big Al went to four hearts. Then J.B. went to four notrump."

"That's right," confirmed Big Al, satisfied with the auction. "And we get 150 honors in notrump!"

Pete the Poet nodded, also in approval. "This got passed around to Stanley, who doubled. J.B. redoubled and that ended the whole thing."

J.B. looked up at us. "*Quiet!* I'm trying to concentrate, guys."

We leaned over and studied the hand. It seemed that all J.B. needed was to guess one of the missing queens. He had three minor-suit tricks, and needed only seven major-suit tricks to make 10 tricks. The question was: Who had the queens?

The only clue in the bidding was Stanley's double. He must have been doubling for a club lead (the first suit bid by dummy), perhaps with a long club suit to the king-queen. Maybe he held some unusual distribution, perhaps a void on the side, in case the opponents ran to five hearts.

145

Then there was that diamond-ten lead. Was that a clue to the distribution? Normally one could deduce that the opening leader held a void in clubs, otherwise he would have led the suit his partner doubled for. However, with Les the Mess on lead, it was possible that he missed the double while reading one of his textbooks. It was even more likely that he held a club, but the card was hidden or stuck behind droppings of tunafish.

Pete the Poet whispered to me that *he* would play Stanley for both queens. "Stanley must have at least one of them for his double."

I suggested that Stanley's club length made it more likely Les the Mess held the queens.

Big Al, who was all excited, leaned down and said, "I saw them. I saw them. They're both with Les the Mess. Darn it, if only *I* were playing the hand! Split aces—it's purely mathematical. But *he* doesn't think that way."

Big Al was right of course. J.B. had never even taken a finesse, let alone taken one in the right direction. Still, maybe that was something in his favor. That is, one of the queens might be doubleton and would drop.

I couldn't resist walking around the beds, stepping by accident on Short Larry, who was hunched over kibitzing behind Les the Mess. Short Larry, Big Al's roommate, didn't even play bridge, and seemed to have his eyes glued on Stanley's brunette.

"One hand, kibitz one hand," said Stanley to me. "You know that."

True, that was common etiquette. However, I did get a good enough look to picture the whole layout:

Big Al's Dummy
♠ A J 9 8
♡ A 8 4 3
◇ A Q
♣ A 5 4

Les the Mess
♠ Q 7 6 5 2
♡ Q 7 5　　◇ 10
◇ 9 8 7
♣ —

Stanley
♠ —
♡ 6 2
◇ 6 5 4 3 2
♣ K Q 9 8 3 2

J. B.
♠ K 10 4 3
♡ K J 10 9
◇ K J
♣ J 7 6

One card, the club ten, was missing, and since everyone had thirteen cards except Les the Mess, who had eleven (and should have had twelve after the lead), it was a certainty the card was hidden in one of his other suits.

Meanwhile, J.B. had finally come out of his trance and won the diamond lead in dummy. Stanley, a bit unethically, was thumbing the deuce on the trick while yelling at his partner to look up from his astronomy text. Then, triumphantly, J.B., looked up and said a new word for him: "Finesse." Carefully he pulled the jack of spades off dummy. Stanley followed quickly with the three of clubs; J.B. played low, and Les the Mess won the trick with the queen.

Les the Mess suddenly saw something in his hand. "Uh, oh," he said, pulling the ten of clubs from behind the spade six. Then he asked to see the last trick.

"Can't see it," said Stanley, quoting the rule book. "Last trick is turned over." However, the last trick was not completely turned over. Les the Mess's spade queen was still face up on the table. (It was often difficult to tell whether Les the Mess's card was up or down.)

Then, upon examining Stanley's three of clubs, Les the Mess said, "No spades, partner?" This surprised J.B., who sat up from the pillow on the floor and squinted his brow in consternation. Finally, Les the Mess, having seen discouraging spot cards in both minors from his partner, shifted to a heart.

Big Al squeezed my shoulder in triumph, but with J.B. at the wheel, I thought his elation was a little premature. I was right. J.B. rose with dummy's ace of hearts and finessed the jack through Stanley. "He's got to have one of them," said J.B. stubbornly. It was another nice try despite being given the finesse for free.

When Les the Mess won the queen and returned a heart (feeling he had finally found declarer's weakness), J.B. could count only nine sure tricks. To his credit, and as any decent Classics major would do, he cashed them in descending order of rank, that is, until he reached this position:

Big Al's Dummy

♠ —
♡ —
◇ A
♣ A 5 4

Les the Mess
♠ 7
♡ —
◇ 9 8 7
♣ —

Stanley
♠ —
♡ —
◇ 6 5
♣ K Q

J. B.
♠ —
♡ —
◇ K
♣ J 7 6

Stanley had been forced down to four cards. If he had held ◇ 6 ♣ K Q 9, J.B. could cash the diamond ace and lead a small club, endplaying Stanley for the tenth trick. Rubber bridge players love the endplay, and Stanley, who had become quite an expert in squeezes of this sort, saw it coming. Also, Stanley could see J.B.'s tempo and could reasonably assume J.B. would continue in the same rhythm of cashing his tricks from the top down. After cashing the spades, then the hearts, it was surely no less than 50 to 1 that the diamond ace would be cashed next. So why come down to K-Q-9 of clubs and risk being endplayed?

This was good thinking on Stanley's part. Unfortunately for him, however, he failed to take into account J.B.'s inexperience. Granted that J.B. was a guy who would rarely change course once he was on a roll, but here also was a guy who in a trillion years would never think of an endplay. Then there was Les the Mess to consider. His cards were seemingly irrelevant. But when the time came to discard on the fourth heart, Les the Mess threw the ten of clubs (I believe because it was the stickiest card in his hand, and he wanted to rid himself of it). J.B. lifted his eyebrows when he saw the ten of clubs hit the floor. "Seems like a lot of clubs have been discarded, guys," he said, rubbing it in as he reached for the ace of clubs. "Let's see what drops on this baby."

When the queen dropped, but not the king, J.B. let out a "darn," and then, gentleman that he was, instead of setting up his club trick, quietly cashed his diamond ace, conceding down one.

"Sorry, big guy," he said to Big Al (who, despite being a terrible declarer himself, was reduced to tears watching the play), "I almost had it. But Caesar had ambition too, didn't he?"

When the game finally broke at 4 a.m., Stanley was the big winner, J.B. the big loser. The rest of us were close to even. The stakes had quadrupled since I was last in the game—was it only the night before?—and in addition, J.B. had an extra half-cent with Stanley. The scoresheet was a copy of the one used at the Mayfair, and Stanley had revised the scoring to the modern Chicago version.

Chicago fast became the scoring for the Quad late-night game version, and it certainly was faster and fairer than standard rubber. However, before I could object with any reason behind my protest, Stanley had initiated a slight variation: dealer in second and third chair would be non-vulnerable against vulnerable, the reverse of the vulnerability at the Mayfair Club. This nuance gave Stanley an additional advantage. As a professional, he understood the strategy that went with the favorable vulnerability. For example, Stanley's opening bids became lighter than usual in third seat favorable when he was playing with a weak partner. His attempt was to "kill the deal"—that is, play the deal in a partscore with four hands of equal strength, rather than risk a passed-out hand that might get reshuffled into a big plus for his opponents. Also, as dealer, he could make much lighter preempts on the second and third deals. A couple times he even psyched with no high cards in his hand, taking further advantage of the weaker players. (In later years, I learned that was why Roth stuck to the Hoyle rule of dealer vulnerable in second and third chair.)

Meanwhile, Stanley's brunette seemed to be in charge of the

paperwork and had account cards made out with all our names. She filed these in a box on Stanley's desk. In fact, she was still there recording figures at 4:30 when all the others had gone to their rooms. I was fairly certain there was a "no-girl-overnight" policy in the Quad, but as I took off my shirt and pants, I noticed she had closed the account box and was doing the same. I couldn't care less by that time, and gratefully slipped between the cool sheets of my bed.

I felt something liquid between my toes. It must have been tomato drippings from Les the Mess's tuna sub. The brunette slipped in with Stanley before I could even catch a peek, and I went off to dreamland amid squeaking mattress springs in the distance.

Four hours later, the alarm clock in my head went off. If the torn piece of paper next to Cathy's body matched any missing corner of Pizza's black notebook, it would imply a struggle for the book had taken place—and Stanley was in possession of the book! I looked at the clock. I was late for my 8 a.m. political science class. I ran to my dresser and pulled out a pair of socks from the top drawer. Beneath my underwear was the dreaded thing.

13

A PIECE DOESN'T FIT—TRANSLATION OF A
BLACK NOTEBOOK—CLUES FROM A RUBBER
BRIDGE FANATIC.

WHY DID Stanley put Pizza's notebook in my underwear drawer? Perhaps I should have asked myself this question before I smothered the thing with my fingerprints. But I was too anxious to see if a torn page existed and if the torn section that Detective Kennedy had found by the girl's body would fit.

It took me a few seconds to find the photocopy he had given

150

me. I didn't have a scissors so I carefully tore around the section of the photo as quietly as I could. Then I opened the notebook and thumbed through the pages. I was wrong; there *were* no torn pages. Yet I had been so sure the piece *would* fit! I carefully folded the photocopy so as not to disturb Stanley and his guest, then placed it inside my *Heart of Darkness*, which was lying on the desk.

For a moment I considered contacting Detective Kennedy. Had there been a torn page which fit the puzzle, the evidence would have been too important to withhold. But it was only a notebook—a notebook, however, that was false evidence against me. *My* skin was at stake, not just Stanley's. What was *I* doing with the book? That's the first question he would ask me. What could I answer? That Stanley had the book in his suitcase and then planted it in my underwear drawer? It would be my word against Stanley's. Was it too late to wipe off my fingerprints? I thought so. I had already touched all of the pages. How does one wipe off fingerprints anyway? No, there was no question of informing Kennedy.

However, after perusal of the first page, I became engrossed. As you'll see, there was invaluable bridge advice inside these pages that no ambitious player would dream of destroying. Pizza McCarver had obviously given his life to the study of rubber bridge just as his father had given his life to the study of biochemistry. Yet the book had to be destroyed! Therefore, it was my intention to transcribe the book for future reference, then dump the original into the Raritan River with a heavy anchor tied to its binding.

I glanced over at Stanley's bed. The two of them were sleeping like babies. Taking my pillowcase off the pillow, I put some white tennis socks inside along with my books and a fresh yellow pad. Beneath all this, I placed Pizza's notebook, then slipped quietly out of the room and past the gates of the Quad toward the campus library. This precaution proved to be unnecessary, but I was taking no chances. I stopped at the food truck for a cup of coffee and a hard roll. At the library I took out my pad and opened the black notebook.

Unfortunately, all I can present here is my translation of Pizza's notebook. I say *translation* rather than *transcription* because a large part of the book was unreadable. It was not until I opened the book at the library that I saw the top portion of most of the pages were damp and wrinkled, much of the ink splattered. Also, Pizza's handwriting was very small and often impossible to read—especially when mozzarella or tomato stains covered key sequences.

I have done my best—for the purposes of this account—to reorganize the notes for readability while keeping the spirit of the original. In that original, subjects were found under various headings with 10 or 20 blank pages to fill in at the end of each grouping. At times however, he rambled from one subject to another, and I have tried to eliminate most of that confusion. I have also tried to present the notes in chronological order within each grouping. Observant readers will spot a few comments from the weekend that I was at the club listed at the bottom of some of the groupings.

I should explain a few details about the content as well. First, the notes are not only about the technical side of bridge, but about the players—in fact, every bid and play took on a particular meaning to Pizza not only because of a particular system, but also because of who made the bid, who his partner was and who the opponents were.

Second, the comments made by Pizza are his own and written with italics. In the original, his bridge notes were written with blue and red pens. His more personal comments were written in pencil (perhaps with the intention of erasing them someday). These penciled comments (that are more like a secret diary than a bridge notebook) I have italicized.

Third, I have taken the liberty of writing my own comments now and then. These criticisms and thoughts—which I made both at the time of translation and 20 years later, after longer reflection, are enclosed in brackets and typed in rather than printed—the italics in the brackets being the later commentary so that readers may make the time distinction.

Finally, Pizza had a shorthand, which I have eliminated for ease of reading. For example, instead of suit symbols, ♠ ♡ ◊ ♣, he used "s", "h", "d" and "c". At the end of all auctions, Pizza gave only the last call; three passes were assumed by me. For historical purposes, his shorthand was: N = notrump, M = major, m = minor, r = red suit, b = black suit, d = double, rd = redouble, v = vulnerable nv = nonvul. Now to the translation:

PRIVATE PROPERTY—M. P. McCARVER

WARNING to anyone touching these notes: Unless you'd like to go for a midnight swim in the East River, get your hands off this.

That idiot, Otto, tried to read my notes today while I went to the john. I caught him with it by the window. Next time, I said, he goes out the window! From now on I take the book to the bathroom with me.

THEORY AND PRACTICE
A RUBBER BRIDGE TREATISE
BIDDING AT THE BRIDGE TABLE
MONEY BRIDGE
THE MAYFAIR DIARIES

by Michael P. McCarver

```
[These titles appear here and
there throughout the book; probably
he could not make up his mind. He
had other titles as well, which
were washed out and unreadable.]
```

Chicago Scoring

All money bridge must be played with Chicago scoring. Played once in London and some madman went for seven numbers before we completed the rubber. The English are impossible bidders, passing in the middle of forcing auctions! Only exception is Reese, who knows the value of a bonus score.

By the way—prefer Hungarian rubber clubs to Austrian—far more structure in their bidding, thus easier to comprehend. Young man I met in Budapest club confirms this. *Nice guy. Listened all night to my theories. Name's Marx—not Groucho, ha, ha. Recollected some of the systems I used to play there in the late 30s. Must remem-*

*ber to use influence to get him job in New York.
Good kid.*

Chicago four-deal rubber is:
First deal - no one vulnerable
Second deal - dealer's side vulnerable
Third deal - dealer's side vulnerable
Fourth deal - both sides vulnerable

*[This is the way it was and
still is played at the Mayfair
Club. In the Quad game, second- and
third-deal vulnerabilities were
switched. See next comment!]*

Distinct advantage to playing dealer's side
favorable on second and third deals, but Roth
won't allow it! When dealer is vulnerable against
not, all the rewards of Frankenstein's preemptive
style are ruined. *He has convinced me of this;
and when Roth goes home we're going to insist
on second and third deal favorable.*

Now playing dealer favorable in back room
after midnight when Roth leaves. *He can't run
the club when he's not around!* We all agree it
makes the game more exciting—*except for Doc
B, who is a stubborn bastard.*

It worked! I love it!! Frankenstein opened
3 ♡ on six hearts to the queen-jack and out. Doc
overcalled 3 ♠. I held:

♠ K Q 10 x ♡ x ◇ A Q x x ♣ A J x x

Wham! Bang! Plus 800.

Third deal, second seat: Opened 1 ♡ playing

154

with Frankenstein on:

♠ 10 x x x ♡ A K x x ◇ Q x ♣ x x x

Big mistake. Deal would have been passed
out and reshuffled. Instead, we reached four
hearts down two. Frankenstein went crazy but
made good point. When playing with a good
partner like him, I should not kill the deal with a
light opening.

*Kid turned on me tonight and threatened to
tell Roth about second and third deal switcha-
roo. Think I'll take kid for a ride downtown
tomorrow and straighten him out—he'll do as I
say or cover his own losses.*

[I believe "kid" is Stanley.]

*Played with Chops this afternoon in two-
cent game. She's looking better. Might have to
have another go.*

Overcalls
Asked Roth today how to reach slam on
these cards after North seat opened 1 ♣:

West	East
♠ A 10 x x x	♠ K J x
♡ x	♡ A x x
◇ Q J 10 x x	◇ A x x
♣ x x	♣ K x x x

Roth would not answer at first. Apparently
feels strongly that game is difficult to reach, let
alone slam. I suggested 1 NT overcall to begin
with, and he got upset. Said that the seat *behind*
me might hold the West hand instead of my
partner. Would he double my 1 NT on only
seven points, though?

155

Doc B. held 15 pts. and overcalled 1 ◊ with 1 NT today. I doubled with:

♠ x x x ♡ Q J 10 x x ◊ A x ♣ J 10 x

Down three. Happy to have Gussie as my partner in this venture. She always has her full 13 HCP for opening bid. Don't think I could double with anyone else in the club.

Confusion over sound overcalls. Roth claimed 1 ♠ is correct overcall on:

♠ A K x x x ♡ x ◊ J 10 x x ♣ x x x

Even vulnerable! Frankenstein agreed. But Doc jumped to 3 NT and Frankenstein doubled—down four. They may be great theorists, but Frankenstein and Roth are wrong! Must have structured overcall system.

At supper, Roth heard what my result was and amended his remarks. 1 ♠ is correct, except with weak partner like Dr. B. *With Dr. B. and maniacs like him, always pass. Pass, pass, pass.*

Tall young man was at club today. Wouldn't overcall with full values when holding three small cards in opener's suit. Roth claims this is correct, but more so at the two level.

Big discrepancy. Held:

♠ x x x ♡ A K J x x ◊ A x x ♣ J x

After 1 ♠ opening, Frankenstein claimed if heart suit was minor he would pass, but here 2 ♡ correct because the suit is hearts and that's where money is. Roth is adamant, claims three small spades is deterrent. Can't overcall. Too dangerous.

Roth seems to emphasize plus scores. Frank-enstein emphasizes bonus scores. *Must decide who is right.*

Kibitzed man called Mitchell—guest today. Used to own club in forties, considered expert's expert. Overcalls at four-level on every hand!
Two examples:

♠ A Q x x ♡ K Q J x x x ◇ x x x ♣ —

After 1 ♠, Mitchell bid 4 ♡! Next hand doubled with A 10 9 x x of hearts. Opener re-moved to 4 ♠! Mitchell doubled 4 ♠ for 700. Later:

♠ A Q J x x x ♡ x x ◇ — ♣ A x x x x

After 1 ♡, Mitchell bid 4 ♠. Missed 6 ♣ from partner's side. Partner held ♡ K plus five clubs to king. However, 6 of either red suit cold the other way!

[Must be referring to Vic Mitch-ell, who likes to put pressure on opponents with direct game bids. He became a bridge mentor of mine dur-ing my twenties and believes in reaching games quickly. Often re-sponds in game with decent hands over partner's opening bid as well as overcalling game. Misses a few slams, but in return destroys any chance of a sacrifice and often winds up with a huge profit when the opponent bids, gets doubled, and goes for a number—while Mitch-ell can't even make the game he jumped to.]

Overcalled four-card suits today in preference to light 1 NT. Seems to work well:

♠ A x ♡ A K J x ◊ K x x x ♣ 10 x x

Over 1 ◊, bid 1 ♡. Gussie jumped to 4 ♡, which was going down two. Frankenstein doubled, and Doc removed to 4 ♠, down three. Gussie criticized my call anyway. Can't take her any more. She's getting too old for me. *She's like one of those old worn-out Culbertson asking bids that have no use in modern world. Besides, finally won contested will!!!!!! Entire foundation to me. The only kind of support I need from Gussie now is when I overcall a four-bagger, ha, ha. Must untie some capital—too many charities.*

Vulnerable weak-jump overcalls are killing me! Held vul vs. not:

♠ x ♡ x x x ◊ K Q J 10 x x x ♣ x x.

pass - 1 ♠ - <u>3 ◊</u>

Seemed clear-cut at the time. How could a normal preempt like this lose a thousand points?
Frankenstein ended in 6 ♠ and finessed my partner for queen-third of trumps to make!
Must be careful against good players to preempt only when the bid has strong potential to hurt them. Why not preempt with side queen doubletons? Must look to do that in future.

Opened 3 ♠, third deal vulnerable. Partner, new kid, held three aces and passed. Doesn't understand simple vulnerability rules. Count your tricks and open three-bid when the vulnerability matches correctly. Within one or two tricks of your contract vulnerable, three or four nonvulnerable. Kids!

["New kid" must mean me.]

Tempo

Roth explained that in other rubber-bridge clubs players lose their money slowly. In his, he insists they lose it fast. I told him that because of my genius I. Q. (hereditary), more facts pop into my head than the average bridge player; thus I have more to sort out and require more time.

[Rubber bridge should have helped Pizza's speed. I had a similar problem of thinking too long in those days. Edgar Kaplan once brought to my attention the fact that my time-problems occurred when I would double-check the same analysis that I had already worked out. Ninety-nine out of a hundred times, this double-check produced the same analysis. So all I was doing was wasting time. Really, it was a matter of confidence, which comes with experience. As you become more confident in your ability to analyze, you feel you can afford to stop double-checking. Then there is also the fear of making errors and looking bad. See the next comment:]

Roth told me my game has slowed up too much since I came into my inheritance, trying to be too perfect instead of playing the game. Insists rubber is a game of errors. But I can't stand to make errors! Can't sleep at night after errors!

Learned who's been complaining about my slow play. That idiot, Dr. B. Do they tell him to speed up when he's got a patient on the operating table?!

[Good question. But Pizza is

159

*wrong. I believe surgeons do have
to speed up at times.]*

Frankenstein's complaining about players' tempos. Young girl in club today for first time. *Vavavoom! What a mouth she has!* Nicknamed "Chops." Filled in two hands for Doc, after call to hospital. Got to laydown slam on only 26 pts.:

Me	Chops
♠ Q x	♠ A K x x
♡ A Q x x x x	♡ K x x x
◇ x x	◇ A x x
♣ A x x	♣ x x
1 ♡	1 ♠ (after huddle)
2 ♣	3 ♡
4 ♡	5 ◇
6 ♡	

Frankenstein claimed foul. Said Chops' 1 ♠ call was a "slam alert," coming after a 15-second pause. Claimed I wouldn't have temporized with 2 ♣ without the pause. Had I rebid 2 ♡, the girl would never dream of slam. I told him where to go and pointed to the window. I always temporize when I have a good hand with a six-bagger. Checked it out with Roth. Roth claimed a rebid of your suit is weak-sounding, and with anything above a minimum hand, temporizing in a three-card suit was a wise policy.

*[Pizza's hand was a minimum and
he should have rebid two hearts.
Seems like he did take advantage of
the huddle. This slam is cold, but
looks unbiddable. There's absolutely no wasted honor—not a jack.
    I asked Chops about this hand
later, and she confessed she
paused, but was wondering whether*

to raise hearts directly or start with one spade. It wasn't her fault that Pizza took advantage. He knew after her pause that she wouldn't drop him in two clubs.]

Must admit, Frankenstein is a hell of a player. Picked up on my tempo tonight and I hardly flickered. I held:

$$\spadesuit \text{A x x} \quad \heartsuit \text{x x} \quad \diamondsuit \text{J x x x} \quad \clubsuit \text{A K Q x}$$

Opened 1 ♣ and Doc responded 1 ♠. I couldn't stand to raise him, but 1 NT seemed so wrong with my two little hearts. I just thought about it for a split second, then bid 2 ♠. Frankenstein caught it. He balanced with 3 ♡ and got raised to four:

Dummy
♠ x x x
♡ A x x
◇ K Q 10 x
♣ J x x

Frankenstein
♠ K x
♡ K x x x x x
◇ A x x
♣ x x

I led three quick club honors. He ruffed, drew trumps, and guessed diamonds, playing me for 3-2-4-4 shape. I couldn't believe he played me to have raised an idiot like Doc with only three trumps.

[Frankenstein not only "heard" the pause before raising spades, but probably deduced the jack-

fourth of diamonds when Pizza gave
no thought to shifting to a spade.
The assumption was that Pizza felt
safe—that he had the diamond suit
"locked up."

This type of thinking is devel-
oped almost exclusively from the
rubber bridge table where so many
hands are played without emphasis
on conventions and systems. Thus,
the player, if he has the talent to
begin with, develops an extraordi-
nary sense of timing, detecting the
slightest pause in a bid or play.
Vic Mitchell once labeled this
process "the analysis of a
thought."]

Made my move on the girl, took her to
Patsy's for pizza and vino, then took her home
after the late-night game. Let her resist for a
while, then gave her the old forcing two clubs.
Tempo is equally important at the bridge table
and in the bedroom, ha, ha.

[Oh, God.]

Boys played in the local board-a-match team
tournament over at the Hilton Hotel. We lost by
one board, and couldn't have played worse.
Those tournament players *are* children, like Roth
says. *Had to laugh. Doc looks good among these
guys.* I never saw so many people get so excited
about overtricks. They make me look like a fast
player.

They keep coming to my table (I was playing
with the Kid) and they write W's on their score-
card after Kid gives up three overtricks. Meanwhile, Doc is in game at the other table, making
two less tricks but 500 points more! *Ha, ha. Imagine Doc killing these guys!* We teamed him with

Gussie the first session, figuring Gussie would underbid and Doc would overbid. Perfect match! *Second session that girl insisted on playing. I let her play with Kid—maybe she'll take to him.*

Lost on the last round to Frankenstein and his duplicate associates. *Big shot, plays in our game but won't play on our team.* I played with Gussie and had to find the right lead on this hand:

♠ x x x ♡ A K x ◇ Q J x x x ♣ x x

1 NT - pass - 4 NT

I led a low diamond:

Stayman (Dummy)
♠ K x x
♡ Q x
◇ A 10 x
♣ K Q 10 x x

Me
♠ x x x
♡ A K x
◇ Q J x x x
♣ x x

Gussie
♠ x x x
♡ J 10 x x x
◇ 9 x x
♣ x x

Mitchell (Declarer)
♠ A Q J x
♡ x x x
◇ K x
♣ A J x x

Declarer played low from dummy, so my lead gave up nothing. But then, he ran five clubs and four spades. I had to come down to three cards. Kept queen-jack of diamonds but had to throw a heart honor. He led a heart up and made six!

At the other table, Frankenstein led ace-king of hearts. Disgusting. How can a man like that degrade his bridge game by giving up before the opening lead—and then get lucky enough to beat the contract by two tricks!?

Took the boys to little Italy after the game. Frankenstein tagged along. *Nut case with the meatballs. Had to order my own second pie.* Must admit his reasoning was good: 1 NT - 4 NT showed 29-30 points for opponents. Claimed he counted at least 10 tricks for declarer and saw squeeze coming. Would always lead a diamond at rubber.

Later, took me aside and whispered that Kid had huddled briefly before opening 1 NT. Figured he had an unstopped suit, and that was the vigorish for leading a heart!

Learning to read your opponents' hesitations is the most difficult thing in bridge. *But I'm going to keep trying even if it kills me.*

Frankenstein's partner, young wealthy fellow who hired him to play. Nice boy, Frankenstein said, treats him with kid gloves. Told the boy, take this advice: Play rubber, not duplicate. Nobody coddles you at rubber; that's where you'll learn to use your own brain instead of following the bids and leads of your partner. Frankenstein called me Big Baboon for butting in. I told the boy that was the umpteenth time he's called me Big Baboon and it's never penetrated my thick skin. That's because I train at the Mayfair.

Rebids
Roth laughed at Kid when he heard about the hand that kept us from winning. Roth plays strict 16-18 1 NT. However, claimed the points were not relevant. Automatic 1 ♣ opening with clubs and spades with one suit unstopped. This would lead to proper 4 ♠ contract. Interesting point, spades make an easy rebid.

Got into trouble with Frankenstein. Held:

♠ A K x x ♡ J x ◇ K Q x ♣ K x x x

Opened 1 ♣, planning easy spade rebid. Kid overcalled 3 ♡. Pass-pass- to me. Had to pass. But Frankenstein held:

♠ Q x x ♡ K 10 x ◇ A x x x x ♣ x x

Diamonds were 4-1 and we were still cold for 3 NT. Frankenstein insists on 1 NT with 16-18 regardless of stoppers. Claims it gets across hand type in one simple bid.

Gave the hand to Roth. He opened 1 NT. Said my clubs were too weak, and the heart jack might be partial stopper. This game is too difficult, I think. No one gives me set rules. Always have to think and judge. *Should have stuck with bio-chemistry. But had to beat the old man at something! Damn him!*

[Except for contesting the will, this is the only reference to Pizza's father, Michael McCarver, Sr. Seems there were a number of problems between the Nobel-laureate father and his son. Wonder if I took up bridge myself only to challenge or surpass my own father's success in the game?]

Temporize. Played in the two-center with Chops. She held:

♠ A x ♡ Q x x x x x ◇ K Q x ♣ A J

1 ♡ - 1 NT
2 ◇

Nice idea. Suit's too weak for three hearts,

hand is too good for 2 ♡. Tried it last night with
Gussie:

Me	Gussie
♠ A J 9 x x x	♠ Q x
♡ x	♡ x x x x
◇ A Q x	◇ x x x
♣ A x x	♣ K Q J x

1 ♠	1 NT
2 ♣	2 ♠
3 ♠	4 ♠

Best bid old girl ever made. Evaluated her
clubs. We went down with K-10-x-x of spades
offside and diamond hook wrong. But I was
proud of her. Gave it to Roth. Said I might have
tried 3 ◇ over 2 ♠ to complete my shape.

*Never rebid a terrible suit! Went home with
Gussie last night just for old-time's sake; felt sorry
for her. Hopeless. Started to cry afterwards, and I
had to calm her down. You'd think I pulled one
of her doubles, the way she carried on. Told her,
I'd take care of some of her losses at the club.
She still makes decent marinara sauce, though—
and at least she can't get knocked up like some
of those other tomatoes.*

    [Is "tomatoes" referring to
Chops?]

Don't temporize with idiots like Dr. B!

Me	Dr. B
♠ x	♠ x x x x x
♡ A K x	♡ x x
◇ K J 10 x x x	◇ Q x
♣ A J x	♣ K Q x x

1 ◇	1 ♠
2 ♣	p

Next time I jump to 3 ◇. Dr. B doesn't understand any subtleties. *It's like playing with a Neanderthal.*

Passing
Roth said I must learn to say the word, "Pass."

Confused at first. Everybody's having fun bidding, and he wants me to pass. Dr. B. never passes, I complained. Roth made a good point: Dr. B loses twenty thousand a year. Roth claimed I could listen to Frankenstein in this area. Even Frankenstein knows what an opening bid looks like.

Twelve-point hands seem to be the break-even point. Some twelves are opening bids, some are not.

Two taking tricks on defense—that's the key! So when partner doubles, you're not afraid to leave it in.

Finally got it! The purpose of an opening bid is to reach games and slams—not partscores. So say the masters.

Held the following hand last night, second seat, dealer:

♠ A x ♡ A J x x x ◇ Q x x x ♣ J x

Questionable 12, with a jack doubleton. Passed. Bidding went:
1 ♠ - pass - 2 ♠. Lost the heart suit.
Frankenstein claims with hearts, I must open

lighter because of exactly what happened. Told Roth. He hesitated, but did insist that with spades you can always pass and slip in later.

What's the point of making it harder than it already is? Why pass, then later risk bidding? Roth calls it "listening."

Woke up in my sleep just now. Recalled a hand I went down in last week, where passing would have helped.

Frankenstein
♠ x x
♡ A 8 x
◇ K 10 x
♣ A x x x x

Doc
♠ K 10 x
♡ K J x x x
◇ A x x x
♣ J

Kid
♠ x
♡ 9 x
◇ Q x x
♣ K Q 10 x x x x

Me
♠ A Q J 9 x x x
♡ Q 10 x
◇ J x x
♣ —

Opened 4 ♠, and played it there. Doc led a club and I won the ace, discarding a diamond from hand. A spade finesse lost. He came back a low diamond—can't believe an idiot like Doc would underlead his ace. I ducked. Kid won the queen and led a high club. Doc over-ruffed my 9, cashed his diamond ace and still made a heart trick. Down 2.

Could have made this hand if I guessed diamonds. Go up king, draw trump and lead the queen of hearts. Doc covers. I lead another heart from dummy and when the 9 pops up, I cover with the 10. Dummy's 8 is high. It was an impossible line of play, or so I thought at the time.

At 5 a.m. in bed it came to me. I *pass* as dealer. I pass and "listen." Doc, the idiot, opens 1 ♡. Frankenstein passes and Kid bids his clubs. Now when I reach 4 ♠, I know who has the diamond ace and the heart honors!

Speaking of passing—The boys visited Chops in the maternity ward today, but I passed the invitation. They said she'll be back at the club in no time. She's not a bad girl, but you can't feel sorry for every rotten tomato off the street. The Kid is doing a good job with her, but there's a limit. He's got to start earning his money at the table. They say the baby was terribly handsome.

14

*AN EXPERIMENT WITH THE LIGHTS—
MORE STRUDEL—EVIDENCE IS CAST TO SEA.*

"I HAVE always longed for the dark. I will tell you why."

As usual, Mr. Keewood got off one of his outrageous remarks at the beginning of class. It was my last session, on Thursday afternoon. I had a date with Esther afterward. It had taken me three days to copy Pizza's notebook, and now that the task was complete I felt somewhat relieved. I had it with me, packed in my pillowcase, ready for a sinking to the bottom of the river that very night. I wondered what my fellow students would say if they knew half the adventures I had been through since last Friday night.

Mr. Keewood tossed his shoulder-length blond hair back around his ears and stared at us. His eyes were clear grey.

"It is not a coincidence that we read in the newspaper this

week about the blackout in New York City last weekend. Darkness and light are parts of all things, and all things are reflected in our literature. If you read any of the articles, you will have noticed an inconsistency we have been discussing here in class. That is: the fear of light and the joy of dark. Those fortunate to have experienced the blackout expressed a view that rather than being scared of the complete darkness, they rejoiced in it. Some left their homes, danced to radio music in the street, and shared the moment with their neighbors. Others stayed in their homes and shared the experience with their most intimate partners.

"Psychiatrists had a field day analyzing why some people stayed indoors and others sought refuge outside. Did the darkness force a confrontation with the truth? Couples could no longer watch television or read books; it was too noisy to sleep, so they had to confront each other or escape into the streets. Friends, and some strangers, caught at the time in restaurants, theaters, and even apartments where dinner-party guests were still conversing, and who had no intimate relationship with each other, reported sudden intimacies sparked by the catalyst of darkness.

"By the way, I was in Connecticut at the time. If anyone here was in New York last Saturday night, perhaps you'd care to share your experience with the class."

Mr. Keewood looked around the room. There were only 20 of us. I hesitated, then I saw a girl at my right raise her hand.

"Miss Tilden. Go right ahead."

"Well, I was staying with my grandparents who live on Park Avenue. And my girl friend, Sheila, and I were. . . well. . . you want the truth?"

The class laughed. Mr. Keewood walked over to the door. "I've got an idea," he said. He turned off the lights and asked for some help pulling the shades down. "We can't really achieve true blackness, but we can make it pretty dark."

The room was much cooler. We could still see each other, but most of the sunlight was gone and we were more like sculptures than live people. "Forget about note-taking," said Keewood, "not that any of you take notes. Continue, Miss Tilden."

"We were getting high, you know. Listening to a record, "Magical Mystery Tour"—you *know*? We saw the sky light up for a few seconds and thought it was groovy and all, but put it off to the marijuana (giggle). Anyway, then the stereo stopped. We figured it was just the building—you *know?* Went into the kitchen to make some sandwiches. You *know?*

"Now I remember something funny. My grandparents came out of their bedroom and grandpa was desperate to find the flashlight. But my grandma was really relaxed about it all and insisted we just go to bed and take advantage of an early night's rest. Grandpa said he never sleeps before midnight and *she* knew it! But Grandma found him in the dark and shoved him back into the bedroom. That's all, you know."

The class seemed to enjoy that account. So I raised my hand, then realized nobody saw it. "Ahem. Uh, Mr. Keewood."

"Who's that?"

"Matthew, uh Granovetter."

"What do you have for us, Mr. Granovetter?"

"All right, I was in New York at a woman's apartment." There was a slight murmur in the class.

"Shh," said Mr. Keewood.

"All right, here's what happened. We got intimate like you said happened to a lot of couples who didn't really know each other that well. But the interesting thing was that it would have happened regardless because we had started . . . er, uh, before the blackout. . . . Come to think of it, it was right after the blackout that things developed further. . . ."

There was more laughter now. Mr. Keewood said, "Here, here."

A very indignant and puritanical voice from the corner spoke up. I thought I recognized it, but it couldn't be who I was thinking of. "What has this got to do with English comp?"

Mr. Keewood answered. "Aside from the fact that our friend, Franklin, would have enjoyed studying the psychological effects of a lightning flash had he been alive last Saturday, this has everything to do with our study of symbolism. What is the writer's perception of dark and light? Well, we've discussed the popular view that has taken hold over the course of time: darkness represents evil and lightness, good. Darkness hides lies and light reveals truth. And yet, is this really so? Aren't our deepest senses and feelings revealed in the dark? In the bedroom chambers, do we turn on all the lights before revealing our true self in the most natural and necessary act of nature? No! We turn out the lights! We make it dark, so we can expose our deepest truths.

"There are many other effects of dark and light that run

contrary to literature's perception. Any ideas?"

"Light is hot, dark is cold," said a voice.

"Good," said Keewood. "In this cold we can think ever so much clearer and therefore see—within the endless depths of our own precious minds—the truth. The light and the heat stifle our thinking, don't they? They slow us down and makes our eyes hazy and tearful. The pupils dilate in that disruptive brightness. While in the dark, the scientist and the poet alike meditate and discover cures for disease and truth in beauty. Any other comparisons?"

I spoke up. "At the bridge table."

"Bridge?" asked the professor.

"Yes, the card game. You see, often you play a deal in your head before you actually do it with the cards. And if you make the right play, even if it loses, you feel you've succeeded. What I mean is, what actually occurs in the, uh, light can be insignificant. It's what took place in your head, or the dark, that counts."

"I think we're getting too metaphysical, now," said Keewood. "Why don't you write that up for me in a short paper, Mr. Granovetter? 'The Power of Darkness at the Bridge Table.'"

I agreed, and at the conclusion of class when the other students handed in their papers on Ben Franklin, I admitted that I hadn't done mine. Mr. Keewood said it was okay, to work on the new paper and not to worry. "You can't do everything in one week," he said. "I noticed you at the rally Monday night with young Esther here."

I turned around. There was Esther beside me.

"Did you just arrive?" I asked.

"No, I did not just arrive." She looked at me straight in the eyes. I wish she had slapped me—the sting would have been less painful. "So you got intimate, did you? Was this a homosexual affair with that Chops character, or did you make him up?" She turned and walked out of the room. I grabbed my books and pillowcase, catching up to her outside in the light.

"Wait," I said, "I can explain." Though I couldn't explain anything really.

Suddenly she turned. There was a tear in her eye and she wiped it away. "It's silly of me to be upset. I'm not even that attracted to you. But, well, it's just that you didn't have to lie to me."

"You're not attracted," I said, my head low.

"Well, I'm not, uh, you know—repulsed. It was your mind that

172

I liked, Matthew. Well, until this silly lie."

"I'm sorry," I said. "I don't know how it happens, but I'm often afraid to tell the truth when I think it's going to be bad for me."

"C'mon," she said, "I'll give you a second chance." She went to take my other hand and noticed the pillowcase. "You don't think I do laundry for my boyfriends, do you?"

I laughed. "I'll explain this later," I said, not really sure if I would.

After a Red Tulip supper of cold cherry soup, stuffed cabbage with cucumber salad, topped off with apple strudel plus tea for dessert (they still wouldn't take my hundred-dollar bill, so Esther paid), we took in "Casablanca" down at the Student Union. We ran into Stanley with a cute red-haired girl just as the movie was starting, and he suggested we sit together. Stanley sat down next to me, but I quickly changed places with Esther when I remembered what was in my pillowcase under the seat. At one point, when Esther went to the bathroom and Stanley went for a coke, the girl leaned across the seats and whispered, "Bogart's really cool, don't you think?" I nodded. "Just like Stanley," she added.

When the movie ended, Stanley and the girl made a fast exit, and I suggested to Esther a stroll along the river bank.

"Oh, no," she said. "I know what you have in mind."

"Oh, no," I said, "You don't." I swung my pillowcase over my shoulder and tried to take her hand, but she moved quickly to my other side. There was a three-quarter moon out, and it helped us find the path off George Street down to the embankment. We stepped gingerly forward toward an enclosed brick wall built above the rocks. The hissing of the river became louder and we looked over the edge at the water breaking on the shoreline. How was I ever going to sink the notebook?

"Listen," I said to her. "I brought you here tonight for a very important reason."

"Be careful," said Esther, "We've only known each other a week, remember."

"Look," I said, pointing to the pillowcase. I bent down and pulled out the book. Then I swung around suddenly straight into a flashlight's beam.

"What's going on down there?" said a cop. He came closer and put the light on our faces. "Oh, it's you again. Oh, excuse me, sorry to interrupt. Just don't get too close to the wall."

My hands were shaking. I took a deep breath. Then I showed Esther the name written on the first page of the book:

PRIVATE PROPERTY—M. P. McCARVER

"What is this book?" she asked.

"It's evidence in a crime—I can't tell you any more, except that it's important to both me and my roommate, Stanley, that it be destroyed."

"Does he know you're destroying it?" she asked.

"No, but it's for his own good." Suddenly I got very nervous. "Listen, you've got to promise me never to say a word of this to him if you ever meet him again."

"I'm not gonna say anything, but—"

"Okay, but I still want you to be a witness to the book's destruction. It probably will never be important, but if it is, at least you'll be able to back up my story that I *did* possess it and it *was* half ruined."

"Listen, Matthew. I don't think I'm a good person for you to trust with this," she said, hesitantly.

"Sure you are," I said. "Here, help me with this rope." I pulled it out of the bag.

"Are you crazy? You're not going over the wall!"

"You have any better ideas? I've got to sink this thing."

"There must be some rocks up here. We could just, uh, fling it in." Good, I thought. She'd gotten into the spirit of the affair. Looking around the brick enclosure, we found nothing but a few twigs. Then, at the far end of the wall, she discovered some loose bricks. We tried to force them out scraping and pushing, and finally succeeded by tying the rope around each one and tugging. One of the bricks fell over the wall and crashed on some rocks below. It was a loud crack and we sat down in the dark silence that followed to see whether the cop would return. When he didn't, we put the loose bricks in the pillowcase alongside Pizza's notebook.

"Wait a second," she said, "don't tie it yet." Then she threw in a folded piece of paper from her purse. "Just an old love letter I've been wanting to get rid of. This is definitely the way to do it."

I tied the rope securely around the top of the case and lifted it up over the wall. Then I realized it might not land in the water unless I gave it a strong fling. So, I had Esther stand back on the other side of the embankment and, like a decathlon champion, slowly twirled the pillow round and round, finally letting go at the right angle. It must have been beginner's luck, because the dreaded white case flew across the Raritan like a shooting star in the night, and landed smack dab in the middle of the water. Esther ran to my side and we both leaned over the wall. There it was floating downstream—not sinking—but floating!

"It needed one more brick," she said, gazing across the moon-lit water.

"That's all right," I said. "According to Franklin, it should float out to the Atlantic."

15

A DUMMY IN THE DRAWER—FRANKLIN'S
VIRTUES REVISITED—INNOCENT
COURTSHIP—STANLEY CONCEDES.

THE NEXT day, when I opened the drawer to get dressed, I felt the emptiness under my socks. I wondered if Stanley had put the notebook in my dresser just to get it away from his own things, or to induce me to put *my* fingerprints all over it. If he knew that I had tossed the notebook into the river, he would probably shake my hand. Then again, he might be upset. After all, *he* could have thrown it away himself rather than stick it in a drawer. Suddenly, I wasn't so sure I had done the right thing by destroying it. Suppose he wanted it back. Suppose he checked for it when I wasn't in the room. So I went to the bookstore that afternoon and bought a notebook of similar size and weight. Then I copied the first page from my translation and stuck the whole thing into the drawer. If he just opened the drawer to check it was there, without really examining the thing, he would be satisfied. I believe it worked, because for over a month I never heard a word about it, and in time I even forgot it was there.

It must have been beginner's luck, because the dreaded white
case flew across the Raritan like a shooting star in the night,
and landed smack dab in the middle of the water.

Meanwhile, I had to do something with my translation. The safest thing I could think of was to send it home. I wrapped it up, went to the post office, and addressed it to my dad in Jersey City. I didn't tell him to hide it because that would sound as if something were wrong. So I simply asked him to hold it for me until the end of the semester.

With every passing October day, the late-night game at the Quad was improving in quality. Most of this improvement was due to Stanley. For one thing, Stanley was a double-dummy artist, analyzing every bid and play. He provoked a number of arguments, and was the direct cause of Les the Mess getting his first "B" ever (in a History exam). Stanley flung Les the Mess's history book out the window in the middle of a small-slam contract, in which Les the Mess, his partner, was declarer. Stanley was right; Les the Mess concentrated for the first time in his life, and landed the slam. Unfortunately however, it was a rainy night; the book landed in mud, and was ruined. (The incident reminded me of Pizza's notebook landing in the Raritan River.)

More important to the quality of the game was Stanley's ongoing stake increases. Soon we were up to a quarter of a point, and what was once a friendly diversion fast became a "serious" sport. It's incredible how quickly players' games improve when they can't afford to lose. Going for 800 now meant losing two dollars. In those days, two dollars translated to three tuna subs, two coffees and a one shake from the sandwich truck.

If there were a way to punish bad bids at duplicate, I think matchpoint players also would improve. But what sort of punishment? Take away masterpoints for bottom scores? Why not? Then players who value their masterpoints would be at some risk when they sit down to play. I wonder how many Life Masters there would be under these rules. . . .

Speaking of rules, one night Pete the Poet came to me with a list he had compiled to improve players' games. He had copied Franklin's list of 13 virtues but changed the precepts:

```
     1.  Temperance.  Eat  tuna  subs
while  dummy  only;  never  as  de-
fender.
```

2. Silence. Don't discuss bidding theory with players who don't understand.

3. Order. Keep your tricks in a neat order on one side of the table.

4. Resolution. Decide how many tricks you want to take before you play to trick one (as declarer or defender).

5. Frugality. Waste no spot cards signaling on defense. (Half the time partner doesn't look at your signal anyway. You guys know who you are.)

6. Industry. Lose no time thinking about overtricks.

7. Sincerity. Don't deceive partner in the bidding or he'll never trust you again.

8. Justice. Don't take advantage of meaningless revokes.

9. Moderation. Avoid extreme decisions in the bidding. (When in doubt, take your plus score).

10. Cleanliness. Clean cards after double-sub nights.

11. Tranquillity. Don't be disturbed when partner does something stupid. Keep in your shell and play your best.

        12. Chastity. No sex on the
card-bed. (You guys know who I
mean.)

        13. Humility. Imitate Stanley
and Matthew: two great teachers who
are still students of the game,
themselves.

The list was posted on the dormitory wall outside J.B.'s room
where Pete the Poet thought it would do the most good. I was
quite flattered over number 13, though I really wondered if
Stanley's name should have been included.

I saw Esther regularly throughout the month of October (except
for the night the October *Bridge World* arrived). We went to
flicks at the Student Union, ate at the Red Tulip—they finally
changed my hundred (that's what I owed by now)—and did a lot
of studying together, mostly on weekday nights when the Quad
game could afford the loss of a player. I think if it were not for
her, I would never have studied. As to deepening our physical
relationship, things were going slowly. If I were lucky, I received a
peck or two on the cheek before I said goodnight. She explained
to me how she wasn't ready for anything serious yet.
    One night, while doing a little calculus to the music of
Brahms, her favorite composer, I felt her hand massaging the back
of my spine. I told her it felt good. She said, "There, now don't
complain any more."
    On another occasion, she dragged me to an SDS meeting.
SDS stood for Students for a Democratic Society. At the meeting, it was pounded into us how America was run by the rich,
how the elected officials were controlled by the rich, and how the
war in Vietnam was nothing more than a way for the rich to sell a
lot of ammunition to the army and increase their richness.
    It was pretty heavy stuff and I was under the impression at
the time that it was a Communist organization and that I should
stay clear of it. Esther was furious with me and scolded me for
being a coward and a "no-good bum with nothing on your mind
but cards and sex. All you people care about is your own pleas-
ure."

I refuted her insult and claimed virginity. "Also," I lied, "I haven't touched a card since that escapade in New York a month ago."

One evening early in November, she suggested we study at my place. I tried to talk her out of it, but she insisted. She already thought I was a card bum at heart; what would she say if she saw what went on in my room? The game didn't start until 10 o'clock, so I figured maybe I could rush her out of there before then. After supper, we returned to the Quad. Pete the Poet caught site of us and rushed over before we could enter. "Don't go in there unless you're prepared for blood."

"Blood?" said Esther.

"Yeah," said Les the Mess. "J.B. challenged Stanley to a set game. Half-a-cent a point. I went to get my physics notebook and Short Larry filled in for a hand. When I got back, J.B. was in one notrump doubled opposite a yarborough! I couldn't watch."

Before I could stop her, Esther had opened the door. The place was warm and smoky. Stanley had a cigar in his mouth, he was drinking a beer, and there was a half-finished pizza on my bed. Underneath the sheets was Stanley's brunette, taking a snooze. I think she was not wearing any clothes, either. More important, Big Al had just led the king of spades and Short Larry had just floored a 4-3-3-3 honorless dummy. "Nothing wasted," said Short Larry. I took a quick peek around Stanley's bed.

Short Larry (dummy)
♠ 8 7 5
♡ 6 5 4
◇ 4 3 2
♣ 6 5 4 3

Stanley
♠ K Q 10 4
♡ K Q 10
◇ K Q 10
♣ K Q 10

Big Al
♠ 9 6 3
♡ 9 8 7 2
◇ 9 8 6 5
♣ 9 7

J. B. (declarer)
♠ A J 2
♡ A J 3
◇ A J 7
♣ A J 8 2

"How'd the auction go?" I whispered to Short Larry.

"Not too bad," he answered, "but we're not in game."

I later learned that J.B. had opened one club, Stanley doubled, and Short Larry passed. Big Al bid one heart and J.B. made a simple one-notrump call. Stanley doubled, and that ended the auction.

The play was interesting. J.B., who was fast becoming a hold-up expert in notrump play, ducked the first four tricks as Stanley led out all four kings. On the fifth trick, Stanley retreated back to spades and J.B. was forced to win the jack. He then led out ace and jack of clubs, establishing the fourth club, and I couldn't help but admire that he had preserved the deuce for an entry to that dummy! Stanley cleared the spade suit, and this was the position with five cards left, J.B. on play and needing four tricks for his contract:

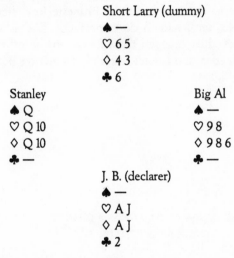

Short Larry (dummy)

♠ —
♡ 6 5
♢ 4 3
♣ 6

Stanley

♠ Q
♡ Q 10
♢ Q 10
♣ —

Big Al

♠ —
♡ 9 8
♢ 9 8 6
♣ —

J. B. (declarer)

♠ —
♡ A J
♢ A J
♣ 2

J.B. led his deuce of clubs and Stanley had to make a crucial discard. In theory, he was dead. If he threw a red card, it would set up one of J.B.'s red jacks. If he threw the queen of spades, J.B. could play ace and jack of either red suit to endplay him. In practice, however, Stanley probably couldn't go wrong. J.B. had carefully unblocked clubs to reach dummy, no doubt to take one of the finesses through Big Al, probably the heart finesse (Big Al having bid the suit).

Suddenly a strange thing happened. Stanley looked around the room for a few seconds, took his cigar out of his mouth and crushed the butt. Then he tabled his cards face up.

Wham! J.B. banged his palm into his forehead. "Both finesses off! Can you believe that?"

"No, no," said Stanley, rising from the table. "It's all right. Look, man, you have me endplayed."

J.B. was startled at first, but with a little help from Big Al, who had seen the position from the start, and me, J.B. grasped what had happened. He was very proud, and graciously accepted congratulations from everyone. Les the Mess returned instantly upon hearing the incredible news, and I took over in Stanley's seat for the last deal of the rubber. When Pete the Poet arrived at 10 o'clock, we cut for a regular wheel.

It wasn't until I was out, on the third rubber, that I realized I had totally forgotten Esther. I looked around the room. She must have left hours earlier. It didn't matter. I still had a paper to write. As soon as the game broke, I woke the brunette from her midnight nap and told her I had to do some work. She asked me where Stanley was, then dragged herself over to the other bed. She was a good sleeper, and I don't think my typewriter bothered her.

16

THE POWER OF DARKNESS—A CHANCE
ENCOUNTER WITH DR. B.

```
              Matthew Granovetter
      English Comp. 1 - Sect. 9
                   Mr. Keewood
```

```
  The Power of Darkness at the Bridge Table
    (A brief comparison of bridge and bedroom
activities, using the literary themes of light
and dark to demonstrate how truth may be found
in darkness rather than in the light.)
```

The following is a card position from a
bridge game:

Dummy
♡ A Q 4 3 2

West   East
♡ J 10 9 7 5   ☐   ♡ K

Declarer
♡ 8 6

Declarer leads the eight of hearts toward
the dummy. No matter what West plays, declarer
puts in dummy's queen—losing the trick to
East's king. This is called a simple finesse.
With no knowledge of the East-West cards (which
are hidden from declarer's view), declarer
takes a 50% chance—it is equally likely that
West or East holds the king.

The finesse is considered declarer's "only"
chance, because the play of the ace will almost
never win. A singleton king in the East hand is
a miniscule possibility. Add to that some
knowledge of the distribution—say, during the
course of the deal, declarer learns that East
has length in three suits—therefore is likely
to hold only one heart—and the finesse, which
was a 50% chance before the deal began, is now
a five-to-one shot, or approximately an 83%
chance!

And yet the truth is that the king *is*
singleton offside, and the *successful* play on
this particular deal is to go up with dummy's
ace—or is it? A philosopher might ask: Is
success achieved by doing wrong things that
turn out right or by doing right things that
usually turn out right, but occasionally turn
out wrong?

The novice bridge player, sitting in the
dummy position, screams at his partner, "You

lost to a singleton king, you numskull!" The expert bridge player understands the odds perfectly and is a supportive partner: "Too bad, but you played it correctly." The expert is being fair and philosophical. The truth, to him, lies in darkness, where the opponent's cards cannot be seen. The truth is not what is exposed in the double-dummy light of the card table, but what is conceived clearly in the darker depths of declarer's brain.

The sinister light can be cruel to the bridge player. It may taunt him with bad luck and near-impossibilities! But the better bridge player cares little for what the light's curse can do. And the great bridge player does not even let such ugly lies pass his thoughts! He is immune to everything but the inner truth.

The Bedroom and the Bridge Table

Let's take the case of a woman who loves a homely man and thinks he is beautiful (in the dark, especially), while the rest of the world thinks he is ugly. Which is he, beautiful or ugly? This is a case of artistic judgment. (Let a committee decide—if it can get all the facts.)

But wait, you say! This is not bridge. This is passion, this is love. Bridge is a game, a science. You cannot judge truth by what you think. You must judge it by how the cards actually lie. (And they do lie.)

However, you would be in error. For the cards on the table last only a few minutes. The possible lines of play of the cards last not only all night (like that woman's homely man), as the bridge player tosses and turns, thinking, working, picturing the hand until he has the solution in his dreams! No, they last forever. In the case of a singleton king offside, every good bridge player knows the correct line of play—and will know it until he

goes to his grave: finesse, finesse, finesse!
That is the only truth; and damn the light!

*Nice work, though you get carried away at
times. As a chess player, I understood much of
what you said about thinking about a position
in the darkness of your mind, but I wonder if a
non-games-player would understand. Have a feeling there's a good story here in your bridge
world—if you ever decide to write, it might
make an intriguing novel. Missed you at the
latest rally. J. Keewood.*

I had missed the last rally because Esther came down with a cold.
The truth is I only went to those rallies to accompany Esther. I
wasn't *against* protesting the U.S. involvement in Vietnam; but I
was involved too heavily in two other worlds to get worked up
over politics. Had there been a rally against traditional black
symbolism in literature or bidding notrump without stoppers, I
would certainly have attended—with or without my girlfriend.

Some time around mid-November, a week before Thanksgiving break, Esther caught the flu. I found it harder to study without her influence, and started rereading Bridge World magazines
instead. Even when I wasn't reading or playing bridge, I would
often think about hands. I doubt that a bridge enthusiast can ever
get truly bored.

One day, while studying a trump squeeze outside the College
Bookstore on George Street, I did a double-take. Was it really the
same man? I walked back a few steps and caught his eye. Either
he didn't recognize me or he was thinking about something else.
But I was sure who *he* was—the very same Doctor B. with whom
I had won my 42-point rubber at the Mayfair Club. He was asking
directions of a young man, but quickly turned away from him
when he heard me speak.

"Hi," I said. "Don't you remember me? The one who made six
spades on the suicide trump squeeze." It's funny how it all came
back to me, as if by shaking his hand I had pushed a memory-
button. I tend to associate memorable events with the acquain-
tances I've shared them with; so when I saw Doctor B. outside

the College Bookstore, I remembered the cards I held with him on the fourth deal of the rubber two months earlier at the Mayfair. Then, suddenly, a flash of lightning passed through my brain and I could see the girl at the window as well.

"Excuse me," said Doctor B. "Yes, I do remember, though you'll forgive my not recalling your name."

I woke from my brief trance and stared at him. It's amazing how dignified he was, considering his coarse manners at the bridge table. But then, I guess that most people are more polite away from the table.

"My name is Matthew Granovetter. I go to school here."

"Granovetter, Granovetter, ahh, very interesting." He put a finger on his temple as if he were trying to remember something. "So you go to school here. Very good. What's your major?"

"Uh, I'm not sure yet. I'm only a freshman, you see."

"Only a freshman! Well, my goodness. I thought you were older than that. Take my advice then. Go into science—any of the sciences, medicine, engineering, even the new computer science. That's the field of the future."

"To tell you the truth, I like to write."

"Ahh, writing. Wonderful, but dangerous—listen, I have to go now; I'm sure we'll meet again sometime in a New York bridge club." He nodded his head and started to walk off.

"Wait a second," I called after him. I ran up and put my hand on his well-tailored pinstripe suit. His blue tie flapped across his lapel like a compass in the late autumn breeze. "How is that little girl?"

"Eh?" he asked, his eyes squinting a little. He glanced quickly up and down the street, then looked back at me.

"You know," I said. "Frankenstein's girl, the one who fell out the window."

"Shhh. Not so loud. I'm not so old that my eardrums can't hear you if you talk in a normal voice."

"Sorry, but I read all about it in the paper and a detective was here from New York to interview me and—"

"A detective?" He glanced around again and put his hand on my arm, leading me to a more deserted area by a nearby oak tree. "Now settle down. Here now, you shouldn't get carried away by these things. I have so many patients, but . . . wait a second—now I remember who you mean. Oh, it was a nothing case. In fact it was fortunate it was my last night on late-call. Of course the other doctors, the younger ones, are adequate, but I'm quite friendly with Frankenstein, and was very happy to make certain the girl received the best attention possible."

"Yes, I—"

"Now don't you interrupt. I'm sure you know a lot about everything; but the girl is perfectly okay. She was in a coma for only a few hours, and she did lose some of her speech, but she's improving every day. There never was a more devoted father than Frankenstein. He's there every morning, reading to her, working with the therapists; of course if they hadn't halted operation on the new wing, she might have had more available to her— the child—"

He suddenly stopped. He had been rambling, realized it, and checked himself. For a brief period, he just stood there looking past the tree into the cloudy November sky. I was happy the little girl was all right. Of course, Detective Kennedy had *said* he would call me back only if the girl did *not* come out of her coma. But wasn't that almost 48 hours *after* the accident? According to Doctor B., she was out of her coma in just a few hours.

"Tell me," said the doctor, "do you know where . . . ."

"Where what?" I asked. "Are you giving a lecture at the, uh, medical school?"

"Eh? Yes, yes. Just direct me to the office of the dean of the medical school, if you will."

Suddenly I realized I had no clue where the medical school was. There was a science department and I gave Doctor B. some rough directions, which he seemed to comprehend almost too quickly. Then a quick handshake and he was gone. It wasn't until the next day, when I was talking to Les the Mess, that I learned why I couldn't recall where the medical school was: Rutgers didn't have a medical school.

17

I wish I could say that this was one of my most carefree periods of my life. It should have been. There I was, closing in on my eighteenth birthday, a happy-go-lucky freshman who enjoyed his classes, had his first nice girlfriend, and was the toast of a great bunch of card players at the dormitory. So I had had an adventure in New York! Surely, all vestige of guilt was removed by the knowledge that Frankenstein's little girl was on her way to recovery. Besides, all that had happened a long time in the past (nearly two months), and now I could relax for a while in the comfort of my scholarly surroundings. In poetic terms, you could say that I had climbed a mountain and had finally reached Shangri-la on the top.

However, I was not *so* innocent; nor was I *that* blind. I had only to look a little more closely and I could not fail to notice the pebbles beneath my feet starting to loosen. But on that blustery November day, the very same day I had bumped into Doctor B. outside the College Bookstore, I refused to look.

Oh, I was *much* too sure of myself—*much* too smart to see that I was not on top of that mountain, but descending it! I didn't see that while my interest in English was plentiful, my grades in other courses were rapidly declining. I didn't see that two months and 30 miles are not nearly far enough to escape the consequences of lying to a New York City detective or jilting a beautiful, older woman named Chops. I didn't see that dumping black notebooks over the Raritan River Bridge or discussing politics in a Hungarian restaurant was not always the best way to secure romantic feelings. Finally, I didn't see Stanley—period. That is, for the last week he hadn't made a single appearance in the late-night Quad game, which is why I was relieved at first when I arrived back at my room from dinner at the Red Tulip to find him there.

The first rubber was not due to start for another hour, which was just as well because our room was in terrible disarray—clothes strewn over the dressers, bedspreads turned over, desk drawers on the floor.

"Long time no see," I said, observing that a torn notebook was lying across the lampshade on my desk. I began to feel the pebbles beneath my feet.

"Where the hell have you been?" Stanley asked.

"Me? I, uh, just finished some veal paprikash you'd have died for."

"You and your stupid restaurant!" he said, though it didn't make sense to me at the time.

"Now maybe *you* should tell me what happened here," I retorted. "Did the police raid us for your little white pills?" I walked over, opened the top drawer of my dresser and started putting back some socks that were on the floor.

Suddenly I felt something on my left shoulder. It was Stanley's arm. He was trying to force me around, but he didn't have the strength to do it. I turned 45 degrees the other way and he tried to grab my shirt. I pushed him back and he stumbled to the floor, hitting his head against the desk chair. I gave him my hand to help him up. "What's wrong with you?" I asked, more confused than angry.

I looked down at him and spotted a tear in his eye, a single tear that was there for only an instant before he quickly wiped it away with his dirty sleeve. "Where is it?" he asked.

"Where's what?" I answered, suddenly feeling those pebbles start to spread.

"You know. Where is it?"

All at once my legs were rubber, my face flushed; I had to sit down. Instead, I grasped the top of the open dresser drawer, the one where I had found the black notebook hidden beneath my underwear. "I don't know what you're talking about," I lied.

"Listen to me," Stanley said, his voice quivering. "You want to see your friend Stanley at the bottom of the East River? That's where I'm headed if you don't hand over that book."

"Does the Raritan River flow into the East River?" I said.

"What the hell does that mean? Where is it, you idiot?!"

I looked at him. I swear his mouth was foaming.

"What's so important about a bunch of bridge notes?" I asked.

"What did you do with it?!"

"It's at the bottom of the Raritan River. That's where!"

"Are you crazy? You stole my book and threw it into the river?!!"

"What was it doing in my underwear drawer if it was so

important? Besides, I copied the text, if it makes you feel any better!"

"*You copied the text? What right did you have to read that text? It wasn't your book, you fool. It belongs to Pizza. He asked me to hold it for him. Now he wants it back. What am I supposed to tell him? That my roommate threw it into the river? That he read a private diary and copied the text?—*"

"Not all of it! A lot of it was ruined by rain."

"WHAT RAIN, YOU *IDIOT*?!!!"

"THE RAIN THAT FELL ON THE LITTLE GIRL—REMEMBER HER, HUH?—LYING IN THE BUSHES? THE ONE YOU STOLE THE BOOK FROM—GO AHEAD—TELL ME ABOUT THAT ONE!!!"

Stanley staggered backward to his bed, sat down and put his hand on his forehead, then looked up at me and spoke in a whisper. "Who told you this story?"

"Nobody," I said. "I deduced it. I saw the book in your suitcase on the night we returned from New York. Then Detective Kennedy mentioned a black notebook. Well, here it was, and I didn't say a word; but I when I saw the book in my drawer and accidentally put my fingerprints all over it, I realized how much trouble it could be for me, err, for you if they found it here—you know—with a search warrant or something. Anyway, I took the book and transcribed what I could, but much of it was rained on. I put two and two together—obviously the book was with Frankenstein's girl when she fell from the window, and since you had it, *you* were obviously the one who took it from her. Really, Stanley, I've been protecting you all along."

"You haven't been protecting *me*," he said. "Kid, kid, kid, you've been protecting. . . listen to me. Where's your transcription?"

"I, uh, mailed it home—you know, for safe keeping."

Stanley got up and went to his dresser. There, from beneath some tissue, he took two white pills and popped them into his mouth. Then he reached in and pulled out some other pills, wrapped them quickly in tissue, and walked out of the room without another word. I didn't see him again until 5 a.m., when he stumbled noisily through the open window and into his bed. If I had known where he'd been all night, I would never have helped him up from his tumble earlier that evening. I would have punched him again and again . . . and again.

The next few nights Stanley did not show at all. On Tuesday night (I remember the specific day because I remember the deal— as you will too when you see it), Stanley's brunette took me aside before the game.

"I'm quitting," she said.

"Who's going to keep score if you quit?" I complained.

"I don't care any more."

"Well, what will Stanley think?"

"I don't care about Stanley either. I don't know if you've noticed or not, but Stanley and I have stopped sleeping together."

Since she was in the next bed to me on those occasions, you'd think I would have noticed, but I guess I was too much in my own world. It suddenly occurred to me that despite keeping accounts in the Quad bridge game for an entire month (among other more personal endeavors in the same room), she had never revealed her name. I held out my hand and she shook it.

"Look me up sometime. My name is Ramona."

"Whatever are you going to do with yourself?" I asked, as if keeping score for our late-night game was a job one should treasure.

"I'm going back to school."

"Are you registered at Douglass?"

"No, silly. I'm still in high school. I live with my parents in North Brunswick."

This took me by surprise. Before she left, I asked her to show me the bookkeeping procedure. Then, as she packed a few things from Stanley's dresser, she started to get upset. Before slamming the door, she gave me a mean look and made a vow.

"You know something?" she said. "I'll never go with a bridge player again!"

As I said before, that night, a remarkable deal was played, which, by coincidence, reflected the theme of my recent English paper on the power of darkness at the bridge table. The declarer was none other than J.B., who was fast becoming a dummy player par excellence. Let me show you the deal from his perspective.

Me (dummy)
♠ Q 10 3
♡ Q J 7 6
◊ K 6 5
♣ K 7 3

J. B. (declarer)
♠ 6 5 4
♡ A 10 9 8 5
◊ A J 2
♣ A 6

Les the Mess	Me	Big Al	J. B.
1 ◊	pass	pass	1 ♡
pass	2 ♡	pass	2 NT
pass	3 NT	(all pass)	

Les the Mess led a thoughtful queen of clubs. How would you play it?

Despite the spade weakness, J. B. ducked the lead all the way around. This was now routine for him, and a very clever routine. Les the Mess continued clubs to Big Al's nine and J.B.'s ace. Now, J.B. laid down the ace of hearts and, when the king dropped singleton on his left, claimed nine tricks.

Here was the full deal:

Me (dummy)
♠ Q 10 3
♡ Q J 7 6
◊ K 6 5
♣ K 7 3

Les the Mess
♠ A K 9
♡ K
◊ Q 10 8 7 4
♣ Q J 8 2

Big Al
♠ J 8 7 2
♡ 4 3 2
◊ 9 3
♣ 10 9 5 4

J. B. (declarer)
♠ 6 5 4
♡ A 10 9 8 5
◊ A J 2
♣ A 6

Lucky? Well, had this deal occurred in September when J.B. was still a novice, I'd have ascribed his play to not knowing how to take a finesse. But J.B., because of his nightly rubber-bridge practice, was coming into his own. Amid the commotion after the hand, J.B. put out his palm for quiet; then, his eyeglasses practically fogged with tears of pride, he stood up and explained his reasoning:

"There was nothing to it, guys. There were 16 points out against me. Les the Mess had 12 or 13 at least. If Big Al's solitary high card was the king of hearts, I could finesse in hearts and make nine tricks easily. But if it were offside, my only chance to make the contract was to drop it. So I asked myself, as any student of Plato would, what if I spurned the heart finesse, but, alas, found the king guarded to my right?" With this, his arm practically jumped out of his socket and pointed to the wall.

"Then I pictured in my mind what would happen: Big Al, upon winning the second heart, would return a club to dummy's king. I would cash my heart tricks coming down to five cards. Les the Mess must keep three diamonds to the queen and the ace-king of spades. Therefore, he would have to discard his club winner. Then I play spades for my ninth trick.

"Having thus reasoned, I laid down the ace of hearts. If the king were on my right, I was always cold; and if it were singleton on my left, finis." With a flair, he produced a handkerchief and swept it through the air. Then he sat down and wiped off a spot of mayonnaise lingering on the king of hearts.

"J.B.," I said, "If you could only learn how to play a trump contract, I could take you to the Mayfair Club in New York and challenge any two rubber-bridge players in the world."

J.B. beamed. "Someday, guy. . . someday."

18

I WAS late to class because I had forgotten the change in schedule. Due to the upcoming Thanksgiving holiday, Thursday's classes had been switched to Wednesday. Mr. Keewood was already lecturing, so I tried to be inconspicuous as I slipped into a seat in the third row.

"Fiction is a dreamlike version of reality. The author's job is to explore not what is, but what might be. The possibilities in a given situation are endless, which is one reason why the writing of fiction is so difficult. The choices that the author must make at every turn of events, at every twist of the plot, at every detailed description are not only artistic ones, but personal choices based on the author's own experience.

"Our last two authors of this semester, Joseph Conrad and Edgar Allan Poe, wrote fiction, but used their own lives as frameworks for their stories—in different ways. When Conrad described Marlow's journey in "Heart of Darkness," he based the plot on his own trip to the Congo in 1890. Thus, he took a slice of real life and fictionalized it. Poe, on the other hand, took only the *moods* and *feelings* of his experiences and set them to fictionalized plots. He was obsessed with darkness, enclosure, death and life beyond the grave, things that were part of his youth—the early deaths of his parents and his wife."

I looked through my pile of books on the desk and saw "Heart of Darkness" second from bottom. I still hadn't read it, and wasn't ready to follow the lecture. Every now and then, Mr. Keewood had the habit of selecting a particular student to answer a question. Somehow, he had the knack (as all good teachers do) of selecting the student least prepared. I was glad I was in the third row behind a girl with bee-hive hair.

"In 'Heart of Darkness,' Conrad's narrator tells the tale of a journey into the unknown. There is an air of tension and mystery in the narrative, images of death popping up in various places. Then, of course, there are the images of black and white, the so-called darkness of Africa and the fierce, horrible, white blaze of the sun—"

Bang!

My books dropped to the floor. Everyone turned to look. I quickly retrieved them and put Conrad on top of the pile.

"For those of you busy activists who haven't had time to read the book, let me review the plot briefly. Marlow is sent by the greedy manager of an ivory-import firm deep into the Congo to locate a company man named Kurtz. When he finds him, he sees that Kurtz has fallen into an abyss of degradation, engaged in abominable rites—the killing of natives, impaled heads, and so forth. You get the picture. Now Marlow gets caught up with the world he enters, embraces the darkness of life, but manages to retain his power to distinguish right from wrong, to function in the dark without succumbing to its moral decay."

Two loose pieces of paper had dropped out of my book and were still on the floor. I had to get out of my seat to pick them up.

"Mr. Granovetter, you seem to be in a chaotic mood this afternoon. Can you tell us what you think Conrad meant by his title, 'Heart of Darkness'?"

"Uh. Perhaps he meant the heart of Africa?" I sat down and held tight to the papers while leaning my neck around the bee-hive hair in front of me.

"Possibly. But the narrative evoked other meanings, inner depths of feeling, those of the heart itself. The heart is an emotional port. We give our heart to others, in love; but we're jealous and hateful from the heart as well. Needless to say, mankind spends much of its time destroying hearts. In Poe's story, 'The Tell-Tale Heart,' you'll read about a madman who murders his master, but continues to hear the old man's heart beat after his death. For Poe, whose narratives rarely had more than two characters—the murderer and the murdered—that heartbeat implied that time was running out for both the victim and the killer. Conrad's heartbeat is a larger, more symbolic pulse—that of the white European civilization invading the heart of black African culture. What is happening in *today's* world that resembles the horrors Marlow saw in the Congo?"

Hands rose. A few voices said, "Vietnam."

"Of course. In Vietnam, the American Marlows have been sent by the capitalist rice dealers. . . ."

I was staring at the papers that had fallen out of my book.

They matched perfectly, the left fitting into the right. They were a copy from the first page of Pizza McCarver's notebook. But they were not a copy of *my* handwriting. No, they were the careful handwriting of a . . . of a . . . *7-year-old girl:*

Chicago Scoring

All money bridge must be played with Chicago scoring. Played once in London and some madman went for seven numbers before we completed the rubber. The English are impossible bidders, passing in the middle of forcing auctions! Only exception is Reese who knows the value of a bonus score.

By the way—prefer Hungarian rubber clubs to Austrian—far more structure in their bidding, thus easier to comprehend. Young man I met in Budapest club confirms this. Nice guy. Listened all night to my theories. Name's Marx—not Groucho, ha, ha. Recollected some of the systems I used to play there in the late 30's. Must remember to use influence to get him job in New York. Good kid.

Chicago four-deal rubber is:
First deal - no one vulnerable
Second deal - dealer's side vulnerable
Third deal - dealer's side vulnerable
Fourth deal - both sides vulnerable

The bottom-right part was the photocopy that Detective Kennedy had given me, the torn piece of paper found in the bushes near the little girl. The remaining part . . . the remaining part . . . I didn't know where the remaining part came from. What was it doing in my book? What was *I* doing with the fitting piece? What did it mean? My head started to get dizzy. Was there something in the air or was the physical sensation caused by the enigma? I looked down at the fitting pieces. The little girl must have been copying out of the black notebook. Was she doing it to practice her penmanship? Or was she doing it for a purpose?

". . . rarely asks how it is possible to kill a person you don't even know. The atmosphere, the power of the setting, takes hold of a person's mind and reshapes it to fit. The human in a soldier's uniform may not take on the persona of a soldier until he enters that other world, a world filled with signs and symbols of death, darkness, and evil . ."

Suddenly I realized the meaning of it! The torn paper was in the girl's hand when she fell! There must have been a struggle for the paper to tear in half. The little girl took the bottom right half with her to the bushes below, while the other half was in the hands of the person who. . . who *what?*. . . who struggled with her before she fell or *pushed her out the window?!!* My head was really spinning now. What the hell was *I* doing with the fitting piece?!!!

"Mr. Granovetter, *Mr. Granovetter,* are you all right?"

"What?"

"Your face is all white. Are you with us?"

"Yes, yes."

"I asked if you, as a bridge aficionado, considered any of the playing cards as symbols of good or evil?"

I stared at him. Why was he bothering me with these questions? I tried to get my thoughts together. "Well. . . I think there are good plays and bad plays made in the course of every bridge deal, so the cards don't have a symbolic meaning but, well, depending upon their setting, they could become good or evil in the eyes of a particular player. Excuse me." I rose from my seat and rushed out of the class to the men's room. There I stayed until the end of the hour.

When I returned, Mr. Keewood was still at his desk. I gathered my books, folded the two halves of paper into my jacket pocket and started out. He stopped me at the door and asked if there were anything troubling me. I shook my head, no, but he suggested that I try to relieve my worldly worries by getting a head start on my Poe.

"There's nothing like a good mystery or a gruesome coffin tale to take your mind off things."

I had my collected short stories with me, and he took the

book and marked off a few pages in the introduction and table of contents. Handing it back to me, he said, "Try 'The Tell-Tale Heart' first. It will take your mind off things. Then the whole class is going to read 'The Murders in the Rue Morgue' just for the fun of it. Not all literature has to be so serious, you know." He gave me a pat on the back and my books tumbled to the floor again.

I had so much work to catch up on, I wasn't even annoyed when Esther stood me up at the library. Maybe she had mixed up the scheduling also, or maybe she had left school early for Thanksgiving weekend because she still wasn't feeling well. I decided I wasn't going home for the holiday. I telephoned my mom and tried to explain the situation. I was too far behind in my course work—for once, that was the truth. She accepted my excuse, and I spent all of Wednesday afternoon at the library. But it was difficult for me to concentrate when all I could think about was Frankenstein's little girl and her copy of Pizza's black notebook.

Later that night, back at the Quad, I lay awake in bed imagining the scene in various ways. The possibilities were endless.

There was the manslaughter scenario: The girl was copying from the book, Pizza saw her copying, grabbed the paper, there was a tug of war, and, with him pulling one way and her the other, the paper tore, he fell back into the center of the room and she fell out the window in the other direction.

There was the accident variety: She was copying from the notebook, she went to sleep while leaning on the window, the lightning struck, the window broke and she fell out, tearing the paper in half—one part flying into the room and one flying out.

There was the second-degree murder possibility: She was copying from the book, Pizza saw her and deliberately pushed her out the window in a fit of rage, the paper tearing in half as she went out.

But no matter how it happened, I was now involved. Somehow I had come into possession of the missing piece.

Finally, I tried to go to sleep, but couldn't. What was I to do? I got up and started to pace. Then I had an idea and opened up the top drawer of Stanley's dresser. Underneath some tissue, there were still three pills. Two were white, and one was pale yellow. Hmm. Which was the tranquilizer? I certainly didn't want to take an "upper" by mistake. After some contemplation, I decided to go with the odds and took a white. Then I returned to my bed and closed my eyes.

In about 15 minutes, I felt rather rubbery all over, and rather heavy in both the head and legs departments. Good. I had definitely avoided the "upper." Then I began to dream. At least I thought it was a dream—it may well have been a hallucination.

I was viewing a scene as if I were far away looking though binoculars. A young boy was at the Mayfair Club on a dark night—*that* dark night. He was walking slowly into the back room of the club. All I could see was the boy's back as he stalked forward toward a half-opened window. Then the little girl came into view. She was writing on a piece of paper on top of the black notebook. The boy came upon her and ripped the paper in two. He was angry and pointed to the paper. I couldn't hear anything, but I knew he was upset because she had left out an important bridge theory. He grabbed the notebook and threw it out the window. Then they both forced the window open further and looked down at the ground. It was raining, and he told her to go get the book so that he could copy the notes properly. Then he pushed her forward. Only I was no longer watching from afar. No, I was the young boy. And I started calling after her. I could see her heading down to the ground as if we were forty, fifty, sixty stories up. Suddenly I was dizzy. And suddenly I was the one heading to the ground. I fell and fell and fell and fell and fell.

I awoke just seconds before dawn. The smell of fresh rain came from the window. Stanley was not in his bed. I hadn't seen him for two days and nights. Suddenly, the night's hallucination came back to me. I was the killer. It was possible. There were plenty of cases of amnesia in situations like this. Why not? It would explain my possession of all the incriminating evidence. Maybe Stanley was merely a scapegoat for my own crime, which my dark subconscious had conveniently whitewashed from my memory. Maybe *I* was the one who had a Heart of Darkness!

I turned my head upon the pillow and stared at the blank wall. A morning shadow appeared. No, I was getting carried away. If I had amnesia, how would I have remembered the spot cards on a bridge hand I had played that night?

It must have been a dream—that's all. But what a dream! Dear God, I hope that's all it was. Yet so much of the last two months was not a dream. I thought back to all the things I had done since my journey to the Mayfair Club, and they were not good things.

Hadn't I gambled and lost money at the Mayfair, eaten dinner there without paying the bill, then fled the club without paying my losses? Hadn't I stolen money from Stanley's wallet and never returned it? Hadn't I stolen Stanley's *girl* and then jilted her in the middle of the night? Hadn't I lied countless times to Detective Kennedy, to Esther? Hadn't I destroyed an important piece of evidence because I had fingerprints on it? These things were not dreams—they were real, and somewhere, somehow, down the line, I was going to have to answer for these crimes.

I tried to go back to sleep but tossed and turned upon the evidence any decent district attorney would use to lock me up and throw the key away. But wait. Wasn't I getting carried away again? What would I be prosecuted *for?* The girl was all right. Doctor B. had said so. The girl was fine, recovering nicely from her fall.

So I owed a few dollars to the Mayfair—I could make that up. So I had failed to return to Chops' apartment—I could send her some flowers. So I had gotten a little confused and nervous during Detective Kennedy's grilling—I could straighten that out. So I had tossed a piece of evidence into the river—I still had a copy of the notebook.

The important thing is: The girl is recovering. By the time she's able to talk again, she can tell the whole story and they won't even *need* my testimony. Rest easy now, rest easy. Lock me up? For telling a few lies? C'mon, c'mon, back to dreamland. . . relax . . . think about a bridge hand. . . .

I had another dream that morning. My dad was in it. He was lecturing me not to tell lies. Suddenly he became Mr. Keewood, and I was playing a hand in the Congo. I was there to find Stanley. But then he turned into my partner. Chops was there too, and Doctor B. I kept trying to concentrate on my bridge hand. I held four aces with two major suits, something like:

$$\spadesuit A x x x \ \heartsuit A x x x \ \diamondsuit A x \ \clubsuit A x x$$

—though there might have been 14 or 15 cards in the actual dream-hand.

Suddenly my dad was kibitzing and whispered his rule, called "Appreciation of Aces."

I turned around. There was Gussie, not my dad. I opened one notrump with my 16 points. My partner bid four hearts. Was it a transfer? I couldn't remember.

Then I was playing the hand. I held something resembling:

$$\spadesuit K Q x \ \heartsuit K J x x x x \ \diamondsuit x x x \ \clubsuit x$$

Cold for six. Missed another slam. Chops tried to slap me across the face, but someone grabbed her arm and stopped her.

Then I picked up the same four aces again. This time partner opened one heart. I bid one spade. I should have raised hearts, but I wanted to make a "convenient bid." Partner rebid two hearts. I jumped to four hearts. Suddenly I was declarer again. I held:

$$\spadesuit K Q x \ \heartsuit K J x x x x \ \diamondsuit K x x \ \clubsuit x$$

Making *seven*. Missed a grand slam.

Chops had a gun this time. She aimed it at me. "Stop with the points!" she screamed.

I ran away, into the bush. I came to a clearing. There was Frankenstein dishing out soup from a huge boiling pot. There was Pizza being served by Maggie. There was the little girl holding hands with the baby.

I ran further into the bush. It was darker and darker. I heard someone following me. I turned. It was Stanley.

We got into a cab. He was carrying the notebook. We turned around the corner and stopped at the train station. I refused to go in. Not the train, I thought. Not the train.

I ran in the other direction. In the clearing was another bridge game. It was the Quad game. There was Big Al, Pete the Poet, Les the Mess, J.B., even Short Larry. Ramona was there keeping score; she turned around and asked if I was knocking in. I nodded my head, yes.

She got up and started to cry. She was Esther. She started to beat my chest. I pushed her aside and sat down.

I picked up a hand with four aces! My partner opened two hearts, weak two-bid. I bid two notrump. He bid three spades. I bid four hearts. Suddenly I was declarer. My hand was

$$\spadesuit K Q J \ \heartsuit K x x x x x \ \diamondsuit x x x \ \clubsuit x$$

Making six. "Makes six notrump as well," said J.B. "You should have bid it. Didn't my three-spade bid wake you up?"

No, no, must sleep some more. Must forget. "I said, wake up." No, no. . . "C'mon, guy, wake up!"

I opened my eyes. J.B. was standing there in his bathrobe.

"There's a phone call for you. It's that detective from New York."

"Hello?"

"Sorry to wake you, but I'm back on this case again and I want you to come to the Mayfair Club in two weeks."

"Two weeks?"

"From tomorrow. On Friday night, December 12th. Be there by 9 p.m. at the very latest. Best really if you arrive sooner. You got it?"

"Yes, sir. But, wait, did something happen to the girl?"

"I'm sorry to tell you, she's gone. Is your roommate there?"

"What? No, she's, er, he's not here. Whad'ya mean, she's gone? She died? Are you saying she died?!"

"When you see him, tell him to phone me immediately. I want him there too."

Click.

19

STRANGE RELIEF—ROMANTIC VOID—
A SMART REDOUBLE—WHAT HAPPENED
TO ESTHER.

I T'S STRANGE and sad (and horrible to face), but I believe the death of the little girl *relieved* me from the stress I was feeling. It lifted a veil of uncertainty from my mind; and, poor as my prospects were for unraveling the deceitful web I had spun myself into, the case had at last become serious enough for me to give up any thought of further cover-ups. The truth had to come out now, regardless of friendship, regardless of the consequences.

With this "comforting" thought in my mind, I was able to catch up on my school work during that Thanksgiving weekend. I reviewed calculus, conjugated Latin verbs, wrote a paper on Roman civilization, and finished a book on Indian political systems without disturbance.

Then again, upon reflection, it might have been the opposite case. That is, perhaps I was so fallen, so worried, so sick with what had happened and what nightmares were still to come that my mind forced the whole matter into one of its remarkable guilt-closets and locked the door—permitting me to concentrate on less threatening matters.

Many times in my bridge career, I've played my best game under the pressure of outside troubles. Because I was ill, or because some terrible problem was bothering me, I forced myself to play harder, concentrate deeper, to the point where those outside influences seemed to vanish from my state of mind. Thus, bridge, or study, or any pursuit, can become an escape from one closet of the mind to another. It's only when we go to bed and dream that we can no longer prevent the wrong closet from springing open.

On Monday night following Thanksgiving, I went to dinner alone after returning from the Douglass campus. Esther still hadn't returned from her weekend, and I was afraid to call her at home. It was more than a week since I'd seen her, and even in the week before I had only pretended to myself that we still were anything beyond a brother-sister type of friendship.

Now that I was set on telling others the truth, I crossed the biggest bridge between fiction and reality by making the decision to tell *myself* the truth. The romance I had imagined from the first shady afternoon in early October had withered as fast as the November leaves. The reason—I wasn't sure yet. But I soon would learn that it wasn't simply nature taking its course—there was a fox in my woods.

The game that night at the Quad consisted of Big Al, Short Larry, Pete the Poet and me. Les the Mess was on a first-week-of-the-new-month rampage of studying and J.B. had to attend a meeting of the Rutgers Classics Society. Stanley still was missing.

The hands were rather boring until about midnight, when an eerie thing happened on the first deal of the fifth chukker: I picked up a hand that looked familiar, and after the auction had proceeded a few rounds, I realized it was the same hand—albeit a different sequence of bids—that I had kibitzed a few weeks earlier.

Big Al
♠ A J 9 8
♡ A 10 9 3
◇ A J
♣ A J 5

Pete the Poet
♠ Q 7 6 5 3
♡ Q 8 5
◇ 10 9 7 6
♣ 10

Me
♠ —
♡ 6 2
◇ 8 5 4 3 2
♣ K Q 9 8 3 2

Short Larry
♠ K 10 4 2
♡ K J 7 4
◇ K Q
♣ 7 6 4

Pete the Poet	Big Al	Me	Short Larry
—	1 ♣	pass	2 NT
pass	4 NT	pass	5 ♣
pass	5 ♠	pass	5 NT
pass	pass	double	pass
pass	redouble	(all pass)	

Although my spot-cards may have been slightly different, my hand was what Stanley had held against J.B. when J.B. reached the contract of four notrump. I remembered that Stanley had doubled four notrump and, though Les the Mess—who was sitting in Pete the Poet's chair—did not lead a club (it being hidden behind some tunafish), J.B. had gone down one, misguessing both major-suit queens and failing to execute a strip, squeeze, and endplay to recover at the wire.

This time, the auction was more straightforward. Short Larry, who was still studying the point-count system, bypassed his majors to show 12-14 points. Big Al made a quantitative leap to four notrump, but Short Larry, unable to distinguish the bid from Blackwood, responded five clubs—no aces. Big Al bid five spades and at least Short Larry understood this properly as asking for a return to five notrump.

I doubled. After all, if Stanley could double *four* notrump, I could double *five*. I knew the suits were breaking poorly, and a club lead would be to our advantage.

Big Al, a math major, redoubled on his enormous hand—a sound mathematical bid because he would lose only 100 points if the contract failed by a trick, but would gain 320 points if the contract made. The redouble accentuated the downside of doubling final contracts.

Pete the Poet led the ten of clubs, Short Larry played low and so did I. My partner switched to a diamond and Short Larry, also a math major, had no trouble counting my hand for six clubs. Therefore he went with the odds that Pete the Poet held the missing queens—making his contract.

This hand taught me two lessons: 1) Never make a psychological double against two mathematicians, and 2) Don't double for the lead when you have too much length in dummy's first-bid suit—it will help declarer work out the rest of the distribution. Had I not doubled, Short Larry wouldn't have known about the club suit and would more than likely have taken at least one finesse through me.

As the first week in December slipped by, I tried not to think of the upcoming meeting at the Mayfair. Instead, I concentrated on my class work and retreated in the evenings to the serenity of the Quad bridge game. If I were falling down a mountain, I had at least managed to stop for a brief rest on a precipice. But that rocky ledge was weak and when I entered the Red Tulip on Saturday evening and saw Esther at our usual table, working on a bowl of cabbage soup, the ledge started to give way.

"So there you are," I said, trying to keep my shoulders back, trying not to reveal my sad state of affairs.

"Yes, here I am," she answered.

"Mind if I join you?"

"I don't care what you do."

I sat down. Why was she angry with me? She was eating well, I thought. There was a lot of food on the table, bread, cheese, butter, tomato and onion salad. I called the waitress over and ordered some chicken paprikash. "Just for old-time's sake," I said with a smile aimed at Esther. Only the waitress smiled back. "Oh, and some wine. Would you like some of the Hungarian red—"

"No wine for me," Esther said.

"Do you want your goulash now, or do you want me to wait for his main course?" asked the waitress.

"Now," she answered, "oh, and more of those rolls, please."

For a few minutes I just sat there watching her eat. I never realized she had such a hearty appetite. Finally I had to say something, so I asked her when she had gotten back from vacation.

"Yesterday."

"Oh," I said, "You took off a whole week. You missed a rally this Wednesday."

"I'm sure you weren't there," she scolded, wiping the remains of her soup bowl with some crust.

"No, I wasn't. I guess it's not the same without you."

She looked up at me quizzically. "What are you talking about? You were too busy playing cards. That's why you weren't there. The two of you are two peas in a pod—dirty, nasty, disgusting card players."

The two of us? I could feel the precipice shaking beneath me.

The waitress brought her goulash and told me my order would be right out.

"Okay, so you don't like cards," I said. "Don't take it out on. . . on, uh, a deck of cards."

"Don't take what out?"

"That's what I'd like to know," I said. "What's eating you?"

She dug into her goulash with relish. Then, balancing a forkful of potato and string beans, she broke my precipice in half. "Believe me, you don't want to know, but because you're such a busybody, I'll tell you. Your best friend is going to be a father. Congratulations." Pop, in went the fork as I started my free-fall.

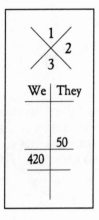

Trapped

20

*A DIFFERENT BLACKWOOD—SECOND
MISSION—NOTE FROM HOME—LEAD
IN THE DARK—STORY OF REVENGE—
NORTHWARD BOUND—LOSS OF NERVE.*

"I S EVERYBODY here?"

We all looked around. There were 22 students in the class. Everyone was accounted for.

"Fine." Mr. Keewood walked over to the door, took out a key and locked it. Then he went to the windows and shut them. Finally, he returned to his center stage. "Anybody uncomfortable?" He looked at us intensely. "How does it feel to be locked in?"

One guy in the second row cried out in jest and we all laughed. The way I was feeling these days, I just sat there in a numb state, vaguely paying attention.

"Not enough, I'm afraid," said Keewood. With that, he walked over to the switch and shut the lights off. A minute of silence passed; there was a little coughing, then one girl in the back got up, ran to the window, and tried to open it. It was locked.

"Hey, c'mon now," she said. Then she moved quickly to the door and put the lights on. "Unlock the door," she demanded.

Mr. Keewood took out the key and unlocked it. "Sorry, Miss Tilden," he said. He pulled the door open and shut it again to prove it was unlocked. Then Miss Tilden returned to her seat. Mr. Keewood brushed back his long blond hair and addressed the class.

"In Poe's story, 'The Cask of Amontillado,' the author locks his friend in a crypt. It is an example of Poe's fascination with being buried alive. In another piece, 'The Premature Burial,' he wrote 'The boundaries which divide Life from Death are at best shadowy and vague.'

"Like our other authors this semester, Poe lived the life he wrote about. His personality had the same strange twists and turns as his literary characters and plots. It might be interesting for you to know he was a gambler at college, and often fictionalized his own life when talking to others. That he drank and took opium is well-known. However, he was also a hard-working writer, and loyal and devoted in his personal relationships.

"I know that some of you aspire to the profession of writing. You've seen from the books we've read this semester that it takes not only hard work and talent to write a good book but some interesting experiences in life. You should try to record what you experience—keep a notebook. Poe once advised, 'Should you ever be drowned or hanged, be sure and make a note of your sensations.' This comes from 'How to Write a Blackwood Article.'"

My head shot up. I raised my hand and called out, "Would you repeat that, please?"

"'How to Write a Blackwood Article.' Who here knows about Blackwood?"

The girl with beehive hair raised her hand.

"I do. My aunt in Scotland subscribes to *Blackwood Magazine.*"

I never knew Blackwood published a magazine.

"Correct," said Mr. Keewood. "It was founded in Edinburgh by William Blackwood in 1817. It was a Tory publication—you history scholars know those feuds between the Tories and the Whigs. The magazine contained satirical pieces that, in those days, were thought of as depraved, impious and anti-patriotic. There were also stories, poems, and serialized novels. I believe *Blackwood's Magazine* provoked the founding of another periodical, *London Magazine*, and the rivalry between the two publications once led to a duel in which the editor of *London Magazine*—let me think . . . his name was Scott—he lost the duel— mortally wounded and all that sort of thing.

"So, what does all this have to do with Mr. Poe? Well, in the early 19th century, writers were able to read most of the good material produced in the limited marketplace, and, like great painters, built their own works upon the works of those who had come before. Many of Poe's stories were takeoffs on what he had read in *Blackwood's Magazine*. One of these, which I'm sorry to say is not in your collection, was called 'The Scythe of Time,' based on the *Blackwood* thriller, 'The Man in the Bell.' In the *Blackwood* story, a man is tolled into madness by a funeral bell, while in Poe's version the victim faces decapitation by the hand of a clock while standing upon his servant's back, looking through an opening in the clock-tower.

"The exploration of darkness, destruction and death pervaded Poe's tales. In 'The Pit and the Pendulum,' Poe makes the narrator a prisoner of the Spanish Inquisition waiting for deliverance from forces of darkness. This darkness was not a void, however. Poe described it in this way: 'It is evident that we are hurrying to some exciting knowledge—some never-to-be-imparted secret, whose attainment is destruction.'"

On Tuesday, in my room at the Quad, a note from Esther was waiting for me:

> *Dear Matthew,*
> *Sorry for being so mean to you at the Red Tulip. You can't help it if your roommate is a scoundrel. If you see him, tell him nothing. The last human I want to lay eyes on is him. Besides, I might be able to work this whole thing out over Christmas week.*
> *At least we had a good time at the Raritan. See you some day in a Hungarian restaurant.*
> *Esther*

On Wednesday, J.B. called me into his room. "Stanley is missing again," he said.

"No kidding. So what am I supposed to do about it? Am I his keeper?"

"Don't get so excited, guy. I just want you to look at this." It was a copy of Stanley's grades to date. In those days, freshmen at Rutgers were given status reports to take home to their guardians. Up until Thanksgiving, my grades had been so-so in all my courses except English (where no status was reported). Stanley had straight A's down the line!

"How does he do it?" I asked, hating him even more than before.

"I don't know," said my preceptor, "but he's hardly the sort of guy the college wants to lose. That's why—"

"That's why you want me to go bring him back again, right?"

"Now, now, guy, just be reasonable. I happen to know you have to make the journey anyway. Just see what you can do when you see him."

"You realize," I said, "that he could be anywhere. Nobody's seen him in a week. And even if he does show up for the inquiry, he may end up in jail, and I may be his cellmate."

"What are you talking about, guy? You haven't gone and gotten yourself deeper in this than I've been told?" J.B. looked at me with sincerity and innocence. He was a shepherd, I thought, and Stanley and I were just slightly spotted sheep in his eyes.

I shook my head, no. "I'm sure it'll turn out all right, and we'll both be back here by Saturday morning."

"You had me worried there for a moment, guy." J.B. wiped his brow. "I'll pick up the two of you at 11:00. I'm going into town Friday for the National Classics conference at NYU. Come to think of it, if you're supposed to meet Detective Kennedy at 9:00, it might not be a bad idea to check in with me at 8:45—just to let me know that you got there safely." He took a slip of paper from his desk and wrote a New York phone number. "Say, guy, would you like a lift in as well?"

"No thanks," I said, folding the phone number inside my Poe. "I'm going in a day early . . . just to get my bearings."

Then he gave me a little fist to the shoulder. "You're a good kid, guy. . . ."

———————

On Thursday morning I rose at 7:30, packed a small overnight bag, picked up some coffee and a buttered roll at the food truck and went to calculus.

At 9:30, I checked my mailbox at the post office. My November *Bridge World* finally had arrived. Actually, I had no idea it was late until the date dawned on me. It was December 11th. I remembered because there were birthday cards from my mom and dad and brother. Eighteen years old tomorrow, I thought—legal age for capital punishment.

Inside my father's envelope was a 50-dollar check. I put it into my wallet. Inside my brother's envelope was a brief note:

> Stanley was here looking for
> that package you mailed us last
> month. I told him that dad had
> given it to a man — an old army
> buddy I think — who stopped by
> last Wednesday night.

What old army buddy? What did it all mean? Could my dad possibly have done that to me—given my copy of Pizza's notebook to some old army buddy? I slipped the note into my back pocket. Maybe I could figure it out later.

At 10:00, I bumped into Les the Mess at the food truck. He was having an early lunch—a tunafish sub and chocolate milk. Said he needed the energy for an astrophysics exam. I had another cup of coffee and headed across town, forgetting to stop at the Quad to pick up my Poe.

At 10:30, I went into the Douglass library and took the New York *Times* off the rack. Balmy weather with possible showers was the forecast. There was a sex scandal in Washington and a counter-feit-money racket in New York. There was an all-city alert by Con Edison: an electricity turn-off for five minutes at exactly 9:00 p.m. the following night. This was the security test they had promised the mayor when the lights had gone out earlier in the year. Funny, I thought, that's the time we were supposed to meet at the Mayfair with Detective Kennedy. I turned to the bridge column:

Blackout Causes Killing Lead
by Alan Truscott

I looked at the headline again. Was that "Blackout" or "Black-wood?" No, it was "Blackout."

> With the upcoming test by Con Edison, it may never happen again, but during the city's electrical shortage on October 4 of this year, a contract of six spades was headed for defeat after an accidental opening lead.
> The deal occurred at Al Roth's Mayfair Club on 57th Street in Manhattan. The players, passing a flashlight around the table, completed the bidding in the dark. Then,

West accidentally pulled the "wrong" card from his hand, the only lead to defeat the contract. A few moments later, fate struck back and logical defensive play actually allowed declarer to make his contract.

Looking at all four hands, see if you can solve the mystery: What was the accidental, killing lead and what was the logical defense that permitted the slam to make?

South dealer
All vulnerable

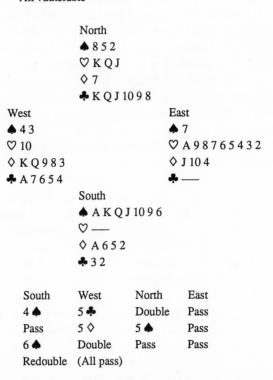

North
♠ 8 5 2
♡ K Q J
◊ 7
♣ K Q J 10 9 8

West
♠ 4 3
♡ 10
◊ K Q 9 8 3
♣ A 7 6 5 4

East
♠ 7
♡ A 9 8 7 6 5 4 3 2
◊ J 10 4
♣ —

South
♠ A K Q J 10 9 6
♡ —
◊ A 6 5 2
♣ 3 2

South	West	North	East
4 ♠	5 ♣	Double	Pass
Pass	5 ◊	5 ♠	Pass
6 ♠	Double	Pass	Pass
Redouble	(All pass)		

I recognized this as the deal Detective Kennedy had asked me about during my grilling. It was the fourth deal, the one after the partscore on the night the little girl fell from the window. I admitted to the detective that I hadn't made the winning lead, that I had left before this deal, and he admitted to me that he was only testing my honesty by putting my name in the West position.

I studied the hand again now. Hmm. Some bidding! I tried to remember who sat where. According to Detective Kennedy, Otto and Gussie had filled in on that last deal. The five-club bid by West *looked* like a bid the mad Hungarian would make. Then I observed the East hand—never making a bid with nine hearts! East *must* have been Gussie. As for North and South, it looked as if Pizza would have opened only *one* spade with the South cards, following the Theory of Exhaustion. Therefore he was probably North—yes, I remembered now—Frankenstein was declarer.

What about the accidental opening lead? Let's see. The only opening lead that will defeat the slam is the ace of clubs. If West continues with another club, East can ruff, and that's down one.

Therefore, West *must* have led the ace of clubs; but then, by what logic would he not continue the suit? Did Gussie signal with a high heart? Hmm. Then Otto would have switched, thinking perhaps that partner held a void in trumps.

On the other hand, East held a nine-card suit and dummy had three more. Clearly, if West switched to hearts, declarer would be void. It was ridiculous to signal a high heart. Then what happened?

I was not in the mood to analyze further, so I looked at the answer:

> The winning lead was the ace of clubs, a card that Mr. Otto Marx, an engineer from Manhattan, admits was led in error after he dropped the flashlight on the floor. On this lead, his partner, Miss Gussie Addles of the Bronx, demonstrated that the correct defense is not always the winning defense.
>
> Staring at 12 hearts between her hand and dummy, it was necessary to decide who held the 13th heart. If it was South, it would be vital to trump the opening lead and lead a heart. Add to that the logical assumption that West held six clubs for his overcall and Miss Addle's only correct, but losing, play was to trump her partner's ace and try to cash the ace of hearts.
>
> In the postmortem, Mr. Marx was chastised for not overcalling four notrump with both minors. However, many experts play this as a *three*-suit take-out rather than a *two*-suit bid. It was South, Mr. Frank Stein, one of America's premier players, who pointed out that he was less likely to have bid six spades with two singletons than with a void. Perhaps, but in the dark, anything is possible!

Hmm. Interesting hand, but one thing bothered me. I couldn't quite believe that Gussie was up to trumping her partner's ace. Yet the bidding of the East hand looked like Gussie's. Who else would never bid with nine hearts to the ace? It had to be Gussie . . . . I suddenly saw the time and realized I was late.

At 12:00, I arrived at my last English class of the week. When I entered the room, Mr. Keewood was discussing the origins of mysteries, and I tiptoed over to an empty seat by the window.

"'The Murders in the Rue Morgue' was the first real mystery. As Arthur Conan Doyle does later in the century with his Watson and Holmes, Mr. Poe writes in the first person as a friend of his detective, Monsieur Dupin. This immediacy and intimacy with the reader forces the narrative into a camera lens in which we see only what the narrator sees, and are therefore faced with the same problems of deduction.

"Is there any similarity between this mystery and his shorter tales of murder? Miss Tilden?"

"It's in the first person," she said.

"Correct," said Mr. Keewood. "However, many of his shorter tales are in the first person of the killer himself. Can someone give me an example, please. . . ."

"The Cask of Amontillado," said a boy in the back.

"Tell us about it."

"Well, there's this guy called, uh, Fortunato, who has insulted another guy, uh. . . ."

"His name is Montresor, the one who's telling the story," said Mr. Keewood.

"Yeah, and he's planning revenge some day, so it happens that during the carnival season he leads this Fortunato guy through his wine cellar. Fortunato loves wines and the narrator, he tricks him into searching for a rare drink or drug called Amontillado." (Giggles.) "Well, he gets him into the cellar and through a lot of human bones and crypts and things until the end when he suddenly locks Fortunato in a little hole in the wall and leaves him there to die."

Mr. Keewood smiled. "You've got it, more or less. And I don't think you've spoiled it for those who haven't read it yet. You'll note that Poe used wine, one of his own vices, as the object of the victim's desire and downfall. Here, as in many of his short stories,

Poe gives us the solution to a mystery—he reveals who the killer is and what happened. However, unlike the detective tale 'The Murders in the Rue Morgue,' which is a whodunnit type, nobody is going to be found and no investigation will be made—the emphasis is on the psychological joy of revenge of a man who escapes punishment for the crime.

"It would be interesting and instructive for one of you budding authors to rewrite 'The Cask of Amontillado' as a detective story—if you'd like to try it for your final paper, let me know."

At the end of class, Mr. Keewood took me aside to ask if I had read "The Murders in the Rue Morgue" yet. I admitted I hadn't, and didn't even have the book with me, because I was about to travel to New York and did not want to risk leaving the book there as I had done with my Franklin. He told me when I did read the story, not to skip the "truly remarkable passage at the beginning in which Poe gives a short discourse on analytical game theory."

At 1:00, I walked across the street to the main campus area and decided to take a breather. I sat down under the huge oak tree where I had waited for Esther two months earlier. I wondered if she were attending class in the old brick building across the walking path. It was a cool day and my jeans felt rough on the hard earth. Something was sticking out of my back pocket. It was my brother's note. I read it again:

> Stanley was here looking for
> that package you mailed us last
> month. I told him that dad had
> given it to a man — an old army
> buddy I think — who stopped by
> last Wednesday night.

Old army buddy. . . . How could my father give anyone my package when I specifically asked him to hold it for me? Then I realized who it was: Pizza McCarver. I remembered now, in the Daily News report there was a passage about McCarver being a veteran stationed at Fort Dix during World War II, the same Fort where my own dad had spent the war years—as the fourth in a bridge game with a Colonel and two officers. One of those officers must have been Lieutenant McCarver.

216

Stanley, that rat, must have told Pizza where I sent the transcription. Now Pizza would know I had been through his notebook, seen his personal remarks, and copied them. Would I end up at the bottom of the East River as he had warned on the first page of the notebook? Or would he see fit to spare the son of an old army buddy? Wait a second—Stanley couldn't have told him— my brother's note said that Stanley was looking for the notebook himself.

At 1:30, I spotted Esther coming out of the building. I quickly got up and walked in the opposite direction. It was strange, but I no longer felt I was part of her world; I had slipped past the boundaries of Douglass College, past Rutgers as well. I was shooting down into some hole inside the earth now, with nothing to hold onto—into my own dark well, and down at the bottom of the pit was a bridge club with characters like Pizza and Frankenstein and Chops waiting for me to join them.

At 2:30, I stopped back at the Quad for my Poe. What the heck. Maybe it would come in handy as reading material if I were thrown into the clink. Then I realized it was a good thing I had stopped back because J.B.'s NYU phone number was inside the book.

At 3:00, I left for the train station, checking again that I had everything: my overnight bag containing one change of clothes, one toothbrush, one towel (in case I slept at the Mayfair), one comb, one notebook and pencil (as prescribed by Mr. Keewood), one "Collected Short Stories of Edgar Allan Poe" with one November *Bridge World* as a book mark. In my rear pocket I still had the fifty-dollar check, fifteen dollars in cash, the photostat of the little girl's handwriting and the matching torn page that somehow had come to be in my possession.

At 3:15, I stopped at the bank and cashed the check. The teller handed me a fifty. I looked at the photo, half expecting to see Edgar Allan Poe. No, it was Grant.

At 3:45, I bought a round-trip ticket between New Brunswick and New York and stuck it inside my shoe, taking no chances of losing it if I were robbed in the Pennsylvania Station men's room.

Then I remembered that J.B. was driving me back, so I returned to the ticket-window for a one-way fare.

At 3:48, I bought a cup of coffee at the New Brunswick coffee shop across the street from the station, taking no chances of getting locked out between doors while going for a cup of coffee inside the moving train.

At 3:55, I boarded the train on the local track for Edison, Metuchen, Rahway, Linden, Elizabeth, Newark and New York. Seven stops. This time I could change my mind at any point if I lost my nerve, and return to the Quad for one more peaceful night.

At 4:05, I lost my nerve, but decided to go as far as Edison since the train was already moving over twenty miles an hour.

At 4:06, I looked out the window at the Raritan River and thought I spotted Pizza McCarver's black notebook sitting on a rock at low tide. I was sure it was my imagination.

At 4:09, I began to wonder how I had gotten myself into this mess. I was sure my parents had brought me up right.

At 4:11, not being able to come up with a good excuse for my failings, I put the blame on the game of bridge. That was the cause of my fall into the abyss. Esther was right, it was an evil game and had evil consequences. It must be a curse in my family, like a black cat or an unlucky uncle, or something.

At 4:12, I decided that I would give up the game of bridge. I would go to the Mayfair, kibitz a few rubbers, have dinner, then watch a backgammon chouette.

At 4:13, I stood up to get my Poe out of my overnight bag on the rack above me. The train screeched to a stop at Edison. I spilled the last of my coffee on my pants, and knocked my head against the bottom of the rack.

At 4:13 and 30 seconds, I jumped the train at Edison.

21

*A DISSERTATION ON WHIST OVER A CHOCO-
LATE MALTED—TWO DEALS REAPPEAR—
UNRAVELLING THE PAST—
REQUEST FROM THE FAT LADY.*

I PICKED up my bag from the tracks. My left knee was cut, but not bleeding badly, and when I pressed my pants to the wound it stopped altogether. The Edison station was empty, and I checked the schedule for the next train—5:05. I considered going back to New Brunswick for the night, then changed my mind again. I had to stop doing that, I told myself. Switching back and forth, gaining confidence, losing confidence, heading into town a day early, then jumping the train at the first stop. I don't know what made me push the panic button this time—probably the fear of what was in store for me at the Mayfair on Friday night with Detective Kennedy. I still hadn't worked out the mysterious sequence of events that had brought me to this juncture, and, if truth be told, I was scared—scared to go face to face with the players at the Mayfair Club without a clear idea of who was friend and who was foe. The motives of people are rarely as defined as those at the bridge table, I reflected. There, partner is on your side—or supposed to be—and the opponents are . . . well— the opponents.

I glanced around the station's exterior—there wasn't much to see. Then I spotted a drugstore down the block on the far side of the street.

It was an old-fashioned country store with a clean white soda-fountain counter along the right wall. I was the only customer, and I took a seat on a stool. There were some rainbow colored straws sticking out of a glass container, and I decided to splurge with a chocolate malted and fries. The waitress was petite and dreamy-eyed, and if I had been somebody else maybe I would have asked her out on a date and spent the rest of my life in Edison, but I wasn't.

I took my Poe from my bag and turned to the index. Then I flattened the book on the counter, put some ketchup on my potatoes, and started reading "The Murders in the Rue Morgue." So this was Mr. Keewood's remedy for worries—a good murder mystery.

> The mental features discoursed of as the analytical, are, in themselves, but little susceptible of analysis. We appreciate them only in their effects. . . .

Pretty heavy stuff, I thought. I started skimming a bit rather than reading every line.

> As the strong man exults in his physical ability, delighting in such exercises as call his muscles into action, so glories the analyst in that moral activity which *disentangles*. . . . He is fond of enigmas, of conundrums, hieroglyphics. . . . The faculty of re-solution is possibly much invigorated by mathematical study. . . . Yet to calculate is not in itself to analyze. A chess-player, for example, does the one, without effort at the other. . . .

Weird little discourse, I thought. I wondered why Mr. Keewood wanted me to read it. Was it because of the comparison with a chess player? I downed a third of my malted in one long slurp, then went back to the book.

> Deprived of ordinary resources, the analyst throws himself into the spirit of his opponent, identifies himself therewith, and not infrequently sees thus, at a glance, the sole methods (sometimes indeed absurdly simple ones) by which he may seduce into error or hurry into miscalculation.
>
> Whist has long been known for its influence upon what is termed the calculating power; and men of the highest order of intellect have been known to take an apparently unaccountable delight in it, while eschewing chess as frivolous.

So there it was! Poe was a whist player and thought highly of the game. Well, maybe bridge isn't as bad an influence on me as I thought. If "men of the highest order of intellect" enjoy it, it must have its merits. I continued my reading:

> Beyond doubt there is nothing of a similar nature so greatly tasking the faculty of analysis. The best chess-player in Christendom *may* be little more that the best player of chess; but proficiency in whist implies capacity for success in all these more important undertakings where mind struggles with mind.

Wow! I took a quick peek at the back of the book to make sure this was Poe I was reading.

> When I say proficiency, I mean that perfection in the game which includes a comprehension of *all* the sources whence legitimate advantage may be derived. These are not only manifold, but multiform, and lie frequently among recesses of thought altogether inaccessible to the ordinary understanding. To observe attentively is to re-member distinctly; and, so far, the concentrative chess-player will do very well at whist; while the rules of Hoyle (themselves based upon the mere mechanism of the game) are sufficiently and generally comprehensible. Thus to have a retentive memory, and proceed by "the book" are points commonly regarded as the sum total of good play-ing. But it is in matters beyond the limits of mere rule that the skill of the analyst is evinced. He makes, in silence, a host of observations and inferences. So, perhaps, do his companions; and the difference in the extent of the infor-mation obtained lies not so much in the validity of the in-ference as in the quality of the observation. The necessary knowledge is that of *what* to observe. Our player confines himself not at all; nor, because the game is the object, does he reject deductions from things external to the game. He examines the countenance of his partner, com-paring it carefully with that of each of his opponents. He considers the mode of assorting the cards in each hand; often counting trump by trump, and honor by honor, through the glances bestowed by their holders upon each.

He notes every variation of face as the play progresses, gathering a fund of thought from the differences in the expression of certainty, of surprise, of triumph, or chagrin. From the manner of gathering up a trick he judges whether the person taking it can make another in the suit. He recognizes what is played through feint, by the manner with which it is thrown upon the table. A casual or inadvertent word; the accidental dropping or turning of a card, with the accompanying anxiety or carelessness in regard to its concealment; the counting of the tricks, with the order of their arrangement; embarrassment, hesitation, eagerness, or trepidation—all afford, to his apparently intuitive perception, indications of the true state of affairs. The first two or three rounds having been played, he is in full possession of the contents of each hand, and thenceforward puts down his cards with as absolute a precision of purpose as if the rest of the party had turned outward the faces of their own.

I paused to slurp up the last of my malted while I digested Poe's dissertation. There were two amazing things in this piece of writing. First, it was incredible and exciting to me that this famous writer was speaking over 100 years ago about the game I was consumed with today. Second, he was talking about a part of the game that I had never seen in print, let alone heard anyone speak of. Wait a second! I *had* read this before. In the black notebook, Pizza had referred to reading the thought processes of his opponents. But he had not been nearly as eloquent as Poe—nor as precise. Why, if a bridge player could learn to analyze the players the way Poe described, he would be the greatest player in the world.

This was a new dimension, and I stepped into it with my eyes closed and my mind open. How could I learn to read the slightest hesitation or the countenance of a player's face? Who could teach me? It struck me that it might take years of practice to become such an acute analyst. To observe so closely as to distinguish a grimace from a frown or a split-second hesitation from an accidental pause might mean a sacrifice of many years cultivating such instincts. Certainly it had to be done continuously as in other sports, like the golfer who hits a thousand golf balls a day, or the tennis player who volleys for hours every morning, or the baseball player who goes into the batting cage for hours, hitting the ball with his bat again and again and again.

But where was the bridge player's batting cage? Where could I deal, bid, and play hundreds, thousands, millions of bridge hands? Certainly not at the duplicate club, certainly not at the average of two deals every 15 minutes. Certainly not with opponents who moved to the next table every round and didn't give me time to exercise my analytical prowess.

No. It had to be someplace where everybody stayed put, where all they did was play bridge, eat bridge, sleep bridge. It had to be among other students of the game, not there for master points, or an ego trip, or a social diversion; it had to be against players who were there for the sport of it, for the thrill of each hand, each bid, each card. There was only one place I knew where I could study this religion, this drug, this sport of detection—the Mayfair Club.

I marked my place in the book, and checked the time: 5:03. I still had two minutes before the next train. I flipped a couple of singles on to the counter and told the waitress to keep the change. Maybe she'd remember me to her future grandchildren. Then, filled with my newly found ambition, I sauntered out of the drugstore at a future-champion's gait, knowing there was a world filled with mysteries out there waiting to be explored and conquered by a young lion named Matthew Granovetter.

Little did I realize that trains do not wait for young lions to saunter across the street. And when I heard the whistle blow, I told myself sometimes young lions have to run a bit to catch their prey. Down the block, across the street, across the tracks, this young lion reached the caboose just as it started to sputter up the Northbound line. A kindly railroad porter gave me a helping hand as I narrowly avoided the electric sparks of the steel tracks. "Is this the train to New York?" I asked.

Looking back on it now, I believe it wasn't more than a 50% finesse that I was on the Northbound line rather than the Southbound—young lions not having a very good sense of direction when their heads are full of mad dreams. But at the time, when the gentle porter gave me the nod, I was sorry I had bothered to check. After all, the direction in my life had taken a new turn, and I should have been completely confident that there *was* nowhere to go but up.

This train was filled with commuters and the only empty seat was by the East window, next to a heavy-set middle-aged woman wearing granny glasses. She was reading the newspaper, and I tried not to bump her going past, but it was impossible. After squeezing and rattling between hard knees, thick thighs, and some round container between her feet, I finally managed to hurl myself into the seat. Embarrassed by it all, I averted my eyes to the scenery outside and I could see the landscape moving forward. I was trapped in a seat facing Southbound, and that recent feeling of moving toward a new day, a new dream, a new destiny, started to fade as fast as the December sun.

Suddenly I felt I would never return—that the future was flying past me. There it was—poof, it was gone—like the millions of bridge hands played during the course of a lifetime. There were no recap sheets, no comparisons, no postmortems. Backwards, backwards, and further backwards the train took me, leaving the signs, highways, farmland, and rivers in the unreachable future. Good God, was I going back in time? Back to the days my dad used to travel on the train to New York? Back to the days when he played his rubber bridge?

I grabbed hold of my Poe. I had been hallucinating, and I needed something to hang onto—something real and present. I opened to where I had left off, but changed my mind when I noticed my *Bridge World.* There on the cover was the date, "November, 1969." I took a deep breath, then noticed something strange about the cover. The label was type-written with my name and address from the Quad. This didn't make sense because the subscription was in my father's name and the magazine always went to him first; then he would put it in an envelope and mail it down to me in New Brunswick. There was something else suspicious also. It was an article listed at the bottom of the cover entitled, "Partscore Tragedy by Edgar Kaplan." It couldn't be, I thought. But with trepidation, and a sudden rumbling of chocolate malted in my stomach's pit, I turned to page 31 where the article started. My eyes quickly moved to the diagram midway down the right-hand column. Yes, there it was:

Third deal – Scoring: Chicago variation
East dealer
North-South vulnerable
Partscore: 40 on for N-S

NORTH (McCarver)
♠ A 7 3
♡ J 6 4
♦ K 10 8 6 4
♣ 5 4

WEST (Dr. B.)
♠ K 10 4 2
♡ Q 9 2
♦ 7 2
♣ A 10 9 7

EAST (Kesselman)
♠ J 9 6 5
♡ A 10 3
♦ Q J
♣ J 6 3 2

SOUTH (Stein)
♠ Q 8
♡ K 8 7 5
♦ A 9 5 3
♣ K Q 8

SOUTH	WEST	NORTH	EAST
Stein	Dr. B.	McCarver	Kesselman
—	—	—	Pass
1 ♦	Pass	2 ♦	Pass
Pass	Double	Pass	2 ♡
Pass	Pass	3 ♦	Pass
Pass	3 ♡	4 ♦	(All pass)

Finally! What a relief for me to see Stanley's name on the East hand rather than my own. Yes, all the names seemed to be accurately in place now—just as Gussie had told Detective Kennedy in her testimony. Even the variation on Chicago scoring was correct: as Pizza had written in his notebook, the vulnerability was switched on the second and third deals during the late-night games after Roth left the club.

Still, a sea of jealousy flooded my veins, as I stared at Stanley's name. Despite being cleared from the scene of the crime, I was boiling mad. Why couldn't they have reported the deal on which I had made six spades earlier in the evening? Why this stupid partscore deal, with *Stanley* making the killing shift? My eyes turned back to the beginning of the article.

The battle for the partscore is one of the least discussed features in the game of bridge. Yet, at duplicate

225

it is crucial, while at rubber bridge it builds or completes a game bonus.

The diagrammed deal, played at New York's Mayfair Club, has kept analysts at the Bridge World offices awake at night trying to find a sound reasoning for a killing defensive shift. I'll get to that in a minute. First, readers should note the auction, which is so typical of Chicago partscore battles. With North-South needing only 60 points to complete their game, East-West were aggressive in their attempt to push North-South one trick too high.

Astute detectives will observe immediately the rather questionable (to put it nicely) double by West. At this point in the auction, the opponents were only in two diamonds, a contract that could score 40 points, not the 60 points needed for game. Here is where rubber bridge and duplicate part paths, for the double at duplicate is clear and admirable, while the double at rubber is tantamount to playing with a loaded gun.

The bid of two hearts by Mr. Kesselman, sitting East, shows the imagination that some of our younger experts employ. I doubt that many veteran players would make that call, and rightly so, since had a more patient player been sitting North, he would have found a pass to three hearts rather than a four-diamond call.

I stopped reading for the moment and savored the criticism of Stanley's two-heart bid. Mr. Kaplan had certainly converted my jealousy to joy—

"Your ticket, please."

It was the porter. I told him how I had gotten off at Edison and my ticket was in the train that preceded this one. He nodded and suggested I get off at the next stop as well. So I coughed up another three dollars and quickly returned to my *Bridge World.*

Players who like to bid their cards two or three times must think their partners are somewhat deaf. Frank Stein is hardly deaf and is wise enough to know what to do in a competitive auction with four trumps to the king. Needless to say, had North passed the three-heart bid around to Stein, young Kesselman would have learned a thing or two about the dangers of imaginative bidding.

Now let's go to the play of four diamonds. The heart lead turned out not to hurt the defense. Had East bid spades, and had West led them against four diamonds, declarer would have made his contract easily. Opening leaders should realize that when they force their partners to bid a suit, the suit does not promise a high honor. Personally, I think a trump lead would have been safest (and wisest), but after the actual heart lead the defense still had a chance.

East had little to go on, and, as I mentioned earlier in the article, upon analysis, after East wins the first trick with the ace of hearts, it is difficult to find sound reasoning for the spade shift—that is, without looking at all four hands.

In fact, young Kesselman returned a club, naturally enough (necessary on many other layouts), and declarer had no further trouble. He forced the club ace, won the club continuation, drew trumps and played king and a heart to West, who was endplayed.

I put the magazine down. Stanley told me he had shifted to a spade. He bragged to me about it all the way from New York to New Brunswick—the stinking liar! Oh, how glad I was to see the truth in print, how very glad!

The train was at another station, and some people were standing in the aisle. I looked outside and saw the dim lights of the station turning on, one after another. Night was approaching rapidly now. There was a reading bulb below the luggage rack and I turned it on. Suddenly, it occurred to me my overnight bag was not in the rack. Of course it wasn't! Darn it, I had left it in the drugstore back in Edison. Oh well, I still had my Poe and my *Bridge World*. With that comforting thought, I returned to the article.

All right, readers. I leave it to you for the moment. Can you analyze the deal and come to the winning defense by proper reasoning? (Answer on page 52.)

I looked at the diagram that I had looked at so many times before. Then I stared out the window into the cloudy grey sky and tried to analyze it again. No, I couldn't see why one play was much better than another. Declarer could have held the ten of spades, which would make the spade shift disastrous. The ten of clubs could also have been with South, making it necessary to lead back hearts. It was frustrating. I looked back down on my lap. Hmm. Two Edgars, Kaplan and Poe, each in his own way telling me that the clues to the puzzle were there in front of me, if only I could detect them. Suddenly I felt a newspaper page scratch me on the cheek. It was the fat lady's paper—she had turned the page. She folded it back again, and I glanced over. She took a huge green pencil from her black handbag and started the crossword puzzle. Hmm. It was on the same page as the bridge column:

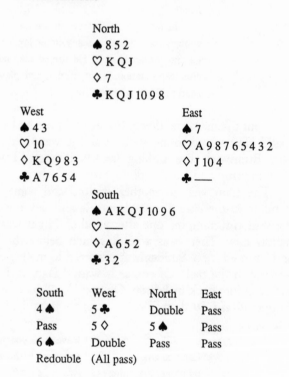

South dealer
All vulnerable

North
♠ 8 5 2
♡ K Q J
◇ 7
♣ K Q J 10 9 8

West
♠ 4 3
♡ 10
◇ K Q 9 8 3
♣ A 7 6 5 4

East
♠ 7
♡ A 9 8 7 6 5 4 3 2
◇ J 10 4
♣ —

South
♠ A K Q J 10 9 6
♡ —
◇ A 6 5 2
♣ 3 2

South	West	North	East
4 ♠	5 ♣	Double	Pass
Pass	5 ◇	5 ♠	Pass
6 ♠	Double	Pass	Pass
Redouble	(All pass)		

There was that slam hand again. I looked back and forth from the slam in the newspaper to the partscore in the magazine. The partscore had been the third deal in the chukker; the slam, the fourth deal. If Frankenstein and Pizza were partners in the third deal, they had to be partners in the fourth as well. It was here when, according to Detective Kennedy, Doctor B. left for the hospital and I had left the game also. Of course, I had left earlier and Detective Kennedy simply had me confused with Stanley. This is when Otto and Gussie filled in, Gussie making the remarkable play of trumping her partner's ace. Did Gussie really do that?

I decided to double-check the players' positions by the dealer's position. The dealer on deal three was Stanley. It then would have passed to his left, to Frankenstein. Yes, that made sense, and it left Frankenstein as South on the slam deal, with Pizza North. It also confirmed the mad Hungarian's position as West and Gussie's as East.

"Young man, do you mind?!" The fat lady pulled her newspaper to her chest.

I turned back to the window. We were passing the port of Elizabeth. I could see the lights on the tails of the Esso tigers strewn across the huge oil tanks. I remembered them from the train ride with Stanley—when he had bragged to me about his partscore triumph, lying to me about the spade shift . . . wait a second . . . in my pocket, the hand on the schedule. I stood up slightly to pull it out of my pants, and I jarred the fat lady's pencil. She gave me a big huff. There, finally I got it. Let's see:

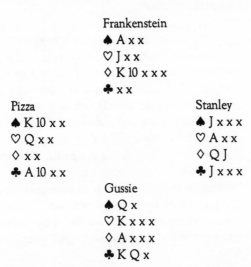

Frankenstein
♠ A x x
♡ J x x
◊ K 10 x x x
♣ x x

Pizza
♠ K 10 x x
♡ Q x x
◊ x x
♣ A 10 x x

Stanley
♠ J x x x
♡ A x x
◊ Q J
♣ J x x x

Gussie
♠ Q x
♡ K x x x
◊ A x x x
♣ K Q x

Hmm. Stanley had lied to me about the players as well as the layout. But he definitely was East . . . hmm . . . *something's*

229

missing—a ten, the ten of hearts. I remembered now: Every ten was recorded except for the heart ten. Was there any significance to the missing card?

My eyes darted back to the fat lady's newspaper. Hmm. The heart ten was certainly an important card in that deal. I thought back to my interview with Detective Kennedy. I didn't remember the ten of hearts being a singleton when *he* showed me the slam. Of course I was nervous then; I may not have seen it. No, surely I would have recalled a glaring singleton like a ten. . . . I glanced back at the partscore. Could there be any reason to play the ten of hearts at trick one *instead of the ace?*

Suddenly I could hear my own heart beat. I was excited; I had discovered a new play—I was sure it was the solution to Kaplan's question. It wasn't just an "x" that was led, but the *deuce.* After the lead of the deuce of hearts, East knows that declarer has at least three of them because partner can have no more than four. Therefore, instead of going up with the ace at trick one, when you have no idea what to do next, you insert the ten and give yourself time to learn more about the deal. As long as declarer holds at least three cards in the suit, you can hardly lose. If he holds the queen, the defense will still take the ace and king; if he holds the king, the defense will still take the ace and queen. I turned eagerly to Kaplan's solution:

Solution to Part-Score Tragedy

East should play the ten of hearts *at trick one*. This temporizing, or convenient, play gives East time to analyze more clues before making a shift. On the actual deal, declarer will win the king. If he now draws trumps and plays clubs, East eventually will realize the necessity of a spade shift. Therefore, declarer's best play at trick two is to return a heart, keeping East in the dark. However, West can relieve East of any further worries. West rises with the heart queen and exits. There is no more possibility of an endplay, and by the time East wins the ace of hearts, it does not matter what suit he returns: in due course, West will make his ace of clubs and king of spades for down one.

I let out a sigh of content. I had solved the hand. The fact that it took me two months to come up with the solution didn't enter my head. Suddenly I felt strong again, like that young lion back at the Edison drugstore. On to the mysteries of life, I thought.

Why had Stanley lied about the partscore deal? Obviously, he had an ego problem. Surely, he had never considered the ten-of-hearts play and that's why he subconsciously left out the card when he showed me the hand.

Why had he lied about the players? He had put Gussie in Frankenstein's chair as declarer. There didn't seem to be any reason for that. He had Pizza as his partner instead of Dr. B. That made no sense either. According to Gussie's evidence to Kennedy, which was now confirmed by Kaplan's article, Pizza was dummy on the hand. Wait a second! Now I remembered. The detective told me that at first Pizza also said he was in the West chair—that he was my partner. Then, after Gussie gave her evidence, Pizza changed his evidence, claiming he couldn't remember an insignificant partscore. Pizza had lied about his position, and Stanley had lied about Pizza's position also. But why? Were they in league?

Think back. What did Stanley say on the train? He had played the partscore deal, then left the club. Yet he knew about the girl's fall. How could he have known about her fall, while nobody else knew? For if anyone else knew, he wouldn't have continued to play the fourth deal, especially not Frankenstein, the girl's father.

Let's assume that the lights went out during the partscore deal. If it happened later, Stanley would not have left the game. Perhaps it happened between the bidding and the opening lead. How would the players have reacted? Obviously they didn't hear the girl fall out the window or they'd have stopped the game. She was in the back room; they were in the front. Okay, what did they do? In the newspaper column, a flashlight is mentioned. Hmm. Otto got his flashlight. The game continued. But how did Stanley know about the fall?

Only two answers to that question: Either he saw her fall out the window or someone told him about it. Wait. One more possibility—he passed her on the street when he left the club. Hmm. That would be quite a coincidence, but then surely he would have stopped to call the police, rather than hop into a cab and leave her lying there. No, either he saw her fall out or someone told him about it.

Now, he couldn't have seen her fall out if he was playing bridge, so let's eliminate that possibility. Unless he were dummy—only dummy can get up from the table in the middle of a hand. *Who was dummy?* Pizza was dummy! Yes, that's why he had testified he was in the West seat! And later, he tried to excuse himself by saying he couldn't remember the partscore deal. And he had Stanley to back up his story!

I was on track now—I was sure of it. Pizza was dummy, he got up from the table, perhaps to go to the bathroom, then passed through the back room, and spotted the little girl by the window. What was she doing? Copying out of his precious diary. He lunged at her. Perhaps the thunder and lightning came at that point, drowning out the scene. Maybe she threw the notebook out the window rather than give it back. Pizza, in a fit of rage, threw *her* out of the window! Then the lights went out. Pizza realized he had to do something because his incriminating notebook was with the girl's body. What now?

The partscore deal was still being played in the front room with the help of Otto's flashlight. Stanley . . . Stanley finished the deal and got up to leave. No, that made no sense. Why would he leave before the completed chukker? Unless . . . somehow Pizza had gotten Stanley aside and told him what had happened. But how could he do that without raising suspicion?

Wait, wait. I think I got it. The deal was over. Pizza was still in the back room. Somebody from the game was sent to get him. That's it. *Stanley* was sent. Maybe Stanley even came in at the crucial moment! Maybe he saw everything! Maybe he took the opportunity to blackmail Pizza! Yes! Yes! Yes! He forced Pizza to give him some money immediately. Those Franklin notes on the train! I remembered now when he opened his wallet! The missing five hundred from the cashbox! Of course. Pizza had given Roth the money earlier in the evening to cover Gussie's account, and now when he needed it, he somehow stole the money in the dark and gave it to Stanley.

Then, in return, Stanley covered up for the man. He went downstairs, found the black notebook *and* the piece of paper that little Cathy copied on. But he made a mistake. The paper had torn, and one small piece still remained in the bushes—the corner that Detective Kennedy came across later.

Suddenly I remembered something else. On the train, when I went to get coffee, Stanley *gave me that crumpled paper and told me to throw it out.* But in my horrible journey with the coffee, I had forgotten. That's why I possessed the missing piece!

I double-checked my rear pocket. There it still was next to the detective's photocopy of the missing corner. I folded it again and switched it to my jacket pocket, which had a zipper. *This* was the evidence that would send Pizza to the electric chair! And maybe Stanley, too . . . Stanley too. . . .

When the train stopped in Newark, most of the passengers got off. However, the fat lady remained, and I didn't feel like climbing over her again. So I remained in my seat up against the window. There, I gazed at the stars that were beginning to appear in the December sky. No, they weren't stars, they were airplane lights. Suddenly I saw drops of water on my window pane. Soon the train was rolling through the Jersey marshlands toward the Hudson River. I was confident I had most of the facts in order. But I was bothered by one question: If the little girl had died two weeks ago, why wasn't the inquiry called then?

"Cough, cough. Oh, my." The fat lady put down her newspaper and began to make strange sounds. "Ugh, ugh. Ahem. Cough. Oh my."

I tried not to notice. Then she addressed me.

"Young man. Ugh. Oh my. Young man, will you please get me some water? It's my, ahem, I need some water, please."

We were only a few minutes from New York. Couldn't she wait? I got up and stepped over her, bouncing against various flabby things, until I fell into the aisle. "Do you know where the water is?" I asked.

She raised her finger and pointed forward. "Down by the coffee concession. Hurry."

22

WATER ON A TRAIN—STOLEN PANTS IN THE
MEN'S ROOM—OLD LEROY TAKES ME
FOR A RIDE—A NEW SET OF THREADS.

T HE LAST place I wanted to go was the coffee concession. But
when the fat lady makes weird sounds, you don't worry about
things like getting stuck between train doors. So I weaved and
stumbled my way to the rear of the car and slid open the first
door. Aiiiii. Outside. New Jersey chemicals flying in my face. I
slid open the next door. No problem. I was safely inside again.

Pushing my way forward, traveling became difficult when
some of the passengers got up to get their belongings from the
racks above. We hadn't reached the tunnel yet, so I didn't know
what their hurry was. At the rear of the car, I braced myself and
opened the door. Aiiiii. Outside. Marshland dust. I tripped over
the iron connection to the two rail-cars, but landed against the
red emergency stop. Luckily I didn't pull it when my elbow
hooked around it. Next door. Good, it opened nicely and when it
closed I was face to face with a little man smoking a cigar.

I pushed around him and he squawked. There at the end of
the car was the concession stand! Thank goodness it wasn't any
farther up the line. When I arrived, I ordered a cup of water, but
the porter shut the window and stuck out a "closed" sign. "Hey," I
said. "I got a sick fat lady next to me; fill my order, please." The
porter muttered something and opened the window. Then he
shoved out a huge pitcher of water. I took it off the counter and
almost dropped it—it weighed so much. "Don't you have any
cups?" I called into the window. But the window was shut again
and the "closed" sign was out. Suddenly I heard thunder. *Oh god,*
not a storm!

I headed back through the car, this time traveling backward
against the forward-speeding train going the other way. Trying to
stem the tide, I found myself moving too fast with the heavy
pitcher in my arms and I was heading straight for the little guy
with the big cigar. What the hell was he doing standing by the
door, anyway?! He turned—it must have been instinct—and saw
me coming. Quickly, he opened up the door for me and I heard it

slide back as I passed through. Aiiiii. Outside. Icy water in the face. I hung onto the pitcher and reached for the door handle. It clicked. I tried it again, and it opened. *Whew. Into the dry car.*

The water was spilling a little on the floor. There were three coeds up ahead who were laughing. Onward, water on my pants, water on the seats, water on a tall guy with dark glasses who cursed me as I bounced by. Finally the last door. A red-haired kid with black freckles opened it for me. I loved him. I loved kids. Then he shut the door behind me and stared through the window, his nose pressed up like a squashed tomato.

Aiiii! Outside. Ice. Slipping. I try to save the pitcher, but it's me or the pitcher. Aaaaaagh. It hits a wall. Blackness and screeching noise as the train passes into the tunnel. Nightmare, living nightmare, as sparks fly and lights flash in the horrible blackness. I curse Franklin and his electricity. I curse Edison and his lightbulbs. But most of all, I curse the fat lady and her water.

Somehow I find a dry place to grip. Lying flat against my stomach on the one-foot-length of train ledge, I try to tuck my right leg in from the width of the car. I don't bother screaming. What good is it? Eeeeeeh. Dust flying. I cover my eyes. Then I just lie there, hoping that one day the train will come out of this tunnel.

We slowed as we reached the station and I lifted myself up and opened the door. Squeezing through the passengers who were ready to exit, I reached the fat lady. She was drinking out of a thermos. When she looked up at me, she closed the thermos and tucked it into a duffel bag under her legs. *If only I had a gun. . . .*

It was a quarter to six on the huge clock in the middle of the station. There weren't as many commuters as my last excursion and I headed straight for the escalators. Somebody snickered as I walked by, so I looked down at myself and saw that my left pants leg was ripped from the ankle down. But it wasn't that. When I passed the Orange Julius stand, I saw my face in the counter's reflection. Soot, ice, rain, dirt, chemicals. I spotted the men's room and wondered if I should risk it. Then I saw Otto!

I caught up with him as he entered the restroom. He gave me a big hello and said, "It's a clazy theeng, but you don't look so hot." I tried to explain briefly how I had gotten a little messy riding between train cars, and he was kind enough to understand. "That's why you get a seat," he advised.

Otto told me he was on his way to Jersey City to feed his sister's cats. I didn't really pay much attention to the rest of his story; I was just glad he was there while I washed up. Unfortunately, however, he had to catch the next train and I still had to make a pit stop. There were a couple of young fellows hanging around the sink area who looked like they had knives up their sleeves, so instead of the urinal, I went into one of the cubicles and locked the door. I opened up my *Bridge World*—a reflex, I think—and sat down. After 10 seconds, I heard a voice.

"You black or white?"

I got up and tucked the magazine back into my Poe. There were a lot of cubicles in the Pennsylvania Station men's room. Maybe the question wasn't for me. So I sat down again.

"Hey, you deaf? We asked you a question."

I made up my mind quickly and decided to scream. "HELP!!!!!!!"

A few seconds passed. It seemed longer. Then I heard the voice again.

"Ain't nobody here but us and the cleaning lady, and she don't hear a thing."

"What do you want?" I asked.

"We want to know if you're black or white."

"Will my answer have any bearing on the situation?"

"If you lie, you die. If you're white, you fight."

"Well, to begin with, I'm not a liar."

"Take off your pants and let's see your legs."

I took them off. But instead of sneaking a peek, someone grabbed the pants and ran off. They ran off with my 50 dollars. They ran off with my train schedule. And worse, they ran off with the evidence against Pizza McCarver and Stanley Kesselman.

I was despondent, to say the least. After about 10 minutes, I opened the door to the cubicle. Maybe they had dropped some of the evidence on the bathroom floor. The place was business as usual, commuters at the urinals and the sinks. I started combing the floor, then I looked through the trash bag. Nothing. I started to walk to the exit and realized I had no pants on. Back at the mirror I considered my situation. No pants, no money, no evidence, no nothing—except my Poe and my *Bridge World*. What was I going to do?

Then I remembered! I had switched the evidence to my jacket pocket. Yes, it was still there. Things were not all bad. I looked around me, suddenly embarrassed. But strangely enough no one seemed to give a damn whether I had pants or not. I wondered if I could actually go into the station without pants when an elderly but spritely man, with a Yankee baseball cap and red-rimmed sunglasses, asked me if I needed some help.

The rain was coming down heavily. I watched it from the back of his cab. At least he called it a cab. There was a broken down meter in front, but the old white Studebaker had no cab sign on top of the car and no license in the front paneling. I was still wrapped in the tar-stained towel he had brought from the car when he asked me if I were a Yankee fan or Met fan. I had no problem with that one—unless he were a Met fan wearing a Yankee cap. He smiled at me and started the cab. "So, man, you going to 57th Street and Seventh Avenue. That's what you said, all right?"

"That's right. I don't know how to thank you . . . ."

"That's okay, sonny. You don't have to thank Old Leroy. I knew what happened to you minute I seen you. Besides, I got a niece works up that way, so I don't mind stopping."

What a nice man, I thought. I wondered when he was going to start driving. We'd been sitting there for five minutes. After another minute, there was a tap on the window. Old Leroy opened the door. Suddenly my door was opened and about six or seven people pushed into the Studebaker, two or three in the front, and four in the back, one on my lap and one laid out at my feet across the floor. "The *two* horse," he said. "The two horse, my eye, you ask Stella," said another. "Hey Stella, which mother you have, the two or the four?" asked the first guy. A whispery voice from the front said, "Move it." There was a screech of tires, and Old Leroy made like a front-runner in the Indianapolis 500.

Under other circumstances, I would have admired his show-manship, weaving in and out of lanes, coming within inches of other cars, driving through yellow lights only split-seconds before they turned red. However, I was too concerned with my company in the back seat to observe Leroy's prowess with a kibitzer's keen eye. It wasn't that they weren't nice guys—they joked a good deal and had a lot of interesting insights into why the favorite lost the seventh race at Belmont; no, it was more the black things that they were emptying from their revolvers that had my attention.

In the meantime, I sat there quietly, trying to remain inconspicuous. The man on top of me was rather thin and light, so I had no major physical complaints. However, when the guy on the floor asked, "Who got the white ankles?" the other two in the seat to my right gave me the once over.

"Hey, Leroy," said the man in the middle, with the mustache. "This guy new?"

"No, no, ha, ha," said Leroy, swerving the cab to the left, almost hitting a woman crossing the street. "He just got caught with his pants down, ha, ha. In the men's room!"

Suddenly everyone was laughing, and I had to chuckle a bit too. But one of the guys in front, a mean looker, told us all to shut up. "I lost count," he said. From my angle, it seemed like he was counting green bills with Franklin's picture on them, dividing up piles and passing them to another guy in the front. Only he wasn't a guy, he was a girl with a man's hat on. And he, I mean *she*, was eyeing me in the rear-view mirror.

"Where you going?" said the guy next to me, still chuckling.

"Fifty-seventh street," I answered, smiling nicely.

Suddenly there was another roar of laughter. "We already passed there 50 blocks ago! Ha, ha."

"Maybe we can fix him up with Queen Louie," suggested the guy on the floor. There was tremendous laughter now. God, they were having a grand time. Personally, I was not happy to hear we had long passed 57th Street, and even less happy about the notion that I should be fixed up with anyone called Queen Louie. Suddenly, I felt in more trouble than I had realized. But when the girl in the rear-view mirror took off her hat and let her long red locks fall over her ears, then turned around to look at me, I felt safer. She was the one they called Stella. Her smile was warm, her wide eyes captivating. I gave her my most charming grin to gain her confidence.

"*Kill* the dummy," she said. Then she took out a compact and powdered her nose.

Old Leroy must have been going at least 60 miles an hour. I wondered why no police car bothered to pull him aside. The money was finally counted out and I saw bunches of it passed to the other fellows in the back seat. I was given a bunch myself but

"*Kill* the dummy," she said.

told to pass it down to the guy on the floor. "We're here," someone said.

The cab stopped and the doors opened. Everyone stormed out of the car and seemed to go his separate way. I stood next to the open car door and looked around. The rain had let up, and I noticed a sign at the corner—128th Street. Then I saw a subway entrance across the street. Could I make a run for it? Could I bear another train ride? There was nobody around except for Old Leroy and Stella. She was talking to him in a businesslike fashion. I didn't like the way he was shaking his head back and forth—but the real scary thing was that his smile had disappeared. She gave him a bundle of loot and rushed through an old boarded-up entrance way to a deserted-looking brownstone.

Meanwhile I had lost my chance. Old Leroy took my arm and invited me back into the car, this time the front seat. When he got in, he saw the back door of the car was still open. So he got out and slammed the door shut. I noticed the key in the ignition and took a chance. Before Old Leroy could get back in, I was behind the wheel.

After about seven or eight blocks, I realized I was heading uptown instead of downtown. I turned at the next corner and found myself going the wrong way on a one-way block. I managed to get to the end of it without incident and turned back downtown. When I had gone about a mile, I remembered I had never driven a car before.

For some reason my failure to keep a straight path as I headed down the streets of New York didn't give anyone pause to notice. This was the way all the people drove on Broadway. Unlike Leroy, however, I seemed to hit all the red lights. At one point I stopped near a parked police car. The cops were drinking coffee and stared at me. Looking down at the towel around my waist, I decided not to ask for help. It was a good thing too, because when I pulled over for a breather at the corner of 96th Street, I noticed the gun and the wad of Franklin notes on the front seat.

I took the gun and hid it inside my shirt. Then I retrieved my Poe from the back-seat and stuffed the money into a story called "The Gold Bug." There were Old Leroy's sunglasses, too. I put them on, shut off the car, put the key in my jacket and closed the door. Then I started to walk briskly down the street.

At 96th and Broadway I spotted Fortunato's, a men's store,

and walked in. There I purchased a fresh pair of socks, a pair of brown patent-leather Italian shoes, a white silk shirt, a navy blue cashmere suit, and a black wallet. When no one was looking, I transfered the gun to the jacket; then I dabbed on some French cologne as well. Mr. Fortunato accepted my Franklin notes with much graciousness and even helped comb my hair. Suddenly I remembered the drizzle outside, and tried on a new coat as well.

I told him to burn my old clothes, and he told me he'd save them for the "Sal-a-vation Army." Then he gave me a big "Gracias, Senor," and I walked to the next corner where I hailed a yellow cab and gave the driver the address of the Mayfair Club. This time I was arriving in style.

23

JUST DESSERTS—RECURRING HANDS—
THE PLAYERS BEHIND THE CARDS—
SOME BAD FRANKLINS—A QUICK EXIT.

I WALKED up to Mr. Roth's desk and saw Stanley sitting in Roth's seat, working on the accounts. So there was no need for Detective Kennedy to call Stanley to the inquiry tomorrow night. He was staked out right here, in his habitat. Out came my new wallet, and four crisp Franklins hit the table. Stanley looked at them and stopped in his tracks. "Put 'em in my account, kid," I said.

"Yes sir," he answered. "Oh, wait a second. Which is your account, mister?" Then he took a closer look at me behind the sunglasses. "What the hell—?"

I strutted away from the desk and took a deep breath of musty air into my lungs. Gosh, the club smelled good; I had forgotten *how* good. I left my overcoat and Poe in the TV room and headed into the back. Everyone was finishing his supper—all the old crowd were there. Hi Gussie; she was sitting with Mr. Roth. Hi, Doctor B; uh, oh, there was Pizza next to him, pontificating on some obscure bridge theory, no doubt. Hi Maggie—long time no see; she was serving dessert to Frankenstein. Next to him was Chops.

Good God, I'd forgotten how gorgeous she was! I could see the pupils of her dark grey eyes standing two tables away. They were big and slanted and luminous like a cat's. She saw me now, but had to look twice to make sure who I was. I wondered if we could start up where we left off. Then I remembered I had jilted her, and she might not be such a friendly kitten after all. Someone was missing. Of course, Cathy, Frankenstein's little girl. I felt a pang of remorse and wondered how the man could sit there and eat his ice cream sundae so close to where the accident—I mean the murder—took place.

Suddenly I felt an arm around my shoulder. Stanley was breathing his nasty breath down my fresh silk collar. "Hey, man, you're looking pretty neat. What's the good word from the Quad?"

I wanted to tell him what the good word was: pregnancy. But Esther had asked me to keep my trap shut, so I just brushed his arm off and gave it to him right above the belt. "You're in big trouble, Stanley. I've had it with your crap. When we meet with the detective tomorrow night, I'm telling the whole truth."

"Hey, of course you are," said Stanley. "We all are."

I didn't like the way he said that. But I was too busy eyeing Chops to get further concerned. I walked over and sat down at her table. I had to break the ice sometime.

"Hi," I said. "You don't hold any grudges, do you?"

Chops looked at me and turned back to Frankenstein again. She must really be angry with me, I thought. They were discussing a bridge hand. From what I could gather, the opener had a nice six-four hand, something like:

$$\spadesuit \text{x x} \quad \heartsuit \text{A K J x x x} \quad \diamondsuit \text{A K J x} \quad \clubsuit \text{x}$$

The opening bid was one heart and the opener's partner had responded one spade. Now it was a question of rebids.

Maggie came over to pour some coffee and asked if I'd like some. "You know," she said, "I got an uncle in the Bronx who's got a pair of sunglasses just like those." I quickly took off the sunglasses and put them in my jacket pocket. Was it possible this town was too small for me? I wanted to ask if her uncle's name was Leroy and if he drove a white Studebaker, but I didn't have the guts. "Would you like some pie?" she asked.

"Yes, ma'm," I said.

"Say, I know you," she said. "You're that lost little kid who was here the night. . . " She eyed Frankenstein and stopped in mid-sentence. "I'll get your ice cream."

"No, no, no," said Frankenstein. "if you jump to three diamonds, you're gonna give partner a migraine."

"But take a hand like this," said Chops. She wrote on the tablecloth:

$$\spadesuit \text{K x x x} \ \heartsuit \text{x x} \ \diamondsuit \text{Q x x} \ \clubsuit \text{Q x x x}$$

"You can't expect partner to keep the bidding open. And game is on one of two finesses."

There was an urgency to her voice, as if reaching game on these two hands were the most important thing on earth. I had forgotten about that voice, and how it fluctuated up and down between bass and falsetto tones.

"You're wrong," said Frankenstein. "That hand *should* keep the bidding open. There are a lot of hands that produce game, so you take a false preference to two hearts just in case."

"All right," said Chops, "then take away the queen of clubs; now you'd pass two diamonds."

"Take away the queen of diamonds. Now you make nothing, and if you jump shift you could end up in four-hearts doubled."

"Excuse me," I said. "But how about a hand with a singleton heart honor like this one." And I wrote down a similar hand to the one I held the last time I saw Chops, in her apartment on the night of the blackout:

$$\spadesuit \text{J x x x x} \ \heartsuit \text{Q} \ \diamondsuit \text{Q x x} \ \clubsuit \text{x x x x}$$

"*Now* I know who you are," said Chops, "Stanley's friend."

Stanley's friend. Very nice, I thought, so she hadn't said hello because she didn't even remember me! And when she did, I was nothing to her but "Stanley's friend."

Frankenstein looked at my example hand and shook his head. "You're a baboon. If you want to find hands that make miracle games, you can always come up with some. But the idea of bidding is to reach the right game on 99% of the likely hands. Besides, somebody may balance."

243

My ice cream arrived, and I was pleased to find a slice of blueberry pie underneath. Of course, when Chops and I had bid those hands in the serenity of her living room, we never considered our opponents. We had no opponents. I took a big forkful. It was true, the opponents held almost half the high-card points. If they balanced, the opener could rebid his hearts and responder could re-evaluate for game.

"You're here a day early," said Chops.

I nodded nonchalantly. "I figured I'd get in some tough rubber bridge while I was in town," I said. So she was coming to the inquiry too! I guess everyone was a suspect. "How's the baby?" I asked, then kicked myself for asking right in front of Frankenstein. I looked at him. He didn't seem to flinch behind those thick-lensed glasses.

"Oh, Bobby's fine. We have a TV now, and he loves it."

"I hope I'll get to see him while I'm here," I said, meaning I hope I'll get to see her.

"That depends on Pizza," she said.

I finished my pie. What the heck did she mean by that? I looked over at Pizza. Stanley was talking to him, rather confidentially. Was he telling him what I said about my intentions to reveal the truth? Well, too bad. I could handle him if it's trouble he's after. I patted my inside jacket pocket just to make sure. Yes, Old Leroy's revolver was still there.

The game had increased to 10-cents-a-point, five times what I had played for the last time I was here. That was okay by me. I still had 15 Franklins in my pocket, enough to last me quite a while. The players were Frankenstein, Pizza, Doctor B., Chops and me. Chops had somehow acquired money and had moved up to the high-stake game. Stanley was now working for the club as a house-man, and could only play if the game needed a fourth. The stake was too high for Gussie, so she kibitzed.

We cut for the wheel. Doctor B. was high and I was second. Third was Pizza, fourth Chops, and low man was Frankenstein. I gave Doctor B. a big nod and asked if he remembered me from outside the Rutgers Bookstore, but all he returned was, "Stayman and Blackwood." Pizza, on the other hand, was quite friendly and offered me his hand to shake. I simply kept my hands in my pockets and nodded. I didn't feel like getting grease on my clean cuffs.

Just as I picked up my first hand, I noticed the building's janitor, Otto. He was being scolded by Maggie for missing supper. Apparently she had prepared his favorite dish, chicken paprikash with noodles. I was sorry now that I, too, had missed the main course. Otto asked why she wouldn't save him a portion, and she claimed she did, but somebody ate it.

"Hey, it's your bid," said Pizza. "What are you dreaming about, sex or food? Ha, ha."

♠ 8 7 6 5   ♡ Q 7 3 2   ◊ 3 2   ♣ K 4 3

Doctor B. had dealt and opened one notrump. Pizza had passed. So did I. Chops passed and Doctor B. went down two tricks. I think he could have made it, but before he played to trick one he declared 150 honors. It was a good idea so he wouldn't forget later, but I believe the knowledge that he held all four aces enabled Pizza and Chops to pick him clean on defense.

Behind me I heard Otto whispering to Gussie. "It's a clazy theeng, Guss, but I think if he bids Stayman, he gets to two hearts and makes it."

"Shut up and eat your cookies," said Frankenstein, who was kibitzing on my right. "Here, give me one."

A small roll of crust and raisins passed by my right elbow. Hmm. Should I have bid Stayman? I asked Frankenstein.

"Yeah, and over two diamonds, you could go back to one notrump," he said, sarcastically.

♠ A 8 3 2   ♡ 10 8 6 4 3 2   ◊ —   ♣ A 10 8

Pizza passed and I passed. Chops opened one spade in third seat and Doctor B. overcalled two clubs. Pizza passed again and I had a problem. My hand was too good for only two hearts or three clubs, but a cue bid would not solve my problem, and with Doctor B. cue bids were generally not the wisest of actions. So I bid only two hearts and took a chance it would not be passed out. Over this, Chops bid two spades and Doctor B. bid three clubs. Pizza now came alive with three spades, and suddenly I recognized a "Theory of Exhaustion" situation. I quickly reviewed the auction in my mind:

Pizza	Me	Chops	Doctor B.
pass	pass	1 ♠	2 ♣
pass	2 ♡	2 ♠	3 ♣
3 ♠	?		

I was certain we could make a game, maybe a slam—even with Doctor B. at the helm. The bidding told me that Doctor B. couldn't hold more than one spade or one or two hearts, and he had to have at least a six-card club suit, if not seven. Now it was a question of buying the contract. The rule said, if I wanted to play five clubs I should bid only four and allow them to push me to five. Hmm. Then again, what was I afraid of? If I jumped to five clubs and pushed them to five spades, I could double and collect a nice penalty. After all, they were vulnerable and we were not.

Back to plan one. I jumped to five clubs. Chops took the bait and bid five spades. I doubled, and Doctor B. led the king of clubs.

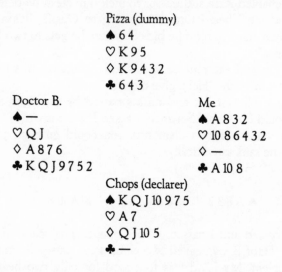

```
                        Pizza (dummy)
                        ♠ 6 4
                        ♡ K 9 5
                        ◇ K 9 4 3 2
                        ♣ 6 4 3
Doctor B.                                   Me
♠ —                                         ♠ A 8 3 2
♡ Q J                                       ♡ 10 8 6 4 3 2
◇ A 8 7 6                                    ◇ —
♣ K Q J 9 7 5 2                             ♣ A 10 8
                        Chops (declarer)
                        ♠ K Q J 10 9 7 5
                        ♡ A 7
                        ◇ Q J 10 5
                        ♣ —
```

Making five. I was furious with myself. Here I had worked out the theory's application in my head, figured what bid I should make, and then failed to execute the plan. What was wrong with me? I wasn't nervous. I wasn't short on capital. I wasn't tired from playing too many deals. Then what was my problem, psychological?

Doctor B. was called to the phone. When he returned, he told us he had to go to the hospital. There was a question of finishing the rubber. Mr. Roth was called, but was away from the desk. Stanley suggested that Frankenstein fill in for the last two deals, but Pizza was adamant—it wasn't fair; Frankenstein was too good a player to fill in for Doctor B. What about Gussie? Gussie refused—she was still reading her evening paper, so finally we compromised on Otto.

Maggie brought him some more tea and cookies—I think they were Hungarian cookies called "rugaluch"—and I dealt the cards to the third deal.

♠ 6 4 ♡ Q J 8 4 3 ◇ A K 9 8 ♣ 7 2

I don't know what made me do it, but I opened the bidding with one heart. I did have two quick tricks, but the hand was still too short of highcards. Not only that, but playing with the weakest and craziest player in the game was not the time to start opening light hands. Pizza, on my left, passed, gazing at the ceiling. And Otto was studying his cards with relish. It reminded me of what Poe had written on how the players' countenances give away their cards. Otto obviously held a nice hand, and I could feel we were about to get into some wild auction, two or three tricks too high. Suddenly—I believe by accident—my deuce of clubs fell face up on the table. If I had done it on purpose, it was surely a subconcious action. In either event, I jumped at the chance and threw in the rest of my cards.

"Sorry," I said. "Let's redeal."

Everyone threw in his hand except Otto, who looked up at me and shook his head. "I don't theenk you should have done that," he said. Then he tabled his cards:

♠ A K Q J 7 5 2 ♡ — ◇ 5 3 ♣ A K Q J

I apologized profusely. What could I say? Then I thought of one way to make it up to him. I took out my wallet and passed a Franklin across the table. I'm not sure if I did it for Otto or for the effect it would make on the others, but it caused some excitement. Otto resisted for a moment, then gave in and took the bill. Pizza eyed me with new respect. Gussie looked up from behind her newspaper. Even Maggie spotted the gesture from across the room and came over to look. Only Chops failed to show any

247

acknowledgment. Good old Chops was all business, studying her cards for the next deal. It turned out to be a slam in diamonds, bid and made against us. And when I glanced at the scorepad, I noticed we were down quite a lot.

WE	THEY
	500
150 x	100
	850
	420

♠ A 7 6 4 3 ♡ K 10 4 3 2 ◇ 2 ♣ Q 2

Pizza passed, my partner passed, and Chops opened one notrump. If I were playing Landy I could bid two clubs for the majors. Then it came to me that Otto and I had had this problem once before, that he bid *Landy* and I thought he was bidding *natural*. So, this time, confident we were on the same wavelength, I bid two clubs. Pizza, on my left, jumped to three notrump and Otto started to think. Finally, he came out of his trance with four clubs, which Chops doubled.

My head was starting to throb. Did Otto think I had clubs? Why had he hesitated over three notrump? Obviously he was also thinking back to the time I had misinterpreted *his* Landy call. Maybe he was catering to me, just as I had catered to him. If he thought I had clubs, his four-club bid was natural, and we had better escape into a major. What were my options? I could bid four hearts and he would get the message, but would he really correct with three spades and two hearts? He might think I had a six-card heart suit, for if I had equal length why wouldn't I simply redouble four clubs? Redouble had to be S.O.S. Suddenly I realized everyone was staring at me. I had been thinking much too long. If I now redoubled it would be totally unfair, since my pause had given away my thoughts. That's when I got the bright idea to bid four diamonds. Then, after getting doubled, I could redouble

248

that—in tempo—and force Otto to pick a major.

Four diamonds, I said. Pass, said Pizza, a glint in his eye. Pass, said Otto, happy I had clarified the auction. Pass said Chops, serious as ever. Pizza led his fourth-best diamond. This was the full deal:

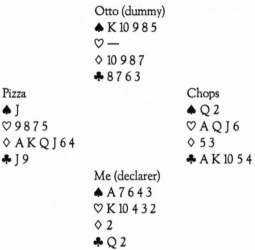

Otto (dummy)
♠ K 10 9 8 5
♡ —
◊ 10 9 8 7
♣ 8 7 6 3

Pizza
♠ J
♡ 9 8 7 5
◊ A K Q J 6 4
♣ J 9

Chops
♠ Q 2
♡ A Q J 6
◊ 5 3
♣ A K 10 5 4

Me (declarer)
♠ A 7 6 4 3
♡ K 10 4 3 2
◊ 2
♣ Q 2

The defense was merciless. After four rounds of trumps, Pizza switched to a club. Chops cashed three clubs, as Pizza discarded his singleton spade. Next, Chops led a fourth club, which Pizza ruffed. A heart to Chops' ace, a fifth club, and finally the queen of hearts to my king. That was the only trick I took—down nine, minus 900 points, or, at ten cents a point, $90. I took out another Franklin and told Otto to keep the change. Then I realized there was no change. Another hundred points went to their side when Chops reminded us that Pizza held honors.

She opened the big white scorepad, jotted in all our names and put "- 27" next to mine. No problem, I thought, as I checked to make sure my wallet was still intact.

We all got up to change partners. Otto was out of the game, and Frankenstein was in. There were only the four of us now. We cut for partners, with the proviso Pizza could not repeat with Chops. I cut Chops and high card was Frankenstein's. Since Roth hadn't returned, we agreed on dealer's side not vulnerable vs. vulnerable on the second and third deals. I noticed Otto in the corner, looking at his Franklin bills. Maybe it was stupid of me to give him the money, I thought.

♠ 87 ♡ — ◊ A 9 8 6 4 ♣ K J 9 8 7 6

Two clubs on my left by Frankenstein. Pass by Chops. Two hearts on my right by Pizza. I tried three clubs; I had to do something. Suddenly I heard four clubs on my left, four hearts on my right, six notrump on my left. Chops led the three of clubs. This was the deal.

```
                      Pizza (dummy)
                      ♠ 10
                      ♡ A 8 7 4 3 2
                      ◊ Q 10 7 5
                      ♣ 5 4
    Chops                               Me
    ♠ 9 6 5 4 3 2                       ♠ 8 7
    ♡ K 10 9                            ♡ —
    ◊ 3 2                               ◊ A 9 8 6 4
    ♣ 3 2                               ♣ K J 9 8 7 6
                      Frankenstein
                      ♠ A K Q J
                      ♡ Q J 6 5
                      ◊ K J
                      ♣ A Q 10
```

Frankenstein won the trick and led the king of diamonds. I ducked and ducked the next round of diamonds as well. Had I won either trick, Frankenstein would have four spades, two hearts, three diamonds, and three clubs for a total of 12 tricks. However, now Frankenstein, after finessing in hearts, was forced to give up a third heart trick to Chops, and hope she had no more diamonds to return. She had no more.

Chops gave me a very mean look and shook her head in frustration. Had I not bid three clubs, we probably would have defended a slam in *hearts* instead of notrump; six hearts would have been down one. I had not only tipped off the location of both club honors, but had warned Frankenstein of bad distribution as well.

♠ A 8 7 6 ♡ — ◊ A 10 8 7 ♣ A 9 7 5 4

Nice hand, that is until Chops opened with three hearts. Pizza passed and I was about to make a pass, in tempo, when I recalled a very similar hand. I think my partner on that occasion had been Pizza, and he, too, had opened a vulnerable vs. non-vulnerable three-bid. I was glad I checked myself. At unfavorable vulnerability, a three-bid shows around seven tricks. I had the other three and dutifully raised to four hearts. This was passed around to Pizza, who dutifully doubled. It was a loud double, a nasty double, a vengeful double, and when I tabled my dummy, Chops lost her composure.

"Give me a break!" she said.

"But-but-but we're vulnerable versus not. Surely you have a good sui—"

"We're not vulnerable versus vulnerable!" cried Chops.

"The Little Baboon forgot we switched vulnerabilities," said Frankenstein.

I won't give you the gory details, but Chops' hand was basically queen-ten-seventh of hearts and out. Down three meant another 500 in the minus column. Chops was furious and when Stanley came in to tell her there was a phone call for her, I was glad. I couldn't face her any more. As she left the room, she suggested that Gussie pick up the next hand for her. Ordinarily I would have objected, Gussie not being close to the caliber of Chops. But in this case, I kept my mouth shut.

♠ A 7 4 ♡ A K J 10 4 ◊ J 2 ♣ 6 5 3

Another good hand, that is until Pizza opened the bidding with one heart on my right. Oh well, I passed. Frankenstein raised to two hearts. That was interesting. Gussie passed and Pizza said four hearts! I was about to double, and it would have been a mean double, a nasty double, a vengeful double, when I realized I had been in this position before—a bird in hand, and all that sort of stuff. The last time I had doubled a similar auction and my partner had pulled it with a void in hearts and two five-card suits. Why take any chances with a sure plus? So I passed, as did the rest of the table.

The contract went down four when Gussie showed up with

the king of spades and the queen of diamonds. Including my 100 honors, we made 300 points above the line. Not bad, I thought, until I felt a cool hand on the back of my neck squeezing the skin. Ouch! She had clawed me!

"What are you doing," asked Chops who was back from the phone, "dumping?"

I tried to explain my bird-in-hand business, but Chops just shook her head and pointed at my partner. "Gussie never pulled a penalty double in her life!!" She was right, of course. I had forgotten who was across the table from me. But then, what the heck, I thought, it wasn't Chops' money, it was Gussie's.

When Chops sat across from me for the fourth deal, she thanked Gussie for the plus score, and I remembered that when a player sits in for another player, it is the *initial* player who is responsible for the finances. Suddenly I thought of Otto. He had been filling in for Doctor B. Hey, where was he? I wanted my two hundred back!

"Deal the cards," said Pizza.

$$\spadesuit 987 \ \heartsuit A2 \ \diamondsuit QJ \clubsuit AKQJ10\,32$$

I dealt and opened three notrump. There, take that. Frankenstein passed and so did Chops, though I thought I detected a slight hesitation. Pizza doubled and it was back to me. Hmm. Surely I had full values for my bid. The gambling three notrump is often played without any stoppers on the outside, so I couldn't have a better hand. However, Pizza doubled. As rotten a person as he might be, his human nature shouldn't be confused with his bridge ability. He wasn't *that* rotten a player. In fact, it was very likely he held a long, solid spade suit, and maybe some diamond tricks as well.

Then I remembered Pizza's own words two months earlier, "You don't run from a double, kid, or they'll be doubling you out of cold contracts from here to Canarsie. That's game theory." Now that I knew the man's nature, I knew he was not to be trusted. He was using his own words to trick me into sticking it out in three notrump doubled. Besides, if I went for another number, Chops might never speak to me again. So I ran to four clubs.

Pass, said Frankenstein. Five clubs, said Chops. Everybody

passed and Frankenstein led a spade. Chops put down:

♠ 6 5 4 3 2 ♡ K Q J ◇ A K 10 ♣ 9 5

Of course she had hesitated over three notrump. She must have been thinking of slam. Unfortunately, however, in five clubs, Pizza took the first three spade tricks for down one. No only that, but three notrump was laydown. Pizza held the A-K-Q-J fourth of spades and nothing else of value.

Chops got up from her chair, and I braced myself for a tantrum. Instead she put on the most sinister smile I have ever witnessed and whispered, "I'll get even." Dare I say a word in my defense? The deal was over and my mistakes were blatant. I had run from a double with no knowledge of my partner's hand. I had bid in front of her, not even giving her the chance to redouble. I had made a decision for both sides of the table, when my partner was the one who knew my hand and would know what was best.

I changed seats with Pizza and faced Frankenstein. He smiled at me from behind his thick glasses. "Listen, Little Baboon. Forget the score and remember who you're playing with." What *was* the score? I looked down at the sheet. I had lost 11 points more. Not so bad for so many catastrophes, I thought. On the other hand, not so good for so many high cards. Still, it was only one more Franklin note, and now I was playing with the best player in the club.

♠ K 7 4 3 ♡ 8 6 4 ◇ 8 7 ♣ 10 5 4 2

Frankenstein passed and Chops opened one spade. I passed and Pizza bid three spades, forcing. Chops bid four clubs and Pizza cue-bid four diamonds. Chops went back to four spades and Pizza bid five hearts. Chops bid six spades, and that ended the auction. I led the six of hearts. This was the deal as I pictured it in my mind:

Pizza (dummy)
♠ Q 9 8
♡ A Q 10 9
◇ A K 3 2
♣ 9 8

Me
♠ K 7 4 3
♡ 8 6 4
◇ 8 7
♣ 10 5 4 2

Frankenstein
♠ x
♡ K x x x 2
◇ J 10 x x
♣ K Q 7

Chops (declarer)
♠ A J 10 x x
♡ J
◇ Q x x
♣ A J x x

Chops rose with the ace of hearts, dropping the jack from her hand, while Frankenstein signaled with the deuce. I could tell a subtle false card when I saw one. Frankenstein probably held five hearts to the king, and didn't want to tip off the king to declarer.

Chops led the eight of spades off dummy and finessed into my hand. I refused to win the trick without hesitating. With king fourth, it was best to duck the first round, because on the next round I could get a clue from partner. That clue turned out to be the seven of clubs, which was discarded on the second round of trumps (Chops led dummy's queen and played the ten from her hand).

I won the trick with my king and turned the four cards face-up. Yes, that seven of clubs was certainly a come-on signal. But I had learned my lesson on a similar deal two months earlier. I believe Gussie was my partner at the time. She had also signaled a come-on and I had blindly shifted and given away the contract. The important principle to remember in "come-ons" is that partner's signal is not a *demand* for a shift, but merely a *piece of information* to be analyzed and used to best advantage.

In this case there were other clues as well: Chops had cue-bid four clubs over three spades—she probably held the ace; then there was that subtle play of the ten of spades beneath dummy's queen on the second round of trumps. That Chops is really getting to be a clever declarer. She must be saving a low spade in her hand as an entry to dummy—but why?

Let's say Frankenstein held the king-queen of clubs for his seven-of-clubs discard; what would happen if I played one? I imagined the scenario. Chops would win with her ace, and go to dummy's nine of spades. Then she would lead the queen of hearts and pass it if Frankenstein did not cover. When this won, Frankenstein would certainly cover the next round of hearts, and Chops would ruff it. Pulling my last trump with her last trump, Chops would discard dummy's last club, and this would be the five-card ending:

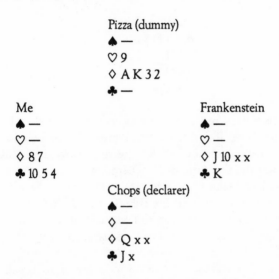

Pizza (dummy)
♠ —
♡ 9
◊ A K 3 2
♣ —

Me
♠ —
♡ —
◊ 8 7
♣ 10 5 4

Frankenstein
♠ —
♡ —
◊ J 10 x x
♣ K

Chops (declarer)
♠ —
◊ —
◊ Q x x
♣ J x

Next, she would lead a diamond to dummy and cash the nine of hearts, squeezing Frankenstein in the minors.

How could I stop this scenario? I thought about it for a while, and finally realized a diamond shift was the answer. If declarer won the diamond in her hand, she would lose her entry to the club jack in the end-position. If she won the diamond in dummy, she could ruff out the king of hearts, but could not return to dummy to cash the last heart without blocking her diamond suit.

It was a brilliant analysis, I thought, and with a bit of flourish I flung the eight of diamonds onto the table. With less flourish, but more acumen, Chops tabled her cards. This was the actual deal:

Pizza (dummy)
♠ Q 9 8
♡ A Q 10 9
◊ A K 3 2
♣ 9 8

Me
♠ K 7 4 3
♡ 8 6 4
◊ 8 7
♣ 10 5 4 2

Frankenstein
♠ 6
♡ 7 5 3 2
◊ J 9 5 4
♣ A 7 6 3

Chops (declarer)
♠ A J 10 5 2
♡ K J
◊ Q 10 6
♣ K Q J

My face turned red in embarrassment. I didn't dare look up this time for sure. If I caught Frankenstein's eye behind those thick lenses I would be cursed for the rest of my days. But then there was the shriek: "Aiiiiiiiiiiii!" There was no escape now, and when I tried to make a dash for the men's room, Frankenstein followed me in. From behind the cubicle, I could hear him.

"You have to watch my cards! You can't sit there for an hour and play another suit! You can't *escaaaaape* me, Little Baboooooon!"

"I'm sorry," I called out, "but I was trying to break up a squeeze if you had the king-queen of clubs—"

"*Awwwrrrrrr! Are you out of your mind?!* If there was a squeeze, I would have asked for a diamond switch, *myself!*"

"Yes, but, I had a similar hand with Gussie, a one-notrump contract—"

"Aiiiiiiiiiiiiiiiiiiiiiiiii! Do *I* look like *Gussie?!*" Frankenstein's head appeared over the cubicle. He looked like Dr. Frankenstein peering into a grave, and I was the corpse. "What are you doing in there anyway, Little Baboon?"

Somehow, that last "little baboon" sounded somewhat affectionate, and I opened up the door and apologized profusely. I had failed to realize that there is a human being behind every bridge hand. A signal is as simple or complex as the person who makes it. When a *bad* player signals, he is simply telling you what he holds; when a *good* player signals, he is telling you what he has analyzed and now wants you to play.

As we went into the hall, I offered him one of my Franklins, but he refused.

"That's not the way it works here," he said. "The partnership loses, the partnership pays. Besides, this is a counterfeit bill. Now you've got to trust Frankenstein from now on. Let's go back in there and get it back. Let's—"

"What? Counterfeit?"

I grabbed the bill and looked at it. There was Franklin's picture; it seemed perfectly fine to me. Then I turned it over. There was Franklin's picture again.

As we returned to the back room, I thumbed through the rest of my Franklins. All of them were the same—Franklin's mug on both sides. These weren't even *attempts* at counterfeit bills; this was play money! Suddenly we ran into Mr. Roth. He nodded hello, and headed toward his desk. Oh no, the money I had given Stanley was there.

When we entered the back room and took our positions, I noticed Otto seated behind me on my left. He gave me a pat on my back. I guess I was his good friend now, but what would happen when he discovered the two bills I had given him were no good? As I sorted my cards, I remembered the men's store where I had passed the bad bills as well.

"Get with it, kid. Time is money." Pizza was chomping on one of his enormous cigars, and sent a little puff into my face.

"What happened?" I asked.

"You better wake up, Little Baboon," said my partner.

I turned to Chops. "One notrump," she repeated.

♠ A 6 3 2 ♡ A Q 7 2 ◇ 3 ♣ 7 4 3 2

Pass, I said. Two hearts on my left. Pass by Frankenstein. Two spades on my right. I passed. Two hearts was a transfer, I guess. Pizza passed on my left and Frankenstein balanced with three diamonds. Chops passed and I passed. Now Pizza came back with three hearts. Frankenstein passed and Chops bid a quick three spades. What was going on? Somewhere in the back of my mind I had heard an auction like this. It had been a confusing auction, and I couldn't remember it.

Let's see now. Pizza bid hearts twice—did he forget to trans- fer? Of course! These are the opportunities that you can't afford to miss at rubber bridge. I doubled three spades. Everybody passed. When I led my singleton diamond, dummy came down with five spades to the jack and five hearts to the king-jack. Chops made an overtrick.

Frankenstein jumped out of his seat and ran to Roth's desk. We could hear his voice from the back room. "YOU GOTTA GET THAT KID OUTA THE GAME; I'm *telling* you, Al, he's gonna *kill the game.*"

How could I have done such a stupid thing, I thought—doubling them into game? Then I realized it was *Otto* who had been sitting on my left the last time. Otto *would* forget a transfer, but Pizza—no, Pizza would *never* forget a convention!

When Frankenstein came back, he gave me a big smile. I believe he thought I was a lunatic—someone he had to pacify. I dealt the cards, my hands shaking.

♠ K J 4 3 ♡ 9 8 7 ◇ A J 9 8 3 ♣ 2

Pass, I said. Pizza opened one heart. Frankenstein passed and Chops responded one notrump. I passed and Pizza bid two clubs. Frankenstein passed and Chops returned to two hearts. With five-four in the unbid suits, it seemed right to double. Playing the forcing notrump, Chops could easily hold three hearts, and even if she didn't, we probably had a fit in spades or diamonds.

Pizza redoubled. Suddenly two passes came around to me. Did this mean Frankenstein wanted to play two hearts redoubled, or did it mean he simply had no suit to bid and wanted me to pick one?

Sweat began to run down my brow. Must try to think. Pizza had five hearts and Chops had at least two, so Frankenstein couldn't hold more than three of them. Really, it was a choice between bidding two spades and three diamonds. Perhaps partner held a 4-3-3-3 type hand with four clubs, or maybe he held five clubs and two diamonds. Do I want to play a four-three spade fit or risk a five-two diamond fit? I looked up from my cards. There was Stanley, peering over Frankenstein's shoulder. I caught his eyes for about two seconds. His pupils seemed to move laterally. Good God, was he trying to tell me something?! But why *would* he? He must hate me by now, it being only natural to hate someone who threatens you. Then again, maybe he was trying to make things up to me for old times' sake, maybe he was sending me a message with those lateral eyeballs—but *what* message?

I had to do something, so I bid two spades. Maybe I wouldn't get doubled.

No luck. Pizza pounded me and Frankenstein bid two notrump. Chops passed and I removed to three diamonds. Pizza pounded me again. Everyone passed and Frankenstein laid down:

♠ 9 8 6   ♡ A Q 10   ◊ 4 2   ♣ A 10 9 8 7

The K-Q-10-x of diamonds were on my right, the rest of the high cards were on my left. Had I passed two hearts redoubled, we would have collected 1,000 points. Had I passed two notrump—I surely had no reason to bid over this—we would have been plus 70. Instead, I was in three diamonds doubled, down one, minus 200.

I could never look up from the floor again. Not only did I never want to look my partner in the eyes, but I didn't want to see the scorepad. I just kept my eyes glued to my patent-leather shoes and wondered if I would be permitted to take them with me when I went to federal prison.

Staring under the table, I could hear a lot of carrying-on above it, but I tuned it out. Stanley's lateral eyeballs must have been saying no to me—"No, don't bid." So he was trying to help me after all. But it was unethical. And even if it weren't, it was too late. I was deep in a hole now, and I was going to drag him down with me.

Without moving my head I reached up for my cards and brought them down into my lap; then I sorted them for the last deal of the rubber.

♠ Q 10 9 8 3   ♡ Q J   ◊ Q J   ♣ K J 10 4

I heard Pizza pass and Frankenstein open one heart. Chops bid one spade and I lifted my head up and passed, waiting for a reopening double. Pizza raised to two spades and Frankenstein jumped to four diamonds. Chops passed and I stared at my hand in shock. My red honors were incredibly well-placed. After all, Frankenstein must hold two big suits, headed by at least the ace-king. That he was void in spades, I was sure of from the opponents' bidding. Why if he held the ace of clubs as well, we might be laydown for a grand-slam!

So I came up for air and bid four notrump, Blackwood. Frankenstein responded five spades, three aces, and I bid five notrump. Frankenstein responded six hearts, two kings, and I considered further action. The main problem was whether to trust Chops and Pizza. Did they have an eight-card spade fit for their bidding or had Chops overcalled on a four-card suit, or perhaps Pizza had raised with only a doubleton.

Hmm. Where were all the high cards? In Frankenstein's hand. Chops would never overcall light on a four-card suit; therefore she must have five spades. Pizza might raise with a doubleton ace or king, but obviously Chops had both those honors for her skimpy overcall; so Pizza must have jack-third. What the hell, I thought, I can't do worse than I've been doing; I bid seven hearts. Everyone passed and Chops led the king of spades. I placed my dummy down on the table and shut my eyes. Soon I heard a lot of cards hit the table, but no scream. How wonderful that silence was!

"Good evaluation, Little Baboon. Now you see how it pays to trust Frankenstein."

He held:

♠ — ♡ A K 10 9 6 3 ◇ A K 6 5 4 ♣ A 2

Plus 2210. A horrible, heavy weight lifted from my shoulders. Maybe the tide had turned. Unfortunately, when I got up to pick a card for the new wheel, I spotted a man in the kitchen doorway talking to Maggie—an elderly but spritely man wearing a Yankee baseball cap. I covered my face in my hands and sped past him to the hallway. As I went past, I called out, "96th and Central Park!"

"Hey, man," I heard from behind me. I ran past the TV room, grabbed my Poe and overcoat, then rushed out to the elevators. Still there were footsteps behind me. The elevator was only seconds away. I crouched to defend myself. Then I remembered the gun, so I reached into my jacket.

24

I HELD my fire. It was Chops. The two of us went into the
elevator and down to the foyer. She complimented me on my
grand-slam decision and I told her I may have lost a little in my
card play, but my bidding was improving.

"That's the way it always is," she said as we got into a car
waiting downstairs. "You work on one part of your game, and lose
a little in another. But eventually it all comes together; that's what
Frankenstein says."

Suddenly I realized we were in some kind of limousine. She
turned to me and asked where I was heading. I suggested a night-
cap at her place—told her I'd like to see the baby. She said okay,
on one condition.

"What's that?" I asked.

"You're out by 1 a.m.," she said in a whisper. "That's when he
gets back."

I didn't ask who "he" was. I had taken it for granted she was
again living with Stanley. But when the limousine stopped at 77th
Street and Park Avenue, I had grave doubts. A doorman with an
umbrella opened the car door, and we were ushered into an
enormous hallway where another doorman bowed his head and
gave the okay to let us up.

The elevator stopped at the 39th floor and we got out into a
tiny corridor with two entrances. There were only two apartments per floor in this building, and I soon learned that Chops'
apartment had a total of nine rooms, lush red carpeting throughout. There were lots of decorations too, chandeliers and vases, art
deco stuff, and Picasso-like paintings on the walls. No, this wasn't
Stanley's apartment—not by a long shot.

Little Bobby was in his crib and the baby sitter, a very charming woman, told us he had just fallen asleep. When the sitter left,
we took a peek in. The boy was wrapped in a soft blue blanket.
His room was quite large; the walls light blue and green with
posters of Winnie the Pooh and Mickey Mouse. I noticed the
windows had iron bars on them.

We passed from one room to another, living room, dining room, kitchen, pantry . . . library . . . bedroom . . . guest room . . . bedroom. It was impressive. Chops finally sat me down on a small couch at the foot of a four-poster bed. Then she asked if I wanted some coke. I told her to make it diet, and she laughed.

"You still have that weird sense of humor," she said. I had no idea what she was talking about. Then she handed me a deck of cards from a posh velvet box. "Take out the little ones," she ordered, "while I slip into something more comfortable."

She walked into a closet in the right-hand corner of the bedroom and called out, "Hey, give me your coat. It must be wet." I got up, deck in hand, and walked enthusiastically to the closet. It wasn't just a closet. It was a long dark dressing room, and the only thing white inside was a silver framed clock that seemed to light up in the dark. When I passed her my coat and Poe, I noticed her grey outline; she was in her underwear and stockings. It was black underwear, silky black that matched the color of her hair. I also noticed that the underwear did not include a bra. "The light went out in here," she said. "Pizza always forgets to change it. Would you reach up behind the top shelf like a good boy—there's a flashlight there."

I fished for it on my toes and took it down. When I turned it on, the beam of light hit her in a particularly fascinating area, and it took all my self-control not to slam that dressing room door and shut off the flashlight. "Here," she said, passing me a light bulb. "Screw it in." I boosted myself up on a box and screwed it into the socket. The bulb came on and I stared down at Chops. "Now, up there," she pointed, "in the box."

I lifted the box and passed it down to her. Inside was a little tin container, and in that was some white powder. She took a little on her pinky and sniffed it. "You sure you're not partaking?" she asked. I shook my head. The truth was, I was innocent in these matters, and the last thing I wanted was white powder up my nose.

She put on a pink silk night-robe and slippers. Then, before I knew what was happening, she had me by the arm and was forcing me down onto a stool. "Give me that," she said. "Oooh, the cards are all sweaty. Uh, oh, you haven't been doing your sorting," she teased. She sat on the dressing-table stool and flipped through the deck like a Las Vegas baccarat dealer. The twos and threes dropped to the floor. "You deal," she ordered.

♠ A K 9 5 ♡ A K 8 6 ◇ K 7 ♣ A K 9

I opened two clubs; she responded three diamonds. I tried five notrump; she jumped to seven diamonds. I corrected to seven notrump; she passed. Her hand was:

♠ 8 7 6 ♡ J 7 ◇ A Q J 6 5 4 ♣ Q 8

Nice queen of clubs, I thought.
"Nicely bid," she said. Then she dealt.

♠ 7 6 ♡ K Q 7 ◇ J 8 7 ♣ 10 9 8 5 4

One spade by Chops; one notrump by me. Two diamonds by Chops; two spades by me. Three clubs by Chops; pass by me. Her hand:

♠ A K 9 5 4 ♡ 9 ◇ A Q 10 5 ♣ K J 7

Nice stop, I thought.
"Only a partscore," said Chops.
What did she want? A slam on every hand? Suddenly she looked at me, eyes ablaze. "Let's go all the way," she said. With that she skimmed through the deck and flipped out the fours, then handed the deck back to me.

♠ — ♡ J 8 7 6 ◇ A K Q 8 5 ♣ K Q J 9

I opened one diamond; she responded one heart. I rebid three clubs. She raised to four clubs. I retreated to four hearts; she cue-bid four spades. I tried five diamonds; she bid five notrump. I jumped to seven clubs; she passed. Her hand was:

♠ A K Q 7 ♡ A 10 9 5 ◇ 7 ♣ A 10 7 6

Nice grand slam, I thought.
"Where'd you find that jump shift?" she asked.
"With a nice fit, I don't count points," I answered. "How'd you know which suit was trumps when you bid five notrump?"

263

"With two fits for you, I didn't care, darling," she responded.

I swept up the cards and shuffled them. "Hey, mister," she said, "hand those cards over; it's my deal."

$$\spadesuit \text{A K 4} \quad \heartsuit \text{10 9 4} \quad \diamondsuit \text{7 5} \quad \clubsuit \text{J 10 9 7 4}$$

One diamond by Chops; one notrump by me. Two clubs by Chops; two spades by me. Three hearts by Chops; three notrump by me. Pass by Chops. Her hand:

$$\spadesuit - \quad \heartsuit \text{J 7 6} \quad \diamondsuit \text{A K 9 8 4} \quad \clubsuit \text{A K Q 8 6}$$

Nice shape-showing three-heart call, I thought.

"Hey, you remembered the 'impossible bid,'" she said.

"And you did likewise," I responded.

"But you stuck the fours back into the deck," she chastised.

"But you're the one who dealt it," I answered.

"But you're the one who shuffled," she returned.

$$\spadesuit \text{A 9} \quad \heartsuit \text{Q J 10 9 8 5} \quad \diamondsuit \text{A 5} \quad \clubsuit \text{K J 5}$$

I opened one heart. She responded one spade. I temporized with two clubs. She temporized with two diamonds. I returned to two hearts. She returned to three clubs. I jumped to four hearts; she passed. Her hand:

$$\spadesuit \text{K 8 7 6} \quad \heartsuit \text{7} \quad \diamondsuit \text{J 7 6} \quad \clubsuit \text{A Q 10 8 7}$$

Ah, the convenient one-spade response, I thought.

"If you had rebid two hearts, I would have passed," she said.

"My heart spots were too good," I answered.

"Still, it's only a game," she said.

"Can't you be satisfied with a game?" I returned.

"I'm never easily satisfied," she responded.

She took the cards and placed them neatly in a stack on the dressing table. Then she stood up and moved to the door. I heard a switch, the lights went out, and the door slammed. For almost a minute nothing happened. I just sat there in the wonderful pitch blackness of the closet listening to the ticking of the luminous clock, breathing in the smell of her perfumes and dresses. It was my fond hope that Chops was on this side of the closet door.

Suddenly a silk robe hit me between the eyes, and I knew a college freshman's dream was about to come true. I turned my head and noticed the clock again. It was ten before one. A warm leg reached across my arm and a hand moved down to my jacket. How was it possible I was still wearing my suit, darn it! Quickly, I loosened my arms out of the sockets and let the jacket fall to the floor. Next came my shirt, and suddenly I felt something tingly on my chest. She was tickling me with one of the twos (or was it a three?) that had been tossed to the floor in the shuffle.

Finally my shirt was off and my pants were on their way down as well. My shoes were still on, however, and with great discomfort I forced them off, my back against the stool. Finally, I was as bare as she was, and one of the great moments in time had arrived. That's when we heard the door slam.

"Oh shit," she said. "I told you to be out of here by one."

She was suddenly gone, the closet opened and closed in a split second, but it was too late. I heard voices now and quickly felt around for my pants. All I could find was her robe, so I slipped it on. Then I heard a slap and cry. There was a baby in the background crying as well. Suddenly I remembered the gun—good Old Leroy's gun. Where the hell was my jacket? I felt for it on the floor. There it was, inside the pocket. Thank goodness, the gun was still there. I pulled it out and pointed it at the door, then waited impatiently for someone to open it.

25

T HE SECONDS ticked by, and I continued to hear sobbing. Then there were heavy footsteps and I steadied my arm, my finger around the trigger. Suddenly I heard the doorknob turn. No, it wasn't the doorknob; it was the lock. Then there was a laugh, a huge, uproarious laugh that wouldn't stop. Then there was nothing but sobs again.

I inched my way to the door and slowly turned the knob. I pushed forward. Ummmph. Nothing happened. The darn thing was locked. I put the gun down and peered through the keyhole. The bedroom light was on and I could see the foot of the bed. Suddenly a pair of fat legs passed by the bed poster and Pizza McCarver sat down on the couch. He was undressing.

The sobs had subsided now, and I considered my options. For one thing, I could try to shoot my way through. But after the first shot, Pizza would be alerted and there would be a fight, maybe a gunfight; but whatever kind of fight, it was going to be bloody. No, that's no good, I thought.

I could wait it out for a few hours and then shoot my way through. Possible, and I'd have an edge in a few hours with Pizza half asleep. But then again, what if I missed the lock? Was I so sure I knew how to shoot one? At what point in the door was the lock, anyway?

Hmm. What if I spent the whole night in the closet? I could watch, listen, gather evidence of the character of Pizza McCarver. But what for? I knew what he was: an ape, an inhuman scoundrel, a woman-beater! And now he had me locked in his closet! He was a kidnapper! Good god, I had to get out! What was his plan for me in the morning?

He was undressed now and leaning over the bed. I could see Chops now, too. Oh God, she was naked also. I moved back from the keyhole. I couldn't bear it. I moved back further, until my head bumped into a box by the wall. It was a metal container. I opened it. Inside was the white stuff. I took out a few grains and sniffed it. It wasn't bad, so I tried some more. I started to get happy, happier and happier.

Strange sounds were coming from the bed now—groans and grunts. How nice, I thought. Suddenly the grunts and groans got louder, less musical to my senses. So I placed my palms around my ears and heard sweeter tones. Then, feeling a little woozy, I sat down on one of the stools and rested my head against a soft velvet thing hanging from the rack.

After a few minutes, maybe longer—I couldn't tell—I seemed to awake from a daydream. My palms were stiff as I removed them from my head. Silence. Wonderful silence. Wait, was that a soft shuffle I heard? I opened and closed my eyes—there was no difference. The darkness inside me and the darkness outside were the same. Suddenly I was scared. I got up and felt myself all over. Was I alive? Maybe I had taken a poisonous drug and had fallen into a sleep of death. Maybe I had awakened in hell. But wait. No, hadn't Chops sniffed the same white powder? It was a good powder, a fine powder; you could trust Chops not to be sniffing a poisonous powder.

I took a few steps to my right. Should I scream out? Then I would know if I were alive. But then, Pizza would come, and I wasn't ready for him. I had lost the gun. That's it—the gun. If I could just hold onto something physical, I would be sure I was alive. I felt around. Dresses, of course—I was in the closet. I tripped on the stool, but did not fall. Wait. Up on the shelf. I stepped up and felt into the back. Got it! The flashlight! I turned it on and almost scared myself to death. The light hit a mirror and the reflection was me.

My heart was beating rapidly, but I took a deep breath and let it out slowly. I was alive, buried perhaps within a Park Avenue dressing room, but alive. Then I noticed the reflection of my Poe. Well, I thought, why not? There's nothing like a good mystery, said Mr. Keewood, to lighten one's troubles.

I took some of Chops' softer dresses from their hangers and made a cushion for my head. Then, positioning the flashlight between my shoulder and the wall, I opened to "The Murders in the Rue Morgue" and continued where I had left off. It was an interesting murder story in which a woman and her daughter were found mauled to death in their apartment on the Rue Morgue. I won't spoil the outcome for those readers who haven't tried it, suffice to say that the French detective, Dupin, does solve the crime. After that, I turned to a cute little tale of vengeance entitled, "Hop-Frog." Then I realized I had never read "The Cask of Amontillado," but I couldn't last till the end of the story. Somewhere, around page 89, buried alive deep within a skeleton-strewn wine cellar, I laid my head down on a cashmere blazer and fell into a deep sleep.

When I awoke, I thought I heard a baby crying in the distance. I looked around. The first thing I saw was a stream of light through a window on top of the door. I had not noticed that window before. Then I saw a small piece of rolled paper. Then it dawned on me where I was, and I grasped the paper and opened it. The handwriting was shaky, but it read:

> *Bedpan on top right shelf—*
> *don't damage the clothes.*

Thank you very much, I thought, but I would prefer a key to the door. There was another bit of scribbling. It read:

> *ISM 15*

What did that mean?

Turning my head, I saw the clock. Strangely enough, it was harder to read with the light pouring in than in the black of night. Five to eleven. Hmm. I moved over to the door and stuck my eye to the keyhole. There were some feet sticking out of the bed-spread—and they weren't nice feet either. I got up on both of my legs and stretched—arrrrrhhh, terrible cramp in my left thigh.

After a few minutes of soft curses, I took off the sweat-stained robe and located my clothes. Then I noticed the dressing table. I pulled over the stool, sat down, and opened the drawer. There were some lovely perfumes and lipsticks and things. There was also a pad and pencil, and on the top was a little typewritten note on the Blackwood convention. It read:

```
4NT followed by 5NT promises
all the aces. Responder, instead
of answering kings, may jump to 7
with a good source of tricks.
```

Interesting, I thought. Then it came to me what Poe had written in his takeoff of a Blackwood article: If you ever found yourself buried alive, you should take the opportunity to keep an account of the affair. So I took the pencil in hand and wrote of my experiences (as best I could remember) from the night before. Then, looking around me, I thought I might make a few notes on the particular nature of my "tomb":

> Some readers may wish to know what the temperature conditions are like in a locked dressing room of a Park Avenue apartment; and, for the record, I'd like to say that they are significantly better than the living room of the average brownstone walk-up. The reason is, I believe, that Park Avenue residents have more pull with their landlords and the heat comes up much faster than in smaller apartments. You get what you pay for; and looking at the incident from a writer's view, I offer words of advice to other young boys of amorous ambition: Stick to the wealthy neighborhoods—when things go against you, they are seldom as bad as when things turn in a poorer section of town. Not only are the closets roomier and warmer, but the men of the house are more inclined to the eccentric revenge—such as locking you up— rather than the old-fashioned and less-reasonable knife through the heart.

This was ridiculous, I thought as I finished the paragraph. It was time to get the hell out of here! But when I saw myself in the mirror, I knew I couldn't leave until I had at least done something with my hair. Another advantage of my high-rent 'entombment' was the mirror and hair brushes. I was able to doll myself up, and for a guy who had spent the night in a closet, I had to admit I was looking quite spiffy. There was quite a lot of make-up about, too, so I rubbed a little pink stuff onto some blemishes around my chin. Then I spotted the cold cream, and wondered if I should have given myself a facial first.

The right-hand shelf was higher than the left and I had to lift

myself up on some shoeboxes. There was the bedpan that Pizza
had mentioned in the note, and behind it were some books.
Hmm. They were mostly bridge books, the same ones I had seen
at Chops old apartment on the West Side. In particular, I noticed
the Roth-Stone book, *Bridge is a Partnership Game*. I took that
down along with the bedpan, and after certain operations, which
I will spare the reader, I sat down on a stool and opened to the
table of contents. There it was again! Of course, I should have
remembered what the scribbling meant: "IX. Roth-Stone 'Isms'."

About a quarter of the way down page 188 was the "ISM 15"
previously referred to. I read with growing interest the following
passages:

15. Freaks Require Special Strategy
in Competitive Auctions.

a. A score of plus 510 (4 ♡ making 7) is better than
plus 500 (7 ♠ doubled down 3). If you feel that you can
make game or slam, try to buy the contract as cheaply as
possible. Don't leap to slam. This tips off your hand and
invites a cheap save by the opponents.

b. As a corollary to the above, if you are not sure you
can make game or slam, tend to jump so as to encourage a
sacrifice. This particularly applies to total points. (They
may be suspicious of your actions, but they cannot afford
to risk your making a vulnerable game or slam).

Illustrations

You hold (vul vs. nonvul):

♠ A 10 x x x x
♡ A
◊ J 10 x x x x
♣ ———

Total Points		
Part	Opp	You
1 ♠	2 ♡	?

2 ♠. There is going to be plenty of bidding by the
opponents, unless by some chance all the power shows up
in partner's hand. If the opponents become aggressive,
this hand must be bid as if you were not anxious to go to
slam. (You have no sure slam in any event, depending
upon partner's diamond holding.) The actual bidding proceeded as follows:

Part	Opp	You	Opp
1 ♠	2 ♡	2 ♠	3 ♡
4 ♠	5 ♡	P	P
D	P	5 ♠	P
P	6 ♡	P	P
D	P	6 ♠	7 ♡
D	P	7 ♠	P
P	P		

The opponents refused to sell out cheaply, and the eventual bid of 7 ♠ was an out-and-out gamble. (The profit could be great and the loss insignificant.) Fortunately, 7 ♠ was made. The opponents would have been down 3 at 7 ♡.

You hold (neither vul):

♠ A J 9 8	You	Opp	Part	Opp
♡ K 10 x x x	1 ♡	1 ♠	2 ♡	2 ♠
◊ A J 9	?			
♣ x				

4 ♡. Here is a hand on which you think you can make game, but not slam, and you are sure that you can take care of a 4 ♠ sacrifice. On the actual hand, the opponents bid 4 ♠ and went down 700 points.

You hold (vul. vs. nonvul): Total Points

♠ x	You	Opp	Part	Opp
♡ A 10 x	1 ◊	2 ♡	3 ◊	3 ♡
◊ A K J x x	?			
♣ A 10 x x				

6 ◊. Partner's free bid makes it probable that you will have a reasonable play for 6 ◊. Therefore, leap to slam and let the opponents then guess whether to sacrifice.

It was a brief essay, but a brilliant one. The psychological strategy of keeping the opponents in the dark during the bidding when you have a good idea where you are heading was not new to me, however. It was, in more recent terms, "The Theory of Exhaustion," and its corollary: Go slowly and buy the contract—go quickly and encourage a sacrifice.

Why did Pizza want me to read this? Was he bragging that he had the same theories as Al Roth and Tobias Stone? I thumbed to the beginning of the book. "Copyright 1958." Hmm. It was written more than 10 years earlier. I wondered how many bridge players were familiar with the concept—certainly a lot more now that Pizza's article had been published in the Bridge World.

I heard some coughing from the bed, so I returned to the keyhole. Pizza was up now. He looked horrible. His face was red and ruddy. His body was pure flab. I considered rapping at the door. He had probably calmed down from the night before. And surely he didn't intend on keeping me in there all day.

Then, studying his horrible face, I realized the bitter truth! Tonight was the meeting with Detective Kennedy. All the witnesses would be there, but only one had read the black notebook and knew what its disappearance implied. That witness was *me*. And hadn't I warned Stanley with my big mouth that I was going to squeal? And hadn't I seen Stanley confer with Pizza last night during supper at the club? How stupid of me, I thought. Pizza had not locked me up in a sudden jealous rage. No, he had locked me up in a cold and calculating plot to prevent my appearance at the inquiry.

The question was: What would he do with me afterwards? Surely he couldn't let me go free—not after he'd locked me up and incriminated himself even further.

I watched him as he put on his socks and boxer shorts. I could see a white bald spot in the middle of his head as he bent over the couch. In the light of morning, his premeditated plot became clear. My destination was the East River, and the sooner he could sink me the better off he'd be.

I turned to the floor and found my gun. The time had come to make a break for it—while he was still a little sleepy and off his guard. I could climb to the window on top of the door and shoot first. Then I could crash through and leap into the bedroom—no, that was impossible—I would surely kill myself jumping through the glass. So I went back to the lock idea. I tried to measure the area where the lock would be, maybe an inch beneath the door knob. Then I put the muzzle against the door. Counting to three, I closed my eyes and squeezed the trigger. As I did, the door suddenly opened and Pizza was standing there in a red-stained T-shirt.

26

*ONLY A CLICK—CHINATOWN—GOOD AND
BAD FORTUNE—A RUN-IN WITH OLD LEROY—
SPILLING BEANS OVER TEA—STYLE.*

I HEARD the gun click and continued to stare at the red stain on his T-shirt. I wasn't sure if the red stain was there before I squeezed the trigger or after. He reached for the gun and took it from me without a struggle.

"I assume you knew this thing wasn't loaded," he said. Then he pointed it at my head and squeezed the trigger himself. He started to chuckle. "Where'd you get it?" he asked. "I haven't seen one of these old German pistols since the war."

"I got it from a cab driver in Harlem," I answered, swallowing hard. I noticed some dried blood on his left cheek. It looked like a wound from an animal's claw.

"C'mon outa there, you look like you spent the whole night on the floor."

I moved into the bedroom, my knees shaking. The bed hadn't been made and there were old *Bridge World* magazines strewn across it. One was opened to the partscore tragedy I had read about on the train. An idea struck me, and I checked the address of the publication at the bottom of the first page. Then I noticed some twos and threes on the floor next to the bed. There must have been a lot of action last night, I thought. He showed me to the bathroom, where I washed my face and hands. There was no sign of Chops or the baby. I asked where they were.

"The kid's out with his nanny. We're meeting Chops for lunch, so let's get going, huh?"

When I came out, Pizza was dressed in a white shirt, red tie and navy suit. I wondered what his plan was. He was certainly playing it smooth. Maybe he was waiting to get me near the river. But if he wanted to bump me off, he'd certainly blown his opportunity back in the closet. He tossed me the gun and told me to be more careful where I aimed it in the future.

At 12:30, we entered the back seat of a black limousine. I expected the driver to be some mug with a heavy revolver in his pocket, but he turned out to be the same young driver as the night before. After a few minutes, however, my worst fears emerged as he headed straight for the water. Soon we were speeding downtown on the FDR Drive, the East River to our left. I looked forward and could see that we were passing the United Nations; then, to my right, I spotted the Empire State Building sticking up over the other skyscrapers. We were little people in a town of enormous proportions, and nobody would miss me—I was sure.

I thought of opening the door and bolting out, but the way the traffic was moving, I would be dead within seconds of my exit. Would I rather drown or be hit by a car? I thought. Hmm. Where were we going for lunch? Not Little Italy, I hoped. He probably had his Mafia connections ready to assault me in the middle of my pasta primavera.

Suddenly his hand was on mine. I tried to pull my forearm away, but he held it firmly in his pudgy grip. "Look kid, I don't want you to worry over last night. These things happen all the time. A misunderstanding—let's call it that."

"Is Chops your wife?" I asked.

"My wife? Ha, ha, ha! Are you outa your ------- mind? Take the advice of a man of experience—women are like a good hot plate of spaghetti. You poke at 'em, you twist 'em, you devour them, but you don't marry 'em. Not unless you're a meatball, ha, ha."

For what it was worth, this confirmed my suspicion we were headed for a cozy Mafia hangout. But when we turned off the highway to Canal Street, we made a sharp left onto Mott, straight into the heart of Chinatown.

She was waiting by a table in the corner on the second floor. There was a window behind her, overlooking the corner of Mott and Pell. When we sat down, she took off her sunglasses and I noticed two things, one obvious and one rather shocking. First, her left eye was black-and-blue with a large bandage over the eyebrow. This must have been Pizza's work from the night before. Second, her eyes were slanted more than I ever realized, making deep almond-shaped caverns above extraordinarily high cheek-bones. There was no doubt in my mind—she was part Asian, and all the more beautiful for it.

This last realization was confirmed when she ordered our lunch for us, speaking half English and half Chinese to the waiter. Then she put her shades back on.

We started with a plate of noodles, and Szechwan hot red sauce on top. I tried to use the chopsticks like the two of them, but mangled the noodles. I did better with the steamed crabs in garlic sauce and chicken with red pepper and peanuts. Chops dipped her food in a bowl of white rice and handled her sticks with agility. Pizza was less skillful, especially with the sauteed stringbeans, but still not bad for a man who had no table manners to begin with. I tried to emulate Chops, and after a while got the hang of it.

We talked about bridge hands from the Mayfair, and which players you could rely on for having their values, giving proper signals, or not bungling the dummy. We discussed the advantages of vulnerability and the weather. Finally Pizza came to the point.

"You see, kid, we can all be friends. It just takes a little understanding. As I said to Chops this morning, let bygones be bygones." He smiled, a few kernels of rice trickling down from the corner of his lip, and again I noticed the scar on his cheek. "Pretend you got me for 800 and I got you for 800. New rubber now—the slate is clean." He wiped his face with his napkin and turned to Chops. "Don't you agree, my dear?"

She nodded and gave me one of those rare warm smiles that I was used to only after we had bid to a successful slam. Obviously, he was referring to the inquiry that night. He wanted to make up with me, but instead of threatening me with a visit to the bottom of the East River, he was bribing me with a Chinese lunch. Granted, the food was great, the company fascinating, and the conversation educational—but it wouldn't take. My mind was set on exposing his wickedness, his fight with the little girl by the window, her murder, and the cover-up. That is, until he leaned over, placed his grubby hand on my shoulder and whispered, "You know, for a kid who lives at 33 Harrison Avenue, Jersey City, New Jersey, and has a telephone number of 434-4467 and has a brother and two lovely parents who think their son is a scholarly fellow doing his homework this weekend at Rutgers University, you're not that dumb.

Then he paused for a few seconds, just enough time for him to devour the last crab claw on the platter. "You see what I mean about letting bygones be bygones?" he added.

"Friends don't rat on each other," I said with honest conviction.

At the end of the meal, we had fortune cookies and lichee nuts. Pizza insisted we read our fortunes. "Oh, that's so silly," said Chops, behind her sunglasses. "Anyway, Chinese fortunes are personal, and shouldn't be read out loud."

"We'll read them," he insisted. He opened his and read, "'Long life—happiness; short life—fame.' I'll take both," said Pizza, and started to laugh. It made no sense, but I chuckled anyway out of respect for my blackmailer. Then Chops read hers, "A tall dark man will soon enter your life." Pizza and I had a good laugh over that one as well. When it came time to read mine, though, Chops' took off her glasses and gave me one of those "red alarm looks." I read the fortune to myself: "ISM 15." A lichee went down the wrong pipe. When I stopped coughing, I looked at my fortune again and read out loud, "Life is a partnership game." What a stupid thing to say!

"Well, that's true," said Pizza. I drank some tea and slipped the fortune into my pocket. I realized now that the note to me in the closet had been from Chops, not Pizza. *She* was the one who wanted me to read Ism 15 from the Roth-Stone book. But why? All it did was repeat Pizza's Theory of Exhaustion. No, I guess you wouldn't say the book *repeated* it, but that it worded it differently from the way Pizza had worded it ten years later. . . . In other words, *Pizza* was the one who repeated it. I suppose some people would say he had *stolen* the idea from the Roth-Stone book, and that his so-called original theory was nothing more than a plagiarized Ism.

But what of it? To what conclusion did the evidence lead? Perhaps Chops was merely trying to get even with Pizza by exposing his plagiarized bridge theory. Perhaps she was merely trying to tell me, "Here's another piece of evidence against him. I'll be in your corner tonight at the inquiry."

After lunch, Pizza took me aside and told me I had one week to return his notebook. I nodded. In one week he'd be behind bars, I thought. So Stanley had told him I still had the notebook. *Very nice of Stanley.* Suddenly Pizza grasped Chops' wrist with hand-cuff precision, seemingly forcing her into the car. Then he asked me if I needed a lift. I shook my head no, although I did have some stops to make before returning to the Mayfair. However, I was not about to get back in that limousine if I could avoid it. I stood there in front of a Chinese newsstand watching them drive off into the traffic.

Then I turned my attention to my own position, first checking my wallet. There were still the bad Franklin notes, but nothing else. I was furious with myself. Why hadn't I changed one of them last night at the club? Then I thought, it might not be too late—I quickly put on Old Leroy's sunglasses, ran upstairs to the restaurant, and checked the table. The tip was still there—three dollars and seventy-five cents. I had to give Pizza credit: he was a decent tipper. The waiter would hardly miss fifty cents. So I scooped up two quarters for a subway token and dashed downstairs. Then I ran over to Canal Street and Broadway and down into a subway station. I boarded the first train that came in. It was a sign of good fortune, I thought, that the train was heading uptown, instead of for Brooklyn.

I picked up a *Daily News* that had been left on the subway seat. Friday, December 12th, 1969. I had forgotten it was my birthday. Eighteen years old today. It occurred to me that my parents might expect me home tonight, and that somewhere along the line I should make a phone call to let them know I wasn't coming.

There was a headline in the news about a Vietnam massacre and a smaller headline at the bottom concerning Con Edison. The electricity test for tonight had been postponed due to possible thunderstorms. The train was getting crowded now, and I noticed the time on someone's watch. It was 2:45. The subway car was screeching and clattering, people bobbing back and forth like human balloons.

We stopped at a big station and I could see outside the window, "14th Street — NYU" written on a huge post amid red and orange graffiti. I wondered if J.B. had arrived for his Classics conference. Somehow it didn't seem possible that a guy like J.B. could be in this city. He didn't belong here, at least not in the city I had come to know.

I thought it was a sign of very good fortune that a map of subway stops hung directly over my head on the train wall. Had

277

the map been at the other end of the car, I would never have been able to reach it. The train was shaking so violently that I could hardly stand up. The map was multicolored for different-lettered routes. Since we were making many stops, I assumed I was on a local, and though I couldn't read the lettering behind the red smears on the door, I could follow the stops on the map.

When we reached 42nd Street, a crowd of people got off, and I figured only four stops to go; 51st Street was next, then Columbus Circle. Seventy-second street followed, then 86th. That was *my* stop, but some idiotic slowpoke was in front of me and the door suddenly closed, almost taking my foot with it.

I grabbed onto the railing and positioned myself firmly against the door even though the sign said, "No Leaning." Suddenly I was scared. What if the next stop was Harlem? What if I ran into Old Leroy and his gang? It was a sign of fantastic fortune that the next stop was only 96th and Central Park West, and I bounded onto the platform in relief.

It was a sign of bad fortune, however, that when I bounded from the train, I bounded into a tall grayish character with skull bones on his T-shirt and spike bracelets on his wrists. He gave me a little shove and I landed about seven yards back against the wall. Quickly, I ran to the exit, and when I climbed to the street level, I thought it a sign of worse fortune to be standing precisely in front of the white Studebaker that I had abandoned the day before. And it was surely a sign of *terrible* fortune that Old Leroy was sitting on the car's hood, looking extremely unhappy.

"Hey man, what's wrong with you?!" Old Leroy had his forefinger in my face. "You steal my sunglasses—here, give me them—" He removed the glasses from my eyes and started waving them in the air. "You steal my cab, and you take the key!"

"The key?" I hadn't realized I'd taken the key.

"Yes, the key! How'm I supposed to make a living? You some kind of psycho or something? I could have you arrested, you know. Why, if it weren't for my niece Maggie who works down at that gamblin' club—"

"Bridge club," I corrected.

"Bridge club, my eye! You think I don't know what goes on down there? Why, I played bridge-whist before you were born, sonny. You come up to my territory and I'll show you how to play *bridge.*"

I checked my pockets for the key, but came up with nothing but my wallet. I took out my remaining Franklins and handed them over.

"What I want with this junk—it's phoney baloney, man." He smacked the money from my hand and the bills flew up westward into the December wind. Suddenly he caught some of it in the air and put it in his own pocket.

"You haven't been passing this junk, I hope."

I shook my head, no.

"Good, man, cause you already in enough trouble as it is."

I took out his gun and handed that over, too.

"Yeah," he said, "I forgot about this thing. You got a lot of nerve, you know that, boy?"

"I'm sorry," I said. "If you'll come with me, I think I know where your car key is."

We headed west to Broadway, and I asked him why he and his friends were carrying counterfeit money and guns.

"You think I'm gonna discuss my racket with you? Why you know too much already, you stupid dummy. How you play bridge, man? Bet you get faked out a little, then next thing you know you start running with the scorepad downtown?" He waved his fingers in the air. "Boy, oh boy, I seen everything now!"

At 94th Street we entered Fortunato's men's shop. Mr. Fortunato spotted me immediately and rushed over—but it wasn't to shake my hand.

"Senor, you take-a off that suit, thees instant! You give me fake-a bills."

"Yes, sir, I'm sorry," I said. "That's why I'm here. Do you still have my clothes from yesterday?"

"You mean-a those rags that you walked in with?"

"Hey man," said Leroy, "Let's get going. It's nearly four o'clock and I got a pick-up downtown."

"You, Senor, may wait . . . outside."

"My eyeball, I'll wait outside," said Leroy brandishing his pistol. "You go get him his threads—and make it snappy, Romeo."

Fortunato rushed into the back and came out with a bag of clothes. Inside my jacket pocket was Leroy's car key. He took the keys, nodded, and I told him I'd see him someday in a Harlem bridge club.

"You mad, you know that? If I was you, I'd get myself outa town."

Old Leroy walked out of the store, looked to his left and right, then started back toward Central Park. I went into a dressing room to change into my old clothes, and when I came out, I offered to send Fortunato the money for the pants, the one article from his store that I needed.

"I theenk is best if I never see you again," said Fortunato.

With those kind words, I put my Poe under my arm and left the store.

Two blocks East, in the middle of the street, I stopped and checked the addresses: 43 . . . 41 . . . 39. Hmm. That was it, but it was not a shop or store front, just another old brownstone. I climbed the stoop and opened the door into the foyer. Above the bell, the sign read, "Bridge World Magazine."

A tall, distinguished man with a pipe and grey cardigan sweater answered the door.

"Ah, you must be young Matthew. Come in. My name is Edgar Kaplan. You may call me Edgar."

He opened the inner door and led me through to his living room on the right of the stairway. I was vain enough to be flattered that he know who I was, even though we had never met before. I was stupid enough not to analyze *how* he knew.

"I'm here because I'm looking for some information," I said, sitting down on a comfortable armchair. There was something furry near my head, and it jumped onto the rug.

"Well, that's interesting," said Edgar. "I sincerely hope you'll find some." Edgar offered me a cup of tea and I accepted. He walked through a dining room, past a piano and into a kitchen. I heard water boiling. Edgar had already been brewing and in just a few minutes he came back with two very strong cups of tea. In the meantime, I had gazed around the room. It was a warm, cozy place, with small pillows and quaint rugs, and plenty of dark brown books on the shelves. He handed me one cup, then took his cup to the couch. Then he took out a pack of matches from his sweater pocket and went to work on his pipe.

I didn't know where to begin, so I started by asking him if he was aware of what was going on at the Mayfair, including the inquiry scheduled for that night.

"I'm not *unaware* of it," he responded.

"Oh, Mr. Roth told you what happened," I said, sipping some of the tea. It had a strange taste, but it made me feel very relaxed.

"Now that would be nice, but I haven't spoken to Alvin since our last team together."

"But you published that partscore hand from his rubber bridge game—the one where the ten-of-hearts play at trick one would have defeated four diamonds. Can you tell me who gave you the details of the deal?"

Edgar sat back on the sofa and puffed away. "Yes, I can."

I stared at him and he gazed back at me. "Well?" I asked.

"Well, what?" he answered.

"Are you going to tell me who gave you the partscore hand?"

"Certainly not."

"Why not?" I asked.

"Because it's none of your business."

It was a smack in the face, and perhaps I deserved it, acting the young upstart and all. He offered me some softer words to lessen the sting: "But if you tell me why it's so important for you to know, maybe I'll tell you *why* I published the hand."

So I spilled the beans, as they say in the detective trade. I trusted him completely, and to this day, I believe there was a truth serum in the tea. I told him everything about everyone, including how I had lied to the detective and thrown Pizza's notebook into the Raritan River. I told him my theory on what happened the night of the little girl's fall, how I believed Pizza was in my dad's regiment during World War II, how Pizza had stolen the Theory of Exhaustion from the Roth-Stone book, and I even told him about my escapades with Old Leroy.

He was a good listener and never interrupted with questions or comments except perhaps to puff a little harder on his pipe during my more romantic descriptions of Chops. When I reached the point of returning to 94th Street that very afternoon, switching clothes and ringing his own bell, he downed the last of his tea and heaved a little sigh.

"Ah, yes, well, it all sounds like something right out of a novel, doesn't it?"

I nodded, then waited for him to give me some answers, which he did in his own fashion.

"Before I tell you why I published that hand, I would like to correct your notion about the so-called plagiarized bridge theory. You should not be so quick to accuse a man. You see, the inventor of a bidding convention, or theory, is rarely the same person who promotes it. I doubt very much that either Roth or Stone first came upon the idea of playing poker with their opponents. However, they *may* have been the first people to express it in their particular language.

"You profess to be a scholar of literature," he continued, noting my volume of Poe, "so you must realize that rarely, if at all, is a work of art totally original. Even a scientific invention is the reinterpretation of something that has come before, perhaps restructured in some new manner.

"In short, young Matthew, so-called original thinkers build upon the past. Whatever Mr. McCarver's shortcomings are as a human being—and between you and me, you are probably right in your assessment of him—he is not the thief of a bridge theory. No, you might say, in fact, that he has done service to the bridge community by redefining some very interesting concepts about deceiving one's opponents in the auction."

Edgar took a long drag from his pipe. I asked him if *he* applied the theory when he played.

"Personally, I don't subscribe to the concept—which doesn't necessarily mean it's not a useful theory. And if you'd like a small insight into what editors of bridge magazines are up against when they receive articles from unknown bridge authors, I will tell you one. Mr. McCarver sent me a rather incoherent essay and, with the help of one of my co-editors, Estee Griffin, I rewrote the piece, inventing the nomenclature, 'Theory of Exhaustion,' myself."

"Oh," I said. "It must be a difficult job, editing a bridge magazine."

"I heartily advise against it."

"But why don't you like the theory?" I asked.

"It simply doesn't suit my style. You see, I prefer to play a straightforward game with my partner. I try to tell him what I have in my hand, and he tries to do likewise. If the opponents are listening in and pick up on it, and even figure out how to use the information by sacrificing against our game or slam, well, I congratulate them. It's very seldom that I run into such astute opponents, and in the meantime, my partner and I are very comfortable knowing that we can trust each other to bid exactly what we have rather than to plot some evil trap for the opponents."

"Then you don't think I should try it?"

"That's entirely up to you. It's a perfectly good ploy—for the person who can get away with it. Take Roth and Stone. They enjoy chicanery. They like to trap-pass on certain awkward hands, and later in the auction guess whether to balance. That's their *style*. The important thing about a bidding theory is not how good the theory is but whether it suits the person who is playing it. For you, I dare say, the Italian Roman Club system is probably a very poor system; or if I were to ask one of my beginning students at the Card School to judge whether a 15-point hand is a good 15 or a poor 15, I would be doing her a disservice. Yet you and I both know that the best way to play 16 to 18 notrump openings is to include some strong 15's while eliminating some strong 18's."

"True," I said, though I must admit I was getting a free lesson myself. "But don't you favor the *weak* notrump?"

"There, you see. Strong notrumps don't suit me, but I still don't disapprove of them."

"But how does a player know what his style is? I mean, I hear this convention or that concept or this type of play and I try to adapt them to my own game. Does that mean my style is just a mishmash of everybody else's?"

"It's reasonable to try everything—especially when you're young, like yourself. Then you can see what works for you and what does not. Your style may simply be what you feel most comfortable with. For example, take the weak notrump. If you feel comfortable opening a 12-to-14-point hand with one notrump and enjoy it, you should adopt it. If you feel nervous every time you open one notrump with 12 points, you shouldn't do it."

I had always thought the merits and flaws of systems were strictly scientific. But Edgar was rating the effectiveness of a system by the player who uses the system. It was like the lesson I had been learning at the rubber-bridge table: Make an intricate cue bid or difficult defensive play with a guy like Doctor B., and it would be like giving caviar to a child for dinner. Hmm. When Chops used the Theory of Exhaustion against me, it worked perfectly; but when I tried it, it blew up in my face. I was too nervous with it—I wasn't able to play the bluff. Hmm. On the same track: Put a clean, well-oiled gun in the hands of someone who's never used a gun, and that so-called precision weapon is no longer so effective either.

Bridge, like life, is a game with people in it. The bids, the plays, the events of day-to-day, deal-to-deal, are rarely black and white; most of the time they can only be interpreted by knowing the people behind them.

Edgar rose from his seat and looked at a clock on the mantel. "Well, young Matthew, I hope I've helped you in your admirable quest for knowledge. It's getting late and I have some work."

I rose also, but then, as I put on my jacket, I realized he had not told me why he had printed the partscore deal in this month's issue. I reminded him as he showed me to the door.

"Ah yes, you remembered that, did you?" He heaved a big sigh and thought for a few seconds before continuing. "Let me put it this way. Say you were the editor of a certain bridge magazine, and you were requested by a certain party, whom you had a good deal of respect for, to publish a particular deal in a particular fashion to further the cause of justice. What say you, young Matthew, what would you do?"

"I uh, I don't know; I guess I would publish it."

"Ah, then there you have it. I bid you good evening."

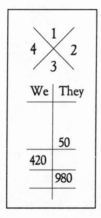

Everybody's Vulnerable

COURTYARD

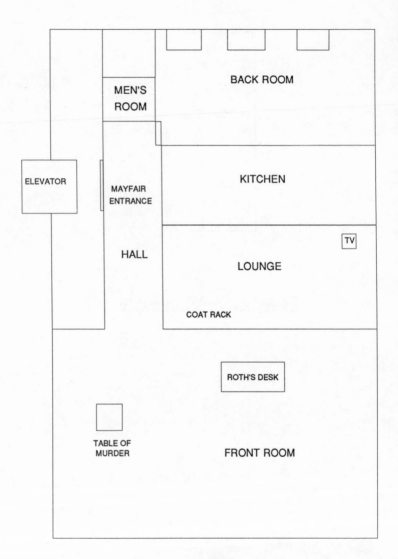

57TH STREET

Positions after the shooting, when the lights came back on:

PIZZA

OTTO

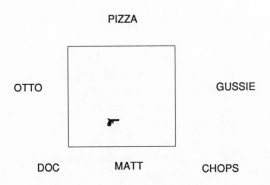

GUSSIE

DOC   MATT   CHOPS

ROTH

27

*A REVIEW OF THE PLAYERS—BLACKWOOD,
BLINIS, AND MORE BLACKWOOD—
CAUGHT IN THE ACT.*

L OOKING BACK on the conversation with Edgar, which took
place nearly 20 years ago, I have come to understand why
most bridge players reach a certain level and do not improve
beyond that level: stubbornness. Even if they find the systems and
ideas that suit their style—even if they learn to relax and feel comfortable—they still fail to take into account the people behind the
cards.

These stubborn experts, as well as amateurs, are locked in by
their own blinders. They don't realize that a one-spade opening
with Alvin Roth as their partner is not the same as a one-spade
opening with Otto Marx. They play a hand the same way against
Frankenstein as against Gussie Addles.

When given an opening lead problem, they rarely ask: Who is
my partner? Who are my opponents? What are their characteristics? No, instead, they analyze the auction as if it were an entity
unto itself, and choose the same lead no matter who is at the
table.

You often hear: What's the best percentage play? Or: How do
you play this hand with a low-club lead? But rarely do you hear:
How do you bid this hand with Kaplan as your partner?

If there was one lesson I learned that day, and continued to
learn from rubber bridge, it was: Learn the players. Yet, even
today, as we enter the 1990s, bridge players of the highest caliber
are sent to World Championships with their opponents' bridge
notes to study; rarely are they briefed on *personality traits.*

The weather was balmy for December, and as I walked downtown along Central Park West that Friday evening, I thought about these things, and tried to concentrate on the players I was about to face both at the table and in the upcoming inquiry.

Pizza McCarver: Horrible person. Blackmailer. Violent with women. Slob. Egotistical bridge player. Knowledgeable about systems but fails to apply the knowledge at the right times. Overbidder. Good card player, though. Almost certainly murdered the little girl in a state of frenzy when he discovered her copying from his black notebook. Yet, he never showed his temper to me, even when I "shot" a gun into his belly. Could I be wrong about his killing the girl? Was it some kind of weird accident, after all?

Stanley: Lifelong friend until he became envious of my bridge ability. For some reason, seems to be attractive to women—dammit. No scruples. A flair for the bidding, maybe too much of a flair, always looking for something tricky, some edge. Certainly he tends to misanalyze the play and defense. Talks a better game than he plays. A liar, a gigolo, but a grade-A student. How is it possible? He's definitely in league with Pizza, but as against that, he's scared of him, too. Does Pizza have something on him? Hmm. I must remember that I'm supposed to bring him back to school after the inquiry—assuming we are both free to leave. I hate him for what he did to Esther. He's got to be punished, somehow.

Chops: What can I say? Sharp, clever, expert bidder and crackerjack defender. Weakest part of her game is declarer play—too much in her shell and does not take advantage of the defenders' carding. Certainly plays her partner and opponents. A beautiful dark cat, but with claws intact. Has a sudden temper, and a personality that seems to switch back and forth between ignoring me and showing affection, depending on the current state of my bridge game. Unfaithful. Few scruples, that's for sure, having compromised herself with Pizza. I think she still has it in for him, or why else would she have wanted me to read that Roth-Stone Ism?

Frankenstein: A great bridge player in all departments. Terrible temper, though. However, he does tend to forget the last hand after exploding at partner, plays on without being fazed—must be a tremendous psychological advantage to bury the last hand.

Really, he's kinder than he appears at first. He may use insulting nicknames but talks bridge theory without talking down to you. Hmm. Seems to have taken death of daughter very well. It's hard to believe, considering his devotion to her.

Doctor B: Terrible bridge player in all departments. Most dangerous in the overbidding department, but his card play is not nearly as bad—most rubber-bridge players seem to excel at card play; I wonder why. Epitomizes Roth's concept of the rubber bridge player who loses his money quickly rather than slowly. No patience for conventions. Strange man. What was he doing at Rutgers? Seems to be a dedicated doctor away from the card table. Hmm. What was it he started ranting about that day outside the College Bookstore? Didn't he get upset about conditions in the operating room? There's some connection here to Pizza, but I can't remember . . . was it in the notebook? Something to do with the McCarver Foundation—Yes! There was a grant for a new hospital wing! But then, that wing was never built, or Doctor B. would not have been so upset.

Gussie: Nice woman, I suppose, even if she does have a high squeaky voice. Terrible bidder, mostly because she underbids too much. I can hardly remember her ever taking a bid! But then again, you can count on her when she *does* bid, especially when she doubles. Steady, but nothing special in the card play. She'll signal on defense what she has—Gussie doesn't fool around with deception or deep analysis. Pretty wise old woman. Stays out of the game after supper to digest her food, reads the paper, doesn't take flak from anyone, especially Pizza. Hmm. Remember from the notebook. She used to keep Pizza, before his inheritance. Then if she has money, why doesn't she play in the high-stake game? Maybe she's prudent. But then again, didn't I see Pizza take care of her minus account the first time I was at the Mayfair? That would mean she once had money, but now doesn't. How did she lose it? It couldn't have been at two-cents-a-point. Was it in the stock market? Wonder how she feels knowing that Chops is Pizza's girl. That must be hard to take, being around both of them, day in, day out.

Otto: A bit of a crackpot, but what of it? He plays bridge as though on a roller-coaster, always doing things in the bidding.

Totally unpredictable, that's for sure. Interested in the stock mar-. ket too. Resourceful fellow, had the flashlight handy during the blackout. Well, of course, it must have been in his toolbox—he *is* the janitor. Very sharp temper—banging the table during supper when he read about his Hungarian bidding theory stolen by Pizza. But then there was something in the notes. . . hmm. . . didn't Pizza help him get his job? Yes, which means Pizza knew him when he first came to New York. Maybe Pizza *did* "adopt" the Budapest bidding theory—that would mean the theory was not only Roth-Stone's but used in Hungary as well. Yes, Edgar was right—he said that a bridge theory was not likely to be totally original. The Theory of Exhaustion may go back to the days of Culbertson, maybe further back to the days of whist. . . to the days of Poe?

Maggie: Didn't play bridge, of course, but is a great cook. Was she there the night of the girl's fall? Of course, I remember she got upset at Pizza for throwing his noodles at Frankenstein, but hitting her by mistake. According to the newspaper account, she left early that night, before the lightning hit. Then how could she have been so insistent that I was not involved? I wonder if she'll be at the inquiry. On the other hand, she was interviewed at the time. Seemed to be very protective of the little girl. A very nice woman, that Maggie. Funny that she's the niece of Old Leroy. I wonder if she knows about what kind of gang he hangs out with? Actually, when I think about it, Leroy isn't such a bad guy.

Roth: Great player and theorist, but doesn't play much in his own club. He also left early the night of the blackout. Seems to say what he thinks about his club players without fear of insulting them and losing their business. Calls them "children." Also seems to be lenient about collecting on minus accounts. Never once asked me for money—and two months went by without my reappearing. Must be hard up to get a night-man to hire the likes of Stanley. Then again, Stanley is smart, and maybe Stanley owed money on his account and is working it off. Hmm. If that were the case, Pizza was certainly not taking care of Stanley's losses in return for Stanley's helping him cover up a murder. Do I have Stanley and Pizza's relationship all wrong? Is Stanley blackmailing Pizza or is Pizza blackmailing Stanley? Naw, Pizza's got too much money.

Detective Kennedy: Young for a detective. Pretty naive about his bridge ability, having played only a few duplicates. Seems to be slow. Why did he call for an inquiry two weeks after the death of the victim? Hmm. Was a bit tricky with me during my grilling at the Quad, trying to trap me with that slam deal. Perhaps he's just overworked and fits things into his own schedule. There must be a lot of homicides in New York, and the death of the girl may very well be an accident—but doesn't sound like the way a homicide detective would go about his business. . . .

I had turned the corner at 57th Street, and by the time I finished reviewing the players, I found myself across the street from Carnegie Hall. The Mayfair was farther down the block, and I paused to record the moment in my mind. Perhaps a notebook would have helped, as Mr. Keewood suggested, but in matters of senses and occasions of this sort where something serious that will forever affect me was about to take place, using my mind as a notebook was more accurate—I did not wish to lose the sensation of what I was feeling by trying to record it in written language. That I would remember this feeling of being on the doorstep of a horrifying adventure, I had no doubt; that I could never satisfactorily describe that feeling, I had no doubt either. And to emphasize this foreboding moment in my life, nature placed an exclamation point across the sky.

It was a terrible, wonderful lightning bolt that flashed above the East River lengthwise between two giant clouds hovering like ghosts above the New York skyline. The ugly whiteness of the sky invoked a shriek from some of the people waiting in line across the street on the steps of the concert hall.

I decided to cross over and see who was playing tonight. The billboard read, "The New York Philharmonic" and underneath was the evening's program:

First Symphony by Johannes Brahms
Piano Concerto #1 by Easley Blackwood

I took a second look. Yes, that's what it said: "Blackwood," and to frighten me further it was "*Easley* Blackwood." It was much too much of a coincidence not to be the same man who had invented the convention for asking aces. Something was in the air all right, something that nightmares were made of, something I could not escape. For just a moment, I thought I *could* escape! I could attend the performance, and skip the inquiry. But they would find me, no doubt, with that *Blackwood* clue, written in red across the billboard.

So I started walking again, toward the club, when I passed the Russian Tea Room and felt a rumbling in my stomach. Except for Edgar's tea, I hadn't eaten since lunch. Curtain time at Carnegie Hall was 8:00, and people were still dawdling; there must have been at least an hour, an hour and a half until the inquiry was called for. But was there any way I could really have a meal here? I had no money in my pocket—counterfeit or real—so my chances were very poor. Nevertheless, I brashly entered the door, making sure my jacket was buttoned to the top. My pants and shoes looked somewhat presentable, and maybe I could pass for an eccentric tourist who suddenly finds his wallet missing when it came time to pay the bill. It was a stupid and sinful thing to do, but I ventured inside anyway, believing I was following some preordained path.

That path was suddenly sparkling with gold, red and white Christmas ornaments strung across the silver mirrored walls. There was a line from the cloakroom to the maitre d', and most of the line was a perfect mixture of dark black cashmere and pure white diamond.

I elbowed my way in amid haughty looks, and in less than a minute I was at the front. The man with the tuxedo gave me a quizzical look and asked what name my reservation was under. I took my best shot and said, "Michael McCarver." There was a small chance, I thought, that Pizza had a following here. After all, he loved food, had recently come into lots of money, and the restaurant was just down the block from the Mayfair.

To my astonishment, the maitre d' said, "Right this way." In a few seconds he had ushered me in front of a small booth in the corner, and sitting there, making short order of a bowl of Beluga caviar and wheat blinis (with sour cream) were Pizza, Chops, and Stanley! For a moment, I thought I heard Pizza say, "Shut up." Chops was still wearing her sunglasses. Stanley looked completely out of place between the two of them. If truth be known, it's a good thing I didn't examine myself too closely in the mirror or I would not have criticized *Stanley's* appearance.

"Always room for a fourth," said Pizza, a squirt of melted

butter dripping down his chin. A chair was called for and before too long I was also feasting on caviar—although mine was red because Pizza insisted there was no way I could distinguish the black from the red anyway.

He ordered me a Stolichnaya on the rocks as well, and the waiter asked how old I was. I told him I was 18 that very day, and everybody wished me a hearty congratulations. "I remember your last birthday," said Stanley suddenly.

And the other 16 as well, I thought. After all, we had been best friends from childhood. So what happened to us?

"We've just been discussing a new form of Blackwood," said Pizza. "It's called, you know, kid, uh . . ."

"Roman Blackwood," said Chops, her lips moving, but not another facial muscle.

"I'm thinking of calling my new baby, 'McCarver'—What do you think?"

"It's very original," said Stanley.

"Give us all a break," said Chops.

The waiter was back with my vodka and blinis by the time Pizza had outlined his "new baby." Pizza ordered three glasses of tea, one Napoleon, one Chocolate Mousse, and one Strawberries Romanoff. In a nutshell, his new system was similar to Roman Blackwood but with an added safety device on the following round. Over four notrump, five clubs showed zero or three aces, five diamonds showed one or four aces, five hearts showed two aces with nothing extra, and five spades showed two aces with an important king (for example, a king in the trump suit). The added wrinkle was that the four-notrump bidder, over five clubs or five diamonds, could check to see if responder had zero or one ace rather than three or four aces. He did this by bidding the next suit. It was then responder's duty to return to the trump suit with the lower number, but cue-bid or bid a slam with the higher.

"Listen, man," said Stanley, "it's nice, but I don't think it's possible to mix up a three-ace differential. I mean, by the time you reach the five level, you should have some idea of partner's strength."

"Why not have the four-notrump bidder simply return to the trump suit over five clubs?" suggested Chops, adding a slight yawn at the end. "Then responder passes with zero aces and goes on to slam with three aces."

"That sounds easiest," I added, slicing into my third blini.

Suddenly Pizza shouted, "No, no, no! Who's the bidding theorist around here?"

From behind the sunglasses, I could see Chops' eyebrows lift a half an inch.

"My way avoids confusion," he continued. "You ask for aces, you get your reply, and you ask for a clarification. Three steps, simple and clean."

"Fine, man," said Stanley. "We'll play it."

"Good," said Pizza. "Any time two of us are partners, agreed?"

"No, we'll play it when we're *opponents*," said Chops.

"You're getting to sound like Gussie, you know that?" said Pizza, his finger near her face.

"Must be *your* influence," she returned.

"Hey, man," said Stanley, "it's getting late. We better get back to the club."

"You take the kid," said Pizza. "She and I are having dessert."

"I don't want dessert," said Chops.

"I ordered it for you," insisted Pizza. "Don't you know about the people starving in China?"

I could just barely see his heavy hand holding her wrist under the table. Personally, I wanted to support those starving people myself if eating one of those desserts could help—but Stanley grabbed me by my own wrist and edged me to the door.

"What do you think you're doing?" I asked when we were outside, under the canopy.

"Let the two of them have it out alone," he said.

"The two of them have already *had* it out."

Stanley and I had a lot more to say to each other as we crossed 57th Street and walked to the Mayfair, but no words were spoken. The air was heavy with dew and I could almost feel the electricity building to a crescendo. When we got to the club, I went straight to the men's room and did my best to refresh myself for the ordeal to come.

When I came out and walked back into the TV room to check my Poe on the coatrack, I noticed Stanley bent over a deck of cards. There was no question about it—he was fixing the deck!

28

RATTING—LOTS OF INS AND OUTS—
SHADOWS—A BLACKWOOD DISASTER—
SECOND BLACKOUT—COLD STEEL—
A SHOT—ONE BRIDGE PLAYER LESS.

I LOOKED down at Stanley and shook my head. "This doesn't surprise me," I said. He started to object—said I had no idea what was going on, called me a nincompoop, and told me to go back to the Quad where I belonged.

"Oh yeah?" I said. "Well, what about Esther? I suppose I should take up where you left off."

"You mean like you did to me with Chops," he said.

"I wouldn't mention the two in the same breath," I said.

"Why not? You think Esther is some sort of saint? Well, let me tell you she makes Chops look like the Virgin Mary!"

"SHUT UP !" I screamed. "Who are you to talk? You already did enough damage to her."

"What the hell are you talking about?"

"I'm talking about PREGNANT. That's what I'm talking about!"

Half the deck fell to the floor. He took off his eyeglasses and wiped them on a handkerchief. Then he dabbed an eye, pretending it was only dirt. "Did she tell you she was pregnant?" he asked, in a very subdued tone.

I nodded, then placed my book up on the rack. The last thing I saw as I walked out of the room was Stanley, on all fours, gathering up the cards from the carpet.

There were no players in the back room, although Mr. Roth was there helping Maggie set a long row of tables with some kind of smorgasbord. There was some salad, bagels, cream cheese, olives and other delicacies. Apparently this was for the inquiry. It was nice of Maggie to make a party of it—it would probably be somebody's last good meal. As Mr. Roth set down a bowl of egg salad, he nodded at me.

"You're back," he said. "Check with me later at the desk. Your account has to be settled."

Wonderful, I thought. So he knows about the counterfeit bills and wants me to make good. I wondered if I could work it off the same way as Stanley—maybe work the weekend shift as the house-player. Then I did a mean thing: I ratted on my ex-friend, just to get his job:

"Mr. Roth," I said, "I just caught Stanley in the TV room—he was fixing a deck of cards."

Roth looked past me and said, "Is this true, Kesselman?"

Stanley was standing there, the cards in his hand! I ran out of the room before he could answer, so I don't know what he responded. But in all my short life of 18 years, I had never felt so ashamed.

In the front room, a few people were just sitting around drinking coffee and smoking cigarettes. There was Frankenstein in the far corner, gazing out the window. Gussie was reading her newspaper at a table right in front of me, with Otto leaning over her shoulder.

"You see," he said, pointing to the paper, "down only two points. It's a clazy market, Gus, and now is the time to get back in."

"You want I should go back in, Mr. Rockefeller? And I could also jump out the nearest window—and maybe you'll hold my hand."

"I'm just tlying to help, Gus. You got to have patience with these theengs."

I cleared my throat, and they looked up at me.

"Excuse me," I said. "Is the inquiry to start in here, or is the whole affair in the back room?"

"They're holding it at the Ritz," squealed Gussie, "black tie."

"In here, in here," said Otto, who seemed to be looking forward to the affair. "And by the way, these are yours." He handed over the two Franklins with the faces on both sides.

"I'm sorry about that," I said. "I didn't know they were fake."

"That may be," said Otto, "but I don't know they're fake either, and when I give them to Mr. Roth to pay my account, he says there's plenty where these come from."

I nodded in agreement. The man was a lunatic, the type you opened light with in fourth seat just to end the rubber. Suddenly he had his arm around me. "Hey, why don't we play a few deals to make the time go by, eh? We got enough players now for a two-penny game."

Gussie looked up. "I'm in," she said. "I'll get Stanley."

She went to find Stanley and I fetched a scorepad and pencil. The two of them soon appeared, and Stanley had two decks with him, red and blue. He spread the red ones across the table. Gussie picked the seven of clubs. Otto picked the six of hearts. I picked the jack of hearts. Stanley pulled the ace of hearts. Funny how Stanley always started the rubber with the best of the other three players.

Gussie shuffled the reds, passed them to Otto to cut, and Stanley dealt the first hand. I noticed his hands were sweaty and unsteady. No doubt he was nervous about the upcoming meeting with Detective Kennedy. No doubt he was furious with me, also.

♠ A J 6 5 2 ♡ K J 9 ◊ J 10 9 ♣ 4 2

Stanley opened one diamond, Otto passed and I responded one spade. Gussie overcalled two clubs and Stanley raised to two spades. Otto passed again and I invited game with three spades. Gussie passed and Stanley raised to four spades. Everyone passed and Gussie led the king of clubs. Here was my hand and the dummy:

Dummy
♠ K Q 7
♡ A 4 3 2
◊ A 8 7 2
♣ J 9

My Hand
♠ A J 6 5 2
♡ K J 9
◊ J 10 9
♣ 4 2

Gussie continued with the queen of clubs, Otto playing up-the-line with the five and the six. Then, without thinking further, Gussie switched to the four of diamonds. I ducked and Otto won the queen. Otto sat back in his chair and started contemplating the dummy. After a while he shifted to a low trump. I won

Gussie's ten with dummy's queen. I cashed the king of spades, Gussie discarding a club, then cashed two more trumps, Gussie throwing two more clubs.

On the fourth round of trumps, I had to discard a red card from dummy in this position:

Dummy
♠ —
♡ A 4 3 2
◊ A 8 7
♣ —

My Hand
♠ A 6
♡ K J 9
◊ J 10
♣ —

The obvious discard was a low heart. If Gussie held the king of diamonds, I could finesse again in diamonds and use dummy's fourth diamond to throw my nine of hearts. However, what was the likelihood that Gussie held the king of diamonds?

The odds were clear—the success of one of two finesses was 75%. That's what any mathematician would say. But against that, Gussie had switched to a diamond at trick three *without apparent thought.* Hmm. What would Poe's detective, Dupin, say if he knew Gussie? It would be unusual for a player like her to lead away from a king when she could make a safe exit with a trump. And to do it so fast was double evidence she did not hold the honor. Poe's detective would laugh at the percentages—and so I discarded a diamond from dummy and led a fifth trump, discarding another diamond as Gussie threw a diamond and Otto a club. By then I was down to five cards in each hand:

Dummy
♠ —
♡ A 4 3 2
◇ A
♣ —

Gussie   Otto

Me
♠ —
♡ K J 9
◇ J 10
♣ —

This time the percentage play was to finesse Otto for the queen of hearts. However, against that, there were two pieces of evidence no jury would fail to find convincing. First, Gussie had overcalled between two bidders. Sure, she had six clubs to the ace-king-queen. But knowing Gussie, I was certain she would never make that overcall with only nine points. Second, Otto's pause after winning the third defensive trick made no sense unless he was thinking about shifting to a heart (and then stopped himself because a trump looked safer). That meant he certainly didn't hold the queen of hearts because with that card, he would never even consider the shift.

Confident that these Poe-like readings were accurate, I led the jack of hearts from my hand. Gussie covered with the queen, and after winning the ace in dummy, I led a heart back to finesse through Otto's ten. A third round of hearts pulled in the rest of the suit, and dummy's ace of diamonds was my entry to the fourth heart. This was the whole deal:

```
                    Dummy (Stanley)
                    ♠ K Q 7
                    ♡ A 4 3 2
                    ◊ A 8 7 2
                    ♣ J 9
Gussie                                  Otto
♠ 10                                    ♠ 9 8 4 3
♡ Q 8 7                                 ♡ 10 6 5
◊ 6 4 3                                 ◊ K Q 5
♣ A K Q 8 7 3                           ♣ 10 6 5
                    Me
                    ♠ A J 6 5 2
                    ♡ K J 9
                    ◊ J 10 9
                    ♣ 4 2
```

After the hand, I half-turned toward the windows and noticed that Frankenstein had sat down behind me on my left.
"Little Baboon," he said, "you're improving." When you're in deep
concentration at the bridge table, you don't notice the kibitzers;
and it was a good thing in this case, because had I been aware of
Frankenstein's presence, I believe I'd have been too nervous to
work out the clues.

It was at this point that Pizza and Chops arrived. When
Gussie noticed them come through the door, she stopped shuffling and rose from the table. "I'm sorry," she said, "but somebody
has to fill in for me." She walked over to Pizza, and edged him
into the TV room. In the meantime, Frankenstein took Gussie's
seat at Otto's suggestion, and Chops, her mink still wrapped
about her, sat down in the kibitzer's chair vacated by Frankenstein.

My initial reaction was to object to Frankenstein's filling in
for a weak player like Gussie. But I decided to let Stanley do the
objecting, as I knew he would. However, there seemed to be a
strange aura about Stanley—not only did he appear less tense,
suddenly, but he appeared to be happy! Yes, he was suddenly
smiling—as I had not seen him do in more than three months. It
was as if he had sweated out a problem and had finally come to
some monumental decision, probably a sweet revenge, I thought.
That settled, he was completely relieved and enjoying the moment at hand.

As Frankenstein shuffled the blue deck, Stanley looked at me, and said, "C'mon, kid, let's show what two guys from Jersey City can do."

♠ A K Q 9 8 7 ♡ A ◊ 10 9 4 3 ♣ 4 3

Otto passed in front of me. And I passed in second seat. Clearly I should have opened one spade, but Stanley's last words surprised me so much that I lost concentration. When I saw what I had passed, I decided it wasn't *that* bad. We were not vulnerable, and with long spades, you can usually back into the auction later; in the meantime, I could learn quite a lot about the opponent's distribution by allowing them to bid first. This wait-and-listen tactic—albeit an accident—was a tactic that I felt very comfortable with and would utilize many times in my future bridge career. In later years I thought of it as my own adaptation of the Theory of Exhaustion. My name for it is "Lion-in-the-Bushes."

Frankenstein opened the bidding one club, Stanley overcalled one diamond, and Otto responded one heart. After only a few bids, game in spades seemed almost a certainty. However, rather than let my opponents know this, I decided to continue what I had started—this was definitely the "Theory" in all its glory.

I bid a gentle one spade.

Frankenstein raised to two hearts and Stanley passed. Now Otto jumped to four hearts. We were not vulnerable and they were. Was he trying to get me to sacrifice in four spades? I knew he was a madman, and I could not trust his jump, but this time I had played my part perfectly, even to the point that it sounded as if Otto were pushing me into my four-spade contract. Everybody passed my four-spade call. I suppose it was too much to expect to get doubled.

Frankenstein led the king of clubs and dummy came down:

Dummy
♠ 6 3
♡ 9 6 3
♢ A K J 5 2
♣ 9 5 2

Frankenstein   Otto

Declarer (me)
♠ A K Q 9 8 7
♡ A
♢ 10 9 4 3
♣ 4 3

Otto followed up the line as Frankenstein continued with the queen and jack of the suit. I ruffed the third round and took stock. Hmm. Had I opened one spade, I might not have reached game. For example, if the opponents had passed, Stanley would have responded one notrump and I would have had to mention diamonds to locate the double fit. A more likely rebid of two spades would have ended the auction.

"Are you going to be long?" asked Otto, "because I have to go do something."

I was wasting time thinking about the bidding when I should have been concentrating on the play. The hand was practically cold. The trump suit or the diamond suit had to behave—that's all. But before I could lay down a spade honor, the whole table was startled by the sound of thunder. I turned to the window; lightning had lit the dark sky again. Hmm. It made me think back to the storm in September. Suddenly, it occurred to me that reviewing the bidding was not a waste of time if it gave me a clue to the play.

The mad Hungarian would have opened a weak two-bid with six hearts, so his first-seat pass and subsequent jump indicated only five. I looked at him—as crazy as he was, he wouldn't jump to a vulnerable game with a balanced nine-point hand—not with Frankenstein as his partner. He had to have a singleton. If it were in diamonds, I could always make the contract by finessing later. If it were in spades, I was dead . . . unless . . . hmm . . . I remembered a similar position many months ago. Was it at here at the Mayfair? No, it was at the Quad. Big Al was learning about

303

finesses. He had taken the Quad-variation of a backward-finesse! That was it! If Otto held a singleton honor in spades. . . .

I led a diamond to dummy's king and played a spade off dummy. Otto followed with the ten and I played the queen. Then I led the nine of spades from my hand. This was the whole deal:

```
                    Dummy
                    ♠ 6 3
                    ♡ 9 6 3
                    ◇ A K J 5 2
                    ♣ 9 5 2
Frankenstein                        Otto
♠ J 5 4 2                           ♠ 10
♡ 10 8 7 4                          ♡ K Q J 5 2
◇ 6                                 ◇ Q 8 7
♣ A K Q J                           ♣ 10 8 7 6
                    Declarer (me)
                    ♠ A K Q 9 8 7
                    ♡ A
                    ◇ 10 9 4 3
                    ♣ 4 3
```

Frankenstein studied this nine of spades as if he were Sherlock Holmes examining the final clue to a murder mystery. "What are you trying to do to Frankenstein?!" he roared. I knew I had him. With four spades to the jack he was thinking that his partner held the ace. After all, how could I pass in second seat with six spades to the A-K-Q and then not play for a three-two split? Obviously, I held five spades to the king-queen and five diamonds to the queen. Something like:

```
                        Dummy
                        ♠ 6 3
                        ♡ 9 6 3
                        ◊ A K J 5 2
                        ♣ 9 5 2
Frankenstein                            Otto
♠ J 5 4 2                               ♠ A 10
♡ 10 8 7 4                              ♡ K Q J 5 2
◊ 6                                     ◊ 7 3
♣ A K Q J                               ♣ 10 8 7 6
                        Declarer (me)
                        ♠ K Q 9 8 7
                        ♡ A
                        ◊ Q 10 9 8 4
                        ♣ 4 3
```

If he went up with the jack, he would crash honors. Yes, Otto could then give him a diamond ruff or play another club to tap me, but would he? If Frankenstein imagined this position, he would realize that if he crashed trump honors, Otto would probably switch to a heart, allowing me to draw trump and claim 10 tricks.

I waited, noting Chops cool hand crawling up my back—a sure sign that I was once again on the right track.

However, in due course, Frankenstein went up with the jack of spades and defeated the contract. Chops' hand quickly fell to her lap while her chair inched closer to Frankenstein's. She asked him how he guessed the position.

"The Little Baboon had me for a minute," he whispered within my hearing. "But then, with K-Q-9-8-7 of spades, even *he* would know enough to play the king-queen of the suit, hoping for J-10 doubleton."

"But couldn't he have made an error?" asked Chops. "After all, he passed an opening bid."

"He might have made an error in the bidding," said Frankenstein, "because he passed in tempo. But how could he have made a technical error in the play after studying the deal so long?"

So I was too slow! I cursed myself for wasting time considering what might have been. I should have had their distribution pegged before the opening lead! Still, Frankenstein had played me to make the deceptive play, and even though it failed, I was proud he thought that highly of me.

Otto jumped up from the table. "I got to go," he said. I asked what time it was, and Doctor B., who must have just walked in, said it was 10 minutes to nine. Suddenly I remembered a phone call I was supposed to make. In the cloakroom, I retrieved my Poe and looked up the number written on the inside-cover. However, while I was in there, I couldn't help overhearing Pizza and Gussie going at it full steam:

"After tonight, that's it!" said Gussie.

"You can't do this to me; I told you everything in confidence." said Pizza.

"I won't have it!" cried Gussie. "She goes or you go!"

"And the boy, then what happens to my little boy?"

"I don't care any more, do you hear me? There's only so much the heart can stand."

"But, Gussie, Gussie, Gussie—"

"Shh, the kid."

I quickly moved back to the front room and asked Mr. Roth, who was sitting at his desk, working on the account cards, if I could use the phone. He nodded, and I dialed the number. My preceptor's voice came on the other end.

"Guy? Is that you?"

"Yes, I'm here at the Mayfair. Everything is okay, but I don't know if I'm gonna be able to bring Stanley back. We haven't even started the inqu—hello? . . . hello?" The connection was broken. I hung up and tried the number again, but there was no dial tone.

"Phone's dead," I said. Roth nodded, but didn't seem concerned.

"Maybe it's the storm."

Darn, I thought. I had forgotten to call home, too. Well, I would do that after the inquiry; at least then I would know how much I had to tell my parents. I was a calculating fellow back then, and was about to learn a lesson that I would never forget.

Back at the table, Chops had taken Otto's seat. If Stanley didn't object to this switch, I didn't either. What the hell, it might be our last rubber together for a long, long time. I dealt the cards as Stanley stared at the windows, in deep reflection. Suddenly I saw a shadow on the wall behind him; it was his shadow—no, it was mine! Had someone turned the angle of the lamp, or had I simply never noticed?

I heard a loud beating sound and turned toward the window. The rain was coming down hard against the glass. It was good to be in the club, I thought; it was dry and warm and safe in here. And despite my anxiety over what was to come, I felt that if I could only stay put in that chair, I would avoid the problems of the real world. It's a feeling that many people long for, and most rubber-bridge players attain—a warm, relaxing, comfortable feeling of spending time in another world.

Suddenly I noticed Doctor B. kibitzing on my left in the chair vacated by Chops. He glanced at his watch and muttered something about the detective being late. Time was running out, darn it, and soon we would have to throw in the cards and deal with that harsh reality.

♠ Q 5 2 ♡ A 7 5 ◇ K Q 8 7 4 ♣ J 9

Not a bad hand, but not a great one either. We were vulnerable and I could open one diamond or pass—it was close. Finally I decided to open one diamond; I had already thought too long to pass, anyway. Frankenstein, on my left, passed, and Stanley started to think too. This wasn't like him, but after a couple of seconds—though it seemed longer to me—he responded one heart. Chops overcalled one spade and I considered for a split second raising to two hearts, then thought better of it and passed.

Frankenstein peered into his cards and came up with two diamonds, a cue bid. Stanley passed, and Chops rebid two spades. I passed, and Frankenstein now tried three diamonds. After Stanley passed, Chops considered for quite a while, then jumped to four spades. I passed, and Frankenstein surprised me by bidding again. He said five clubs. Chops now jumped to six spades, and everybody passed. This was the auction:

Me	Frankenstein	Stanley	Chops
1 ◇	pass	1 ♡	1 ♠
pass	2 ◇	pass	2 ♠
pass	3 ◇	pass	4 ♠
pass	5 ♣	pass	6 ♠
(all pass)			

I had no problem on lead, and flung out the king of diamonds. There was no reason to panic by leading the ace of

307

hearts—if dummy held a big club suit for discards, I could ruff the third round with my queen-third of spades. Besides, I thought, as dummy appeared on the table, Chops' leap to slam must include second-round control of the heart suit, the only suit unbid by their partnership. When I saw dummy, I recognized the hand. I had played it before!

Dummy
♠ K 10 6
♡ Q 9
◇ A 6 5 2
♣ A K Q 8

Me
♠ Q 5 2
♡ A 7 5
◇ K Q 8 7 4
♣ J 9

It was about seven months earlier. We were sitting in my kitchen snacking on chocolate chip cookies and milk. It's funny how a detail like that came back to me now. Stanley had wanted to learn bridge—or so he said. He dealt out a random deal and showed me up by out-analyzing me. Hmm. On that occasion the dummy's hand was the opening bidder, and I had suggested an overcall of two diamonds with my hand, in between two bidders. If I remembered correctly, the entire deal looked like this on that occasion:

Dummy
♠ K 10 6
♡ Q 9
◇ A 6 5 2
♣ A K Q 8

West
♠ Q 5 2
♡ A 7 5
◇ K Q 8 7 4
♣ J 9

East
♠ 9 8
♡ J 10 8 6
◇ 10 9 3
♣ 10 7 6 5

Declarer
♠ A J 7 4 3
♡ K 4 3 2
◇ J
♣ 4 3 2

After the king-of-diamonds lead, Stanley showed me how to make the "cold" six-spade slam. Win the ace of diamonds and lead the queen of hearts to West's ace. After a diamond return, ruff in hand, finesse in spades with the ten, lead a heart to the king and ruff a heart in dummy. Then cash the king of trumps, ruff a diamond back to hand, and cash the ace of trumps:

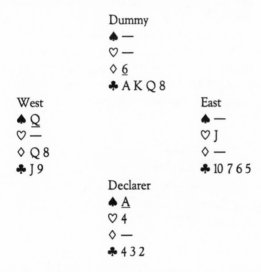

Dummy
♠ —
♡ —
◇ <u>6</u>
♣ A K Q 8

West
♠ <u>Q</u>
♡ —
◇ Q 8
♣ J 9

East
♠ —
♡ J
◇ —
♣ 10 7 6 5

Declarer
♠ <u>A</u>
♡ 4
◇ —
♣ 4 3 2

On this trick, East would be squeezed, and the slam would make.

"Wake up, Matt," said Stanley. I looked up. I was in a trance. What had happened? Everyone but me was on the second trick. I asked to see the first trick again, and Chops insisted it was illegal. Frankenstein, of all people, however, told her to let me see it, and the four cards were turned up.

As I pictured in my trance, Chops had won the ace of diamonds in dummy, Stanley played the three and Chops the jack from her hand. So far, trick two consisted of the queen of hearts from dummy, the three from Stanley, the four from Chops. Hmm. If I won the trick, I knew we were doomed. But if I ducked . . . if I ducked . . . hmm. By ducking, I might deprive declarer of an entry to her hand. Let's see. . . .

Even if she played another heart and ducked Stanley's ten, a diamond play would pump her down to four trumps. She might ruff out my ace of hearts, but another diamond ruff in her hand would reduce her to three trumps and she could not finesse my spade queen, cash the king, and return to her hand to draw the last trump.

So I refused to win the trick. But as I played my five of hearts, it didn't seem fair. This was the deal that Stanley had fixed in the cloakroom, I thought. But wait a second! Why bother to fix a slam, then deal it to the opponents? Were these the red cards or the blue? This was the third deal; had Chops shuffled these before I dealt? If she had, maybe this was just a fluke, one of those rare times when a hand repeats itself in some variation.

Meanwhile Chops was playing the hand and I was following suit. After the queen of hearts won the second trick, Chops led dummy's six of spades to her ace, felling Stanley's jack; then a spade back to dummy's ten, finessing my queen. This was the actual deal:

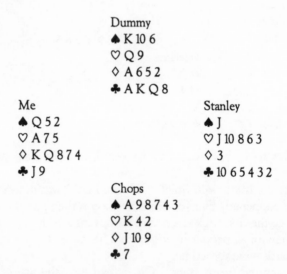

Dummy
♠ K 10 6
♡ Q 9
♢ A 6 5 2
♣ A K Q 8

Me
♠ Q 5 2
♡ A 7 5
♢ K Q 8 7 4
♣ J 9

Stanley
♠ J
♡ J 10 8 6 3
♢ 3
♣ 10 6 5 4 3 2

Chops
♠ A 9 8 7 4 3
♡ K 4 2
♢ J 10 9
♣ 7

Chops cashed the king of spades, drawing my queen, played ace-king-queen of clubs, discarding her remaining hearts, and led a diamond to my queen, claiming the balance.

I swallowed air. How could this have happened to me? What was I doing—thinking backwards on hands from the past instead of watching the cards in the present? Stanley had played the three of hearts on the queen, clearly a count signal.

Meanwhile Frankenstein was impressed, very impressed. "Mrs. Baboon," he cried, "I've never seen such play in my life!"

She blushed. (Yes, it was still possible for her—at the bridge table.) "I thought I knew the whole deal after trick one," she said proudly. Then, in contrast to her usual businesslike demeanor at the table, she clutched in her hands the 52 cards that had just been played and told Frankenstein her thought process. "Of course, even before the lead, I knew quite a lot. The boy—"

The boy!

"—had shown exactly 12 points and no singletons. With 13, he would never have thought so long before opening one diamond; with 11, he would have had some shape to open. But his failure to rebid after my one-spade overcall denied that shape. If he held a singleton, he surely would have bid a second suit or raised hearts. Yet his slight hesitation over my one-spade bid meant he had a conceivable alternative; my intuition told me it was three-card heart support, but he was so ashamed of his opening bid, he decided not to raise.

"Anyway, with him holding 12 points, Stanley must have responded with two, probably the jack of hearts—even *he* —"

She pointed to me.

"—would not fail to raise with ace-jack-third. I hoped Stanley held the jack of spades as well. That's because with spades three-one, I needed to find Stanley with an honor in order to pick up the suit."

"Wait a second," I said. "How did you know the spades were three-one?"

"Gimme a break," she answered, exasperated. Then she addressed Frankenstein, again. "His speed-of-lightning diamond lead practically screamed 'queen-third of trumps'. If he held the queen doubleton of trumps, he would at least have *thought* about leading the ace of hearts.

"Of course, it was a long-shot, but what I hoped for was that the boy would read Stanley's three of diamonds as an odd number of diamonds, and play him for three of them rather than a singleton. As you can see, I couldn't ruff a heart in dummy *and* pick up the trump suit, so my only hope was to sneak by a heart trick early. Luckily I was playing against this one—"

Me again.

"I figured he was barely good enough to duck the queen of hearts."

Suddenly she turned to me, saw my stricken face, and showed some compassion. "Believe me," she said, patting my hand, "I never would have made this hand against a weak player."

Thanks for the bone, I thought. But what good was it? My variations in tempo had given her three separate clues to my hand. I was despondent, and when I cut the cards for the fourth deal, I had completely lost track of the passage of time. It was now 9:15, and Detective Kennedy still had not arrived. Nor did I even care. I had lost interest in everything but the game, my mind swept into the waves of Chops' thought processes and her incredible deductive reasoning. I did not even notice the terrifying storm outside, the wind, the rain, the thunder, and the bolts of lightning that were transforming 57th Street into a sea of chaos. Nor did I notice the return of Otto and Gussie to the game, at least not until the auction to the fourth deal began.

$$\spadesuit - \heartsuit J98764 \diamondsuit 872 \clubsuit KJ82$$

Otto passed, and Stanley opened the bidding with two notrump. Gussie passed and I responded three diamonds, a transfer bid to three hearts. Stanley, however, rebid three spades instead of three hearts. To me, this meant he loved his hand for hearts and was cue-bidding. Granted, my heart suit was weak, but my overall distributional strength was certainly worth a slam try in return. The question that concerned me was: How do I make that slam try? Do I bid my club suit or do I cue-bid my first-round spade control?

As I pondered this question, I realized someone was breathing deeply over my right shoulder. I turned for a second. Chops was kibitzing again, now on my right. She was still excited from the last hand, no doubt. Hmm. What was the most important feature of my hand? My spade void, of course. So I bid four spades.

Suddenly I heard Roth's voice commenting from his desk. "Sounds like two children." Then I heard Chops inch her chair over behind Gussie—the ultimate insult! Of course, I should have bid my club suit as Chops prefers. "Bid your suits first; otherwise how can partner know how to evaluate his hand?" The words came back to me now like a haunting.

Stanley's next bid was four notrump, Blackwood. I responded five clubs, no aces, and Stanley bid five diamonds. It was a great bid, I thought. He was obviously confused with my zero-aces response after my prior spade cue bid, and was checking for a spade void for slam. I started to bid six hearts when I stopped myself again. This time it was the shadows that stopped me!

Behind Stanley, I saw my own still shadow and that of my two kibitzers, and for a split second I thought I saw another shadow also. No, it was my mind playing tricks in the middle of the auction; when I returned to the auction, however, it occurred to me to bid six clubs on my way to six hearts. It was possible that Stanley held four clubs and the hand would play better in the 4-4 fit. Then I stopped myself a second time. Stanley might take six clubs as a grand-slam try. It would be nice to get him to evaluate his queen of clubs, if he had it, but I had a feeling I had already bid too much.

So I bid six hearts, expecting it to end the auction; but the next thing I heard was *seven* hearts. Suddenly someone doubled. I looked up from my cards—Gussie. This was a terrible thing, because when Gussie doubled, you not only didn't make your contract—you ran for cover.

Everyone passed, and Gussie, her fingers shaking, pulled out three different cards from her hand, then put them back again. In the meantime, Stanley had gotten up from the table and left the room. There was Pizza, to the left of Stanley's chair. He must have been kibitzing over Stanley's right shoulder. Then I remembered! At the Russian Tea Room we had discussed the new Blackwood responses. Five clubs showed zero or three aces. Five diamonds asked me how many. Six hearts said I had all three!

I couldn't bear the wait. I peered over into Gussie's hand: three aces! Another flash of lightning filled the sky. There was a booming round of thunder. The ace of spades hit the table, and I tabled my hand. Suddenly, Pizza, eyes alight like I'd never seen them, jumped up and said, "Here, I'll play it."

What did I care if he took Stanley's seat? It was all so hopeless anyway. He reached for the four of hearts with a big smile on his face. Could I be wrong? Was there a chance for this grand slam, even missing three aces? Suddenly the lights went out.

"I thought they called it off," somebody said to my left.

"It's a clazy theeng. I'll get my flashlight," said Otto, his accent unmistakable.

We waited in the dark for 30 seconds, maybe 35. I could barely see the outlines of the cards, and Pizza's head bent over in thought. I heard Otto at Roth's desk. It sounded like he opened up a drawer or a toolbox. A few more seconds passed in silence.

"Where's the dummy?" someone asked in a whispery voice, a

voice I couldn't quite place.

"Here I am," I said.

Suddenly I felt the cold steel across my cheek. I stiffened. The arm across the left side of my neck rested firmly on my shoulder. I started to resist. There was a shot. A match was lit and I felt hot and faint. I was sure I had been shot. I was sure it was Stanley taking revenge for my having ratted on him earlier in the evening. Another match was lit. A red liquid was spreading over declarer's cards, which were lying face down on the table. That is except for one card, the queen of clubs, which was face up, a piece of the upper right corner blown to bits. I hadn't given my partner the chance to evaluate that card in the bidding. Now I was glad to see it was there. Then there he was, facing me, head downcast, with a red hole through his shirt pocket. Was that the tomato stain I had seen earlier that day on his T-shirt?

"He's still thinking," said Gussie.

"It's a played card," insisted Chops.

Feeling very dizzy now, I grabbed the closest thing to me— something, anything to hold onto. It turned out to be the gun. That's when the lights came back on.

29

I RUIN THE FINGERPRINTS—SURPRISE
RETURN—A WELL-CATERED INQUIRY—THE
DETECTIVE'S STRATEGY—STANLEY'S TALE

I DROPPED the gun on the table, and when I realized my finger-prints were all over it, I picked it up again and wiped it clean against my shirt. Then I looked back and forth around the room. There was Otto on my left, all hot and sweaty. There was Gussie on my right, a white ghost, staring at Pizza's huge head. There was Doctor B. on my left, standing up, examining Pizza's pulse. There was Chops on my right, looking into Gussie's hand and leaning

"He's still thinking," said Gussie.

over to see what Otto held as well. There was Roth at his desk, his hand on the phone. Who was missing? Stanley was missing; so was Frankenstein; and of course Maggie—she was probably in the kitchen. Another person was in the room: Detective Kennedy.

The detective was looking very unhappy. His head was held like a cradle in both of his hands and he was shaking it. Then he looked up at the ceiling and spoke to someone—I think it was the Lord.

Pizza, in the meantime, looked even less happy than Detective Kennedy. The side of Pizza's face that you could see was slowly turning grey, but you couldn't really say he looked any the worse for it. Suddenly an additional little blob of human tomato sauce burst out of the corner of his mouth and Gussie let out a horrid scream. His head jolted forward and I lunged for his cards before he fell on top of them and ruined the hand altogether.

"Don't touch anything!" screamed the detective. "Never . . . touch . . . anything . . . ever . . . AGAIN!"

I had already moved the cards over and was not one bit sorry. There was still my account to consider, and if a competent declarer like Pizza thought we had a chance after the ace of spades lead, I wasn't about to let his demise cost me 2470 points. I wanted his hand preserved.

Detective Kennedy walked over to the table and gave me a warning. "From now on, you're gonna do as I say and you're going to tell the truth—and that goes for *all of you!*"

There was silence in the room. The rain had suddenly stopped outside the window. But there was still a dripping sound. At first I thought it was Detective Kennedy's raincoat dripping on the floor. But the floor was carpeted. No, it was Pizza, and, unless Maggie had a very strong bleach under the sink in the kitchen, the card table would have to be replaced.

As Detective Kennedy wrote down the positions of the players, Gussie continued to sob. She was the only one showing any sign of remorse, and I had a feeling nobody else was very saddened by what had happened. I was saddened in my own way, however; saddened for my own position in the affair. After all, when the lights came on, I was the one holding the gun, and though, given a different time and opportunity, I might have shot Pizza McCarver, I was not the guilty party in this particular case. Still, I was currently the chief suspect in a homicide, and was feeling pretty bad about it.

The detective asked where the phone was, and Roth, who still had his hand on it, lifted the receiver. When the detective took it, I knew it was working fine, because he called the bureau and told them to send the rest of the homicide squad to the scene of the crime.

"*I'd* like to make a call," I said. No longer did I wish to keep my activities a secret from my family. The fact was, I needed a lawyer, and I wasn't going to get one without my father's help.

"Wait a second," said the detective. "Of course you're all entitled to call your attorneys and I have to warn you anything you say may be held against you. But, off the record, I'd like to give you all a chance to avoid a lot of hassle. That is, let's make a group effort and get to the bottom of all this right here and now. I suggest—and nobody's gotta go along with me—I suggest we go into the back room, sit down and go over the facts. Think about it. It's a lot more comfortable here than in a police station—"

"I'd like to call my babysitter," interrupted Chops, who had finished examining the deal.

"What time is she on until?" asked the detective.

"Until midnight," she replied, "but—'

"I promise to have you back there by then." He looked at his watch. "It's only ten to ten. Just sit tight. If you're hungry, I'm sure we can arrange something."

"We have a spread in the back," said Roth.

"You hear that? Great, there's some good food back there too. On the house, Mr. Roth?"

"All right, all right, on the house," said Roth. "What's the difference? They don't pay their accounts anyway."

"So what do you folks think? Okay? Everyone want to cooperate? Good, let's go in, because I want to start things off with an announcement."

I looked around. It sounded strange. Don't police detectives like to book everyone and get fingerprints and things? Well, maybe everyone in the room was innocent, or maybe they just wanted to appear innocent, because they all nodded their heads in accord—that is, except for Pizza.

We headed out into the hallway and across to the back room. Only Doctor B. remained, to examine the corpse.

When we had all entered the back room, most of the players went straight to the buffet without pausing to hear Detective

Kennedy's announcement. I noticed Stanley was already there carrying two full plates of smoked salmon, Bermuda onions and bagels. The detective was standing on a chair, telling us to stop eating for a minute and prepare ourselves for a small shock. I didn't really think he could shock this crowd, but lo and behold, he made a nice try: Out of the kitchen walked Maggie, followed by Frankenstein, followed by Frankenstein's little girl!

It's a good thing we had napkins under our plates. Tears streamed down all of our faces—except for Roth's and Gussie's. I think Roth had known she was okay all along, and Gussie had simply shed all of her tears over Pizza. The girl's father kept telling everyone to stop acting like emotional baboons, especially Stanley, who seemed to appear out of the blue with two empty plates and tears in his eyes.

"It's a clazy world," said Otto, drying his cheek, after spilling a large blob of cream cheese on the floor.

I noticed Doctor B. come in and go straight for the chopped liver. He was the one who told me, during his visit to Rutgers, that the little girl was all right. Detective Kennedy buttonholed him and whipped out his notepad. I figured the doctor had examined the corpse and was relating the gory details. If they wanted to know what he had for lunch and dinner, I could be of assistance.

I remembered now that Kennedy was the one who had told me the girl had died. Was that another one of his detective tricks? I saw Doctor B. nod to Kennedy and leave the room. He did not come back for a long time.

I hate to admit it, but I gorged myself, too. Besides what I had seen before, there were two chocolate layer cakes and a bowl of jello. "It does seem a shame," I overheard Maggie say to Mr. Roth. "Chocolate layer cake was Pizza's favorite dessert." Stanley was back for more. He stabbed into the chocolate cake with an over-sized knife, designed, I believe, to cut the bagels. I wondered how he could eat so much only a couple of hours after his Russian Tea Room dinner. Then I decided to try the egg salad. . . .

We ate pretty fast—there was almost no talking, it being somewhat of a wake. Still, everyone ate pretty heartily. I wondered if the detective was watching for this. Personally, I took care to notice if anyone was forcing food down just to *appear* innocent and relaxed. In the corner, I saw Chops hugging and kissing the child, who, by the way, had her neck in a frightening

Out of the kitchen walked Maggie, followed by Frankenstein,
followed by Frankenstein's little girl!

brace. Maggie came over and led the girl to the chocolate cake, from which she took two extra-large helpings, showing signs of becoming a future Mayfair-ite. The girl never said a word, I noticed, but just smiled a lot and ate.

Finally we all took some good burps and the little girl sat down next to the window—just for old time's sake, I imagine—and started on her second slice of cake. This time, however, both Frankenstein and Chops moved next to her, forming a protective and—what shall I say?—*loving* fence around her. Then they started to whisper about a bridge hand; I think it was the fourth deal.

Through all this, I couldn't help remembering that Pizza Mc-Carver was lying face-down on the bridge table in the other room—it was a nasty fact that just wouldn't go away. And as I began to get curious as to exactly when rigor mortis sets in, Detective Kennedy called the inquiry to order. All of us grabbed our coffees and desserts as the detective asked us to form a semi-circle; then he brought out his notepad again.

"Let me first apologize for being late tonight. If I had been here on time, this inquiry would have been as planned, a review and explanation of little Cathy's accident of October 4th. But getting across town in the storm tonight was nearly impossible! Of all nights, my siren goes on the blink, too!" His hand flew up in the air in disgust.

"It's a clazy theeng, but I used to work on sirens, and those theengs never did work right," said Otto.

Detective Kennedy raised his palm. "Let's try to do this in an orderly fashion. Pretend you're playing bridge and you have to wait for your turn to speak, please." The detective obviously was used to duplicate, not rubber. "The storm seems to have had a terrible effect on things here, and now we have an inquiry into a homicide. I'd like to solve this case tonight if we can. As I said before, it'll be a lot easier for everyone."

Otto raised his hand.

"Yes, what is it now?" asked Kennedy.

"If you don't mind my saying so, I theenk it is quite obvious who the killer is. I don't like to be the one to point fingers, but we all know who was holding the revolver when the lights come back on."

Thanks a lot, Otto, I thought. *I'll return the favor someday.*

"We'll get to that," said the detective, "but first I'd like to clear up little Cathy's case, because I believe it may have a bearing on this one." He reached into his coat pocket and took out some cigarettes. They looked a bit damp. "Anyone have a cigarette?" he asked. Gussie gave him one from her pack and the detective lit up. After some inhaling and gazing at the ceiling, he started to pace around the semicircle of suspects.

"To begin with, let me tell you all that Cathy is going to be fine. And I apologize again to those of you who came here tonight under the impression that she was uh, gone from us. However," and he looked firmly at me now, "many of you have not been square with me either, so take it as your own doing."

He took a look at Cathy by the window. "She suffered multiple bruises, two sprained wrists and sprained neck, but her most serious problem stemmed from a coma that left her with a speech problem and slightly blurred vision. Doctor Bellyard assures me that she is rapidly recuperating. However, it was this coma that made things so difficult for me—she could not tell me what had happened or who was in the room with her at the time of her fall. Nor could I ask her to write, lift parts of her body or shake her head—at least not for a while."

Little Cathy had a big smile on her face now; certainly her hearing was sharp because she knew she was the subject of the detective's remarks.

"After my initial interviews with you people, I had to put Cathy's case on hold. There were lots of discrepancies in your testimony, but, at the time, I was too busy to delve much further. Unfortunately, we live in an area where crime is rampant, so the case of a fallen child during a blackout—and a child who has survived the fall—was on the low end of the District Attorney's totem pole. Frankly, the only reason I even investigated the case as much as I did was because of the blackout aspect of it, and the report in the newspapers. That I was a bridge player myself made me more interested than usual, I will admit."

He turned and looked at us all, to let his last words sink in—*he* was a bridge player too.

"In November, while at the hospital, I stopped in to see little Cathy around lunchtime. She was not talking, but could point with her finger. Well, I had no time or authority to make a lineup of you people, but I did tell her who I was, and that I was interested in finding out who was with her in the back room that night. She looked around the hospital room to make sure nobody else was there, then pointed at her plate. I didn't understand at first, but then I realized she was referring to her slice of pizza. I made the connection, and wrote on my pad a giant 'NO' and a giant 'YES.' Then I asked her if he had pushed her. She pointed to 'NO.' So I asked her if she had fallen, and she pointed to 'YES' but then pointed to 'NO.' I didn't understand what that meant. The nurse entered and stopped me from going further, so I left and didn't see her again for another few weeks. That was on the day before Thanksgiving.

"I got a call from the girl's father, and he told me to meet him at the hospital. Cathy was up in her bed, drawing pictures on a pad. Mr. Stein told me she was able to draw ragged pictures, but still had problems with letters and words. In fact, the day before she had drawn, what looked to him, like the scene of the crime. I have it right here."

He produced a folded piece of yellow drawing paper from a silver case, and showed the drawing to all of us. There was a little girl holding a notebook by the window. Outside the window was a lightning bolt and black dots, signifying rain. Next to the girl stood a man and a woman. They were only stick drawings and it was impossible to tell who they were. I noticed Chops and Gussie staring at each other across the room—and they weren't friendly stares either.

"Excuse me," said the detective, as he poured himself some coffee. "I think bridge players and detectives drink more coffee than anybody in the world." He took another sip. "Of course, from the beginning, Mr. Stein took all the blame. It was he who had opened the window earlier that evening to let out some of the fumes from Mr. McCarver's cigar. And he also blamed himself for being so intense about his rubber bridge game that when the lights went out he continued to play rather than first check on the safety of his daughter."

We all looked at Frankenstein, and he growled back at us, remorse having dissipated, I supposed, by the recuperation of his child.

"I now returned to my boss," said the detective, "and explained the new evidence. He didn't want me to reopen the case, because I've been very busy investigating a counterfeit scam uptown. But I promised to work on the Mayfair case while I was off-duty, and that was okay with him."

I swallowed hard when I heard "counterfeit scam uptown." *No, it couldn't be,* I thought—this town just wasn't *that* small.

"On Wednesday night, I had a date with my wife to play duplicate—we play over at the Card School—on the upper West Side."

He shouldn't have reminded us, it would only lower our respect for him.

"Anyway, I couldn't really play up to my A-game because I was too busy thinking about your case and how to go about solving it."

Now he really fell in esteem, letting his work disrupt his bridge.

"But then a hand came up—I wrote the whole deal down here somewhere—let me see—ahh, here. Look."

He took out a piece of paper—it was a duplicate convention card.

"The contract was two diamonds," he continued, "and I don't need to remind you people the importance of holding it to two—the difference between minus 90 and minus 110 is pretty important."

That did it; we rubber players had lost the last drop of respect for him. He had us move our chairs closer together and showed us the deal:

```
                    North
                    ♠ Q J 10 9
                    ♡ J 3 2
                    ◊ Q J 6
                    ♣ Q 10 9
West                                East
♠ K 8 7                             ♠ 6 4 3 2
♡ Q 7 5 4                           ♡ A K 10
◊ K 2                               ◊ 9 8
♣ J 8 7 5                           ♣ 6 4 3 2
                    South
                    ♠ A 5
                    ♡ 9 8 6
                    ◊ A 10 7 5 4 3
                    ♣ A K
```

"South had opened with one diamond and rebid two diamonds over North's reply of one spade. My wife led the four of hearts, and when declarer called low from dummy, I was inspired to play the ten."

Suddenly our respect for him returned; there was something interesting about this play, but I didn't realize how fascinating it really was until he continued:

"I had no idea what to do if I won the first trick—I could shift to spades or clubs, or continue hearts. As you can see, if I had won the trick with the king of hearts and cashed the ace and another, declarer would have time to unblock his ace-king of clubs and reach dummy in trumps for a spade discard from his hand. Really, the only way to hold declarer to eight tricks was to find a spade switch, but how was I to know? However, when I stuck in my ten of hearts at trick one and it held, I found myself in a position to get the information I needed."

We all looked up at him. Only Frankenstein nodded, for he was the only one who understood the play.

"I then continued with the ace of hearts," said Detective Kennedy, "and when my wife dropped the queen under it, I knew she was asking for a spade switch."

We all sat down again and memorized the play—after all, we were all students of the game.

"The thing about it was," continued the detective, "that it reminded me of the partscore deal played on the night of Cathy's fall. During my initial investigation, Mr. Stein wrote out the four-diamond deal for me and included all the tens, but when I asked Mr. Kesselman—who actually held the East cards in that deal—he left out the ten of hearts. As a detective, I had no difficulty spotting the missing ten, but I had no idea of its significance—that is, until a week ago Wednesday when I faced a similar situation.

"It then occurred to me that I could lay a trap. The Card School is headed by a Mr. Kaplan, who is also publisher of a magazine called *The Bridge World.* After the duplicate, I ventured to call on Mr. Kaplan, who was still not asleep, luckily for me, and he was good enough to show me the subscription list, which included some of you people. In particular, I was interested in our poor Mr. McCarver and Mr. Kesselman."

He stared at Stanley, who looked down at the floor, and then in the direction of the front room—we all turned our heads with him.

"Originally," continued Kennedy, "Mr. McCarver had lied to me about his position on the partscore deal, claiming he was the opening leader. I knew he had lied because, not only had all the other players at the time refuted this—except for Mr. Kesselman—

but he had compounded the lie by saying that this boy, Mr. Granovetter, was his partner, rather than Mr. Kesselman. It was obvious to me that the two of them were in some sort of cahoots together. And when I confronted Mr. McCarver with the contradictory testimony, he claimed he could not remember an insignificant partscore—which was ridiculous under the circumstances. Nobody forgets where he is or what he is doing in the middle of a blackout.

"Later, with the new evidence of young Cathy's drawing, I decided it would spare the girl trauma and the legal system wear and tear if I could get Mr. McCarver or Mr. Kesselman to confess what took place. My idea was to have Mr. Kaplan write up the hand for his magazine, with exaggerated criticism of both Mr. McCarver and Mr. Kesselman. They were obviously covering for somebody, and we now know that somebody was a woman."

I looked at Gussie, she looked at Chops, Chops looked at Cathy, Cathy looked at . . . Maggie.

"Basically, I was hoping to stir up trouble between Mr. McCarver and Mr. Kesselman. I wanted each to see the hand and each to think the other had been the source for the hand. Fortunately, the *Bridge World* is often late in its printing, and though the blue-lines for the November issue had already been corrected, the Thanksgiving holiday permitted Mr. Kaplan enough time to slip in the extra article in place of an older one and deliver it to the printer on Friday. For the record, it was a letter to the editor that was cut."

The detective smiled, wiped his brow, and took a deep breath. Personally, I thought he was spending an awfully long time on Cathy's fall, when there was a real live corpse waiting in the next room.

"One small problem was that, though Mr. McCarver was a subscriber, Mr. Kesselman was not. One way to get the magazine to Mr. Kesselman was through his New Brunswick address, but we had to be somewhat subtle, so we sent the issue in Mr. Granovetter's name.

"Now it was up to me to cause an incident that would add to the trauma of the article. So I devised a plan that very night. It was a bit off the beaten path, but it had a chance."

I suddenly got the feeling Detective Kennedy was bragging to us about how he played a bridge hand—it was the same sort of post-mortem tone.

"I knew it would take at least a week for the printing and mailing of the magazine, and I was busy with my other case anyway, so I decided to call this inquiry two weeks hence. I even stopped by the offices of the *Times* and had the bridge editor there, Mr. Truscott, write up the fourth deal of the evening in question, with the intention of having it published the day before our meeting, which was done, in fact—I'm sure most of you read it.

"In particular, my plan was to recreate the scene from the night the blackout took place. For that, I needed a blackout and a replay of that final deal. As for the blackout, I chose the same night that Con Edison was planning an electric shutoff. The blackout was to take place at 9 p.m., so that's the time I called for the inquiry. As for the replay of the deal, I enlisted the help of Mr. Kesselman, who, in accordance with my plan, did break down after reading the planted partscore deal. Luckily the Mayfair Club is also on the Bridge World's subscription list, for Mr. Kesselman had left school long before the issue arrived there, but read a copy when it was delivered here at the club on Monday.

"On Tuesday, I got lucky. I ran into Mr. Kesselman at the racetrack, where I was investigating my other case. He had the *Bridge World* with him inside his racing form. Not only was he generous enough to give me the winner of the fifth race, but he told me what happened on the night of the blackout.

"Mr. Kesselman, do you want to tell them what you told me at the track?"

Stanley looked up at us and addressed Detective Kennedy, nervous at first, but then gaining confidence.

"Well . . . okay; I told you that Pizza had left after the bidding of the partscore. He was excited about the auction—thought that he had won another battle with his Theory of Exhaustion. He was wrong, though. I was the one who pushed *him* up in the auction."

Stanley was obviously still upset over the article, and the severe criticism of his bidding.

"Well," continued Stanley, "he went into the back room—I know that because that's where he used to keep his notebook. Meanwhile we were playing the hand and I . . . well I . . . misguessed what to shift to after I failed to find the uh . . . ten-of-hearts play."

The words came out slowly—boy, how he hated to admit that error!

"Anyway, after my play of a club, we heard the thunder and lightning and that's when the lights went out. Otto here was kibitzing, luckily, and had a flashlight in his toolcase under Mr. Roth's desk. He went to get it, using Gussie's matches to find his way across the room, while we waited in the dark. Gussie was also kibitzing, you know, and she can tell you that no one could possibly have been concerned for Cathy's welfare because we all knew where Pizza had gone, and figured that if there were any problem with the girl, Pizza would certainly tell us. I don't think Frankenstein has anything to regret on that account."

It was nice of Stanley to think of Frankenstein's feelings—very out of character for him, I thought.

My friend continued: "Well, Otto seemed to have some trouble finding the flashlight—"

"It's a clazy theeng in the dark—"

"Shh," said Detective Kennedy.

Stanley cleared his throat and continued again: "Well, all we could hear was the rain outside—a lot of the windows were open—and when Otto came back with the flashlight, we finished the hand. Doctor B. was more upset about the time of day than the four-diamond contract, and he had to leave for the hospital."

We all looked around for Doctor B. Where was he?

"Meanwhile," said Stanley, "Pizza had not returned, and I just figured he was having trouble writing up his partscore hand in the dark."

"Doctor Bellyard also smokes, doesn't he?" asked Detective Kennedy.

"Yes," said Stanley, "why?"

"Oh nothing," said the detective, "I'm just checking all the facts. The doctor probably used his own matches to get down the stairway. Please continue. You were waiting for Mr. McCarver to return to the game. . . ."

'Well," said Stanley, "someone had to go get Pizza 'cause Frankenstein refused to let Otto or Gussie sit in for him. So I went to the back room with the flashlight. Two people were by the window; I could hear them whispering real loud, and when I shot the flashlight in their direction, I saw Pizza and Maggie having a spat."

30

MAGGIE'S STORY—SIX-SPADE RECOUNT—
A CHEWING OUT—SOME CHARACTER
IN THE CORRIDOR—RED CHALK.

W E ALL turned our heads to Maggie. She crossed herself and patted little Cathy on the head. Then she came to the center of the semicircle.

"Mr. Detective, I'll tell you my part in this, though the Lord forgive me for speaking badly of the dead."

"Go ahead, Miss Johnson," said Kennedy. "Would you like a chair?"

"Thank you kindly, but I'll stand—right here in the very spot I stood that night. I was working late, cleaning the floor—right under where Mr. Otto is sitting now. You see, Mr. Pizza made a mess of that spot during supper hour."

We all looked at Otto, who had moved his chair away from the spot.

"Well, it was a terrible stain, and I was doing my best with it when Mr. Pizza himself comes running into the room all excited 'bout something. He looks around for his notebook—you know, the one he keeps in the corner, but he doesn't see me 'cause I'm under the table cleaning up the last of his noodle mess from the carpet, like I already told you."

Some of us nodded. I remembered the incident well, with Pizza throwing noodles at Frankenstein and Maggie getting hit.

"I see him all right, looking in the corner, but his notebook's not there. She's got it, po'r little thing. She's writing away in it, probably sketching one of her famous drawings, when he gets kind of upset. But that Mr. Pizza, he never gets *too* upset—I think 'cause he's got a lot of money and all, and those type know how to control their emotions—money being like a fat cushion to their problems.

"Well, Mr. Pizza, he just walks over and tells the girl to hand over the book. Then he says something else to her, but I can't hear it. Must have been mighty mean thing 'cause suddenly she's scared—awful scared—and she clings to the book tightly with her back up against the window. As you said before, that window was half open and I see that, so I step forward and try to grab her by the arm.

"But then the Lord took a hand—and He works in strange ways sometimes 'cause it wasn't a very helping hand—it was a roar of thunder and a *terrrrrrrrible* lightning flash. Fact is, when I grab her, she slips and falls back, and all I come up with is a torn piece of Mr. Pizza's notebook.

"Suddenly everything goes black. And that's when I hear Mr. Pizza start crying. He's saying, 'the book, the book!' And I know he doesn't care 'bout li'l Cathy—no, he's just upset over his notebook.

"I bury my head in my hands and pray. But Mr. Pizza, he hears me praying and comes over to my side. He isn't mean or anything like that. He lets me pray for over a minute at least, then helps me up and asks if I'm all right."

"Excuse me," said Detective Kennedy, "but is that when Mr. Kesselman came into the room?"

"That could be," said Maggie. "But I didn't see anyone but Mr. Pizza. And he told me to go home. Said he'd take care of the matter. Said it was a very dangerous situation we were in, with the police and all, and told me in his opinion, best thing was to go home and never say a word about it. Said he would call the hospital and take care of the child.

"Well, that's what I did, it being usually the best thing to do—taking the advice of a wealthy man like Mr. Pizza. And though I see now I was wrong to keep it all to myself—'cause I sure feel a lot better now that I'm telling it, which is something people just don't realize 'bout the truth they keep inside—well, there wasn't a whole lot I could do anyway."

"Mr. Kesselman," said Detective Kennedy, "you want to finish?"

"All right, man," said Stanley, getting up and giving Maggie his seat. "What Maggie said was pretty accurate, and I was about to go tell Frankenstein the news, but Pizza grabbed me by my arm and told me the phones were dead—told me to take Maggie downstairs and go quickly to the phone booth down the block to call an ambulance. Then he told me to make sure Maggie went into a cab and then to find the kid and wait with her until the ambulance came. He said he'd go inside and break the news to Frankenstein. Well, it all seemed perfectly sound to me, and I did just that. Then he told me one more thing—to see if his notebook was there, too, and hold it until he got there."

"That's right," said Maggie, "I remember that."

"Did you take the flashlight with you?" asked the detective.

"Uh, no," said Stanley, "Pizza took it, and gave me some matches to find my way."

"Did Maggie, by any chance, give you something?" asked the detective.

"Give me something? I uh, no, man, only, yeah, that's right, she gave me a crumpled piece of paper."

"Excuse me," I said, and ran to the TV room. I thought I heard a voice, but I didn't stop to look. I grabbed my jacket off the coatrack and ran back with it. In the pocket were the folded papers I had transferred from my pants to my jacket on the train into New York. One was the photocopy Detective Kennedy had given me at the Quad. "This one," I said, "this is the paper you mean; Stanley gave it to me on the train to Rutgers that night; he meant for me to throw it out when he sent me for coffee."

Detective Kennedy took the papers and examined them briefly; then he told me to sit down, and motioned for Stanley to continue.

"So I ran down the block to the phone booth across from Carnegie Hall and tried to call an ambulance, but it was difficult to get through. The operator kept telling me to hold, that there were a lot of emergencies. So finally, I gave up and tried to hail a cab. Well, that was impossible under the circumstances, but luckily Maggie's uncle drove up."

Maggie nodded. "He often picks me up on weekends," she said.

"Then I went to look for the kid," said Stanley. "It wasn't easy. She was nowhere; then I remembered the back room faced the back of the building. So I went through the foyer to the courtyard. She was there, all right, lying on some bushes. I bent down to lift her out, and then I saw Pizza's notebook. Suddenly I said to myself, 'Hey man, how did Pizza know the notebook was there?'

"Then I figured this was no accident—the guy murdered her. So I listened to her heart, but it was beating, thank goodness. That relieved me some, but then I heard footsteps right behind me and I really got scared. I didn't know whose they were. I didn't care any more. I figured if Pizza had pushed her out the window, he was gonna pin it on me, so I grabbed the notebook, ran down the street, and managed to hail a cab."

"Good, Mr. Kesselman," said the detective. "Now, it was Mr. Marx who found the girl. You want to tell us what happened after Mr. Kesselman left the bridge game to get Pizza?"

Otto put down his tea and addressed us. "I don't mind speaking, you know. It was a clazy theeng, the whole affair. I was waiting for my flashlight to return, and finally Pizza comes back with it. 'Stanley's cut out,' he says. So he takes his place for the fourth deal and I sit down too. And then Gussie sits down. Then we all sitting down and no one knows whose deal it is! So I say, Who dealt last? Then I say, I theenk the kid dealt last. So I take the deck and deal a ghoulie. What do I care? I theenk, it's only Doctor B.'s money. When I finish, I take the flashlight and see I got something good with two long minor suits, so I open one diamond. Then Frankenstein, he says it's his deal if the kid dealt last, and I say, then go ahead and bid. So he bids four spades and I overcall five clubs, to complete the picture. Now Pizza, he don't need a flashlight to double me with six of them and Gussie over there, I don't think she sees anytheeng. But she's so used to passing, she passes and soon I run to diamonds again. Now I pass the flashlight to Pizza, and he goes to five spades, but when Frankenstein bids six spades, I double. Again, it's Doctor B.'s money, and to tell you the truth, I'm having a good time playing bridge in the dark, it finally putting everybody else on my level— or so they theenk. Now when Frankenstein redoubles, I make no mistake about letting overtricks go by and lead my ace of clubs. This is when I make my big blunder, though. I drop the flashlight. Then Gussie trumps my lead—I believe because she theenks her one black card is a club and is meaning to follow suit. But after we turn the trick and examine it under a match, we see she has trumped the ace. Then she says, That's all right, and leads her own ace. But Frankenstein, he trumps it—it was a clazy hand."

He stopped for a sip of tea. We all stared at him. The scary thing was, I believe his scenario was accurate. In fact, Gussie confirmed it!

"How do you expect me to see in the dark, you nut-case?!" she screeched.

"That's the clazy theeng," he responded. "You can't see in the dark—"

Suddenly Detective Kennedy raised his palm. "Please, let's get to what happened *after* the hand."

"Okay, okay," said Otto. "After the hand, we get up and go in the other room to find whoever is missing. By now, I theenk everyone missing. Unfortunately, it turns out even little girl is missing. Soon Frankenstein asks Pizza what happened. He don't know anytheeng, so maybe she go downstairs. I go down in the dark and when I don't see her in the front, I look in the back. Aha! There she is okay. So I run down to the corner and call the police, the ambulance, the whole theeng."

Suddenly there was noise at the doorway. Detective Kennedy rose and went into the corridor. A man with a camera went through, then other men, two wearing white suits carrying a stretcher. I saw Kennedy flash his badge to someone. Then we all heard an argument. In fact, it was pretty much a one-sided argument; actually it was a chewing out:

"Shut up, Kennedy! You'll be pounding a beat by tomorrow morning!"

"All I ask is a little more time with these people, just a little more."

"Time? Are you crazy? For chrissake, Kennedy, There's a reporter waiting in a car downstairs. What do you want me to tell him? That the suspects to a homicide can't be released until they finish the rubber?!"

"Please, Captain, just one more hour, that's all I ask. I know these people and how they think. I can break 'em."

"Awright, Kennedy, one hour, but I want *everything*, you hear me? The weapon, the killer, the motive, and the signed confession, all in one neat package for the D.A. "

"Yes, sir, one hour tops, Captain."

"And then, I want your other report by 10 a.m. tomorrow, you understand? You've been on that case for two months! I want both cases in the cooler—got it?"

"Got it."

Detective Kennedy came back into the room and told us to have another cup of coffee; he'd be right back.

We all sat there and stared at one another. Cathy had fallen asleep in Chops' arms, and she and Frankenstein placed her down on the rug. Then Chops put her mink over the girl as a blanket. It *was* starting to get chilly, and I was glad I had my jacket. Mr. Roth and Maggie began clearing the dishes. I just sat there wondering what was going to happen to me. Although a lot of questions about the girl's fall and Stanley's behavior had been answered, there was still the murder of Pizza to be solved, and I was still the chief suspect.

Detective Kennedy returned. "Now, where were we? Let's see, it was Tuesday afternoon, right. Mr. Kesselman had told me all he knew, and I was pretty convinced he was telling the truth. Of course I had to reexamine Maggie and Pizza, but that could wait until tonight. I had troubles of my own on another case.

"There were other little questions I had concerning Pizza's notebook, and its whereabouts, but that was pretty much answered by Mr. Kaplan, who met with me tonight before I came here." He gave me a quick look. "Mr. Kaplan has his own informants, and many of the facts concerning the whereabouts of the notebook were cleared up through him.

"Now, we don't have much time, so let's get to tonight. That I am to some degree responsible for Mr. McCarver's death, I am well aware—I may have been negligent in my duties, but before we leave here, I intend to learn who pulled the trigger of that gun in there. Understand?"

Chops raised her hand and asked if she could phone her babysitter. The detective looked at his watch and cleared his throat.

"The truth is," said the detective, "the phone is on the blink, Chops, but I didn't want any of you to know it before; in particular, I didn't want the murderer to know it until I had some help here. However, when I sent Doctor Bellyard for the police, I also asked him to go by your place and make sure everything was okay."

That seemed to satisfy Chops, though, personally, I had a growing suspicion of Doctor B. and I wondered if it was so wise of Detective Kennedy to let him loose.

"Detective Kennedy." It was the voice of the Captain in the doorway. "You can have your front room now. And by the way, there's some character in the corridor here who insists on seeing two of your suspects. Says you know him—"

"Please take your hands off me." There was J.B.'s head peeking into the room. "Guys! What's wrong with you? I told you to be ready to leave by eleven."

"C'mon," said Kennedy, motioning to the rest of us, "we're going back to the front room."

I briefed J.B. on what had happened and he took it rather historically. "Et tu, Guy, et tu," he said, his arm around my shoulder.

Because of J.B.'s presence, I felt much more the college student and somewhat out of place at the Mayfair. Or perhaps my feeling was that *he* was out of place. In the middle of the investigation, he was naive enough to congratulate Stanley on his good grades. Stanley's face lit up.

"Even in History?" he asked.

J.B. nodded. The other players looked at our preceptor as if he were something from another world, which he was.

"That was the one course I had trouble with," Stanley confided to me. "Esther helped me write my last paper."

So he studied with her, also. Very nice, I thought. When did they have time for that? In between. . . .

Pizza's body was gone. Instead there was a red-chalk outline of his shape that went from the table to the chair to the floor. Detective Kennedy enlisted my help and we moved the table to the corner, putting another in its place. I noticed the new table had four bridge hands face down on it.

"My original plan for tonight, before Mr. Kesselman spoke with me on Tuesday, was to have Mr. Stein deal the six-spade contract just before nine o'clock. I thought a player of Mr. Stein's stature could fix a deck and slip it past you people. However, Mr. Roth told me that very few card players, especially bridge players, had that talent. Despite this, when Mr. Kesselman talked to me on Tuesday night, I was able to enlist his help. He assured me he could fix the deck and see to it that nobody would notice. You see, I was still bent on going through with the replay because, even though I believed Mr. Kesselman's account, I wanted a confession. Frankly, I thought I could shock Mr. McCarver into admitting his crime, a crime that I see now he never committed. Of course this was an error in judgment on my part—I think perhaps because I was too excited about the prospect of seeing the slam hand replayed. I let my love of bridge get the better of me."

Many of the players nodded. They could empathize with that.

"Now," he continued, "my silly charade, and my late arrival, have somehow instigated a murder—one that we must collectively solve. I think the best way to go about this is to do exactly the same thing, again. But this time, we are going to recreate *tonight's* scene. Would each of you please take the seat you were in when the lights went out?"

31

I SAT down in the chair facing the wall, where I had sat earlier that night. Otto took the seat on my left and Gussie on my right. Then Stanley sat across from me.

"No," said the detective, "that's Mr. McCarver's seat."

"Yes," said Stanley, "but he was kibitzing until the bidding was over."

"Oh, I see," said Kennedy. He rubbed his head and considered for a few seconds. "Say, you, uh . . . J.B."

"Yes, sir?"

"Would you mind playing the part of the deceased?"

"Delighted, sir," answered my preceptor, and Stanley motioned for him to sit in the kibitzer's seat, behind him slightly to his right.

"Now the rest of the kibitzers, please."

Chops took a chair on my right between Gussie and me. Roth returned to his desk in the far corner behind my right shoulder. "This is where *I* was," he said. "I was working on the evening accounts."

"Who else is there?" asked Kennedy. "What about you, Mr. Stein?"

Frankenstein peered down at the detective. I never realized how tall the man was. "I was in the kitchen," he said. "Otto and Gussie had just returned to the table for the fourth deal."

"Wait a second," said the detective. "Let's go back to the beginning of the rubber. Who was North-South and who was East-West?"

We all grimaced at this allusion to duplicate positions. I spoke up. "I cut Stanley as my partner, and Gussie played with Otto, like we are now. No, wait a second, Gussie was on my left and Otto on my right—that's how we started the rubber. But then things changed around after the first hand, Gussie left the room and Frankenstein filled in."

"Where did you go, Miss Addles?" asked Kennedy.

Gussie hesitated. "I went to the bathroom. Must you know every detail?"

"That's not true," I said. "I saw her in the TV room after the second deal."

"How dare you?" cried Gussie.

"She was arguing with Pizza about his relationship with Chops!" I blurted out.

"How dare he—?"

J.B. gave me a low-eyebrow look as if to say, mind your elders.

"Now, now," said Detective Kennedy. "Everything is relevant here, Miss Addles. To the point, what was your exact disagreement with the victim?"

Gussie folded her arms, then said, "Well, if you must know, Pizza was my confidant—even more than that, though I have no intention of describing personal things that you people would have no feelings for."

"Give us a break!" said Chops.

"Especially her!" said Gussie. "She's been taking advantage of him from the start, ever since she made up that ridiculous story two years ago, that Pizza was the father of her child."

Chops shook her head in dismay. I had something to say, although I couldn't prove it: "Excuse me, Detective Kennedy, as you know, I was in possession of Pizza's notebook, and even made a copy of it. Also, as you know, I destroyed the book, but sent the copy to my home for safekeeping. I believe Pizza might have gone to my home and gotten the copy from my dad, who served with him during World War II. Anyway, in that notebook was a confession that Pizza was the father of Chops' baby boy, and also there was a little note about a certain evening he spent with Gussie recently, and his subsequent jilting of her a second time aroun—"

"Shut your face!" cried Gussie. "Have you no shame—"

"Guy?!" said J. B.

"Now, now," said Kennedy, "there's no need to tell everyone

all this, Mr. Granovetter. I've got your handwritten copy of Pizza's notes in my desk at the precinct. If you must know, Doctor Bellyard was the one who visited your home. I sent him there to get the notes."

I sat down. Very nice, I thought. So my dad must know everything by now. Gussie was in tears, and J.B. gave her his handkerchief.

"Sir," said J.B., "all this seems to prove that this woman had the least reason to commit murder. She loved this fellow called Pizza."

"But that's not so," I insisted, turning to the detective. "She threatened him. She was jealous, and she was in debt—why, Pizza has been paying her account here at the club for months. Ask Stanley or Mr. Roth."

Gussie looked up at me, but I avoided her eyes.

"It's true," said Roth. "Pizza took care of a lot of the accounts. In fact, I don't know what we're going to do with him gone."

"Which means," said Detective Kennedy, "that it was in the interest of both Miss Addles and Mr. Roth for Pizza McCarver to live. After all, they were both financially dependent on him. And from my professional experience, money is always the foremost motive for homicide and therefore the foremost alibi, too.

"Now may we please get back on track here. After the second deal, why did you leave the table, Mr. Granovetter?"

"I, uh, went to get my book because J.B.'s phone number was in it. I was supposed to call him at a quarter to nine. I made my call, but the phone went dead right in the middle."

"I can verify that," said J.B.

"Thank you," said Kennedy. "And when you returned to the table, you played the third deal against Mr. Stein and Mr. Marx?"

"No," I said. "Otto wasn't there. Chops filled in for him."

All eyes turned on Otto now.

"It's a clazy theeng, but I don't remember where I went. Oh, yes I do, I was in the men's room. That's why I don't remember. Ha, ha. I go to the men's room and take this with me. That's how I remember." He pulled out a copy of *Bridge World* magazine. I leaned over and looked at the label. It was my November copy. "I'm reading the magazine, and maybe the time passes, and when I come out, I see the third deal is finished. I remember because this boy here—" He pointed to me. "—makes quite a poor play against a slam. He ducks his ace with the setting tlick in his hand."

"Yes he did!" confirmed Gussie with vengeance.

"I was very happy for the play," said Otto, "because it was on my account that the slam was recorded."

"Good," said Kennedy. "Now for the last deal. You played it with Mr. Stein?"

"No," said Frankenstein. "I told you. I went into the kitchen because Gussie and Otto had returned."

"That's right," said Maggie from behind me. "Mr. Frankenstein did come into the kitchen. He likes to poke his nose into my preparations."

"And where was your daughter, Mr. Stein? With you and Maggie in the kitchen?"

Maggie and Frankenstein looked at each other. "Why Mr. Detective," said Maggie, "I don't recall her until after the lights came back on."

Frankenstein turned red suddenly. "That's true," he admitted. "She came into the kitchen with us *after* the lights returned."

I couldn't believe my ears. Were they insinuating that little Cathy was a suspect?

Detective Kennedy nodded. "That's correct. I picked her up on the way to Mr. Kaplan's and she drove over with me to the club. In fact, that's why I was late; I couldn't really speed during the storm with Cathy in the car. Forgive me, I was just double-checking."

I took that to mean he was double-checking the veracity of Frankenstein. If he would not lie to save his own daughter's neck, he would certainly not lie about anything else. If anybody had a good motive to kill Pizza, it was certainly Frankenstein. And he had plenty of time to come from the kitchen to the front room in the dark and pull the trigger. But though he might have been capable of killing, he *wasn't* capable of lying. If he murdered Pizza, he surely would have confessed it.

"Now, that accounts for everyone and we can begin the last deal, right?"

"Excuse me," I said. "I hate to always be the one who accuses everybody, but what about Doctor B?"

"That's right," said Kennedy. "Where was *he* sitting?"

"Between Otto and me on my left," I answered.

"Good, but he's not back yet, so I'll take his place. Oh, Maggie, Mr. Stein, would you please return to the kitchen and try to simulate whatever you were doing at the time? Thank you."

They left the room and we picked up our cards.

♠ 7 ♡ A 9 8 7 6 5 4 3 2 ◇ J 10 4 ♣ —

"Wait a second—"

"Hey man—"

"This is the other—"

"It's a clazy —?"

All four players spoke up at once. Detective Kennedy had fixed the six-spade contract from the *Times*. The fourth deal *we* played was a seven-heart-doubled contract.

"But that's the deal I asked you to fix, Mr. Kesselman," said Kennedy. "You mean you played a different hand?"

"I'm sorry," said Stanley, "but when I was starting to fix the cards, Matt walked in on me. Actually, I was looking at an old hand we had dealt a year ago when he spotted me. I was thinking of putting it into the rubber just for the fun of it—It certainly made no difference financially since the whole rubber was going to be canceled anyway."

"I don't theenk so," broke in Otto.

"Nor do I," said Gussie.

"Okay," said Stanley. "But when Matthew walked in on me, I never got to finish it."

"It wasn't that," I interrupted. "He dropped all the cards on the floor."

"Why did you drop the cards?" asked Detective Kennedy.

"Well, hey, it's got nothing to do with this case. It's really personal."

"Mr. Kesselman, everything that happened tonight has to do with this case. Please answer my question. Why did you drop the cards?"

"If you must know," said Stanley, "the girl I love is pregnant, and I didn't know about it until Matthew told me. There, are you satisfied?"

J.B.'s eyes lit up. Suddenly I thought I heard a high-pitched sound coming from somewhere far away. A couple of the others heard it as well, but we all turned back to the table thinking it had come from the street. Besides, we were all getting anxious to replay the grand slam.

"I hate to use the actual physical evidence," said Detective Kennedy, looking at his watch, "but there just isn't time to reconstruct." So he had each of us, Otto, Stanley, Gussie, and me, go to the other table and take the actual cards that were still lying there. It was not a nice situation for Stanley, because some of the blood on Pizza's cards had not dried. We returned to the simulated table, and, on the detective's nod, replayed the auction:

$$\spadesuit — \heartsuit J98764 \ \diamondsuit 872 \ \clubsuit KJ82$$

Otto passed. Stanley opened two notrump. Gussie passed, and I bid three diamonds, transfer to hearts. Otto passed and Stanley bid three spades, which I took to be a cue bid. I raised to four spades. After Otto's pass, Stanley continued with four notrump, Blackwood.

"Wait a second," I said to the detective. "Do you want everything? I mean, do you want every word that was said at the time?"

The detective, sitting on my left in Doctor B.'s chair, nodded.

"Well," I said, "I think Mr. Roth made a comment before Stanley's four notrump." I really hated to hear that comment repeated, but I did want to make sure we had an exact re-enactment of the crime—maybe, I hoped, there was a clue that would clear me.

Mr. Roth looked up from his desk. "Yeah, I remember. I said, 'sounds like two children.' It still sounds like two children."

After four notrump, I bid five clubs and Stanley bid five diamonds. Here is where we had gone our separate ways. I thought he was checking for a void, and he thought we were playing Pizza's variation of Blackwood, in which five clubs showed zero or three aces and five diamonds asked which.

I bid six hearts, he raised to seven hearts, and Gussie doubled again. We all passed and Otto led the ten of spades. Stanley got up to leave the table.

"Hold it," said Chops. "There's something wrong here. This is not how it happened."

We all paused for a minute to review the auction in our minds:

Otto	Stanley	Gussie	Me
pass	2 NT	pass	3 $\diamondsuit$
pass	3 $\spadesuit$	pass	4 $\spadesuit$
pass	4 NT	pass	5 $\clubsuit$
pass	5 $\diamondsuit$	pass	6 $\heartsuit$
pass	7 $\heartsuit$	double	(all pass)

Funny thing—it *was* Otto's lead.

"Hey," said Stanley, "what's wrong? It was at this point I got up to go to the bathroom. I was the dummy, you see, and I didn't care to stick around and see the bloodshed—you know what I mean—the bloodshed of seven hearts doubled."

"Yes," agreed Chops, "but it's hard to believe you didn't have the curiosity to see your partner's hand before you left."

"What do I wanna see his hand for?! The rubber wasn't supposed to count anyway!"

"Just a second, now," said Detective Kennedy. "Whose lead was it?"

"It was Otto's lead!" cried Stanley.

"Calm yourself, guy," advised J.B.

"That's true," said Chops. "But I think there was confusion with the transfer bid and Stanley's ridiculous refusal to accept the transfer."

Good ol' Chops, I thought, hates it when someone toys with a bidding convention.

"Anyway," she said, "what actually happened was that Gussie led, but no one realized she was leading out of turn."

"That's right," I confirmed. "I think all of us just assumed that once I transferred, Stanley had to become the declarer."

"Good," said Detective Kennedy on my left, jotting a note down on a pad. "Now continue with the actual lead, Gussie."

"Thank you," she said, in a huff. "After all, it *is* my lead." Gussie led the ace of diamonds.

"I think not," I said. "It was the ace of *spades*. In fact she took a long time to lead it, too. I remember because I looked into her hand while waiting for the lead and saw three aces."

"Three aces?" cried Stanley. "What the hell was your six-heart bid?"

"I uh, well, —"

"Shh," said Detective Kennedy. "Let's get that lead straight."

Chops concurred with my statement about the lead, and Detective Kennedy pointed Stanley to the hallway. He wanted an exact replay not only of the cards but of the physical positions of all the suspects. Stanley left the room, shaking his head, and Gussie, remarking that it hardly could matter, led the ace of *spades*.

I started to put my dummy down, then stopped. "There was some thunder and lightning at this point," I said. "Oh, and Pizza—

he jumped up and took Stanley's cards."

Chops nodded. "Yes, I remember his words. He said: 'Here, I'll play it.'"

Nobody said anything for about 15 seconds. Detective Kennedy motioned to J.B.

"Oh," said J.B., getting up from his chair. "Ahem, uh, 'Here! I'll play it!'"

Detective Kennedy motioned for him to sit down in the seat vacated by Stanley.

Then there was silence again.

"Well?" asked the detective.

"This is when the lights went out," I told him.

32

DOCTOR B. RETURNS—VOICES IN THE
DARK—THE SUSPECTS HAVE THEIR SAY—
AN IMPORTANT QUESTION.

DOCTOR B. came through the door. I was surprised to see him. Really, I was hoping he was the murderer and had skipped town.

"Sorry, sorry, sorry I'm late. The boy had hiccups and you know how they are."

Chops looked up, concerned. "Is he all right?"

"Yes, yes, but the babysitter had to go, so I dropped her off and brought the child here. It's all right, he's with Frankenstein and Maggie. She's fixing him a bottle."

Detective Kennedy stood up and looked at his watch with some concern. "Take my seat, Doctor. You're just in time for the blackout. I want everybody to please not say a single word except for what they said at the time of the shooting. If any of you stood up or walked around, please re-enact your movements. I am going to shut the lights out now, except for the lounge, so there'll be enough light to move around. When you hear a gun go off, don't be nervous—it's only blanks. I don't expect the murderer to reveal himself, of course, so I'll take his part. I'm even going to use the actual murder weapon. For your interest, the doctor has confirmed the physical evidence that the bullet came from across the table, from the dummy's position. I want you, J.B.,—excuse me, you, what are you doing?"

J.B. was ignoring the detective. Then he looked up from the cards. "Sorry, but this hand is fascinating."

The detective took a deep breath and instructed J.B. to drop his head on the table when he heard the gun shot. Then he told us again to repeat the exact words we said before and after the shot, and to take our time so as not to miss anybody's line. "I'll give you a few seconds to refresh your memories."

He left the room and went around toward the kitchen. All the lights suddenly went out, except for the one in the TV room. Unlike before, we could see ourselves, but only in grey outlines. Then about a minute elapsed before Doctor B. spoke up.

"I thought they called it off," said the doctor.

"It's a clazy theeng. I'll get my flashlight," said Otto.

We waited in the dark just like the last time for 30 seconds, maybe 35. It felt much longer now that I knew what was coming. I could hear Otto over at Roth's desk. We kept waiting for someone to say, "Where's the dummy?" but nobody said it.

"Anything else before the shot?"

I was startled. It was Detective Kennedy.

"Yes," I answered. "Someone said, 'Where's the dummy?' and then I said, 'Here I am.'"

"Is that correct?" asked Kennedy in the dark. I had an eerie sensation that everyone nodded, but nobody spoke.

Suddenly I felt the cold steel across my right cheek. I stiffened. "It was the other side," I whispered, "my left shoulder." The detective's arm reached across the left side of my neck, resting firmly on my shoulder. I started to resist like I had done before.

"Now?" he asked.

"Now," I said. There was a shot.

A match was lit. It was Doctor B.'s match. I felt hot and faint again, just like last time. I remembered feeling I had been the one who was shot, and thinking it was Stanley who shot me. Another match was lit, again by Doctor B. There was J.B., head down on the table. He was playing his part to the tee.

"C'mon people," said the detective. "Remember your lines. Who spoke next?!"

There was silence for a few seconds, then:

"He's still th-thinking," said Gussie.

"It's a played card," said Chops.

I grabbed the closest thing to me on the table. It turned out to be the gun, again. In a few seconds, the lights came back on.

"J.B.," I said. His head was still on the table. "J.B."

He didn't stir. Then I saw one finger go up in the air and his head moved.

"I've got the solution," he said.

"You solved the murder?" I asked.

"No, the grand slam," he answered.

Detective Kennedy came back in and spoke briefly to Doctor B. in whispers. Then he said, "This is when you, Mr. Granovetter, committed that asinine act of wiping the gun on your shirt." I lowered my head in shame.

"However," he continued, "it probably doesn't matter. I believe I know who committed the murder of Pizza McCarver. Still, in a case like this, you can never be too careful. As you rubber bridge players know from your crackerjack card play, you can never rely completely on one piece of evidence to make a contract. The more corroborative evidence you have, the better off you are. So I would like to ask everyone to come back in now. Mr. Roth, would you please get the others from the back?" Roth nodded and left the room. "What I want from each of you is your idea of who the guilty party is—that is, if you have an idea. We'll begin with you, Mr. Marx."

Otto: "It's a clazy theeng, but I still theenk the kid did it. He's got the gun in his hand and he's got the motive—his partner bid a clazy gland slam."

"That's ridiculous," I protested. "*Stanley* bid the grand slam, not Pizza."

"Now, now," said the detective, "you'll have your chance. Next, you there, J.B., you're new to all of it, but what have you to say?"

J.B.: "I think if we looked at the deal in question, sir, it might help. A murder is committed in the middle of a doubled grand slam. Is it a coincidence? Or is there an underlying motive? If you'll all just turn your cards face up, we might see something."

Detective Kennedy hesitated, then agreed, so long as we made it fast. When the cards were turned, here was the view from the victim's position:

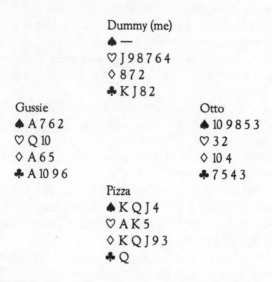

Dummy (me)
♠ —
♡ J 9 8 7 6 4
◇ 8 7 2
♣ K J 8 2

Gussie
♠ A 7 6 2
♡ Q 10
◇ A 6 5
♣ A 10 9 6

Otto
♠ 10 9 8 5 3
♡ 3 2
◇ 10 4
♣ 7 5 4 3

Pizza
♠ K Q J 4
♡ A K 5
◇ K Q J 9 3
♣ Q

"You'll have to forgive me," said J.B., "if I make any subtle errors—this is the first time I've analyzed a trump contract, you know. But, I believe, ruffing may be the only way to bring home this baby."

I shuddered at the thought of J.B. explaining his line of play to this group of veterans.

"As to the bidding, I won't remark except to say I like that two-notrump opening with the singleton queen. Stanley picked up that sort of tactic from me." My preceptor looked up proudly. Where *was* Stanley? I thought.

"Back to the play, guys. After the ace-of-spades lead, dummy ruffed, and that was when the lights went out. Assuming proper play by declarer and defenders, the grand slam could actually be

345

made. A trump is led to the ace and the three high spades are cashed, discarding three diamonds from the dummy. Next the king of diamonds is led. Whether or not it is covered, diamonds are continued, for three rounds if neccessary—ruffing the third round with the jack of trumps, of course. Once the ace of diamonds is forced out, a trump return to the king draws the missing trumps. With four good diamonds in hand, four clubs are thrown from the dummy."

It appeared that J.B. had finally mastered a trump contract, but I noticed Chops shaking her head.

J.B. looked up proudly and cleared his throat. "Therefore, from my special angle, that of the victim, who has been denied the greatest grand slam of his life, I deduce the shooting was a deliberate attempt to stop the fulfillment of the contract. Which defender did it, I leave to you—but I would guess the defender who was more convinced that declarer was about to make all 13 tricks."

"That's a clazy theeng!" interrupted Otto. "Who kills over a bridge hand? Anyway, I had a total yarborough, look at *my* hand and look at *her* hand."

"I had three aces!" screeched Gussie. "You had more reason than me to think the slam was making!"

"Now, now," said Detective Kennedy. "Is that all, J.B.?"

"I can only add this," J.B. continued. "Having lived with Matthew and Stanley for over two months, I don't believe either of my guys could be guilty—based on their characters alone. Granted, neither is a saint, but then let's not confuse the mistakes of youth with the mentality of a murderer."

"Thank you. Now Miss Addles, have your say."

I noticed Frankenstein and Maggie came into the room at this point. Frankenstein was holding little Bobby, and upon seeing the cards laid out on the table, moved behind J.B.

Gussie: "I was going to agree with Otto, until he reminded me what bad judgment he's had in so many other areas." Her eyes darted from him back to J.B. "But perhaps this college man is correct—in the last thing he said. I also believe the boy is innocent." Thank you, I thought. "He may be a horrible gossip and an uncooperative bridge partner, but he did not have the motive to kill my Pizza. No, the motive belongs to *her*."

She pointed to Chops, who had taken her son in her arms.

"You will see," said Gussie, "that when the will is read, *she'll* be the beneficiary. I'm sorry to have to say it, but Pizza—" She looked up to the ceiling—I think she should have been looking downward. "—you really had lousy taste in women!"

"Excuse me," I said. "But during the bidding of the slam, Chops moved her chair away from me and closer to Gussie. At first I thought she didn't like one of my bids. But now, I see it may have been to get a better view of Pizza. Perhaps she was planning to do away with him from that angle."

"Gimme a break!" said Chops.

The detective nodded, "Please, no fights, just your opinion of who did it."

Chops sat the baby in my lap and spoke her mind: "This is not opinion; this is *fact.* His four-spade bid made me sick. It would make *anyone* move his chair!

"As for Pizza—he loved me and I hated him. Last night we had a terrible fight—I'll spare you the details, but I scratched him pretty bad, and he punched me in the eye, here." She pointed to it. "I had a lot of motive to kill him. He was disgusting, a braggart, a slob, and worst of all, a horrible overbidder."

"I could have told you that from the beginning," said Roth, who now appeared in the doorway and walked over to his desk.

Chops nodded and gave a little shudder, then she returned to the crux of her statement. "But, in my defense, you must realize he was my sole support. I've seen his will, and I am *not* in it." Gussie looked up surprised, and delighted. "Nor are *you!* His money goes to the McCarver Foundation . . . with the exception of one savings bond in the name of his son, Bobby McCarver."

I gave Bobby a pat on the head.

"As to who committed the murder, the facts say that Stanley did it. I like Stanley, as you all probably know, and I have no grudge against him; he was very helpful to me after I had Bobby, and before I gave in to Pizza's request to live together. So my observations may be viewed as totally unbiased.

"Fact: Stanley was the one who got up from the table after bidding a grand slam—then left *without first looking at his partner's hand.*

"Fact: Only two people left the room—Frankenstein and Stanley. And Maggie has confirmed *Frankenstein's* alibi.

"Fact: Stanley was the only logical person who could have shut off the lights, gone for the gun, and returned to kill him.

"Fact: His motive was a good one—Pizza was holding him at the club against his will. Pizza used him like he used everybody. Stanley was Pizza's gofer, his coolie, his . . . his . . . deuce of clubs. Stanley owed him thousands from the racetrack.

"Fact: When Pizza saw his notebook go out the window with Cathy, he was afraid he would be arrested, no matter what Maggie said. But later, he started to worry about Stanley. When Stanley couldn't come up with the notebook, Pizza got furious and threatened Stanley. Pizza, of course, is all talk and no action, but Stanley must have been scared. There was no question he wanted Pizza dead before Pizza did something to *him*.

"Fact: And this has nothing to do with the case, but I just can't bear the mis-analysis of the grand slam." J.B.'s head shot up. "The diamond ace must be played on the first round of the suit," she continued, "to give declarer the option of finessing the possible queen-third of trumps. If you wait for the third round to cover, the suit cannot be overruffed, and declarer *knows* where the queen is. If you duck once and cover the second round, declarer will realize you have three diamonds because nobody would duck with a doubleton ace, and he'll realize you're giving him the option of finessing in trumps, a Greek gift he will never accept. That's what I think—take it or leave it."

I handed Bobby back to Chops and congratulated her on both analyses. Stanley still hadn't returned and I was certain this time we had our murderer.

"Mr. Stein? You have anything to say about this?" asked the detective.

Frankenstein: "I agree with Chopsy." *Chopsy!* "That is, in one or two points. However she's essentially wrong and still needs work on her game." He bent over the card table and switched the queen of hearts to Otto's hand.

```
                    Me (dummy)
                    ♠ —
                    ♡ J 9 8 7 6 4
                    ◊ 8 7 2
                    ♣ K J 8 2
  Gussie                              Otto
  ♠ A 7 6 2                           ♠ 10 9 8 5 3
  ♡ 10                                ♡ Q 3 2
  ◊ A 6 5                             ◊ 10 4
  ♣ A 10 9 6 3                        ♣ 7 5 4
                    (Stanley) (Pizza) (J. B.)
                    ♠ K Q J 4
                    ♡ A K 5
                    ◊ K Q J 9 3
                    ♣ Q
```

"Here's what she was referring to. However, after the lead of
the ace of spades, Big Baboon would have had to ruff in dummy
with the six, not the four. The cards are equal except that the *five*
in declarer's hand may be useful as an entry later if the four is
preserved."

"He ruffed with the four, not the six," I said. A small fact, but
I remembered it.

"Well," said Frankenstein, "That proves the Big Baboon was a
bad declarer. However, suppose you ruff with the six. Now you
lead the seven to your king and note the fall of the ten. If you
decide that the ten is singleton, you still have a chance. You play
your three top spades, pitching the diamonds from dummy. Now
lead the king of diamonds, followed by the queen if the king is
not covered. Chopsy here is right that the best play is for the defender to cover when holding the trump queen but not to cover
either diamond *without* the trump queen. Then declarer is kaput—he can't get to dummy to finesse the queen of hearts plus set
up his diamonds. But, can you imagine Gussie-baboon *not* covering in either case?

"After she does cover the diamond king with her ace, declarer ruffs in dummy and leads the jack of hearts. Now Otto's
best play is to cover; but if declarer has preserved the four of
trumps in dummy, he can win the third round of the suit with his
five, and remain in his hand to cash the diamonds."

Frankenstein looked up and shook his monstrous head.

"I'm sure very few of you could follow me, but my point is that the Big Baboon was bound to make his grand slam because he made an error at trick one. He left himself with no option but to play for a two-two split. Be that as it may, neither of the baboons defending are capable of analyzing a hand like this at trick one, let alone now, so neither would know enough to shoot the Big Baboon just to prevent a grand slam from making."

"Thank you," said Otto and Gussie in unison.

"As to who *did* kill the Big Baboon," Frankenstein continued, "I don't know. As Chopsy here said, the Stanley-baboon had the opportunity, but I doubt he or anyone from the ten-cent game did it. You must remember that the Big Baboon was an important fourth in the game. I've read of people killing their spouse or even their own mother, but never of a bridge addict killing the fourth in his game."

We all took a deep breath. Frankenstein certainly was the greatest.

"Maggie?" asked the detective. "Have you anything to add?"

Maggie: "I don't know, Mr. Detective. I'm not a bridge player like the rest of you—although my family does play a little bridge-whist—but I knew Mr. Pizza from a kitchen point of view. He was the best eater at the club, and a pretty decent tipper. But he *was* a slob, and it sometimes made me angry. I've got a temper, and once when he spilled food on me, I said something like, 'I could kill that man.' And I meant it—Lord have mercy on me—but only for a few seconds.

"Now that fellow over there—," She pointed to J.B. "he gets me thinking when he talks about the view from Mr. Pizza's angle. Why Mr. Pizza—he just that moment sits down there, like you people say. It doesn't sound to me like a person could have very much time to kill another person who just sits down there. So I think the person who goes and shoots Mr. Pizza does it suddenly, just on the spur of the moment.

"This person must be angry with Mr. Pizza. Maybe Mr. Pizza has done something bad to him recently and now suddenly he's got the opportunity. But then it would have to be someone who held a grudge a longer time than just a few seconds, like I did. Take last night, for example. Mr. Otto there arrives kind of late and I cooked him chicken paprikash, special. Well, when he gets here, it's all gone, even the portion I save for him. And who ate it?

It was Mr. Pizza all right. Something like that could get someone who's been looking forward to his favorite dish awful angry."

"Now *that's* the claziest theeng!" said Otto. "To kill a man over some chicken paprikash! Besides there were plenty of cookies left; you know that, Maggi—"

"Now, now," said Detective Kennedy, "calm yourself. Anybody I accuse will have ample time to defend himself later, if he can. Who's left? Of course, Mr. Granovetter."

"Okay," I said. Then I cleared my throat. I had come to a definite view. "All night, I've been thinking the murderer was Doctor B."

Doctor B. remained calm and even lit up a cigarette.

"He hadn't returned to the club, and I thought he might have skipped town. But even though he's here now, many clues point to him. Most important, he had the opportunity. Detective Kennedy seems to have a good idea how it happened, and he's right. The gunman put his arm on my left shoulder for aim and shot Pizza. Who was kibitzing on my left? Doctor B. was."

I looked around the room. No one was convinced.

"It would have been easy for him," I continued. "But now please look at the motives:

"One. Doctor B., in his own way, stood to gain the most from Pizza's death—financially. Detective Kennedy can verify from my copy of Pizza's notes that Pizza, upon the death of his father, and subsequent will, had every intention of cancelling the McCarver Foundation's medical donations to NYU's hospital. Construction of the new wing there *was* cancelled and Doctor B. was furious about it.

"Two. I met the doctor at Rutgers where he started ranting about the conditions at the hospital, and how, if conditions were better, little Cathy might have recovered that much sooner.

"Three. This shows that the doctor thought Pizza was responsible for the girl's injuries.

"Four. No one hated Pizza more than Doctor B. Not only did Pizza taunt him for his lack of science in the bidding, but Pizza was a slow player and the doctor was always in a hurry. Add to that the fact that you, Detective Kennedy, sent him to collect Pizza's notebook, and you will see that his hatred could only increase after he read the insults Pizza wrote.

"And finally, five. Doctor B. must have been the one who

said, 'Where's the dummy?' Who else would not know where the dummy was? Only someone who was not used to playing Jacoby Transfer bids would get so confused that he didn't know who was declarer and who was dummy. Doctor B. was the only player in the club to refuse to play any conventions but Blackwood and Stayman, thus he was the only player who would ask that question. And, of course, the person who asked that question is the one who took aim over my shoulder and shot Pizza."

I had a feeling my arguments were not the strongest, but we were running out of suspects, and if no one else did it, I was the one headed for the clink.

"Not bad," said Detective Kennedy.

"But Detective—" complained Doctor B.

"Now, now, just because he's wrong doesn't mean he didn't work a few points out neatly. Just to clear the air on Doctor Bellyard's account, I must tell you that the doctor did hate Mr. McCarver for retracting the hospital wing's funds, and probably most of the other motives were accurate too, except for that last desperate point. Doctor B. was not the only one who would ask, 'Where's the dummy?' None of you knew who the dummy was, and if you want to know the truth, I'm still confused who it should have been. In any event, Doctor Bellyard's trip to Rutgers was a favor to Pizza, isn't that right, Doctor?"

"Quite right," snapped Doctor B., in his usual quick fashion. "Pizza and I had a firm agreement. If I could get his notebook back, he would reinstate the funds for the hospital wing. When I met this young whippersnapper, I did not let on why I was there. Why should I? It was none of his business. If you ask me, he's got too big a nose, and should learn to mind his own affairs. And he isn't half the player his old man is!"

"Calm down, Doctor," said the detective. "Do you have any opinion of your own? Who do you think killed Mr. McCarver?"

"I'm a scientist, not a speculator, sir. I can only speak for myself. The idea of *me* killing the man! How absurd. When I recovered the notes for you, I was assured you would return them to Pizza after this ordeal. I was also confident Pizza would stick to his part of the bargain. But now that Pizza is dead, who *knows* how the Foundation will spend its funds? Probably the lawyers will get all the money!"

I was wrong again. But I did hit on something with that "Where's the dummy?" question. I tried to think: Who else would ask that question?

"Now that's everybody," said Detective Kennedy. "No wait, there's Mr. Kesselman. Where did he go?"

"Here he comes now," said J.B., who had the best vantage point of the corridor. "And there's a young lady with him."

We all looked at the doorway. Next to Stanley was Esther.

"If someone will just give her a seat," said Stanley, "she has a confession to make."

33

HOW THE LIGHTS CAME ON—OTTO UNDER
FIRE—THE GUN—ROTH GETS US BACK ON
TRACK—LOST IN ANOTHER WORLD.

I QUICKLY jumped up and gave Esther my chair. She smiled at me, but before she sat down, Roth suggested his desk chair, which was far more comfortable, and Stanley went to get her a drink of water.

Oh the horror of it, I thought. For I knew exactly what happened before she could confess one word. We had been concentrating on the wrong victim! Mad with passion over being jilted by Stanley, she must have come here to kill him, or perhaps (and I was giving her the benefit of the doubt), to threaten him with a gun. She must have seen Stanley sitting in his seat against the wall throughout the rubber; then, when the lights went out, she took her revolver and asked the leading question—a question that was an obvious give-away of somebody who barely knew how to play the game—"Where's the dummy?" Then she shot, but instead of hitting Stanley, she murdered Pizza.

I looked at her, but saw only a touch of remorse on her face. She took a sip of water and spoke.

Esther: "I don't know you people except for Stanley and Matthew, and I'm a bit nervous—although I shouldn't be—I know what type of people you are. But in the cause of justice, I must tell you that I had something to do with what happened tonight."

Damn, I thought, I hated to be right about this!

"You see," she continued, "I came into the city tonight to hear a concert at Carnegie Hall. One of my favorite composers was featured, Johannes Brahms."

She smiled now—it was a winning smile, and I felt reassured that a judge who saw that smile would not dish out too harsh a sentence—then I thought of the baby that was on the way, and I wanted to weep.

"Well, of course I knew that there was to be an inquiry tonight here at this club. You see, I was—I mean I am—a close friend of two of you."

"Detective, does she have to—" interrupted Stanley.

"Hush," said Esther. "Let me finish. You can't protect me all night."

"You see, I am pregnant and Stanley is—I mean will be—the father of my baby. At first, I had notions of doing away with my pregnancy, but when I was listening to the concert tonight, I started remembering the times Stanley and I spent together listening to the same music, and how wonderful a place the world could be for a little baby, especially one with Stanley's and my genes."

Give me a break, I thought.

"So, here I was down the street, and I decided to come here and tell Stanley—for the first time—about the baby. When I got here, I walked up the stairs to the second floor. I don't take elevators if I can help it; I have claustrophobia. As I started up, I heard a loud sound like a firecracker. Well, I was scared suddenly, but I continued up and even bumped into someone who was on the way down. Then I came into the hallway by the elevators. There I saw the door marked Mayfair Club open, and when I walked in, the lights were all out, so naturally I reached up to the switch on the wall and turned them on.

"I found myself in a small foyer opposite a room with a TV—in there. Then I heard footsteps coming up behind me. I went into the lounge and sat down on a sofa by the corner. From where I sat, I could see a man and a little girl enter the front door. That was you." She motioned to Detective Kennedy. "You went into another room and turned on some more lights. I thought I heard you cry out, and there were a whole lot of other voices, but I assumed it was just the natural arguments that you card players have. I actually felt more relaxed and started out of the lounge into this room. That's when I ran into Stanley."

"May I please take it from here?" asked Stanley.

The detective nodded.

"I came out of the bathroom and spotted you, Detective Kennedy, in the front room. Then I saw Pizza lying there with the blood, and of course put two and two together with the gunshot I had heard. Really, at first I thought the gunshot was from the street; you get so used to hearing these things in New York. You know what I mean? Anyway, I turn around and there's Esther, of all people. So I took Esther into the lounge and told her to stay there until it was all cleared up. I didn't want her to have any part in it, and as you can tell, she waited in there for quite a long time. She was pretty hungry, you know, so I snuck her some food during the inquiry in the back room.

"I'll pay for it, Mr. Roth."

"Don't do me any favors."

"Excuse me," said Esther. "Let me finish. I was reading a book in there—your book, Matthew. And after I finished one of the stories, the one about a murder in Paris, well, I realized it was ridiculous and stupidly old-fashioned of Stanley to try and protect his delicate female.

"You're going to have to realize that women are people, Stanley, accountable for their actions just like everyone else!

"Well, that's when Stanley came back in, but he told me to wait a few minutes more while you finished a reenactment of the crime. I'm sorry for not speaking up at once. I hope this helps you with your case."

Detective Kennedy rose and shook his head. Then he looked up to the ceiling and rubbed his temple. "Anybody have some Darvon?" he asked. At least six of the players reached into their pockets.

"Here," said Chops, "these are stronger." He took the pills and borrowed some of Esther's water to wash them down. Then he shook his head again and cursed.

"Dammit!" he cried. "I had it and now I lost it!"

No one dared speak, and we all waited for him to calm himself.

"Look," he said, banging his hand on Roth's desktop, "I was so close, but your evidence, young lady, your evidence . . . hold it. . .

I could still be right!" He moved into the middle of the room, looked at his watch and grimaced. "Mr. Marx," he said, "do you or don't you know how to use a timing device?"

"A what?" asked Otto, stunned to be singled out.

"Oh for god's sake, you know what I'm talking about." He kicked the side of the chair I had been sitting in. "All right, Mr. Marx, you'll give me some quick answers to my questions and prove me an idiot. But first, Doctor Bellyard, please repeat the words you said when the lights went out."

"I said, 'I thought they called it off.'"

"Called what off, Doctor?"

"The electricity test—the one by Con Edison."

"Do you understand what Doctor Bellyard is saying, Mr. Marx?"

"I theenk so. But I have nothing to do with Con Edison—"

"If the test was called off, then why did the lights go out, Mr. Marx?"

"I don't know, why not ask the girl—she put them on—maybe she turned them off—"

"Mr. Marx," said Detective Kennedy, "Will you answer my questions?"

"I'm not afraid—"

"Good. Then answer this. Did you hate Pizza McCarver?"

"I, uh, it's a clazy theeng, Detective, but everybody hated Pizza."

"Yes, but you held the biggest grudge, didn't you? Haven't you been seething for months over his Theory of Exhaustion article in the Bridge World?"

"I admit he stole the Boodapest system but—"

"And didn't you also get upset when you came here last night and found Pizza had eaten all of your favorite dish?"

"You can't condemn a man on chicken paprika—"

"And didn't you this very night admit that when you went to the john during the third deal, you took the November Bridge World with you and when you discovered your rebuttal was not in that issue—I know about the rebuttal letter because that's what Mr. Kaplan had to drop from the issue in order to fit in the partscore deal—well, didn't you get angry all over again, especially when you saw still another article with Pizza's name?"

"I don't theenk I got so excited as y—"

"And didn't you seethe with anger, Mr. Marx, when you read the hand in yesterday's *Times*, the hand where you let Pizza Mc-Carver make still another impossible slam?"

"I didn't read the *Time*—"

"Admit this, Mr. Marx! Didn't you steal 500 dollars from the Mayfair cashbox on the night of October 4th, the night of the first blackout, when you so graciously offered to get your flashlight from your toolbox beneath Mr. Roth's desk?"

"All right, so you got me on something, but the money I owed to my stockbroker, and I always pay back what I ta—"

"Good, good," said Kennedy, rubbing his palms together like a madman. "Now we're getting somewhere! Tell me, Mr. Marx, during the war, didn't Pizza McCarver meet you at a Budapest restaurant, where *he* told *you* about his bidding ideas? I've got it in the notebook, Mr. Marx, so don't deny it."

"It's a clazy theeng, but that was a long time ago. Let me theenk, I forgot about that restaurant meeting. I don't know now; come to think of it, you may be righ—"

"Aha! And who sir, who would put a child, a little girl of seven years, tell me—who would put a child up to copying from a black notebook while nobody was looking?!"

"Oh that! Okay, so I ask her to copy some notes—I'm trying for a comparison to see—"

"Aha. Now, Mr. Marx, answer me this. Why would a player in a rubber bridge game return to the game for the fourth deal and sit in a different position than he was sitting before?"

"A different position? I don't know. I think, yes I was having bad luck in the other position, so I switch—"

"And Mr. Marx, who would have the best vantage point to kill a man kibitzing between the North player and the West player? Would it be someone in the East position or in the West position?"

"I don't know, these positions are clazy, perhaps one of tho—"

"And tell me, now, are you a lefty or a righty, sir? And remember, I've watched you drink your coffee tonight."

"I admit, I am a lefty, but I drink tea, not—"

"Then Mr. Marx, I put it to you: Who would have more opportunity in the dark to kill a man, someone sitting right up against him or someone standing, taking aim over another person's shoulder, four feet away?"

"I guess the closer the better, but you said the bullet came from the boy's shou—"

"Then who, sir, was the only player to get up from the table after the lights went out tonight, and not return to the table until after the shot?"

"I did get up—"

"And who went straight to Mr. Roth's desk on the pretense of getting a flashlight, but instead took the gun out of the cashbox, stole back to the table in the dark, took aim upon the dummy's shoulder and shot the declarer?"

"I don't *know*, I didn't open the cashbox. I opened the toolbox, but I couldn't even find the flashlight; come to theenk of it I - I - I lend the flashlight to someon—"

"And who is the janitor in this building, the man who knows the electrical system inside and out, and how to turn it on and turn it off?"

"I am the janitor, I won't deny it—"

"Now listen closely, Mr. Marx, very closely. You are aware that I sent Doctor Bellyard tonight to call the police because the phone was out of order, and you undoubtedly have realized that Doctor Bellyard took quite a while to return. That is because I asked him to check on the effects of the electrical storm in other buildings on this block and in other offices in this building. And when Doctor Bellyard did return, he informed me that though the phone was out all along the street, the lights to every other building were unaffected. In fact, the electricity throughout this building was unaffected. So, Mr. Marx, answer me truthfully, why a man who craves Hungarian cooking would show up late on the very night that his favorite dish is being prepared? Tell me, sir, that it was because you were busy fixing a timing device on an electrical switch in the basement—tell me if that was not so. . . ."

"It's a clazy theeng, but last night, right before supper. . . I can't remember, wait, I, yes, I was—I was in Jersey City. I got off work at five, and went to Pennsylvania Station and took the train to my sister's house in Jersey City. I had to feed her cats, my sister is in Miami visiting, and on Thursday night, it is my turn to go feed the cats! So there."

"You expect two cats to be your alibi?!"

"Excuse me," I said, raising my hand. "But I saw Otto yesterday at Pennsylvania Station; it was in the men's room, and he did say he was on his way to Jersey City."

Detective Kennedy slammed his fist down on the card table. "Alibis, alibis, I hate them!!!"

J.B. raised his hand and pointed toward the door. "Forgive me, sir, but I believe somebody's entered the club. It looks like the same police officer from earlier."

The captain appeared at the door. "What the blazes is going on here?" asked Detective Kennedy's boss. "For crying out loud, you've had two hours with these people, Kennedy. What have you got?"

"Uh, here comes another fellow," said J.B.

"Maggie, hey Maggie, c'mon now." It was Old Leroy's voice, and he too appeared at the doorway pushing past the police captain. "I've been waiting for you for hours; what they got you working—overtime?"

"You'll have to wait a few minutes longer, till this Detective says I can go," said Maggie.

Meanwhile, Detective Kennedy had walked over to the Captain. "I have this man on the ropes, Captain. He's about to confess.

"During the third deal tonight, he left the room, went to the basement, and attached some kind of timing device to the light switch. Then, when the lights went out at 9:15, he moved to Mr. Roth's desk, using the pretense of looking for a flashlight, and took the gun that Mr. Roth keeps in the cashbox, and positioned himself over Mr. Granovetter's left shoulder and shot Pizza Mc-Carver through the heart."

"I don't theenk so, I—"

"I was at my desk," interrupted Roth, who was standing by the window. "He didn't open the cashbox."

"Well, then he had the gun *with* him," said Detective Kennedy.

Roth walked over to his desk and opened the cashbox drawer with a key. Meanwhile the captain asked the detective why a man who is expecting a police officer to arrive at 9:00 would set a timing device for 9:15—so that he could be caught in the act of a murder? This was a very good point, and an embarrassing one for Detective Kennedy. Even more embarrassing was what Roth found in the cashbox.

"Nobody used this gun tonight," said Roth, holding it up for all to see.

"Are you telling me that you forgot to check where the murder weapon came from?" asked the captain.

Detective Kennedy stood there in silence and nodded. Then he unclipped his badge. It was a sad sight, and he bowed his head in shame. Meanwhile, Old Leroy, who was just standing there taking all this in, threw up his hands in disgust and wandered over to my table.

Suddenly Roth spoke up again. "You know, Detective, you haven't asked *me* to give *my* opinion, and I was sitting right here at the desk during the entire rubber."

"You got something relevant to say before we all go downtown?" asked the Captain.

"I do," said Roth. "And I'm going to start off by telling you people for the last time, you're all children. You like to plunge into slams and grand slams off three aces, you bid notrump with singletons and Blackwood with voids! But if you want to know what happened, I think I can direct you back to the right path of thinking—which is your major problem—you don't know how to *think*.

"Detective Kennedy actually put his finger on it for a brief moment back there with Otto—though he probably just stumbled on the question by luck."

The detective looked up. Roth continued: "An opening lead was made, and the lights went out. Actually, the lights went out in some people's brains long before the opening lead, but that's another matter. Now, after a half minute or so, the declarer is shot from across the table. Okay? Let me rephrase the detective's question and put it in my terms: In the dark, why would anybody try to kill someone from a distance?"

We all stayed in our places, transfixed on that question. . . . If the killer couldn't *get near* the victim, then perhaps he would shoot from a distance. But it didn't make sense for someone to shoot from a distance when he could just walk up to Pizza and pull the trigger.

Suddenly a voice said, "Where's the dummy?"

All eyes turned to the table. Old Leroy was examining the seven-heart contract.

"Here I am," I answered, pointing to my hand next to the gun.

"Hey, man, it's *you!* How are you?" He recognized me and stuck out his hand, which I shook. Then he turned back to the cards. "What's the contract?" he asked.

"Seven hearts," I said, "ace-of-spades lead."

"Ace of spades! What's *wrong* with you people?"

Detective Kennedy stepped forward. "A person who is looking for the *dummy* asks the question, Mr. Roth! A person who turns out the lights, enters the room and wishes to kill Pizza McCarver asks 'Where's the *declarer?*' But a person who asks, 'Where's the *dummy?*' wants to kill the *dummy!* . . . Mr. Granovetter! You struggled when the gunman placed his weapon on your shoulder! You pushed the gun, didn't you?"

I nodded. *Oh no,* I thought—*Oh my God!* The gunman was after me!

"You!" said the detective to Esther. "You said someone bumped into you on the stairs. What did he look like?"

"He, uh, looked like a man with long hair. That's all I remember—"

A man with long hair? Lots of men have long hair, I thought. *Wait a second!* "Esther," I said, "was he wearing a man's hat?"

She nodded, "Yes, I think he was."

Suddenly I took a closer look at the gun lying next to the dummy. Could it be?! I tapped Old Leroy on the shoulder—he was busy examining the grand slam, very busy. "Look, Leroy," I said, "here's your gun."

He must have heard my voice in the background, for he muttered quickly, without thinking, "Yeah, my gun." Then his head returned to another world—a darker, quieter, analytical world filled with voids and ruffing finesses and diamond discards. However, just when I thought I had lost him, he let his consciousness slip back into this world: "No man, you gave me my gun; that must be Stella's—"

34

"Y OU'RE A lucky kid," said the Captain on his way out. "If you hadn't forced the barrel of that gun away from your temple, well. . . ."

I was glad to see that Detective Kennedy had not placed handcuffs on Old Leroy. I wrote down the address of Leroy's hangout and slipped it to the detective in the hallway along with the two counterfeit Franklins that Otto had given back to me earlier in the evening.

"I want you to stay out of town, Granovetter," said Detective Kennedy, "until we pick up Stella. We may have to bring you in for identification, but then I never want to see you again after that!" He turned and went over some final details with his boss. He had solved both cases and had his badge back where it belonged. In the meantime, I turned to his prisoner and apologized for using him to solve the accidental murder of Pizza McCarver.

"I'm sorry," I said, "I hate to see you get into trouble."

"Hey, man," said Leroy, "You forget it. They got very little on me anyway. Leastwise Stella got the wrong man, huh? But if you want to, you can do me one small favor. Always leave a good tip to my niece, Maggie, okay? And in return, I can do one more favor for you."

"Yes?"

"Here, you go and impress your friends with this one. That so-called grand slam is never gonna make if you defend properly—even with that ace-of-spades lead. Just drop the queen of hearts on the first round of trumps—that's all. You know it's dropping anyway, and now declarer thinks you got a singleton queen. Later on, he'll think he's got to ruff the third diamond high and finesse the ten on the way back, ha, ha. Listen, sonny, when I get out, you come up to the Harlem Bridge-Whist Club and learn what the game is really about."

We waved good-by and went back into the club. Everyone was still there except Maggie and Roth, who left with the two police-men and Old Leroy. Minutes later however, Frankenstein and Chops made their exit with the two children in their arms.

J.B. came up to me and asked if I was ready to go. I nodded, and Stanley, Esther and I all went downstairs to J.B.'s car. On my last glimpse of the Mayfair, I saw Otto, Gussie, and Doctor B. bent over a backgammon board.

When we reached the toll booth to enter the Lincoln Tunnel, Stanley took out a bill and handed it over. It was one of the counterfeit Franklins, and I caught it before it was passed to the toll attendant.

"Where did you get this?" I asked, turning my head to the back seat. Stanley hesitated. I noticed Esther lying comfortably on his lap, sleeping soundly. Then I figured he got it from me when I went to pay my account the night before. It occurred to me to ask him what he was doing with the bill, but then I noticed Esther stirring, and simply ripped up the bill, opened my window, and spread the remains across the New Jersey marshlands. That was the last time I ever came across one of those two-sided Franklins, unless you count the mention of one the following week. While dining at the Red Tulip, the propietor came to my table and asked me to make good the bad hundred-dollar bill I had passed there in October.

We dropped Esther at her Douglass dormitory and returned to the Quad. There some of the boys were up, and listened to the details of the murder. I even laid out the grand slam on Stanley's bed and showed them the queen-of-hearts ploy, giving proper credit to Old Leroy. Nobody really grasped the play until we played out the deal card for card:

363

North
♠ —
♡ J 9 8 7 6 4
◊ 8 7 2
♣ K J 8 2

West
♠ A 7 6 2
♡ Q 10
◊ A 6 5
♣ A 10 9 6

East
♠ 10 9 8 5 3
♡ 3 2
◊ 10 4
♣ 7 5 4 3

South
♠ K Q J 4
♡ A K 5
◊ K Q J 9 3
♣ Q

Ace of spades opening lead, ruffed in dummy with the six of hearts. Seven of hearts to the ace, queen. Three high spades, discarding three diamonds. Diamond king, ducked by West. Diamond queen ducked again. Low diamond, ace by West, ruffed in dummy with the jack of hearts. Now the nine of hearts from dummy . . . three . . .

North
♠ —
♡ 9 8 4
◊ —
♣ K J

West
♠ —
♡ 10
◊ —
♣ A 10 9 6

East
♠ 10
♡ 3
◊ —
♣ 7 5 4

South
♠ —
♡ K 5
◊ J 9
♣ Q

The finesse in trumps and the grand slam is down. Nobody said a word, until Big Al spoke up: "You know, a player who leads the ace of spades isn't likely to find that queen-of-hearts play."

He was right. The players in a bridge game are marked by their consistent characteristics. Though they may improve in time, they do not change from the beginning of a deal to the end.

And so it is for the players of life. . . .

EPILOGUE

*THE TRUTH COMES OUT—WHAT HAPPENED
TO EVERYONE.*

"WHERE'S THE dummy?"

Good question. For six years, I believed a woman named Stella had asked that question in her search for a real-life *dummy* sitting in the dark at the Mayfair Bridge Club.

However, in 1975, at a bridge tournament in Monte Carlo, I met Stanley at the beach club. He was with a stunning Swiss girl, whom he introduced as his child's nanny. After a few drinks, we got around to discussing the murder, and he asked me if I were ever going to thank him for saving my life.

I had no idea what he was talking about, and said so. He laughed and said I was as naive as the police. After all, hadn't he given away the show by admitting he *knew* he was the dummy on the grand slam?

"Got to hand it to Chops—when she said I would never leave the room without first looking at your hand, I thought you guys would catch on."

"Are you trying to tell me that *you're* the one who pulled the trigger?"

"Hey, man, the clues were right there. Even J.B. saw it, but you guys didn't listen to him. He was the one sitting in my seat—didn't he say that he could see people coming in through the front door?"

"Yes, but—"

"And where do you think that phony Franklin came from on our first train ride back to Rutgers?"

"You mean that you were in on the counterfeit racket?"

"Naw. But I was at the track and knew what was going on."

"Just tell me what happened, will you?"

"All right, kid, I'll draw you a map. After you told me about Esther, I was feeling kind of sorry—I'm a very sensitive guy, you know. Anyway, I made up my mind to marry the kid, but I still had Pizza to contend with. Most of my debts had been transferred to his account, and he was getting to be a real pain, you know?

"Well, anyway, after Gussie doubled seven hearts, I really got pissed. There's no way we would have reached seven without that stupid convention Pizza brought up at the Russian Tea Room. I made up my mind right after she doubled that he had to go. How I didn't know. But then fate stepped in. You gotta watch out for fate, kid, it plays a big role in life."

"Gimme a break, Stanley. Just finish the story."

"Okay man, okay. Well, who do I see at the front door? Of all people it's Stella—Stella from the racetrack! Now I heard that afternoon about how she was gunning for you, because you knew too much about their racket and hideout and all; so I knew when I saw her, she was there to plug you. Here's where I saved your life. I jumped up and ran to the door. We had a few words, but I convinced her to give me the gun, and I would take care of you, myself.

"I was never that fond of Stella and I figured I could kill two birds with one bullet. I shut out the lights, went back to the front room, but couldn't see very much. I tried to locate Pizza by asking where's the dummy. See, I knew Pizza was sitting back of my cards, and if I could locate the dummy, I'd put the gun right up against his head."

"But you put the gun up against *my* head!"

"Hey, that wasn't *my* fault. It's *you* guys who had the dummy mixed up. But when I heard your voice, I knew something was wrong. Then I realized it was your head and I was facing Pizza across the table. Well, it was no time to pause, so pow, I gave it to him from where I was standing. You must admit, it was a good shot."

Detective Kennedy exposed a small ring of amateur counterfeiters operating out of Belmont Racetrack. After plea-bargaining and turning state's evidence against the ringleader, a woman named Stella, they all received reduced sentences. Detective Kennedy went on to become a captain in the New York Police Force and recently achieved the status of Advanced Senior Master from the American Contract Bridge League.

Stella was never found. Police records to this day still indicate Stella as the murderer of Pizza McCarver.

J.B. went on to get his doctorate and is currently a professor of classics at Harvard University. He still writes me when he comes across an interesting trump position.

Gussie Addles died in poverty, but not hunger, as she spent her remaining years at the Mayfair Club. She was loved by all, but mostly by her opponents.

Otto Marx writes occasional articles for a Budapest bridge periodical. It's a crazy thing, but in the mid-1980's he went into real estate in Jersey City, and became a millionaire.

Alvin Roth still runs the Mayfair Club in New York City and has recently published an update to his classic, "Bridge is a Partnership Game."

Maggie Johnson left the club in 1981, when she joined a Wall Street firm as head chef for lunches and late-afternoon parties.

Edgar Kaplan is still editor of Bridge World Magazine, and resides in the same brownstone on West 94th Street, NYC.

Esther married Stanley two weeks later. After bearing him two children, she divorced Stanley and returned to school. She was later remarried to a violinist from the New York Philharmonic.

Stanley Kesselman died in a gun-down in a back alley on the lower East Side in 1978. He was a bookie at that time and heavily in debt.

Doctor Bellyard died in 1984 while on vacation in Kingston, Jamaica. He was in a rubber bridge game at the time with three natives, one of them being a woman named Stella (an extraordinary coincidence).

Frank Stein and **Chops** were married in 1970 and moved to an obscure midwestern university town where he taught mathematics and she opened a rubber bridge club. They raised seven children, three of whom are now successful bridge pros. Frank and Chops asked me to mention they sometimes do Bridge Cruises—if readers are interested, please contact me (M.G.).

Mr. Keewood was arrested in 1971 for an obscure income-tax crime. In the serenity of a dark jail cell, he found time to write a book on the power of blackness. He returned to teaching in 1978 at a university he asked me not to name.

Easley Blackwood, Jr. is the son of Easley Blackwood Sr. (the author of the Blackwood convention in contract bridge). He is a famous composer and specializes in microtonal music.

Young Matthew was confined to his room by his parents for the entire holiday vacation of 1969. (However, on the third night, there was a team of four at the local Temple game, and I was let out to make up the team.)

Two years later, I left Rutgers to play bridge, not returning to school for many years. I tried never to lie again, and succeeded to some degree. I did continue to play rubber bridge, but, for sure, I never again went for coffee on a moving train.

At the age of 34 I married. My wife, Pamela, and I currently have two children and live in Saratoga County of New York where, against the advice of a good friend, we publish a bridge magazine.

Old Leroy served two weeks in Rikers Island for illegal possession of a deadly weapon, and was also fined $200 for operating a cab without a license. I met Leroy only a few years ago in a Harlem bridge club—but that's another story.

M. G. – 1989

Recommended readings that may interest you:

The Autobiography of Malcolm X
The Autobiography of Ben Franklin
Heart of Darkness by Joseph Conrad
The Murders in the Rue Morgue
and other Short Stories by Edgar Allan Poe
The Power of Blackness by Harry Levin
Bridge is a Partnership Game by Alvin Roth & Tobias Stone
Bridge World magazine edited by Edgar Kaplan & Jeff Rubens

Books available from Granovetter Books:

I Shot My Bridge Partner by Matthew Granovetter	$12.95
Murder at the Bridge Table by Matthew Granovetter	$12.95
Tops and Bottoms by Pamela & M. Granovetter	$11.95
Spingold Challenge by Allan Falk	$11.95
Bridging the Gap by J. Peter Kichline	$ 9.95
The Best of Eddie Kantar	$13.95
Bridge is a Partnership Game by Roth & Stone	$13.95

Bridge Today magazine edited by The Granovetters
$21 for one year (6 issues — bi-monthly)

Use coupon on next page and mail to:

Granovetter Books
18 Village View Bluff
Ballston Lake, NY 12019

Order Form

Your Name: _____

Address: _____

City/State/Zip: _____

Please send directly to me:

Item	Quantity	Price	Total

Total cost to my address (add $2 for UPS delivery): $_____

Please send these gifts directly to the recipient.

Item(s):

Name

Address

City/State/Zip

Sign card:

Total cost (add $2 for UPS deliv.): $_____

Tax (NY destinations, books only): $_____

Sub total: $_____

Total enclosed: $_____

Please write additional orders on separate paper and mail to:

Bridge Today, 18 Village View Bluff, Ballston Lake, NY, 12019.

If it is getting too close to the holidays, phone 518-899-6670.

Checks payable to: "Bridge Today."

ORDER FORM

Your Name: _____

Address: _____

City/State/Zip: _____

Please send directly to me:

Item	Quantity	Price	Total

Total cost to my address (add $2 for UPS delivery): $_____

Please send these gifts directly to the recipient.

Item(s):
Name
Address
City/State/Zip
Sign card:

Total cost (add $2 for UPS deliv.): $_____

Tax (NY destinations, books only): $_____

Sub total: $_____

Total enclosed: $_____

Please write additional orders on separate paper and mail to:

Bridge Today, 18 Village View Bluff, Ballston Lake, NY, 12019.

If it is getting too close to the holidays, phone 518-899-6670.

Checks payable to: "Bridge Today."